Language and Society

Language is indissolubly linked with the members of the society in which it is spoken, and social factors are inevitably reflected in their speech. In this accessible introduction, Downes surveys the various ways that language can be studied as a social phenomenon. He discusses the known relationships between language variation and large-scale social factors, showing how the variation runs along 'fault lines in social structure', such as divisions between social classes, the sexes and different ethnic groups. Topics covered include domains of language use, language change, code-switching, speech as social action and the nature of meaning and understanding. This thoroughly revised edition includes an up-to-date analysis of language standardisation, language conflict and planning, and a critique of the pragmatic theory of communication. It explains and illustrates the notion of register, and examines the issues surrounding language ideology and power.

William Downes is Lecturer in Linguistics at the University of East Anglia. Previously he taught English and Linguistics at York University, Toronto, and the London School of Economics.

Cambridge Approaches to Linguistics

General editor: Jean Aitchison,
*Rupert Murdoch Professor of Language and Communication,
University of Oxford*

In the past twenty-five years, linguistics – the systematic study of language – has expanded dramatically. Its findings are now of interest to psychologists, sociologists, philosophers, anthropologists, teachers, speech therapists and numerous others who have realized that language is of crucial importance in their life and work. But when newcomers try to discover more about the subject, a major problem faces them – the technical and often narrow nature of much writing about linguistics.

Cambridge Approaches to Linguistics is an attempt to solve this problem by presenting current findings in a lucid and non-technical way. Its object is twofold. First, it hopes to outline the 'state of play' in key areas of the subject, concentrating on what is happening now, rather than on surveying the past. Secondly, it aims to provide links between branches of linguistics that are traditionally separate.

The series will give readers an understanding of the multi-faceted nature of language, and its central position in human affairs, as well as equipping those who wish to find out more about linguistics with a basis from which to read some of the more technical literature in textbooks and journals.

Also in the series

Forthcoming titles include

Language and Society

WILLIAM DOWNES

2ND EDITION

PUBLISHED BY THE PRESS SYNDICATE OF THE UNIVERSITY OF CAMBRIDGE
The Pitt Building, Trumpington Street, Cambridge, United Kingdom

CAMBRIDGE UNIVERSITY PRESS
The Edinburgh Building, Cambridge CB2 2RU, UK
40 West 20th Street, New York, NY 10011–4211, USA
477 Williamstown Road, Port Melbourne, VIC 3207, Australia
Ruiz de Alarcón 13, 28014 Madrid, Spain
Dock House, The Waterfront, Cape Town 8001, South Africa

www.cambridge.org
Information on this title: www.cambridge.org/9780521450461

First published by Fontana Paperbacks, London 1984
Second edition published by Cambridge University Press 1998
Reprinted 2003

Typeset in 10/12 Photina [GC]

A catalogue record for this book is available from the British Library

ISBN-13 978-0-521-45046-1 hardback
ISBN-10 0-521-45046-2 hardback

ISBN-13 978-0-521-45663-0 paperback
ISBN-10 0-521-45663-0 paperback

Transferred to digital printing 2005

Contents

Acknowledgements

I gratefully acknowledge all those works which are referred to in this book, and the scholars on whose research it depends. For permission to quote from published works, thanks are due to Alan Sillitoe, for passages from *Saturday Night and Sunday Morning* © Alan Sillitoe 1958, 1985; McGraw-Hill Ryerson Ltd. Toronto, for stanza from 'Montreal' by A. M. Klein (1948); Walter De Gruyter & Co. Berlin for Figure 2.1 from 'The Social Significance of the Berlin Urban Vernacular' in Dittmar and Schlobinski, 1988; Cambridge University Press (Trudgill, 1974); Edward Arnold, publishers of the series Social Psychology of Language (Hughes and Trudgill, 1979; Ryan and Giles, 1982); Basil Blackwell (Boissevain, 1974; Milroy, 1980); Academic Press (Frake, 1975); Center for Applied Linguistics (Wolfram, 1969; Wolfram and Christian, 1976; Labov, 1966); John Wiley and Sons (Lieberson, 1970); M. LaFerriere whose work on Boston I have used (LaFerriere, 1979); Oxford University Press for the partial entry for 'bear' from the *OED*; Taylor and Francis Ltd. and W. Denis and Peter Li (Denis and Li, 1988); Channel 4 for the exchange from 'Faces of the Family', 4 March 1994; The University of East Anglia for the extract from Draft Regulations; and Norwich Arts Centre for the text from its publicity. The Prayer for the Universal Day of Prayer for Students, 15 February 1953, was taken from R. Quirk (1968), *The Use of English*, Longman, and thanks also to the International Union of Students. Full bibliographical details of all works referred to are given in the text and references. Particular thanks to Peter Trudgill for helping to correct Figure 6.3, to Jack Chambers for his extensive comments on drafts of the Canada section of chapter three, to Dick Hudson and Jenny Cheshire for reading sections of the manuscript, to Jean Aitchison for guiding the whole book, to Michael Gregory and Michael Halliday for introducing me to a social and functional view of language, and a special acknowledgement to William Labov on whom so much of modern sociolinguistics depends, including this book.

1 Linguistics and sociolinguistics

> It is difficult to see adequately the functions of language, because it is so deeply rooted in the whole of human behaviour that it may be suspected that there is little in the functional side of our conscious behaviour in which language does not play its part.
>
> Sapir (1933)

Language is a complicated business. In everyday talk, we use the word 'language' in many different ways. It isn't clear how 'language' should be defined or what the person on the street thinks it actually is! We talk about how miraculously a child's 'language' is developing but how they make charming 'grammar mistakes', like *me maden that* instead of 'I made that'. Here, language is an ability that is blossoming in the child.

But the word is used in a myriad of different ways. For example, people have strong views about how beautiful or how hideous the 'language' is of some region or country or age group; how it sounds to the ear. People say 'I just adore Italian or an Irish accent.' They grimace or smile at teenager talk on television. Here 'language' is being judged aesthetically. By contrast, we remark that you can't *really* appreciate a culture without knowing the 'language', as when we learn French or Japanese for that reason. Then pupils struggle with rules for tenses like the *passé composé* and *imparfait* or have to memorize genders and irregular verb conjugations, matters of grammar which seem a million miles from cuisine, film, high tech or Zen Buddhism. 'Language' here equates with grammar.

Then, people relate the word 'language' to the expression of thoughts. They often say that they 'can't find the words' for their thoughts or express feelings. Or they are 'hunting for the right words'. Alternatively, we say that language is a means of communication. Politicians often use as an excuse the fact that their message 'just isn't getting across' because the media distorts what they say. In negotiations or relationships, when communication fails, we say, 'they just don't speak the same language'. In another sense, 'language' refers to a school subject. It makes sense to say that 'little Mary is behind in her English', although you'd never know it when you hear her chatting with her friends. 'Language' is being viewed as a set of skills acquired in school. We are taught to write Standard English and spell correctly.

At the same time, we use the term 'language' analogically, as a metaphor. We talk of such things as 'body language', or the 'languages' of music, painting or dance. It is fairly clear that these various ordinary uses of the word refer to different aspects of language, and take different perspectives on the sort of thing language is. Or, alternatively, we have simply grouped together under the heading of 'language' a range of diverse phenomena which are only partially related to each other.

In order to clarify our thoughts about language, let's look at some of the ways language is viewed by linguists. We can then give a precise statement of the specifically **sociolinguistic** view of language, and contrast it to other views of language assumed in linguistics proper.

The primary aim of all linguistic scholarship is to determine the properties of natural language, the features it has which distinguish it from any possible artificial language. This means that linguistics will be universalistic in its basic aims. It will examine individual natural languages in the course of constructing a theory of **universal grammar** that explains why the whole set of **natural languages** are the way they are. Natural languages, English, French and so on, are in fact the data for this theory of natural language. Artificial languages are of interest too since they can exhibit certain properties any language has, but they also have features that can sharply distinguish them from any naturally evolved language.

We will look at some artificial languages to illustrate this. The linguist Noam Chomsky, in his influential book *Syntactic Structures* (1957), employed the following languages in the course of his arguments:

(i)   ab, aabb, aaabbb, . . . and all sentences of the same type.
(ii)   aa, bb, abba, baab, aaaa, bbbb, aabbaa, abbbba, . . . and all sentences of the same type.
(iii) aa, bb, abab, baba, aaaa, bbbb, aabaab, abbabb, . . . and all sentences of the same type.

Why would we want to call (i), (ii) or (iii) languages? The answer is that they have certain properties of any language. They have a vocabulary of symbols, in this case two letters of the alphabet 'a' and 'b'. Also, they have a **syntax**. That is, each of the languages has specific rules for joining together their symbols to produce the sentences or strings of that language. If the rule of syntax is not followed, then the **string** or sentence produced is not a sentence of that language.

Consider the syntactic rules of the three languages. In language (i) the rule seems to be that for each sentence, whatever the number of occurrences of the first symbol, a, it is immediately followed by exactly the same number of occurrences of the second symbol, b. In language (ii), the rule is that, for each sentence, whatever the arrangement of a and b in the first half of that sentence, then that arrangement is repeated in reverse in the second half of the same sentence. I'll leave the reader to work out the equally simple syntax of language (iii).

Note that the output of the application of their respective syntactic rules to the symbols of these languages is an *infinite set of strings* which are members of the language sharply distinguishable from another infinite set of strings which are not members of the language.

In brief, then, these artificial languages have vocabularies and syntactic rules for joining their symbols together. And, by following the rules of their syntax, an infinite set of strings can be produced. Natural languages can also be considered in this way. Thus, English can be viewed as a set of strings. And this infinite set is produced by the vocabulary and syntactic rules of English. If linguists can construct a device, a **grammar**, which can specify the grammatical strings of English and separate them from the combinations of symbols which are not English, they have gone a considerable distance towards making explicit the syntactic properties of the language. And if the types of rule in that grammar are also necessary for the grammar of any natural language, then they might have discovered some of those universal properties of language which it is the aim of linguistics to discover. Chomsky, in fact, used languages (i), (ii) and (iii) to rule out a certain class of grammars as candidates for grammars of natural language. Of course, these artificial languages are also extremely unlike natural languages. One very noticeable difference is that the symbols and strings don't bear any relation to the world. They have no **senses** or **meanings**, but are purely syntactic. The study of meaning and how it relates symbols to the world is called **semantics**.

There are other artificial languages which have strings of symbols which are meaningful. An example is arithmetic. Consider '2 + 2 = 4' or '3 × 3 = 9'. These formulae have a syntax and a semantics. And they are true, while '2 + 2 = 5' is false. These are language-like properties. But there is also something very unlike natural language, the language spontaneously acquired by children, about these formulae. Nothing in the world (we feel) could *ever* make '2 + 2 = 4' false, as long as the symbols themselves don't change their meanings. The formulae appear to be **analytic** or 'always true by definition'.

Contrast this with some sentences from natural language:

1.   Arthur *is taller than* Brenda.
2.   Brenda *is taller than* Tom.
3.   Doreen *is taller than* Brenda.
4.   Tom *is shorter than* X?

We can use these sentences to make statements which are true or false, express our beliefs that each sentence designates a state of affairs in the actual world. These sentences are **synthetic**, true or false according to the facts. (Strictly speaking, it isn't the sentences which are true or false, but **propositions** which they express. A 'sentence' may express many different 'propositions'. However, I will ignore the distinction in this book.) We can capture a sentence's relation with the world by giving its **truth conditions**. These are precisely the **possible worlds** – possible **states of affairs** – in which it is true. For example, 1 is true in worlds where the individual designated by 'Arthur' is a member of the class of individuals who are 'taller than the individual designated by "Brenda"'; otherwise it is false. Similarly, if 'Doreen' is also a member of that class, then 3 would be true, otherwise false. Only if we know these truth conditions, can we use the sentences to state what we ourselves believe. Or understand what somebody else using the sentence is claiming to be the case. Intuitively, to know truth conditions is part of the 'meaning' of the sentences.

But sentences also relate to each other. For example, if 1 is true, then Arthur is 'bigger' or 'greater' than Brenda with respect to her 'height' or her 'tallness'. Synonymy is one example of **sense or semantic relations**. Such semantic properties constitute **inferential relationships** between the sentences. Another example. We know that, if both Doreen and Arthur 'are taller than' Brenda, and Brenda 'is taller than' Tom, then Doreen and Arthur 'are taller than' Tom. We don't have to look at the world to know this fact. It is a result of a semantic property of the language: the 'transitivity' of the predicate 'taller than'. Similarly, 'is shorter than' in 4 bears a systematic semantic relation to its **converse** 'is taller than'. Example 1 **entails** 'Brenda is shorter than Arthur'. Entailments are inferences that depend on semantic relations. If one thinks about it, this web or network of sense relations seems to describe features of the very same possible worlds in which the sentences are true. Of course it would, wouldn't it? This is because inferential relations between sentences are just those relations where the two sentences are both true! Hence, to specify sense relations is a way to partially describe the 'worlds' of the truth conditions – the ones in which the sentences are true. Hence it is a way of giving the 'meaning' of the sentences.

So far, no *social* factors have been mentioned. How do social factors figure in the explanation of language? They don't seem *directly* related to either syntax or semantics. We can begin a treatment of this question by mentioning a few social aspects of semantics. A fundamental factor in making both the arithmetic and natural language examples work is **convention**. In the first case, of the arithmetic symbols '2', '4' etc., we have confidence that when we use them, our addressee will understand that we intend to refer to sets of two and four, 2 and 4, etc., respectively. This is an example of co-operative social co-ordination. It connects the sound [tu:] or the mark '2' with any set of two things. It allows an English speaker to use the term with confidence that their intention will be understood. The 'sign' and its 'object' have a **coded** relationship. Similarly with the predicates 'is taller than' and 'is shorter than'. They have a coded relation with the states of affairs they represent. It is important to note that any intrinsic properties that the signs '2' or '4' or 'tall' or 'short' might have *do not explain* the link with their objects. Any noise or mark could just as easily be chosen. This is the property of the **arbitrariness** of the linguistic sign. Signs and objects are arbitrarily linked, by convention. And this is a social phenomenon.

From a different perspective, the connection of world and words *isn't* arbitrary, though it is equally social. Consider the web of inferential relations sketched above. The semantic structure of language describes the possible worlds in which sentences are true. Now to even establish this structure it is necessary for us to use the signs to express belief, what we take as *actually true*, to coordinate 'taller than' and 'shorter than' with the world as we take it to be. In essence, semantics defines possible states of the world based on our beliefs. Truth has to do with 'senses i.e. the inferential net', the relation of 'words and world', and 'our beliefs'. Without the 'possibly true' world set given through meanings, we couldn't inquire, because we couldn't think hypothetically. Without the inferential relations, we couldn't reliably think out the consequences of our hypotheses to test them and thus be right or wrong in our beliefs, assent or dissent in the light of experience. Thus, crucially, the semantic structure of a language is the very resource necessary for humanity to form any **empirical theory** of the world and use language to inquire – to fix belief and hence deal with everyday experience, be able to live. That the set of sentences can form a coherent theory can be seen by the fact that, if you believe that 1–3 are true, then you can give a true answer to 4, without further looking at the world. Tom must be the 'shortest one of all' in this particular universe of discourse. There is no doubt that the process of inquiry is social. We have to co-ordinate our beliefs and inferences for language to work.

Are there other properties of natural language which *require* social explanation? The answer is, 'Yes, there are many such properties.' Next we will look at one of the most definitive social properties of language. This property is called **variability**. Consider the English word 'butter'. On the levels of syntax, vocabulary and semantics, it is a single English item; a mass noun which means something like an edible, yellow, dairy product used in cooking and as a spread. Yet although it is one item, if I asked you to describe its pronunciation in English, you would not be able to give a single answer: there are various **phonetic** realizations of 'butter'.

In British English **Received Pronunciation** the *t* is made by putting the tongue tip on the ridge behind the teeth, and releasing the air in a small explosion without vibration of the vocal chords. The *r*, however, is not pronounced, although it is present in the written form. Instead, a vowel sound, schwa (phonetically transcribed as ə) follows the *t*. The schwa is the same sound that is normally final in the word *sofa*. Thus, the RP speaker and many other British English speakers say [bʌtə].

In Canadian and American accents there is a rule that when explosive sounds like *t* are made between two vowels, the vibration of the vocal chords, called **voice**, continues through the whole sequence. This has the effect of turning the [t], which is voiceless, into [d], which is its voiced counterpart. Thus, a Canadian saying 'butter' in fact pronounces it as if it were 'budder'. However, Canadians and many of their American neighbours also have **r-full** accents (as do the Scots and Irish). This means that, unlike the RP British English speaker, they pronounce the written *r* in butter, giving us the final form [bʌtəʳ].

In many British English accents there is yet another variation in the pronunciation of *t* in this environment. The vocal chords themselves are closed tightly and then released abruptly, giving the impression that *t* is missing. In fact, the gap is filled by a so-called **glottal stop**, symbolized by ʔ. So 'butter' is pronounced [bʌʔə]. Such a pronunciation would typify London working-class speech, familiar to North Americans as a Cockney accent from films like *My Fair Lady*.

This film, from George Bernard Shaw's *Pygmalion*, introduces another feature of the variability we have been describing. For Professor Higgins (modelled by Shaw on the famous phonetician, Henry Sweet) to take such pains to train Eliza Doolittle to pronounce words like 'butter' as [bʌtə], as opposed to [bʌˀə], indicates that the variation must mean something. There is no conceptual difference in the word-meaning itself. The meaning difference of the variation is socially significant and relates to those groups in a social structure who typically use one form rather than another. Such **social meanings** of variants can be further illustrated by looking at two other versions of 'butter'.

In the West Country of England there are some local accents which, like Canadian and some American accents, are *r*-full. Speakers would typically pronounce the *r* in 'butter'. And this can be combined with the use of the glottal stop to give the form [bʌˀəʳ]. On British television an advertisement promoting butter used this regional form, presumably because it had a social meaning to British audiences suggestive of honest West Country farmers genuinely in touch with real, non-synthetic cows.

In New York City a working-class accent will, in casual speech, be largely *r*-less like the British RP. But this would be combined with the voicing of the written 't' between vowels giving the form [bʌdə]. Followers of the 1970s *Kojak* detective series on television will recognize this form. Imagine, however, the different social meaning that would be conveyed if Lieutenant Kojak pronounced the word [bʌdəʳ] as might an upper-middle-class New Yorker, or [bʌtə] as might an upper-middle-class Englishman. It would not be the impression of the 'tough New York cop'.

The diagram opposite gives a summary of the various ways 'butter' can be pronounced which we have looked at. The actual situation is far more complex and interesting than I have indicated, but we will be studying this in more detail later in the book. The purpose here is to merely illustrate the property of variability which natural languages possess.

It is clear that this property requires social explanation. This is in contrast with the arbitrary property of language mentioned earlier. In characterizing the variant forms of 'butter', I needed to make reference to the geographical location in which the form

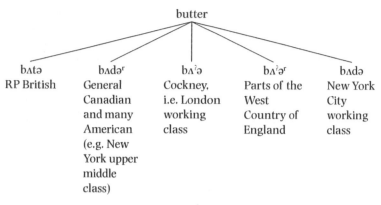

butter

bʌtə	bʌdəʳ	bʌʔə	bʌʔəʳ	bʌdə
RP British	General Canadian and many American (e.g. New York upper middle class)	Cockney, i.e. London working class	Parts of the West Country of England	New York City working class

was characteristically employed, and to the socio-economic class of the speaker. I also described the variants in terms of the social meaning which their use might typically convey. In other words, I was explaining the variants in terms of social characteristics of their users.

So what is **sociolinguistics**? I will now propose a 'broad definition', in order to distinguish this branch of linguistics from other ways of approaching language, and also to try to unite the diverse kinds of inquiry which go under this name:

> Sociolinguistics is that branch of linguistics which studies just those properties of language and languages which *require* reference to social, including contextual, factors in their explanation.

This definition comes with a health warning. As we shall see below, it is broader than usual, including what is normally considered sociolinguistics, and then some. Like all definitions of subjects of inquiry, it is determined by methods of explanation. Here the term 'social' is contrasted with those explanations of language which explain it *sui generis*, just as a system of relations between signs, or in psychological or cognitive terms.

We can also relate our definition of sociolinguistics to Chomsky's conception of linguistic theory. I said earlier that the aim of linguistics is universalistic. It sets out to explain why the whole set of natural languages are the way they are. For Chomsky, the basic answer to this question is that language has the properties it does because the human mind is constructed that way.

Every normal human being 'knows' their mother tongue. This **knowledge of language** is a state of the mind and brain which Chomsky calls **I-language** or 'internalized language'. To 'know a language', whether it is English or Chinese, is to have attained a certain mind/brain state. Every normal member of our species attains this state, called mature linguistic **competence**, during the first years of life. According to Chomsky, the linguist's job is to construct a theory of I-language and how it is acquired (see Chomsky, 1986).

For Chomsky, these two things are ultimately the same. Followers of Chomsky believe that the *only* way to explain the universal features of I-language is to say that we acquire this uniform competence because we are genetically pre-programmed to do so. The answer to the question, 'What is language?' is a theory that specifies this universal genetic endowment. The job of linguistics is to characterize the principles and parameters of our genetically given language capacity that make the acquisition of I-language possible; of course, grammars of individual languages will be predicted as permitted variants of this **universal grammar**. Evidence is advanced that such a capacity – this species specific capacity to spontaneously acquire any natural language – is a separate 'mental organ' or 'cognitive capacity'. This is part of the thesis of the **modularity of mind**, that the mind, and ultimately the brain, isn't functionally or structurally undifferentiated, but made up of distinct faculties. (This very influential view originates with Fodor, 1983.) It follows that the job of linguistics is to tell us about the form and functioning of the **language module**. The inquiry necessarily takes place at an abstract level, but it is clear that language is ultimately viewed as a physical system. Chomsky's conception of language is psychological or **cognitive**, but ultimately **biological**. This is nicely captured in the title of one of the best introductions to Chomsky's thought, Steven Pinker's (1994) *The Language Instinct*.

So where do social explanations fit in? Social explanations will enter into an account of language at the places where we find patterns of language which can't be explained in psychological terms. Characteristically, these are patterns in the use of language. It is quite clear that there are properties of language which *must* be explained either in terms of large-scale social structure or in terms of how people use language to communicate with one another. Social explanations will be concerned with aggregate regularities in group performance and with the explication of acts of communication. Of course, these involve human mental abilities too. We exhibit psychological abilities in social life and action. However, these abilities, according to Chomsky, are not part of our specific linguistic module, however much they may underlie our use of language. Our concern, by contrast, is precisely that use of language. Chomsky calls such use of language, linguistic **performance**, in contrast to competence. These are the places where non-language modules, such as general inferential abilities, beliefs stored in memory, motives and goals etc. interact with language itself. By this methodology, it would appear that explanation by social factors, and hence sociolinguistics by my definition, would only deal with performance.

But just where the boundaries might be between various aspects of the whole complex of things we call 'language', as pre-theoretically sketched out at the beginning of the chapter, is not clear. It isn't obvious which aspects of language are *sui generis*, psychologically or biologically explicable and which could be handled socially. Syntax and accent variability, respectively, seem to be two possible limiting cases. But it partly depends on which aspect of the complex of language phenomena you look at, how and for what purpose you approach it. In part, whether the social function or even origin of linguistic patterns is visible or not depends on how the linguist approaches the investigation – even how the data is generated. Within the Chomsky paradigm, language is highly idealized. Clearly, the use of language to communicate messages, form hypotheses or fix beliefs requires social explanation. But these are not part of Chomsky's language module in any case! Maybe social/contextual explanation does not penetrate to the very heart of the language module – the rules of universal grammar. Alternatively, perhaps the modular conception is an impoverished definition of language, restricting itself to areas insulated from 'language' as it is important to major human interests, or prematurely ruling out accounts in terms of social functions as a theoretical impossibility.

In sociolinguistics, on the other hand, natural languages are much less idealized, they are viewed as the totality of **utterances** which speakers or hearers could make and comprehend in social contexts. Utterances are social behaviour, linguistic acts, requiring explication in mentalistic terms as well. They are where the 'social' meets the 'cognitive'. Chomsky (1986) calls this view of language **E-language** or 'externalized language'. This extension of the object of inquiry, while it adds enormously to the complexity of what we must try to 'fit together', raises the very question of the extent to which the form and functioning of language *can* and *must* be socially or contextually explained. We can ask whether it is *possible* for social explanation to penetrate the formal language system or module and determine its shape. Like *all* kinds of explanation, social explanation is a problematic notion. In chapter eleven we will be looking at this problem as it relates to the explanation of language. But we have already seen how we need to use social factors in accounting for variability. There are other features of language which require a different sort of social explanation. One such is the use of language in small-scale conversational settings. Consider the following exchange from the film *Saturday Night and Sunday Morning* (1961), written by Alan Sillitoe. We will be using excerpts from this film at various points in our discussion. Doreen is talking about a girl at the firm in Nottingham where she and Arthur work. They are sauntering together in a park, arm in arm.

DOREEN: She got married yesterday. She looked ever so nice.
ARTHUR: What was the bloke like, could yer smell the drink? He must have been drunk to get married.

After his utterance of the word 'drink', Arthur physically moves away from Doreen, losing her. Doreen has uttered two English sentences. We are in the same position as Arthur. We have to ask, 'What did she *intend* to convey?' This is the same as asking *why* she uttered it, to me, here and now, in this context. Consider this possible answer. She intended to convey that she believes that the propositions are true, namely that the girl in question got married yesterday and that she looked nice. We can say that Doreen *stated* this. She performed a statement. But now see how we are referring to Doreen's language. Words like 'intention', 'state', 'perform', mean that we are explaining Doreen's utterance as a kind of human action. She *did* something. She performed a **speech act**. This is a crucial concept in the study of discourse, the use of language in interaction.

But there are other possible answers to the 'why' question. Consider these possibilities. Let's first assume something about the context, namely that Doreen and Arthur are 'going together', part of a social institution which can lead to 'marriage'. They have the roles of boyfriend and girlfriend. If we assume this, then it is plausible that Doreen intends Arthur to understand that they also ought to get married. That's what she intended to convey. She performed not only a statement, but also a *request for action*. There are other possibilities. Perhaps she was only *suggesting* that they get married, or *broaching the topic* of marriage. Arthur's job is to construct an explanation of why she performed that particular utterance, to discern the intention behind her action.

Note that all these indirect interpretations would have to be reasoned out by Arthur. Overtly, all Doreen is doing is making a statement. Now consider the context, the sort of things Arthur would have to know, in order to do this reasoning. Much of the context of the reasoning is social, for example, about the institution of 'going together', as well as how their own roles and history together fit into this pattern.

The kind of reasoning involved in decoding conversational utterances is even better illustrated when we look at Arthur's *reply*. Ask yourself whether his reply is to her statement, or rather does it give us evidence that he took what she said as a request or suggestion. Is he rejecting or repudiating a perceived request? Or merely replying to a statement with a question? If he is repudiating her suggestion then try to work out the reasoning required to connect 'X married Y' and 'X is drunk'. We see at this stage how semantics enters into discourse. To do the reasoning, we have to know the conventional meanings of the words 'marry' and 'drunk' and their contributions to sentence-meaning. We also have to know the social background, knowledge without which we could not understand what Doreen and Arthur are doing.

There are some further points to note about this exchange. First, the meanings involved are specific to this particular context. If Doreen had been speaking to her mother, for example, she could not have conceivably intended to suggest or request that they get married. Second, according to my interpretation – and my claim about how Arthur took Doreen's remark – the ultimate message that she intended to convey was something like, 'We ought to get married.' But this message is not 'coded' in the actual words. It is implied by Doreen and inferred by Arthur. It is an example of **intentional communication** conveyed inferentially. Third, it is possible that I could be mistaken about Doreen's intention. In this kind of inference there is always an element of risk. Fourth, since the intention is indirectly conveyed, it is **deniable** by Doreen; she could always say in reply, 'What *are* you talking about? I *only* said she looked nice!' Speaking indirectly allows for tactics in the negotiation of relationships, for treading softly. Fifth, note the element of indeterminacy or vagueness in the message. I gave a number of alternative speech act analyses above, for example, 'to request', 'to broach', 'to suggest' etc. Even leaving speech acts aside, there are many distinct ways we could 'take' the message as alternatives to, 'We ought to get married.' For example, 'Wouldn't marriage be a beautiful thing for you and me?', or 'I'd like to get married myself', etc. The message might be vague! There is another alternative. Perhaps Doreen did *not intend to communicate* to Arthur any message at all in the sense that he recognize her intention. Instead, she merely meant to strategically 'plant the notion in his mind' that marriage is a state worth entertaining, without him recognizing it as a message from her. In this case *the utterance wouldn't be a case of intentional communication at all* although still a speech act, 'strategic insinuation' or 'planting an idea', perhaps.

Finally, irrespective of Doreen's intents, I have used background information to infer that Doreen is the one anxious to marry Arthur, not vice versa. I have also imputed that understanding of Doreen to him. The assumption is that Doreen, in her role as a young woman, might be motivated to manipulate Arthur into considering a married state that he would dismiss or resist if it were raised directly, given the kind of man he is. I have spontaneously made a **gendered** interpretation, one which depends on background information about types of 1950s gender roles. Since neither participant presumably wished to make explicit the topic of how 'laddish' and 'girly' they are ('the drink' and 'looked *ever* so nice', respectively), we are doing a **critical analysis** of this passage. That is, we are providing a social analysis revealing patterns in their relationship and belief systems which are implicit, probably not consciously available to Doreen and Arthur as they interact. In general, the necessity of *social* explanations of conversation ought to be clear.

In this chapter, we have defined sociolinguistics broadly as that branch of linguistics which studies those properties of language which *must* be explained in social terms. Social explanation within linguistics falls into two main types. The first type involves looking at the large-scale social patterning of variation and change. We attempt to correlate variation within a language with social categories such as class, sex, geography, formality, etc. in the context of historical change. This large-scale study is sometimes called either, **correlational sociolinguistics**, **variation studies**, **modern urban dialectology**, or **sociolinguistics proper**. Chapters two through seven cover this approach.

The second way in which language is socially explained looks at small-scale speech situations, like that between Doreen and Arthur. Depending on which of the academic disciplines or research paradigms the study is conducted, this type of small-scale situational study is called **pragmatics**, **conversation analysis**, **the ethnography of communication**, **discourse analysis**, **social semiotics**, **critical linguistics** etc. In the second part of the book, chapters eight to ten, we shall look at these approaches. Chapter eleven examines the social explanation of language in general. In doing so, it shows that the two kinds of approach to language and society covered in the earlier chapters are not unconnected.

2 A tapestry in space and time

> We must be careful not to overrate the uniformity of existing languages; it is far enough from being absolute. In a true and defensible sense, every individual speaks a language different from every other.
>
> Whitney (1875)

Sociolinguistics was defined in the last chapter as the branch of linguistics which studies the properties of language which require reference to social factors for their explanation. One such property is **variation**. We recognize many different 'ways of speaking' the same language; for example, speakers with different dialects or accents. Sometimes we get variation within the same community between two distinct languages; for example, between French and English. In this first part of the book, we shall examine such large-scale patterns of variation.

But first notice that both of these examples of variation presuppose that we know what *a* language is. This is not as easy a question as it sounds. In fact, the title of this chapter is not a bad metaphor for the sort of entity in question.

The question, 'What is *a* language?'

The question, 'What is *a* language?' is not the same as the question, 'What is language?' In the former case we are asking about the nature of particular languages, 'the English language' or 'the French language' etc. We shall see that in this case the answer proves, surprisingly, to be at least partially social. To the latter question, the answer is largely a psychological one. To the universalistic question, 'What is language?' the current best answer is Chomsky's: language is a set of very specific universal principles which are intrinsic properties of the human mind and part of our species' genetic endowment (Chomsky, 1986: 15ff.).

However, whenever we confront language we always confront such principles realized in a particular **variety** of language. A variety is a neutral term which simply means any particular 'way of speaking'; it is applicable to any linguistic phenomenon we want to treat as a single unit. Thus, when we observe an utterance it is always in a particular **language**, in a particular **dialect** of that language, and pronounced with a particular **accent**. Note that I am using the word 'dialect' here as a subdivision of a language, a 'dialect of a language'. A dialect varies from other dialects of the same language simultaneously on all three linguistic levels; phonologically, grammatically, and in terms of its vocabulary or lexically. An accent, by contrast, consists of phonetic variation on its own.

The problem is to explain these varieties and this variation. If, as some people suggest, there are universal principles at work in all human languages, why do we find in actuality so many varieties, and massive and seemingly random fluctuations? There are two answers to this.

One has to do with **typology**, or **language types**. In putting together a language, there must be a systematic way of relating a given meaning to the superficial arrangement of parts of a sentence. For example, there has to be a way of telling apart the subject and object of the sentence. It seems that there are only a limited number of logically possible ways to do this. Therefore, given the available psychological mechanisms we have for the production and interpretation of sentences, and the logical possibilities, it follows that there will only be a certain number of types of strategies which are possible. And these will be reflected in the structure of differing types of languages. Historically unrelated and widely geographically separated languages often are typologically similar in some respect. For example, Eskimo, most Australian aboriginal languages, and languages of the Caucasus of the former Soviet Union all share a highly exotic type of case system, the way in which

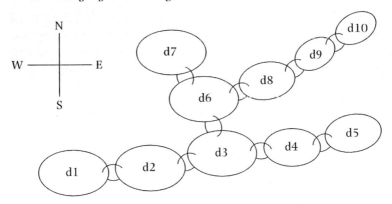

Figure 2.1 A dialect continuum

changes in the endings of words relate to who is doing what, and so forth.

But typology is only one reason why languages differ so much. The other reason is historical and social. Speech is always uttered by individuals who are members of social groups which are both separated from and related to other social groups in space and time. Space and time are both crucial. To begin tackling this, let's consider, in an idealized way, the nature and relationships of the dialects of a language.

The simplest way to consider a dialect is as a language variety associated with a particular place, or a geographical dialect. Indeed, our names for most dialects are geographical: Parisian, Lancashire, Liverpudlian and so on. If we imagine the area in which Figure 2.1 is printed as representing merely geographical space, then the numbered dialects simply occupy different geographical regions. The numbers of the dialects represent the names speakers give to the way they speak, as distinguished from their neighbours.

In general, dialects differ from each other more radically the more remote they are from each other geographically. So, in our model, dialects 1 and 10 would be linguistically the most distinct from each other. The dialects in our model also form what is called a **dialect continuum**. This is a chain of dialects with the following property. Speakers of dialect 1 understand dialect 2 extremely well. The number of linguistic features differentiating the two regional varieties may be quite small. However, speakers of dialect 1 and dialect 3 understand each other rather less well, and speakers of dialect 1 and dialect 4 less well again. There comes a point, however, say at dialect 5, where dialect 1 is no longer intelligible to the local people and vice versa. That is, dialects more remote from each other fade into mutual unintelligibility, while adjacent dialects are mutually intelligible. This reflects the fact that the degree of geographical separation reflects the degree of linguistic difference between the dialects. There are some famous examples of such dialect continua. For example, the West Romance dialect continuum means that one can proceed through rural communities from the Atlantic coast of France through Italy, Spain and Portugal, never losing intelligibility between adjacent villages, although speakers of the standard languages, French, Italian, Spanish, Portuguese, find each other mutually unintelligible.

Separation and divergence

It seems, then, that sheer geographical separation is a causal factor in the differences between dialects. When the distribution of any given variant feature is independently plotted and its boundary, or isogloss, drawn on a map, it is often found that the boundaries of a number of features at least partially coincide forming **isogloss bundles**. These linguistic boundaries tend to coincide with major physical features, such as rivers and mountains, which separate one community from the other. The inference can then be drawn that geographical separation produces linguistic divergence, given time. This kind of conclusion reflects one type of model of the historical processes that lead to language differentiation and the existence of separate varieties. Dialects emerge through time by a process of **splitting** from a single parent variety.

But why should geographical separation lead to linguistic divergence? An obvious answer would lie in the idea of a **communication network**. Consider a population extended over geographical space. Any given person will communicate much more frequently and over a wider range of speech-event types with adjacent individuals, than with those who are more remote. This will produce a pattern of density of communication among those individuals who are immediately adjacent, in contrast to a much lesser density of talk between those who are not. Distinct groups will be nodes of very dense mutual interaction. Boundaries of less dense interaction will exist between distinct groups. Since people mutually affect each other's linguistic habits, there will be a tendency for such distinct groups to evolve away from each other in terms of the linguistic forms they normally employ. And one form of human group is obviously all those people who live in a given geographical locale, hence geographically based varieties of language.

Waves of change

But the picture of separation and divergence is far too simple to account for the facts by itself. Consider the linguistic data. It appears very messy indeed. Dialect continua show that the degree of divergence between the language of groups is relative to distance and accumulates gradually. Isogloss boundaries coincide only very roughly, and sometimes differ substantially for different variant features. Often, the occurrence of a feature spreads out from some centre. Other features radiating from the same centre spread out less far or perhaps farther. These meet and overlap with features radiating from other centres. Some features are intensely local, and others extend over large areas. Some relic areas suggest the preservation in a particular area of earlier forms. The situation becomes even less clear if one examines the linguistic variants in use in a given community. Imagine, for example, that there are different ways of producing the *same* speech sound. The r described in chapter one could serve as an example. You will recall that variant pronunciations of English were r-full, pronouncing the r in words like 'car' or 'guard', while others were r-less, omitting it.

In fact, faced with a real community, one finds very great complexity. Speaker A, who is a middle-aged man, may produce rs, but only a certain fairly low percentage of the times when it would be possible for him to do so. Speaker B, another middle-aged man, may only produce a low percentage of rs in casual speech, but more in formal speech. Speaker C, a young woman, who appears to be middle-class, may produce a fairly high number of rs, but Speaker D, her grandmother, may produce none. Speaker E, who was not born in the locality, may have the highest *r*-score of all. Speaker D, a member of an ethnic minority, may have a different pattern.

We'll be looking in later chapters at how such recalcitrant kinds of data can be explained. At this stage, let's just take an overview. It's clear we're not observing any one relationship to the variants in the community. Its use of the form is not uniform. This lack of uniformity could be accounted for, if a change is in progress, and different individuals stand in different relationships to the change. There is clearly no sudden or abrupt division between those that have a variant and those that do not, as one might expect from a splitting theory.

A **wave theory** of linguistic change accounts for this. In this view, variant forms originate at some point. The variant then gradually spreads by diffusion. In geographical terms, the variant would move in time farther and farther from its point of origin, producing a pattern like a wave that spreads out when a stone is dropped in a pond. Other, later innovations would produce waves which, at any given point in time, are behind those caused by the spread of earlier innovations. Waves coming from different directions, that is, those that have different points of origin, will meet and overlap with these former waves. Some innovations, of course, might not spread at all beyond the immediate vicinity of their point of origin while others might be aborted almost as soon as they begin. Patterns of convergence as well as divergence could be accounted for by this kind of model.

But why do individuals stand in different relationships to the variants? This is because the community itself is not uniform with respect to the variant feature. Up to now, I have been considering space quite literally, in terms of the distribution of population between two points. What is needed is the notion of **social space**. Clearly, there will be weaknesses in density of communication between many different kinds of social group within a given community, and each group will thus form a communication network of its own.

Social space can be viewed as including the geographical distribution of a population. After all, where a person lives determines his or her membership in a social group by virtue of that fact

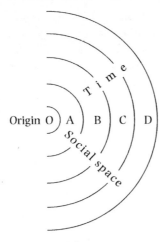

Figure 2.2 Waves of change

alone. Thus urban and rural are important social dimensions in themselves. Relevant dimensions of social space are those that are needed to account for the distribution of linguistic variants. Thus, besides geographical factors, such dimensions as age, sex, ethnicity and social class place social groups in differing relationships to the variable features of language. There is a great deal more to it than this, but that will become clear in later chapters.

Changes propagate through communities in waves. Figure 2.2 displays this process schematically. There is an innovation at point O, adopted by various social groups successively. The change spreads by diffusion through social space. In Figure 2.2, then, points A, B, C, D could represent the fact that a given social group has adopted one variant over the other for any given variable feature. There will be a stage, however, when a given group uses both variants, when the change is passing through that social space. Observed at that time, the group will be distinguished statistically from other groups, in terms of its preference for one variant or the other. Changing features will always be variable and statistical in the overall community, while unchanging features (for example, after a change has completed its propagation through a group) may be categorical in a given group.

But we are talking about time as well. Successiveness entails temporality – thus O, A, B, C and D also represent points in time. B could be the time when both features, but with different statistical preferences, first appear in group B, having crossed a boundary in social space, and so on for C and D. If we are studying a geographical diffusion, the points in time, marked by the successive waves, will coincide with the extension of the variability in literal space. They will be isoglosses drawn on a map.

There is a further subtlety and complication. Variant linguistic features usually have more than one environment in the linguistic system itself. For example, the (r) variable occurs in word-final position, as in 'car', or immediately following a vowel, as in 'guard'. Linguistic changes in which variants occur characteristically move through the language system, environment by environment. The rate at which one variant is chosen also depends, therefore, on which environment the change has reached, as well as on social factors. This can also be represented by a wave diagram. The letters A through D could represent the propagation of the change through the environments in which the variable occurs within the language system itself.

Clusters of features

What then is a dialect? The processes of change explain the fact that any variety, including a geographical dialect, is part of a continuum in social space and time. They are not absolutely discrete entities. One can see, however, how complex boundaries, or discontinuities, can occur which would serve to distinguish one variety from another. These would predictably mirror boundaries in social space and run along lines of weakness of communication. Consider, too, a sort of 'metropolitanism' view of diffusion. Factors of prestige, that is, people's attitude to a variant and, more import-antly, to the group with which it is associated, will lead to its pro-pagation. This will produce similarities in the varieties spoken by those groups under the 'metropolitan' influence of another group. But such propagations will reach boundaries at the limits of that 'metropolitan' influence, where they meet waves from other centres of such influence or from local resistance to outside innovation.

In other words, there are pressures towards both difference and similarity, and these together produce a continuum with internal boundaries which are 'more or less' statistical affairs. This reflects the groupings and processes in the social space in which the speakers are located.

In terms of its linguistic features, no variety of language is a discrete entity. What is true of dialects is true of any variety. We can thus define a variety more precisely. If there is a tendency for variable features to occur together in a cluster and if speakers utter given variants for a similar percentage of the time, and if this also correlates with some common social feature of the group of speakers, then this joint characteristic of speech and speaker is a variety. *A variety is a clustering together of linguistic features within a continuum which is explicable in terms of some dimension of social space.*

In the literature, besides geographical dialects, we find reference to ethnic varieties, men's and women's varieties, and **sociolects**, varieties which are based on features like social class. We can talk about the particular kind of speech which adults use to babies and very small children, or the speech of adolescent peer groups, as varieties. And there are **registers** of speech. These are varieties defined by the social **function** of language; for example, the linguistic choices which characterize advertising copy, scientific prose or sports commentary. And, of course, there are the recognized forms of literary language: poetry, the novel, drama and so forth.

Note that a variety is by definition a social entity. It is not just a type of language but a type of language that is socially definable and explicable. The linguistic side of any variety, however, is always problematical because it is a clustering tendency within a continuum. And any given utterance is multi-dimensional, exhibiting simultaneously the features which correlate with each of the dimensions of social space, and the point in time in which the speaker is located.

Interfaces

I have explained how it is we always confront a variety of language, and not Language, because of the social and historical

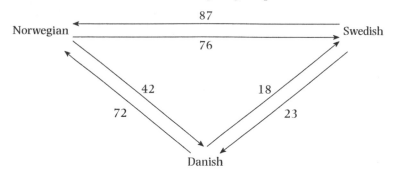

Figure 2.3 Semicommunication in Scandinavia (*from Haugen, 1967*)

processes of differentiation. Now consider again the original question, 'What is a language?', in the sense of the English language, the French language, the German language and so on. Let's try some definitions:

1. A language is an aggregate of related dialects.
2. A language is the aggregate of those dialects which are mutually intelligible.

But neither of these work. They are both refuted by the data of dialect continua. Linguistic relatedness and difference is a matter of degree. These definitions would have the West Romance or West Germanic dialect areas as single languages. I mentioned the West Romance area earlier. A similar situation exists between Holland and Germany. One could proceed, village by village, from the Dutch coast to Vienna and always find mutual intelligibility between adjacent communities, although unintelligibility obviously occurs when the varieties are remote from each other in the continuum. But the Dutch and Germans consider that they speak distinct languages.

Scandinavia, except for Finland, also forms a dialect continuum. In an article entitled 'Semicommunication: The Language Gap in Scandinavia' (1967), Einar Haugen found a considerable degree of mutual intelligibility between native speakers of Norwegian, Swedish and Danish. Figure 2.3 shows the percentage of informants from each country who claimed to understand their neighbours' language fairly easily upon first encounter. This degree of mutual intelligibility is a matter of linguistic distance, but Haugen also found that it correlated closely with the informants' attitudes to the other groups and also with the degree of 'perceived beauty' of the language in question. The fact is that linguistic relatedness and mutual intelligibility between what are thought of as distinct languages is a matter of degree. One study of related dialects and languages from the Algonquin family of American Indian languages, that is, languages and dialects which have diverged from a single hypothetical parent language, found that the degree of mutual intelligibility was precisely related to the degree of linguistic distance. A degree of divergence which results in unintelligibility between dialects, on the other hand, is no guarantee that the dialects will be unambiguously promoted to the status of separate languages. This is the case of Chinese, which has a number of mutually unintelligible dialects.

All the above examples are drawn from clear dialect continua or involve historically related, and therefore similar, languages. (Historically related languages are divergent dialects of the parent.) But are there not clear situations where historically very remotely related languages have clear boundaries? One might expect such situations, for example, where Romance languages meet Germanic languages. It is indeed very often the case that distinct languages come into contact. This is usually the result of some historical process such as immigration, emigration, invasion, conquest or trade. Mass dislocations or movements of peoples, such as the mass enslavement and transportation of Africans to the Americas, often result in populations with different languages coming into long-term contact in ethnically heterogeneous societies.

Consider just for a moment the large-scale population movements which, historically, have contributed to the making of almost any contemporary society. Such situations always bring diverse languages into immediate contact. And, as with dialect continua, there are complex boundaries between the linguistic systems of the different populations. At such interfaces, bilingualism is always generated in the society. Of course, societal bilingualism entails many bilingual individuals in the interacting groups. The distinctness of the boundaries between the language systems, in both the individual and between groups, is closely related to the social processes that are taking place. It depends, for example, on the degree of segregation or assimilation between the groups. And there are always pressures working in both directions. In other words, the processes at the linguistic interface are both dynamic and social. In multilingual situations many varieties may be involved.

In his classic study of **language contact**, Uriel Weinreich (1964) studied factors involved in such interfaces and examined mechanisms of **interference** between varieties on various linguistic levels. He noted that interference was not random, not merely a question of piecemeal borrowing, but was systematic. Systematic changes occurred in the speech of bilingual communities, as foreign elements were integrated into, and restructured, the tightly knit patterns of the interacting languages. The language contact situation which Weinreich studied, between Swiss German and Romansh, a Romance language spoken in Switzerland, was stable. But that is not always the case.

Language death and language birth

In some contact situations, languages can die. In situations of unstable bilingualism when certain social conditions obtain, languages can become the mother tongues of shrinking speech communities. Finally, they become no one's mother tongue, like a star blinking out. When this happens we can speak of language death.

The investigation of this process, of **language shift** from a recessive minority language to a dominant majority language, has only recently been studied intensively (see Campbell, 1994; Dorian, 1973, 1981, 1989; Dressler, 1988). We will be looking at the social conditions for language shift in chapter three, but here let us just sketch some of the structural consequences when contact between languages leads to language death.

There are a number of ways in which a language could disappear. It could catastrophically die in cases of genocide, or if it was systematically repressed. But the most common situation is gradual language loss; in which a population shifts languages over generations. In these situations decay in competence, poor models to learn from and a lack of clarity about norms, produce certain kinds of changes. Nancy Dorian (1973, 1981) made a study of a dialect of Scots Gaelic in the final stages of decay. Three villages on the east coast of Scotland retained the language in an area in which it had otherwise disappeared in the course of the last century and a half. The remaining Gaelic speakers, who ranged in age from eighty to only forty, were *all* bilingual in English. Bilingualism on this scale is a prerequisite for a population to move from one language to another.

Studies have revealed changes in languages that are symptomatic of language death, although these are sometimes hard to distinguish from other processes of change. In fact, one feature is the intensification of change itself. There are many simultaneous linguistic changes and they proceed rapidly. There is massive borrowing of words, which is a reflex of the cultural hegemony of the majority 'way of life'. And these uses of 'foreign' words remain 'foreign'. They are not phonetically integrated into the borrowing language. There appear to be processes of simplification on all levels without any compensating complexity elsewhere. For example, case inflections or gender classes get dropped. Formerly obligatory rules become variable. Morphology, the form of words, becomes simpler and word order plays a larger role. The resources of the syntax become reduced; for example, the ability to modify a noun with a relative clause is lost; e.g. 'The people *who lived in Norwich* caught the train.'

Dorian's (1973) study noted some of these phenomena. The form of Gaelic spoken, compared with healthier dialects in the west of Scotland, was much reduced in grammatical and lexical alternatives. The verb class was lexically 'extremely weak and showed borrowing from English on a truly massive scale'. Since the community lacked a monolingual Gaelic core, there was no reference group to set a clearly focused norm for younger speakers – those in their forties. Therefore, they lacked confidence in the correctness of their speech. Dorian noted that even those who claimed Gaelic as a mother tongue were often more competent in English; they were **semi-speakers**. There was much variation between generations. Accelerated syntactic change was occurring towards simplification. All of these were signs of the loss of competence in a stable set of norms.

By contrast, in contact situations we sometimes also find **language birth**, the relatively rapid emergence of new languages. This can happen if there is an urgent requirement for communication across sharp boundaries where social conditions prevent the normal acquisition of second languages. This process of language birth is called **creolization**.

There are at least two senses of this term, one broad and one more narrow. A broad conception is given by Bailey and Maroldt (1977) in which creolization is the outcome of any language contact of sufficient depth to produce a new language. They write that creolization is a 'gradient mixture of two or more languages; . . . a creole is the result of mixing which is substantial enough to result in a new system, a system that is separate from its antecedent parent systems'. This new system becomes the mother tongue of a speech community.

But creole studies have been the site of intense controversy within linguistics. This has been caused by lack of agreement about the genesis of creoles (for a survey of some of the alternatives, see Muysken, 1988). Among these is another narrower conception of a creole based on one particular type of genesis, which has major implications for our theory of language in general. When people of very divergent tongues are thrown together, for example, under conditions of plantation agriculture or any situation where they are not in a position to become properly bilingual in the most powerful tongue, a functionally specialized variety emerges called a **pidgin**. There is some dispute about how much structure pidgins possess. But they are highly simplified. In Bickerton's view they are not full languages, but 'protolanguages' that serve the specific needs of communication. They lack many of the features of languages which are acquired as 'mother tongues'. However, if a pidgin becomes the only source for the acquisition of first language by children, a miracle happens. A new fully developed human language emerges. In recent creole studies, the term **creole** tends to be restricted to varieties that emerge in this way (Foley, 1988).

The significance of this sort of creolization is important. The children appear to have learned a language without having data rich enough to do so. They seem to have invented syntactic constructions out of thin air. One of the most powerful ways to explain this has been Bickerton's **bioprogramme hypothesis**. This view claims that faced with the impoverished input of a pidgin, children automatically produce a fully fledged language by deploying the universal biological programme which all children use in language acquistion. Bickerton marshals evidence for this from his studies of Hawaiian creole. Such a result would be significant in two ways. First, it provides collateral evidence for Chomsky's views of the biological basis of language. Second, the common features of creoles would reveal just which linguistic features are essential to language. (For example, if the source language had lost number or gender agreement, these would never be reconstituted in the creole. But if pronouns or pluralizers were lost they would always be restored.) However, Bickerton's ideas remain controversial.

Let's return to a broader conception of creolization, to mean simply the emergence of a new language through the gradient mixing of languages in contact situations. Both this and the pidgin-creole definition allow for the rapid emergence of new varieties, sudden language birth. This contrasts with the picture I painted earlier of languages gradually changing through separation and divergence. In the view of the 'divergence' account the reason that English differs from German is that they are on different branches of a family tree which came about through divergence from a common ancestor. But just as a simple theory of divergence cannot account by itself for the complex patterns of contemporary variation (see below, chapters four to seven), divergence cannot account alone for the complex relationships between historically related languages. (For example, English and French share a very large percentage of their 'words', although with variant meanings and pronunciation.) The fact of creolization taken as radical language mix in contact situations offers another model. The picture becomes more complex. Divergence is supplemented by a theory of mixing; separation with contact.

Creolization processes may figure in the history of European languages. Bailey and Maroldt (1977), for example, have suggested that it is needed to account for fundamental features of Middle English which differ radically from the antecedent Anglo-Saxon. James Milroy (1984: 11–12) has suggested that even the stronger sense of creolization may have occurred at some 'language contact'

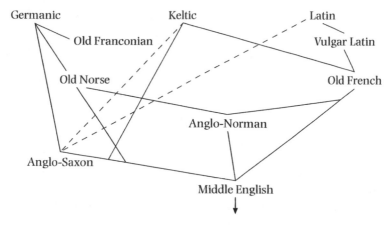

Figure 2.4 A language-mixture view of Middle English (*from Bailey and Maroldt, 1977*)

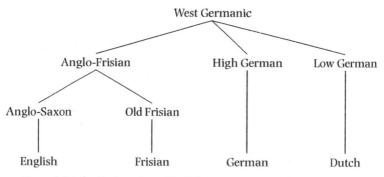

Figure 2.5 A family-tree view of English

stages, with Old Norse and Anglo-Norman French, in the history of English. Evidence for this is provided by certain of the linguistic properties of English; the loss of its case system and overt genders, the massive replacement of vocabulary, the preference for a fixed subject-verb-object word order, and so on. Figures 2.4 and 2.5 contrast the language-mix and family-tree models as they might be applied to English. In Figure 2.4 the interaction is seen as more fundamental than simply interference or borrowing. Similarly, it has been argued that Old French went through a creolization process in its emergence from vulgar Latin.

Standardization: language making

We are confronted with continua in every dimension, including the historical, in our attempt to discover what kind of entity 'a language' is. Obviously, it is wrong-headed, on the purely linguistic level, to think of 'The English Language', 'The French Language' and so on, as discrete 'things' with clear boundaries, internal homogeneity, or invariant rules, either in space or time. All the processes we have discussed point towards variation, heterogeneity and change within a language.

But there is an opposing process, working towards making a language *uniform*. And the fact of importance for our argument is that, just as the diversity was socio-temporal, so are the processes that work towards uniformity. These lead to the evolution of **standard languages** such as **Standard English** or **Standard French** or **Standard German**. (Tellingly, these are often referred to as **national languages**.) Just as the process of creolization happens under certain socio-historical conditions, so does the process of **standardization**. Although the major European and other world or classical languages (e.g. Arabic) have undergone this process, most languages that have existed have not had standardized varieties.

There is an ambiguity in our use of the phrase 'a language'. This has been part of our problem with definition. Consider the following sentences.

1.   (a) ***Nobadi no** gaan a puos yet.*
      (b) No one has gone to the post office yet.
2.   (a) ***Non** a di pikini-dem **neba** si **notn**.*
      (b) None of the children saw anything.
3.   (a) ***No** waata **no** de a hous.*
      (b) There is no water in the house.
4.   (a) ***Nobody don't** like a boss hardly.*
      (b) Hardly anybody likes a boss.
5.   (a) *Over by them bus stops.*
      (b) Over by those bus stops.
6.   (a) *Are you the one what said it?*
      (b) Are you the one who said it?
7.   (a) *You likes him.*
      (b) You like him.

8.   (a) *Do yous want any dessert?* (addressed to more than one person)
         Do you want any dessert? (addressed to one person)
     (b) Do you want any dessert? (addressed to any number of persons)

Sentences 1 (a), 2 (a) and 3 (a) are negative sentences in Jamaican Creole (Bailey, 1966: 92). Sentence 4 (a) is an example of negation in a southern US white Non-Standard dialect from Atlanta (Labov, 1972a: 148). Non-standard examples 5 (a)–7 (a) illustrate the use of *them* instead of *those* as the plural of *that*, the use of *what* as a relative pronoun, and the use of the third person agreement marker *-s* for second person (Trudgill, 1979 and 1984a: 32–7 for lists of non-standard features). Example 8 (a) illustrates the use of *yous* (addressed to more than one person) as a genuine second person plural pronoun, a distinction that Standard English is not able to make. All the (b) variants are in Standard English. It is important to be aware that the non-standard variants follow regular grammatical rules, just like the standard variants. To many people the non-standard 'just sounds *wrong*'. That is one result of standardization.

In one usage of the phrase 'a language', all these sentences are of equal status. 'The English Language' includes *all* the related linguistic systems, *all* the dialects of English. But in another sense of the phrase 'a language' – the one where the term *contrasts* with 'a dialect' – the (b) examples do differ from the (a) examples. Some people would insist that the (b) examples are 'correct' English, and that the (a) examples are 'bad' English. They are taking a **prescriptive** attitude to the language, making judgements between dialects. In this use of the phrase 'The English Language', one particular dialect, Standard English, is placed in a special position above all the other varieties. It is considered to be *the* language. The other versions are considered 'mere' dialects. The standardized variety, on the other hand, is *not* considered by the speakers to be a dialect. Rather, it *is* English to those who speak it.

Standardization is a complex of belief and behaviour towards language which evolves historically. The main features of this process are schematized in Figure 2.6. I will look at these in turn.

In standardization, one linguistic variety, the standard, is raised above or is made **superordinate** to the dialects, which are

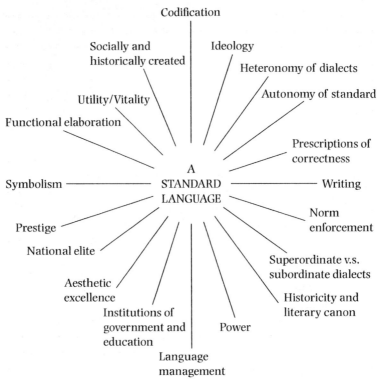

Figure 2.6 Standardization. The social treatment of a linguistic system

subordinate to it. Stewart (1968: 535) introduces a related distinction whereby the standard is viewed as **autonomous** of other historically related varieties, while a dialect is **heteronomous** with respect to the standard. By saying the standard is autonomous, we are saying that it functions as a unique and independent linguistic system and not a part of something else. An autonomous language can be in contact with other languages, even languages to which it has a close historical relation. But one is not subordinated to the other as a dialect. For example, the West Germanic dialect continuum has at least three major **centres of autonomy**: Standard German, Dutch and English. These dialects are recognized as languages. English and Welsh and English and French have had complicated contact but as standard languages they are treated as autonomous. By contrast, a heteronomous linguistic system is one that functions in the linguistic community as a dependent variety of an autonomous system. Therefore, it is subject to correction in its direction (Stewart, 1968a: 535). A variety that is heteronomous to an autonomous system like Standard English is a dialect of that system.

All languages do not have a standard variety. (And in fact most people don't speak the standard where there is one. For example, probably the majority of English speakers use non-standard 'double' negatives.) Whether a standard language emerges from a dialect continuum is contingent because a standard is **socially and historically created**. The roots of varieties like present day Standard English or Standard French have been traced (see, for English, Milroy, 1984; Milroy and Milroy, 1991; Lass, 1987; and for French, Battye and Hintze, 1992; Lodge, 1993; Judge, 1993). As Lass points out, standard languages of the modern type are not characteristic of the Middle Ages. In England prior to the fourteenth century, 'there was no dialect that had much more prestige than any other; to write in English meant to write one's own dialect, using local forms and spellings' (Lass, 1987: 62). Instead of a standard *versus* dialect configuration, the common situation across Europe was dialect diversity in the vernacular and bilingualism, with Latin being used for many prestige functions among a small elite. This configuration of varieties enacted a pre-modern society.

The emergence of the European vernaculars as standard national languages involved their **functional elaboration**. The dialects had to be made adequate for new situations formerly the province of Latin, and in the English case, Anglo-Norman. (That's one reason why English has so many Latin and French loan words.) The new standard languages had to develop adequate resources for functions such as the law, government, literature and the arts, commerce, the 'new science' and so on. European standard languages are social institutions which developed as part of the growth of nation states and the evolution of the modern world.

The standard has **high prestige** as opposed to its dialects. One source of this prestige is its allocation to the high functions mentioned above. For example, the translation of the Bible into the vernacular was an important part of creating both Standard English (the King James version) and High German (Luther's translation). Another source of this prestige is related to its role in the symbolic integration of the larger national or 'ethnic' social identity. Not only does the standard language serve the practical purpose of internal integration and external segregation, it does so symbolically. The language serves as a **symbol** of the nation, a representation of its autonomous identity and unity (Haugen, 1966; Edwards, 1985). People feel **language loyalty** reflecting their sense of national identity.

The potency of this symbolism of identity and exclusiveness is testified to by ubiquitous notions about the **excellence** of the standard, its logical or expressive character, its purity, its aesthetic quality and so on. There is often a feeling that these qualities are threatened by degeneration or innovation or outside influences. These feelings are part and parcel of standardization.

Another source of the prestige of the standard comes from its use by **national elites**, the most powerful and prestigious groups in the society. In England, it was the speech of the Court, the southeast midlands and the London, Oxford, Cambridge triangle that formed the basis of Standard English (Lass, 1987: 67). The standard is characteristically used in the **institutions of government**. Governments actively support and develop its use. Both symbolically and practically the standard language is an instrument of **power** in the society.

The definitive linguistic feature of a standard is its **codification**. This is the linguistic reflex of the acceptance of one variety as 'really' the language. *The attempt is to create a uniform norm of usage through the suppression of optional variation.* As Milroy and Milroy (1991: 22–3) also point out, it is appropriate to think of standardization as an **ideology** since it is a matter of norms to which actual usage conforms only imperfectly. It is impossible to impose 'from above' absolute uniformity on complex, diverse and changing societies. Given this suppression of variation in favour of a uniform norm, it follows that standardization tends to be conservative. A language is not viewed as an essentially dynamic process. Change is often slowed down somewhat because competing variation is smoothed out, especially at the core grammatical level.

The process of codification is carried out through **language management** by a class of **language guardians**. These are people who are professionally involved with language; for example, editors, scholars of language, journalists, creative writers, literary critics, cultural pundits, dictionary makers, textbook producers, educationalists and teachers, and so on. For example, William Caxton, the first English printer, was also one of the first to complain, in the fifteenth century, about the variability of English and the difficulties this created in printing. This is a case where the practical value of a standard is obvious. It was only in the eighteenth century that Samuel Johnson produced the first comprehensive English dictionary. It largely provided the norm for the spelling of Standard English. The culmination of the English lexicographical tradition finds its full expression in *The Oxford English Dictionary*, edited by J. A. H. Murray, in a project spanning the years 1857–1928. Such monumental works of scholarship 'ascertain' a language, specify what is included and excluded, as well as codify. The philosopher Michael Dummett makes the point that such works also establish a language as larger than any one person's linguistic competence. The social institution of the standardized English lexicon is a resource that transcends individuals. It is a form of social 'language making' which is quite different than a language as something someone speaks. Sometimes the control of language has been a matter for the state. This has notably been the case with respect to French (see chapter three, and Judge, 1993; Lodge, 1993).

A standard language is usually the vehicle of a **literary canon and tradition** which exemplifies what critics have selected as the best examples of the language. Indeed, literary works are the source of the citations in dictionaries. It is remarkable how the figure of Shakespeare is central to the ideologies of both the English nation and the English language. Scholars also construct a historical genealogy for the language. They trace its origins and its continuous development leading to the standard, thus guaranteeing its autonomy as regards other languages. This is called the **historicity** of the standard. Johnson's dictionary is prefaced with a history and a grammar of the language. Milroy (1992: 50f.) remarks that many modern discussions of the history of English present it as a 'convergence' towards the standard, as the end product of historical development. This is a view which is both an aspect and a result of standardization and serves to justify it by suppressing consciousness of variation.

Creating a standard is not itself a single process, but has many facets. Different aspects of the language – grammar, lexicon, pronunciation, style and writing – are standardized in different ways. In fact, the notion of a totally unified standard is an illusion. The existence of a **written medium** is a crucial aspect. As Milroy and Milroy (1991) point out, it is in the written language where the imposition of uniformity is most successful and complete. In fact, it is hard to envisage how codification could be achieved in a pre-literate society, or how that sense of a language as a unified, tangible 'thing' could exist without writing. Standardization is interwoven with writing. It is hard to overestimate the impact of this technology on language.

For one thing, a literate public conceives of the written standard as the language in its purest, most 'correct' form. The most complete standardization is that of **spelling** where virtually no variation is permitted. Absolute uniformity is almost achieved on this dimension. An absolute line can be drawn between 'correct' and 'incorrect' spelling and degrees of accuracy can be assessed with precision and 'errors' condemned. Spelling errors in written or printed text would reveal significant social information about the writer. A more nebulous standard exists with respect to **punctuation** and other conventions of **layout**, and with respect to **prose style**. A form of 'plain style', also originating in the eighteenth century and surviving in twentieth-century essayists and writers of editorials, has become a model of 'good English' in yet another sense. The complaint that people 'don't know English' can refer to an inability to write in this style. In fact, there is no single way to write English. Appropriate style varies with function (see chapter eight below).

Standard English is maintained through mechanisms of **norm enforcement**. The very existence of a codified norm is a prerequisite for **notions of correctness**. These are produced and reproduced through the **prescriptive and evaluative** activities of the language guardians which result in general disapproval of 'incorrect' or 'bad' English. Dictionaries not only codify the language, and make it visible to consciousness as a unified homogenous entity, they also prescribe the 'correct' forms of spelling.

Another mechanism of norm enforcement has been termed the **complaints tradition** (Milroy and Milroy, 1991: 31f.). People have been complaining about 'the state of the language' since standardization began in the late middle ages. We noted Caxton's complaints about lack of norms in the fifteenth century. But everyone is familiar with the complaints that regularly appear in the media criticizing 'incorrect' usage, the decline of the language among the young, or the irresponsibility of linguists and educators with respect to protecting good English. (There is another kind of complaint about a use of English that misleads or deceives, the sort of abuse of language highlighted by George Orwell. But that's not what we are talking about here. See Milroy and Milroy, 1991: 44f. and chapter ten below.)

Perhaps the most powerful norm enforcement mechanism is education. The reality of the issues we are discussing can be seen clearly in the controversy over the role of English language in the national curriculum in the period up to 1990. We are now using the term 'English' in yet another way; as a school subject and an academic discipline. The national curriculum for English in England and Wales published in 1989, *English for Ages 5 to 16*, known as The Cox Report, makes it a specific requirement that 'all pupils should learn, and if necessary be explicitly taught, Standard English'. The whole of the report's chapter four is devoted to the Standard. The curriculum confidently says that even though Standard English is just a social dialect, it is a very special dialect. While other dialects – including each pupil's own dialect – must be treated with respect, Standard English has a world-wide role. To participate fully in the society and pursue professional activities pupils will have to speak and write the standard. They have that 'entitlement'. This seems to be an informed and sensitive enforcement of the norm of the standard.

But there are problems which reside in the differing facets of standardization. As we noted, a standard language is not itself a unified thing. In English, there is a separation of accent and dialect. Standard English can be pronounced with any accent, as he national curriculum says. When spoken Standard English first emerged, its codified grammar and vocabulary would, as a matter of course, have been pronounced with its 'home' accent, that of London and the south east midlands. The prestige accent coincided with the prestige grammar; in fact, until about the seventeenth century the primary concern was with the phonology (Lass, 1987: 66). (This did not apply to Scotland where a different standard had developed.) However, as English has spread outside England and with the emphasis on written English, pronunciation can be viewed separately from grammar and vocabulary. Therefore, the prestige accent of England and Wales (**Received Pronunciation** or **RP**, which we shall discuss in chapter five) is not a dimension of Standard English beyond those two countries. Standard English can also be pronounced with non-standard British accents, although in England it tends in fact to go with Received Pronunciation since the two are always learned together. Conversely, an English child who acquires English with a 'non-standard' accent is *not* likely to acquire Standard English with it, but have some dialect markers. Outside England, there are many accents in which Standard English is spoken: General American and Canadian, Australian, Scottish, East African and so on.

Now reconsider the prescriptions of the national curriculum. Children who learned Standard English as their mother tongue also acquired RP or some regional version of it. All other children – the non RP speakers – have to be re-socialized with respect to a small number of grammatical features. Trudgill (1979: 11–12) lists fifteen common dialect features, including examples 5–7 above. At the same time as their *what* relative pronouns are being corrected, they are being told that their pronunciation is acceptable. But a child's linguistic abilities are not easily split this way. (And, in fact, the response of the popular press was the outraged claim that 'bad' pronunciation was to be encouraged, such is the confusion over norms and correctness in the society!) Creole speakers, almost universally black, have a more grievious split, since creoles diverge much more from the standard, as can be seen from examples 1–3 above. In the main, the whole weight of the state is being mobilized against about fifteen grammatical features like *what* relative pronouns and double negatives. This means that most pupils must

not only learn to write the Standard, but must also learn to av
non-standard features while speaking, but only as far as gramm
is concerned. Meanwhile, a pretence is adopted that 'all accent:
are equal' with respect to the standard which is patently untrue in
terms of social response (see chapters four to seven below). Enforcing the norm of Standard English thus poses problems in education (Mitchell, 1994; Stubbs, 1986; Cheshire, 1984).

One aspect of the focused norms of the standard is symbolic and
has to do with identity and social unity. We shall examine this use
of language in more detail below, especially in chapter seven. But
there is a practical side to standardization. The uniformity has a
utilitarian value in that it permits economic and administrative
integration over the whole extent of the state without the impedi-
ment of divergent dialects. It is a centripital force. It facilitates
printing and other technologies of communication. It allows the
free flow of ideas and central control. The practical and the symbolic meet in the **vitality** of standards, their use in the maximum
of situations.

Globalization

The emergence of standard languages is a contingent, historical
phenomenon. This kind of superimposed uniformity was a feature
of the emergence of the European nation states in the modern
world. It is surprising to think that things we think of as natural
like The English Language, The French Language, etc. are particular cultural constructs of a time and place.

A subsequent historical development has been the emergence
of some European national standards as **international languages**. English, French and Spanish are used over wide areas
and so are Russian and German in a more regional way. This is a
consequence, first of colonial expansion and imperialism, and later
of the globalization of the modern capitalist economy and western
culture. As some social and economic forms of life have spread
throughout the world, so have the corresponding forms of language. Cases in which languages have been deployed over wider
culture areas are nothing new in history; Latin, Hellenistic Greek,
Classical Arabic, Written Chinese, Sanskrit and Swahili are all

.mples of this type of linguistic situation. Today, Standard English is often referred to as a **world language** because of its unique status. As regards Standard French, it has been actively promoted as an international language through the concept of a world-wide French speaking community, *la Francophonie* (Battye and Hintze, 1992: 54–6; Sanders, 1993).

A common definition of Standard English is that it is the variety taught to foreigners. Over the last few centuries, especially marked in the post-war period, English has come to have a unique global position (Strevens, 1984; Crystal, 1997; Cheshire, 1991; Bailey and Görlach, 1982). Strevens reports estimates that in 1982 there were around 674 million English users. It is very difficult to assess how many people have learned Standard English around the world, but there are more than 300 million native speakers alone. (Of course, it is likely that most of the latter are non-standard speakers.) The unique aspect of English is its global distribution and its use for international domains.

We can distinguish between the role of **English as a Second Language** in societies like Kenya or India where the language has an officially recognized place in the linguistic repertoire, and **English as a Foreign Language** in countries like Thailand, Russia or China where the language has specialist roles as a link to the international community. Finally, English has **world-wide functions** and **special purposes**; for example, in science and technology. About two-thirds of scientific research is said to be written in English. It is the language of most international institutions and conferences, news and media, international 'pop' culture, trade and commerce, aid and administration and transport. The current information revolutions are inherently globalizing and can only increase the influence of English. There is a major industry in the teaching of the language world-wide and competition for influence (with German) in areas like Eastern Europe.

The results of globalization are transforming the nature of Standard English. We can take the example of East Africa. Kenya illustrates the role of English in a situation of the 'English as a Second Language' type. In Kenya, the linguistic repertoire is complex. First, there are the languages of ethnic affiliation. Each person has their ethnic mother tongue. Second, there is *Ki-swahili*, the regional East

African *lingua franca*. Thirdly, there is English. English has sp
ized functions, for example in education beyond the primary le
in administration, and in the higher levels of commerce. It isr
optional. In practice, it is obligatory. This means that most edu
cated Kenyans are trilingual.

We saw earlier that Standard English evolved with a particular
symbolic value, of 'English' identity and an integrative function for English society. The symbolic and functional roles of the
standard are utterly transformed in the East African context. It
becomes highly ambivalent. On the one hand, English represents
the colonial past, access to the global economy and modernity,
social advancement and education, but also 'the foreign' and
'non-African'. On the other hand, so integrated is English into the
society, it is 'naturalized' or 'made African' (see below). Crises of
identity are clearly visible in **post-colonial literatures** in English.
The language itself makes possible a written 'literature' in the European sense which represents local experience, but at the same time
it conveys non-African cultural values. In many areas of the world,
international languages have also had a role in the language death
of aboriginal languages, which are being lost at an alarming rate.
In this respect, Trudgill has termed the major international tongues
'killer languages'.

Post-standardization?

The spread of English has resulted in tensions which challenge
the standardizing process – the suppression of optional variation.
We saw how the spread of the language beyond England led to the
separation of phonological/phonetic (accent) from other levels of
variation (dialect). Accent apart there are some divergences between British and North American standards. Are we to say that
there is a single Standard English that tolerates minor variation,
or a family of Standard Englishes? In Britain itself, there was and
still is a competing northern English standard or Scots, which has
been largely suppressed since the Union, but which serves as a
symbol of Scottish particularism.

With globalization, there has been the emergence of **new
Englishes** which challenge the ideology of standardization. In

Africa, the Caribbean, India, Singapore and elsewhere the ~ns of the standard that emerge as the language is 'naturalized' ~ bilingual environments or post-creole situations also *differ form-ally as dialects* from the older standard. In terms of accent, East African English has its own distinctive accent which is normatively acceptable and conveys the complex values noted above. These new symbolic values, and the new literatures, transform the meaning of Standard English.

Challenges to uniformity have led at least one commentator to refer to a **post-Standard** situation (Fairclough, 1992: 202). This refers also to the new assertiveness of regional and 'popular' forms (and styles) of speech; in particular, to the acceptance of accent variation. But challenges to the supremacy of Standard English can be overstated. Try writing a job application using double negatives, *what* relatives, misspelt words and slang! The concept of the post-standard draws attention to the heterogeneity upon which the standard is superimposed and which it has repressed from consciousness; and the illusory and multifaceted nature of Standard English.

M. A. K. Halliday (1978) has recognized a variety which stands at the opposite pole from standard languages. An **anti-language** is the idealized antithesis of the idealized uniformity of the standard. Standard languages are 'utopian' – 'the dream of a common language' – unifying *us* in the mainstream dominant society. By contrast, the societies of 'outsiders' such as prisoners, criminal underworlds, youth cultures, travellers, form 'anti-societies' with respect to mainstream norms. The anti-languages generated by such groups are symbolically oppositional and represent alternative social realities. These forms of speech are elusive but generate their own vocabulary and other linguistic features; for example, the extensive use of *like* in some forms of teen slang. In the gypsy dialect **AngloRomani** (also called 'broken language' or 'half-and-half') English word formation, grammar and phonology are mapped onto Romani vocabulary (Hancock, 1984: 374). The language has been **relexicalized**; which makes it inaccessible to non-speakers. Similar relexicalization is a feature of prison talk (*screws, porridge, the nick, the bill* etc.). Areas of cultural preoccupation develop very elaborated vocabulary. They are **overlexicalized**.

It is hard to place all the suprising forms of heterogeneity upc which the idea of the standard is superimposed.

It is now clear that the question 'What is a language?' is answerable in many ways. It depends on the context in which one approaches the question. From one set of perspectives, a language is a *dynamic process*, a changing continuum in many dimensions. From another, it is an *institutionalized entity* deeply identified with the life of a society and intricately involved in its patterns of power and its political and historical development. From this second institutional point of view, a language is a *codified set of norms* in which the heterogeneity, the dynamic ongoing processes of variability and change are repressed from consciousness. The codified set of norms is imposed on the ongoing variability and change. A language seems stable and thing-like to the imagination. From the former dynamic point of view a description of a language would include *all its variant forms and the dynamics of change*. From the institutional point of view a language would appear to consist of *unchanging, invariant structures*. These are important issues within the methodology of linguistics itself. Linguists' intuitions about the object of study cannot but be affected by standardization. Not only is the variation repressed from personal and public consciousness, it can only be discovered through the social investigation of language. It will turn up in partial and apparently disordered ways in the speech of an individual.

We have considered a language as both variable and uniform from different points of view. In the next few chapters, we will look at kinds of varieties and variation in more detail. Three perspectives will be taken into account: from the point of view of the society; from the point of view of the individual in that society; and from a purely linguistic point of view. In any given description, these three will be necessarily interrelated.

3 Language varieties: processes and problems

> Grand port of navigations, multiple
> The lexicons uncargo'd at your quays,
> Sonnant though strange to me; but chiefest, I,
> Auditor of your music, cherish the
> Joined double-melodied vocabulaire
> Where English vocable and roll Ecossic,
> Mollified by the parle of French
> Bilinguefact your air!
>
> From 'Montreal' by A. M. Klein (1948)

Let us now look at some of the differing ways in which linguistic varieties occur in speech communities, beginning with some large-scale variation and then working our way down to differences which occur on a smaller scale.

We will begin with societal bilingualism, the situation in which two or more distinct languages form the repertoire of a community. To explore the complex issues involved in a bilingual society it is interesting to look at one such situation in real historical and political depth. For this Canada will serve as a case study. (For general surveys, see the Further Reading.) We will then turn to those cases in which the society recognizes and names two distinct varieties of the *same* language as the repertoire, and speakers with more than one variety at their disposal switch or fluctuate between the alternatives. This leads us to the problem of relating the larger social pattern of the varieties to what individuals actually do in specific situations; and, even thornier, the problem of

the actual linguistic relationship between varieties which peop‑
perceive as linguistically distinct.

Linguistic diversity in Canada

When one thinks of language in Canada, one thinks of the relationship between English and French. These are the two 'official languages' of Canada. But this relationship, though a central one, is an integral part of a more diverse picture of languages in Canada. I will briefly profile some of this diversity before looking at the relationship of English and French.

The first source of linguistic diversity is the languages of Canada's indigenous peoples. There are said to be between fifty and sixty American Indian languages in Canada. These can be grouped into ten language families. The Inuit, or Eskimo language, *Inuktitut*, makes an eleventh. The ten language families, moving from east to west, are: *Algonquian* (107,000), *Iroquoian* (3,700), *Siouan* (2,000), *Northern Athapaskan* (20,750), *Kutenai* (1,000), *Salishan* (3,500), *Wakashan* (6,000), *Tsimshian* (3,000), *Tlinglit* (2,000), *Haida* (few) (Kaye, 1979; Foster, 1982). The figures in brackets are rough estimates, from Kaye (1979), of the number of speakers. Many if not most of the particular languages within the families have few speakers and are rapidly disappearing. Foster assesses their chances of survival. Some like *Tuscarora*, with seven speakers, or *Tagish*, with five, are almost extinct. Others, like the Algonquian language, *Cree*, with 55,000 speakers spread in a great northern arc from Labrador to the foothills of the Rockies, are more likely to survive. In fact, by the 1991 census 94,000 people claimed *Cree* as a mother tongue.

As noted in chapter two, language death is common in situations of language contact between indigenous peoples and modern 'global' society everywhere. The world-wide loss of linguistic diversity is extremely rapid. There has been a recent surge of activism among Canada's indigenous peoples, although what effect that may have with respect to language maintenance remains to be seen (Gagné, 1979).

A second source of linguistic diversity in Canada is the languages spoken by immigrants. Just as language contact with indigenous peoples is a feature of the global spread of Europe since the seventeenth century, so is the mass movement of peoples through immigration. The history of Canadian immigration has meant that over a third of the non-indigenous population is neither of British nor French origins. Linguistically, the 1991 census reports that out of a population of 26,571,050, English was the mother tongue of 16,516,180, French was the mother tongue of 6,505,570 and 3,549,305 reported a mother tongue that was some other language. Historically, the largest of these language groups have been, in descending order, German, Italian, Ukranian, Dutch, Polish, Chinese, Portugese and Hungarian (Engel, 1979: 226). In the post-war period, the largest group has been Italian (Saint-Jacques, 1979: 208). But most European and many Asian languages are found in Canada. By the time of the 1991 census, the most numerous Other mother tongues had become Italian (512,000), Chinese (492,000) and German (476,000). Chinese was the most frequently reported language used at home other than English and French, by 430,000 speakers.

The central question for immigrant linguistic groups is the relationship to the host society; either the process of linguistic assimilation, or maintenance and survival as a distinct linguistic, ethnic and cultural group. Many factors affect this process. The demographic size and concentration of the group is important. The more than 400,000 strong Italian group in Toronto is stable enough to have generated a contact dialect, *Italese* (Chambers, 1991: 96). Attitudes to the immigrant culture are important. It has been the relative isolation of the self-consciously inward looking religious values of the Russian speaking Doukhobor sect which has maintained their language, and the identity it encodes (Vanek and Darnell, 1971: 267f.). Canada is often thought of as a 'mosaic' of ethnic identities, rather than as a 'melting pot' in which origins disappear. However, it seems safe to say that the overall pattern over time has been language shift. It has been noted that there is 'no evidence to show that assimilation of ethnic groups is occurring faster in the United States than in Canada' (Saint-Jacques, 1979: 209). Almost all Canadians can speak either English or French, irrespective of their origins. The overall pattern in Canada has been towards the adoption of English by other groups, even in

Quebec. This theme will concern us when we look at the relatie
ship of the official languages, French and English.

The history of and variation within **Canadian French** is the
subject of a large and rapidly expanding literature (Walker, 1979;
Blanc, 1993; Bouthillier and Meynaud, 1972; Sankoff *et al.*, 1989).
There are two main French dialect areas in Canada. First, there is
Quebec French, the major variety of French in North America and
mother tongue of the majority, about 83 per cent, of the population of Quebec. This variety has two offshoots to the west. There
are the Franco-Ontarians of eastern and northern Ontario;
464,040 with French mother tongue in 1991 (see Mougeon and
Beniak, 1991: ch. 2). There are the francophones of the prairies,
who also include the *Métis*, a people of French and native descent
who speak a mixed French-Cree dialect, *Métif*. Finally, there is the
Acadian French of the maritime provinces, particularly New Brunswick, where 33.5 per cent of the population were of French mother
tongue in 1986, and its *Cajun* offshoot in Louisiana. The term
Cajun derives from the term for the *Acadiens*, the French speaking
people of *Acadie*, the territory which is now the Canadian provinces of Nova Scotia, New Brunswick and Prince Edward Island.

Broadly speaking, there are three dimensions to the sociolinguistic study of French in Quebec: first, linguistic variation within
Quebec itself; second, its relation to Standard 'Parisian' French;
and third, its contact with English. The technical linguistic side of
these dimensions is fascinating, but we can't discuss them here.
In general, French in Quebec, which originated in the western
regional dialects of seventeenth- and eighteenth-century France,
is spoken in three broad varieties; a 'cultivated' Canadian French
which is different from but approximates to Standard French, various popular rural dialects, and *Joual* (from the pronunciation of
cheval), a non-standard urban vernacular which is extremely vital
and distinctive (Walker, 1979: 139; Blanc, 1993: 247). Up until
recently Canadian French, especially the popular varieties, has
attracted negative attitudes in comparison to Standard French,
but these attitudes have recently changed (Blanc, 1993; Bourhis,
1984). Canadian French is conditioned by its contact with Canadian English. The contact takes place within Quebec, most intensively in Montreal (see below), and in the relatively **stable bilingual**

its on either side of Quebec. These are the main bilingual language contact areas in Canada.

The serious study of **Canadian English** is recent (Chambers, 1975, 1979a, 1991; Bailey, 1982). It is the majority language in all the Canadian provinces except Quebec. In 1991, 63 per cent of all Canadians had English as a mother tongue, as opposed to 25 per cent with French. Canadian English is a variety of North American English, structurally very similar to the adjacent US dialects. This isn't surprising since 'heartland' Canadian English has as its base the eighteenth-century colonial English of the loyalist American colonists, who having sided with the British in the American Revolution, formed the first settlements in what is now English Canada. Today 'heartland' Canadian English and its accent, **General Canadian**, appear remarkably uniform as an urban middle-class standard found everywhere but Newfoundland and in anglophone Quebec. (For a change taking place in the vast area from Toronto to British Columbia, see Hung, Davison and Chambers, 1993.) There is a rich diversity of dialect in Newfoundland reflecting its old and distinct settlement history. Montreal English differs from General Canadian, and the Ottawa valley is purportedly a complex dialect area. In linguistic terms there are only a few clear linguistic diagnostics of General Canadian.

There is **Canadian Raising**, in which the onset of the vowel sounds in words like 'wife' and 'knife' or 'house' and 'mouse' is pronounced higher in the mouth than in Standard British or American accents. But this feature may be disappearing among younger speakers (Chambers, 1991). Be this as it may, Canadian English is an autonomous sociolinguistic entity both in terms of speakers' attitudes and in terms of the selfconscious social and academic treatment it has undergone, which are akin to standardization as discussed in chapter two above.

Canada to 1960: societal bilingualism

Against this background of diversity, let us now turn to the relationship of English and French in Canada. Most of what I am going to say is based on Stanley Lieberson's study, *Language and Ethnic Relations in Canada* (1970). Lieberson's initial concern is

demographic. How much bilingualism is there in society? W
exactly is bilingual and why? Is **language maintenance** or **language shift** going on between French and English?

The primary source of data that Lieberson uses to address these questions is Canadian census information from 1931 to 1961. But the early 1960s is a good starting point for us, because those are the years when what has been termed 'The Quiet Revolution' was taking place in Quebec. Traditional Quebec society, mainly rural and agrarian, was undergoing rapid urbanization and industrialization. First, we will use Lieberson's study, with some updating, to paint a picture of Canadian societal bilingualism up to 1961. Then we shall examine the consequences of this, and changes up until today. Many issues relevant to the study of multilingual language contact, language planning, and language maintenance and shift will be illustrated.

A number of notions are crucial for demographic studies of bilingual communities. The first is **ethnic origin**. This term explains itself: what 'descent group' does an individual belong to, British, French and so on? The second is **mother tongue**. In the Canada census citizens are asked which was the first language learned which they still understand. If a person has replied that his or her mother tongue is different from the language of his or her descent group, then we have evidence that language shift has occurred between generations somewhere in the family's history. Alternatively, if there is no divergence, then the language of the ethnic group has been maintained. Successive censuses will reveal the rate and location of language shift, if there is any.

The number of bilingual individuals in the society can be roughly measured by the 'official language question'. The census baldly asks, 'Can you speak English? French?' Note that this way of obtaining information requires self-assessment and this leaves open many thorny issues about what counts as bilingualism and how it might be objectively measured. This census data, therefore, is only what people *say* about which language is their mother tongue and their ability to speak the other official language. The degree of bilingualism in the community is relevant to the measurement of language maintenance and shift since it is the children of bilingual parents that are at risk in relation to intergenerational

.nguage shift. Another useful census question from this point of .iew is what language is ordinarily used at home. A gap between the ethnic origin of a family and the answer to the home language question is an indicator of language shift.

The conclusions which can be drawn from the census data are extremely interesting. At first glance the official languages look remarkably stable. The percentage of people reporting themselves to be bilingual remained steady at 12 per cent from 1921 to 1961. If one looks at the percentages of persons in each ethnic group and compares them with the percentages of persons in each mother-tongue group for Canada as a whole, there seems to be little evidence of language shift relating to English and French up to 1961.

| | Canada as a whole (1961) | | |
	French	British	Other
Ethnic Origin (%)	30.37	43	27
Mother Tongue (%)	28.09	58.45	14

The major process is the large-scale language shift occurring between Other and English. Those of other ethnic origins prefer English, and assimilate into the anglophone community in Canada.

But these figures concerning the relationship of the two languages are misleading. A clearer demographic picture emerges only when one examines what is happening in each province. Compare Ontario, the largest anglophone province, and Quebec, the province where French ethnicity and mother tongue are overwhelmingly concentrated:

| | Ontario (1961) | | | Quebec (1961) | | |
	French	British	Other	French	British	Other
Ethnic Origin (%)	10	59	31	80.64	10	10
Mother Tongue (%)	6.82	77.52	16.63	81.18	13.26	6

Table 3.1. *A pattern of language shift, 1931–61*

Province	Percentage of French ethnic group with French mother tongue	
	(1931)	(1961)
Prince Edward Island	77.3	44.5
Nova Scotia	67.7	42.8
New Brunswick	94.9	87.6
Quebec	99.4	98.2
Ontario	77.4	61.4
Manitoba	86.0	67.2
Saskatchewan	78.5	54.4
Alberta	70.4	46.8
British Columbia	48.5	33.7

(from Arés, 1964, reprinted in Lieberson, 1970)

This reveals language shift occurring from French to English and from Other to English in Ontario, while in Quebec, although the Other have shifted principally to English, the French mother-tongue group is maintained and only very slightly strengthened.

The extent of language shift from French to English from 1931 to 1961 in all parts of Canada, except Quebec and adjacent New Brunswick, was very substantial indeed. Table 3.1 shows by province the percentage of those of French ethnic origin with French mother tongue in 1931 and again in 1961.

The trend is sharply towards the loss of French as a mother tongue by those of French ethnic origin everywhere except in Quebec, and among the Acadians of New Brunswick. And even in the last two there is some loss up to 1961. We can see the demographic details of these processes in one province, Saskatchewan, in Table 3.2, taken from a study of language loss among the 'Fransaskois', the francophones of that province, done by Denis and Li (1988). Notice among those of French ethnic origin, the systematic relation between the loss of French mother tongue, percentage bilingual, and those who have become unilingual in English, which between 1921 and 1981 has grown from 9.2 per cent to 49.5 per cent of the group. Bilingualism in Saskatchewan

Table 3.2. *Language loss among Francophones in Saskatchewan, 1921–81*

Year	Saskatchewan population			French origin only				
	Total	Per cent bilingual*	Per cent French origin	Number French origin	Per cent French mother tongue	Per cent bilingual	Per cent unilingual English
1921**	757,510	6.1	5.6	42,152	90.4	81.5	9.2
1931**	921,785	4.8	5.1	50,700	82.1	76.3	16.5
1941	895,992	5.6	5.6	50,530	86.5	69.6	23.4
1951	831,728	4.9	6.2	51,930	64.9	61.4	31.6
1961	925,181	4.5	6.5	59,824	54.5	52.8	41.3
1971	926,245	5.0	6.1	56,195	51.1	53.9	43.4
1981	956,440	4.6	4.9	46,920	47.5	49.2	49.5

* Official languages only.

** Statistics on per cent bilingual, and on origin are based on population over ten years of age.

(from Denis and Li, 1988)

has been largely concentrated among those with French mother tongue. Although as an ethnic group they have only marginally declined as a percentage of the population, 5.6 per cent in 1921 to 4.9 per cent in 1981, as a mother tongue group the decline has been enormous. Only 47.5 per cent of those of French ethnic origin retained French as a mother tongue, down from 90.4 per cent in 1921.

So we can discern two major trends up to 1960, trends which are continuing. The other group shifts mainly to English and outside Quebec, there is a loss of French as a mother tongue. One effect of this has been to reduce the percentage of Canadians of French mother tongue in Canada as a whole. While this was 28.09 per cent in 1961, it declined to 25.07 per cent in 1981, 25.01 per cent in 1986, and 25 per cent in 1991. Given that the proportion of people with French mother tongue is being maintained and even slightly increased in Quebec – 81.18 per cent in 1961, 82.8 per cent in 1986, 83 per cent in 1991 – another effect is to increase the 'territoriality' of the two mother tongues. The 1986 census, *Focus on Canada*, tells us that 'Persons with French as their MT are increasingly concentrated in Quebec. More than 85 per cent of persons with French as their MT resided in Quebec in 1986 . . . Furthermore, more than 96 per cent of persons with English as their MT resided outside Quebec . . . There is thus an ongoing polarization of Canada's official languages between two territories: Quebec and the rest of Canada' (Census 1986, *Focus on Canada*: 17).

Asymmetrical bilingualism

Can we relate these processes to the number of people who claim to be bilingual in the various provinces? Although the percentage of bilingual individuals had remained constant throughout Canada from 1921 to 1961, the concentration of that bilingualism was among the French ethnic group, and this was particularly marked outside Quebec. For example, in 1921, 86.8 per cent of those of French mother tongue in Ontario acquired English. In 1961, this was 77.3 per cent. In Alberta, far from the Francophone community of Quebec, 90.8 per cent of those with French mother

gue acquired English. Conversely, the number of people of
itish and Other mother tongues acquiring French in Quebec in
1961 was surprisingly low considering the fact that they were a
minority in that province. The figures for 1921 and 1961 are:

	Quebec			
	percentage learning French		percentage learning English	
	British	Other	French	Other
1921	29.8	38.8	41.1	84.7
1961	26.6	37.0	24.0	66.4

The percentage of British learning French is low. The Other also
prefer to learn English. The percentage of French learning English,
although declining, is very high given the overwhelming French
majority. *It is clear that bilingualism in Canada is asymmetrical and
is generated primarily in those of French mother tongue.* This occurs
very markedly outside Quebec, but also in 1961 significantly within
that province. It is this asymmetric bilingualism that puts the
French-mother-tongue group outside Quebec at risk to language
shift.

There are some obvious questions. What factors lead to this
asymmetric bilingualism? Why has widespread bilingualism among
those of French ethnic origin and mother tongue outside Quebec
led to language shift? Why has similar widespread bilingualism
not led to language shift inside Quebec? Why had not the numer-
ically small British ethnic group in Quebec become more bilingual
up to 1961 and laid the basis for a language shift towards French
in that province? In Quebec, both official languages are maintained.
Elsewhere, French is disappearing.

Montreal

To explore these questions, one tactic is to look very closely
at the interface, the place where the largest number of the two

communities meet and where the largest number of bilingua
viduals are concentrated. That is in the Montreal metropo
area. Lieberson (1981: 131) writes:

> Montreal might be viewed as a battleground between the French lan-
> guage and culture of Quebec and the English-speaking Canadians and
> Americans who surround French Canada. This metropolitan area, con-
> taining more that 10 per cent of Canada's population, is incontestably
> the great centre of English–French contact in North America . . .
> Perhaps 'battleground' is too dramatic a term for describing French–
> English relations in Montreal, although the occasional acts of violence,
> the more frequent verbal expressions of nationalism and the self-
> consciousness about language make our metaphor apt. If inherent in
> linguistic contact is the danger or possibility that one language
> will decline and the other expand, then, in this fundamental sense,
> Montreal, or any other multilingual setting, is a battleground.

The configuration of the varieties in the Montreal metropolitan
area in 1961 as published by the *Royal Commission on Bilingualism
and Biculturalism* is displayed below.

	Montreal metropolitan area (1961)			
	British	French	Other	Total
Population by ethnic origin	377,625	1,353,480	378,404	2,109,509
No. of bilinguals by ethnic origin	101,767	554,929	119,907	776,603
No. of individuals monolingual in each official language	462,260	826,333	` `	1,288,593

The contact of the languages in the city shows some of the characteristics we noted at the provincial levels. There is a preference
of the Other for English, as witnessed by the divergence between
the number of those of British ethnic origin and the number of
those who are monolingual in English. There is also an asymmetric

ation of individual bilingualism in the majority community, relatively little in the British minority. This is the opposite to the situation outside Quebec, where the British majority has virtually no bilingualism generated within it by the presence of a French minority. It is worth adding at this point that these figures show the very real distinction between societal and individual bilingualism. It seems on the face of it quite possible, at least in 1961, to be perfectly monolingual in the heart of the Montreal interface, as the majority of both ethnic groups are. However, one is more likely to be bilingual in Montreal, in 1961, if one is ethnically French.

The functions of the varieties in the city

Why do we get this imbalance? One possible explanation is that this asymmetrically distributed bilingualism results from the use of English in much of the city's economic life, a situation historically imposed on the French ethnic majority by the English-speaking minority. Lieberson's investigation into the uses of the two languages in Montreal corroborates this intuition. There are very marked occupational pressures generating bilingualism within the French majority. These are some of his findings.

The Yellow Pages. One method which Lieberson used to study the allocation of the two languages in the economic life of the city was to examine the distribution of entries for various activities under French and English rubrics in the Yellow Pages of the Montreal telephone directory. An entry might be under a French rubric, an English rubric, or both. One can infer from this which language would normally be used for the activity in question, or whether both languages would normally be used.

It was found that as one moved from retailing (activities which involve face-to-face contact at a local level) to manufacturing, industry and offices, the number of 'French only' entries markedly declined. This suggests that being able to speak only French would be a social disadvantage in these areas. But being a monolingual speaker of English would not be such a handicap.

Appointments columns. Lieberson examined the appointments advertised in the *Montreal Star* and *La Presse*. He noted that the

jobs which required English, for example technicians, accountan̄
managers, clerk-typists and stenographers, were heavily whit̄
collar. Such jobs, it followed, demanded individual bilingualism
from members of the French-mother-tongue group, but not of the
English. Labouring, sales and service jobs were over-represented
in *La Presse*.

Status of occupation. Bilingualism correlated with the status of the
French group, but not with the British one. The number of bilingual individuals of the French-mother-tongue group was 94 per
cent for managerial positions, through 70 per cent to 80 per cent
in sales positions, to 49 per cent for labourers. For the British group,
there was no such correlation.

Income. These patterns were reflected in the average incomes of the
two language groups. As a group, those monolingual in English
had the highest average income of all. The French monolinguals
were at the bottom of the pile. But even French bilinguals, although
better off than their monolingual neighbours, earned less than
people of the British ethnic group, both those who spoke French
and those who did not.

Such factors paint a picture of a city which is vertically stratified
by income and occupation according to ethnic and mother-tongue
group. In 1961, the allocation of English as the principal language
of business and industry produced a high percentage of bilingualism among those of French mother tongue, but did not place a
corresponding demand upon those of English mother tongue. This
also explains the preference of Others for English, and not for
French. When one further notes that the highest concentration of
bilingualism is among French men of working age, the conclusion
is clear that it is occupational pressure which, in general, motivates the individuals to become bilingual and, in turn, produces the
pattern of societal bilingualism.

Residential segregation

Now, given this distribution of bilingualism, what factors lead
simultaneously to French language maintenance within Quebec,
and language shift from French to English elsewhere?

Table 3.3. *Residential segregation by language, Montrea',*
1961

English only and			French only and		Bilingual
French only	Bilingual	Neither	Bilingual	Neither	Neither
64.3	43.4	61.9	24.6	59.4	54.0

(from Lieberson, 1970a)

One factor which is very revealing of the interaction between the linguistic and ethnic groups in Montreal is their degree of **residential segregation**, as explored in Lieberson (1965; 1970a). I must simplify his findings. Segregation was measured by an **index of dissimilarity**. The urban area was divided into tracts (the census tracts). The index was a measure of the number of individuals of each group in each tract. Complete segregation, in which there was no mix of groups at all, would be registered by an index of 100; complete integration, by an index of 0. This method was used to study both linguistic and ethnic segregation in Montreal. The first column, in Table 3.3, illustrates a high degree of segregation between French monolinguals and English monolinguals (64.3), whereas the low index score (24.6) between French monolinguals and bilinguals reveals that segregation between these two groups is low. In fact, the bilinguals of both groups are more integrated with their respective monolingual 'cores' than they are with each other. This means that each group has a spatial 'homeland' where the chances of intelligible communication are higher (you are more likely to be proximate to someone who speaks your mother tongue) than for the city taken as a whole.

Such segregation suggests that the languages have specialized functions within the larger society. One imagines that the situations typical of a residential community (home, shopping, church and so forth) are enacted in the language of each relatively segregated community. But in the larger economic sphere, English is required for many occupations. If this is true, segregation is a measure of the existence of coherent communities based on language and ethnicity, and in which the functions of the languages are specialized.

.It is interesting to note, by contrast, that the segregation ind.
are very low in those Anglophone cities where language shift h.
occurred from French to English. The indices are 21 for Toronto
and only 12 for Calgary. It would appear that a linguistic minority
has to find strategies for resisting language shift if it wishes to
maintain a minority mother tongue in a situation of widespread
bilingualism. Residential segregation is one such strategy, maintaining a 'home base' for monolingual speakers of the minority
language. But that doesn't get us very far into the whys and wherefores of language maintenance and shift.

Language maintenance and shift

A number of factors are involved in whether or not bilingualism leads to language shift. As we saw in chapter two, language
contact, which entails bilingualism for some speakers, always has
linguistic interference effects, if only on the varieties spoken by those
bilinguals. But social factors are crucial in determining whether
the weaker language group loses their mother tongue or maintains it in a stable bilingual situation. At heart, asymmetry of power
is involved in maintenance and shift. Fishman writes 'a problem
area that is so self-evident that . . . it has often been overlooked;
[language shift] occurs because interacting languages-in-cultures
are of unequal power and, therefore, the weaker ones become
physically and demographically dislocated' (Fishman, 1991: 59).
In Figure 3.1, I have tried to disentangle some of the factors
involved in maintenance and shift.

Widespread **bilingualism** among those whose mother tongue
is the weaker language is a necessary but not sufficient condition
for language shift. There are examples of long term stable bilingual
situations where languages are in contact without language shift,
e.g. Switzerland, Belgium. Note also that the weaker language need
not be a minority language, although it usually is. Historically,
French was the weaker language in Quebec, although the mother
tongue of the majority.

A **domain** is a grouping together of recurring situation types
in such a way that one of the languages in a repertoire, as opposed
to the others, normally occurs in that class of situations. And members of the speech community normally judge that the use of that

Figure 3.1 Factors in language maintenance and shift

variety, and not the others, is appropriate to that domain (see Fishman, 1971). Examples are Education, Home and Neighbourhood, Religion, Official and Governmental, Economic and so on. **Domain allocation** is an important factor in language maintenance. A wide range of domains means that a wide variety of areas of life can be led in that language. Clarity of allocation, and general **boundary maintenance**, both linguistic *and* social, where there is no doubt as to which language to use, also favours maintenance. Shrinkage of domains and the obtrusion of the more powerful language into more and more situations favour shift. In studies of francophone communities in Ontario where French is being lost, Mougeon and Beniak (1991) note that **minority language restriction** occurs. *This means that the minority language becomes used less frequently and in fewer social contexts. Use of the majority* *language in the home domain is a powerful sign of ongoing lang[e] shift.* For example, outside Quebec, although 5 per cent have Fren[ch] mother tongue, in responses to the 1986 census question abou[t] which language is used most frequently at home, only 3.6 per cent use French (see also Mougeon and Beniak, 1989: 291). In many minority language situations, the full range of varieties for use in many domains may not exist. If a language is restricted to the home, it may not have the resources; e.g. to deal with technical domains. The words simply may not exist in the language or in the speakers competence in it.

The range of domains to which a language is allocated is also a measure of its place in **the linguistic market** (Sankoff and Laberge, 1978; Dittmar *et al.*, 1988; see below chapter 6). A language is a form of cultural and social capital which can be cashed in economically. Knowledge of the variety with the highest market value generates bilingualism in those with other mother tongues. Parents are also led to prefer that their children acquire the most economically useful tongue. As we saw above, a linguistic market which valued English certainly produced massively asymmetrical bilingualism in Montreal, and also leads to the marked preference of the Other groups for English. But market forces don't operate in a vacuum. They interact with other forms of power in the law and government policy. And **political and legal factors** play a role in language maintenance and shift. Denis and Li (1980) point out that insufficient attention has been paid to *the political process of language loss.* To illustrate their point, they trace the abrogation of the traditional rights of francophones in Saskatchewan between 1875 and 1931. This played a key role in the decline of French in that province. Fishman (1991: 56) also draws attention to this factor, contrasting actual legal prohibitions of language use, frequent in the past in Europe (e.g. Welsh, Breton etc.) but now rare in democracies, with the effects of the moral deafness of the majority, customary indifference and the curtailment of the rights of minorities. With the re-appearance of nationalism and ethnic cleansing in Europe in the post Cold War period, the legal and political suppression of minority languages can't be ruled out. The point here is that **language legislation and language planning** in which language becomes an overt part of the political process can play a ϟ in maintenance and shift. (For a detailed discussion of language law in Canada, see Bastarche *et al.*, 1989.)

Bilinguals are usually more competent in one of their two languages. There is a pattern of **language dominance**. This is related to restriction of the number of domains in weaker languages. Children in minority language groups can also lack the input which they need to learn a full grammar of their mother tongue, or for the full range of vernacular varieties in that language. They become what Dorian called 'semi-speakers' of their mother tongues. The impoverished input is like a 'creolization in reverse' and leads to a simplification of the grammar. As noted in chapter two, this is a feature of language death. If the exposure to the mother tongue is largely restricted to the educational domain, then the variety learned can be rather 'schoolish' and non-vernacular. This could be a result of policies which try to stem language shift by turning a minority language into a 'school subject'. *When minority language mother tongue speakers become language dominant in the majority language, language shift is underway* (Mougeon and Beniak, 1989).

Demographic factors, the statistical distribution of certain characteristics of a population such as the sheer proportion in each ethnic or mother-tongue group, degree of bilingualism, age and manner in which second language is acquired, birth rates, degree of segregation and territorialization, social class, age, sex, patterns of in-migration and out-migration, rates of exogamy (marriage outside the ethnic group), all can have effects, and intersect with or reflect other factors in maintenance and shift.

But demography interacts with **ethno-cultural factors**. There can be a sense that the language is a vehicle for a historical, cultural, ethnic or 'national' identity (see Fishman, 1989, 1991). Maintenance is favoured if the ethno-cultural group values its language as the vehicle of a highly prized culture or way of life, a 'rooted identity', as Fishman puts it. At the same time, this can also be the 'us versus them' factor. A distinct language is a perfect way to inclusively enact an identity, while simultaneously excluding speakers of other languages from that identity. But any group may have positive or negative or ambivalent **attitudes to language** as a vehicle of ethno-cultural identity. The post-famine Irish are purported to have abandoned Irish as an embodiment of old identity and way of life that had led only to catastrophe. Pos. ive attitudes engender **language loyalty** and favour maintenance The identity and the language both have high prestige. Negative attitudes or indifference favour shift. As we shall see below, attitudes to language can be complex, ambiguous and either overt or covert.

The attitudes engendered or symbolized by a language are its **social meaning**. This is an important technical term in sociolinguistics. It designates the set of meanings which a language variety encodes and which it derives from the group whose language variety it is, or the situations in which it is used. The language variety comes to convey the identity of the social group and therefore also the attitudes evoked by the group in question, or the attitudes evoked by the situations in which the variety is used. A positive range of social meanings will favour maintenance.

But the populations involved may also have expectations about what should happen. In language contact which is the result of immigration, the host community may expect assimilation. In other words there may be **ideologies of contact**. The expectations or norms accepted by both or either group about what the relationship between the languages *should be* are a factor in what *will* happen. These may range from models of assimilation to those of linguistic particularism and separateness. This is related to the degree of interference and borrowing which people find acceptable. One model Fishman (1991: 64–5) calls 'cultural democracy'. This is the ethical continuation of democracy into minority cultural and linguistic rights. It entails official guarantees and support for minorities. On the other hand, democracy also requires vigilance against nationalisms that might over-ride human rights.

Canada since 1960: language planning

The way in which the Canadian situation developed after 1961 allows us to see the political consequences of societal bilingualism in crisis, how power and politics are inevitably involved with issues of language, and the ways in which language legislation can be used to effect linguistic developments. The sketch above added up a political and demographic time-bomb, which duly exploded into a demand for change. There have been two basic responses to the perceived crisis. Within Quebec, the response has found political expression through successive Quebec governments, which have embarked, since 1960, on the wholesale modernization of the society, and the assertion and guaranteeing of a predominantly francophone identity for Quebec, as far as is feasible. The power of the ballot box has been used to ensure French language maintenance. The powers claimed by Quebec governments to achieve these aims, and the simultaneous rise of separatism, have precipitated a continuing constitutional crisis in Canada as a whole. Quebec did not sign the new Canadian constitution in 1982. Two subsequent attempts to reach a constitutional accord failed. A separatist *Parti Québecois* government was elected in the province in 1994, which promised to hold a referendum on independence in 1995. So the very future of Canada as a single country is uncertain at the time of writing. Since the 1960s, the response at the federal level has been a major effort in developing policies of bilingualism and multiculturalism throughout Canada.

Quebec language policy

The series of Quebec language laws, Bill 63 in 1969, Bill 22 in 1974, culminated in 1977 with Bill 101, *The Charter of the French Language*. This is perhaps the most extensive example of legislative language planning ever attempted and is worth examining in some detail. It was the first Bill of the first separatist *Parti Québecois* government which was elected in 1976. We must note that official language planning is common today and has a long history. Standardization as discussed in chapter two is a form of language planning. And the development and codification of European Standard languages was usually done by official bodies (Bourhis, 1984: 2ff.; Fishman, 1991; Judge, 1993). A useful distinction can be made between **corpus language planning**, having to do with the codification aspect, and **status language planning**, having to do with the allocation of domains which a variety is to serve, and its official status.

Consider the issues from a Quebec francophone point of First, there are demographic fears. We saw the attrition of Fre outside Quebec and how this was leading to a historically declinin percentage of those with French mother tongue in Canada as a whole. There was the additional demographic fear of a 'Doomsday Scenario' – relative francophone decline within Quebec itself. This fear was based on the fact that since the 1930s immigrants had overwhelmingly opted for English, and had had their children educated in English language schools. At the same time, the Quebec birth rate, once one of the highest in the world – the so-called *revanche des berceaux* or 'revenge of the cradle' – had become the lowest in Canada by 1971. This scenario generated a profound sense of threat among nationalist francophones. Second, there was the historic anglophone economic domination illustrated above and the consequent role of English in the province. The third issue involved identity. There was evidence that historically Quebec francophones had a negative evaluation of their own language. Pioneering social psychological studies in attitudes to language (see below, chapter seven) by Lambert (1967) suggested that francophones at that time viewed 'their own linguistic cultural group as inferior to both the English Canadian and European French groups' (Lambert, 1967: 341). One can see the combined effects of English economic and European French linguistic prestige in these attitudes. Finally, among Quebec nationalists and the intelligentsia, there was a fourth factor, the continuing historical task of *la survivance* as an ethno-linguistic group fed by a sense of moral and historical grievance (for an up to date account of Quebec nationalism, see Ignatieff, 1994).

Bill 101 addressed these issues. On the status planning side, where previously English was also an Official Language in Quebec, French was made the *sole* Official Language. French was to be the sole language of government, of the courts, of civil administration, all public and semi-public bodies, both in their internal and external communication, and in accreditation of the professions – in fact in all public domains, except for specific exemptions, for example to Inuit or American Indian languages.

Two domains were of special significance, the economy and education. French was to be the language of economic activity.

business firms with more than fifty employees were required
obtain 'francization certificates'. Those with more than one
hundred employees were to set up 'francization committees' to plan
and then implement how the firm was to conduct its affairs solely
in French. Sensitive to the international nature of business, head
office and research and development activities were exempted. In
the domain of education, the right to education in French was
established and restrictions were placed on those eligible for
instruction in English, namely those whose parents, at that time
domiciled in Quebec, had received their elementary instruction in
English. This addressed the demographic anxiety by compelling
immigrants to have their children educated in French.

Another set of status functions is very controversial because
psychological and symbolic. There was an intention to create a
French-only 'ambience' in Quebec (Laporte, 1984). Hence all company names, all externally visible public signs, posters, commercial
advertising, were to be solely in French. Geographical place names
not in French were to be replaced by French names. The laws and
regulations regarding signs are very detailed. For example, as of
1989, signs in the interior of premises must also be in French, but
here it may be accompanied by another language. If so the French
must be markedly predominant; e.g. its characters must be at least
twice as large.

The Charter of the French Language has been implemented by
three Boards. There is the *Office de la langue française* which over-
sees francization and engages in corpus language planning and
linguistic research to this end. One aspect of this has been the
development of French terminology, especially in technical domains,
so that status planning can be effective (Daoust, 1984). This is a
codification aspect of standardization, as discussed in chapter two.
A *Conseil de la langue française* monitors the effect of planning and
both the status and quality of French in Quebec. This has had a
positive effect on the prestige of Canadian French as opposed to
European French. The prestige norm of the French language is no
longer the sole possession of France. Finally, the *Commission de
Surveillance et des Enquêtes*, which anglophones call 'the language
police', has powers to see that the law is being obeyed. The overall
purpose of the corpus planning and the 'ambience' aspect of the

legislation must be to affect attitudes, to signify the prest.,
French and to assert francophone hegemony. Daoust (1984: 1
argues that 'by francizing Quebec's *visage linguistique*, a deep
"francization" will follow throughout Quebec society'. Blanc (1993.
249) characterizes the general purpose of this legislation by writing that the language 'became not just a means of communication; it became an instrument of power, a way of gaining control
of the economy and education by securing its future and that of
French culture in Quebec'.

Federal language policy in Canada

The approach of the Federal government in Ottawa to language
policy has been quite different. In 1963, faced with the growing
pressure of francophone sentiment, a *Royal Commission on Bilingualism and Biculturalism* was set up, which reported from 1967–9.
The commission hearings made clear to anglophone Canadians
the demographic situation, the historical record and the depth of
francophone feeling. While Quebec policies have moved towards
explicit unilingualism in that province, federal language policy has
emphasized 'bilingual dualism within a multicultural framework',
and individual and minority rights (Bastarche *et al.*, 1989: 36).
The promotion of conditions for *stable bilingual situations* where
that is feasible has been part of a general response of endorsing
linguistic and cultural diversity, as part of a liberal position which
respects differences (Chambers, 1991: 101). In fact, the policy
espouses Fishman's 'cultural democracy'. Federal policy has had a
leadership role in promoting bilingualism, developing the prestige
of French throughout Canada and promoting a basic framework
of law which protects individual and minority rights.

More specifically, the 1969 *Official Languages Act* affirmed that
both French and English were **official languages** in law, of equal
status in the federal government and all its activities. The principle was established that subject to certain exceptions, Canadians
had a right to deal with central government in either French or
English. This led to intensive 'bilingualization' of the federal civil
service, and the extension of French services in areas such as broad-
casting. Bilingualism was generally promoted as a fundamental

ssion of Canadian identity. One consequence has been a large
.ease in French immersion courses among anglophones. A *Commissioner of Official Languages* was appointed to 'take all actions and
measures within his authority with a view to ensuring recognition of the status of the official languages'.

The new 1982 Constitution and the *Charter of Rights and Free-
doms* go further. French is established as an official language on
the provincial level in New Brunswick. But the other anglophone
provinces did not take this step. Rather, in Ontario, a 'functional'
language policy is employed; minority language services are provided where there is significant demand, e.g. in the 'bilingual belt'
(Cartwright, 1988).

In the crucial and historically contentious area of education,
Section 23 enshrines the principle that Official Language minorities have the right to receive instruction in their own language,
with the caveat that the number of children is sufficient to warrant the provision. This is supposed to guide provincial legislation
in this domain, which can then be subject to legal challenge. Note
that it also serves to guarantee English language education for the
minority in Quebec. Progress in providing French language education for francophones outside Quebec has been made, but the
process has been tortuous (Mallea, 1984). Nevertheless, a legal
framework exists in which Official Language minorities can create
infrastructure. However, as Mougeon and Beniak (1989) have
shown, such infrastructure by itself, e.g. schools, is not sufficient
to prevent language shift if the other conditions in Figure 3.1 aren't
favourable.

Canada and language planning: an update

One must be cautious in evaluating the effects of language planning in Quebec and Canada as a whole. We will look at Quebec
first. Has Bill 101 had the intended effect? Fishman (1991: 318–
19) says that although the French language and ethnic identity
are in fact secure in Quebec, francophones as of 1991 still don't
feel secure and 'French in Quebec has not yet arrived at the stage
of effortless and "taken for granted" existence.' The demographic
situation in Quebec, shown in Table 3.4 for the censuses from

Table 3.4. *Mother-tongue groups in Quebec 1971–91*

	French Number	%	1971 English Number	%	Other Number	%
Province of						
Quebec	4,867,250	81	789,185	13	371,330	6
Montreal	1,819,640	66	595,395	22	328,180	12
Quebec City	458,435	95	18,035	4	4,030	1

	French Number	%	1976 English Number	%	Other Number	%
Province of						
Quebec	4,989,245	80	800,680	13	444,525	7
Montreal	1,831,115	65	607,505	22	363,865	13
Quebec City	513,895	95	15,745	3	12,515	2

	French Number	%	1981 English Number	%	Other Number	%
Province of						
Quebec	5,307,010	82	706,115	10.9	425,275	7
Montreal	1,936,215	68	520,490	18	371,635	13
Quebec City	554,775	96	15,585	3	5,720	1

	French Number	%	1986 English Number	%	Other Number	%
Province of						
Quebec	5,316,925	83	580,030	10	635,495	7
Montreal	1,974,120	68	433,095	15	356,405	12
Montreal	More than one MT claimed				169,439	6

	French Number	%	1991 English Number	%	Other Number	%	Both English + French	%
Province of								
Quebec	5,597,930	81	601,405	9	517,975	7.5	91,590	2
Montreal	2,093,395	67	445,515	14	403,525	13	53,140	1.7
Quebec City	619,370	96	11,255	1.7	7,810	1.2	5,415	0.8

(from *Language and Society*, 8, 1982. Figures for 1986 and 1991 calculated from Mother Tongue data, *Census Canada*, 1986; 1991)

...–91, is quite stable, with the percentage of persons reporting ...ch mother tongue slightly increasing from 1971 to 1986, and ...maining stable at 81 per cent in 1991. The strength of French ...n Quebec is one half of the *increasing territorialization* of the two languages mentioned earlier. French mother tongue groups continue to decline everywhere except Quebec and adjacent New Brunswick. This has been the greatest weakness of Federal policy, and that of the other provinces. It has not been able thus far to prevent or even slow down the rate of language shift from French to English. There is even a slight shift in this direction in Quebec itself, offset by an equivalent shift from English to French. The Other group in Quebec still prefer to shift to English by a majority of 63 per cent to 37 per cent, but the trend is moving in the French direction. There was a shift towards French by the Other group of 28 per cent in 1981, 29 per cent in 1986 and 37 per cent in 1991. These changes may also reflect the effect of Bill 101 with respect to education; by 1984, 65 per cent of the children of immigrant families in Quebec were in French schools. Elsewhere in Canada, language shift from French to English as measured by the divergence between mother tongue and home language is substantial, and has grown between 1986 and 1991; the other side of territorialization.

Among the English of Quebec, a number of trends are observable. There has been a demographic decline which by 1991 appeared to be stabilizing. It was caused by out-migration to English Canada in response to the changes. This is shown in the substantial decrease in the numbers claiming English mother tongue in Quebec between 1971 and 1986, although there is a clear recovery in 1991. A second trend has been a steep increase in the bilingualism among Quebec anglophones. The percentage of those with English mother tongue who are bilingual is as follows:

1961	26.6%
1981	53.2%
1986	57.6%
1991	59.0%

As early as 1982, Caudwell reported that anglophone participation in francophone institutions was increasing rapidly and that 'bilingual anglophone professionals and businessmen are now everyday phenomenon'. By 1987, Cartwright (1987, reported Blanc, 1993: 252) discussed the increased bilingual competence of younger anglophones, and their more frequent use of French. Fishman (1991: 318) points out that within the English mother tongue group in Quebec, 46.6 per cent had switched to the most frequent use of French at home, as compared to 28.7 per cent in 1971. In fact, English is now being maintained in Quebec by the preference for it of the Other groups.

There have been successes of Federal policy in promoting bilingualism. This is especially true among those under twenty-five. The national bilingualism rate increased from 13.5 per cent in 1971 to 16.2 per cent in 1986. The 1986 census revealed that 'On a national scale, francophones continue to be most bilingual, followed by allophones and anglophones. However, in Quebec, it is the anglophones who are the most bilingual, in a proportion almost double that of francophones' (Census 1986, *Focus on Canada*: 35). In the 'bilingual belt' or 'cultural zone of transition' in Ontario, Cartwright (1988) reports that younger anglophones are beginning to accommodate to the French language, favour its acquisition and to use the language more often. *All these trends point to a reversal of the historic situation in Quebec with respect to bilingualism.*

From the Quebec francophone point of view the most extensive evaluation of the effects of Bill 101 is Bourhis (1984a). Most contributors feel that Quebec's language planning has been relatively successful. The prestige of Quebec French over and against both English and Standard European French has increased. One can live and work entirely in French in Quebec. There has been a substantial increase in francophones in managerial positions.

But there are caveats. Coleman (1984: 145) notes that by the mid-eighties the basic ownership structure of the Quebec economy was unchanged and English maintained its prestige as the language of North American business and culture. There are also results by Bourhis that show that francophones in Montreal were more likely to help anglophone students in English than *vice versa*, and that in sales situations the language selected by the customer, and not necessarily French, was the one used (Bourhis, 1984a: 199;

nc, 1993: 252). English speaking Quebecers have protested bout the dangers inherent in the illiberal and repressive nature of the Quebec language laws, especially their more symbolic aspects (for a polemic about the dangers of ethnic nationalism, see Mordecai Richler's (1992) *Oh Canada! Oh Quebec!*). However, many anglophones accept the underlying motivations of Bill 101 (Caudwell, 1984).

Although French language and culture seem secure in Quebec itself, the fact remains that a modernized Quebec remains inescapably integrated into the North American economy and society. This challenges and destabilizes its distinct identity. This would have to be faced whether or not Quebec was part of Canada. In fact, it is probably mitigated by the large francophone and Quebec input into a federal Canada. The problem of cultural challenge is perceived in linguistic terms. Bourhis (1984a: 199) speculates that English may have an attraction to francophone youth as a vehicle of Anglo-American culture. These same anxieties about 'Coca Cola Culture' have also been important in France (Battye and Hintze, 1992: 49–54). But given Quebec's history, its unique situation and sudden modernization, the anxieties are especially intense.

Varieties of the 'same' language

Linguistic diversity occurs not only in strictly bilingual or multilingual settings, but where varieties are those within a single language. Indeed, Fishman has argued that distinct linguistic 'codes' emerge whenever there is any role differentiation in a human group at all. The linguistic variety signals and enacts the social distinction. Another important point is the relevance of notions we have used in describing societal bilingualism to the situation in which varieties of the 'same' language make up the repertoire.

In chapter two, we saw how standardized varieties, or standard languages, emerge. So one possible configuration within a repertoire would be a standard and various dialects, regional or otherwise. Another such configuration is Ferguson's **diglossia**. (This sounds like some kind of sociolinguistic disease; Haugen (1968) describes the preoccupation with 'correct' norms of usage, when faced with varieties of one's own language, as schizoglossia.)

Diglossia may be thought of as a kind of super-standardiza
Ferguson (1959) defines it thus:

> Diglossia is a relatively stable language situation in which, in addition
> to the primary dialects of the language (which may include a standard
> or regional standard), there is a very divergent, highly codified (often
> grammatically more complex) superimposed variety, the vehicle of a
> large and respected body of literature (written) either of an earlier period
> or in another speech community, which is learned largely by formal
> education and is used for most written and formal spoken purposes but
> is not used by any sector of the community for ordinary conversation.

The advantage of examining it at this point is that once again
it is relatively easy to distinguish between the varieties. Ferguson
examines four defining cases where diglossia obtains. In each case
he calls the superordinate variety the High (H), and the colloquial
variety, the Low (L). The four communities are Switzerland, Haiti,
Greece and the Arab world. In the German-speaking parts of Switzerland, the H variety is Standard German, while the L is Swiss
German or Schweizerdeutsch. In Haiti, the L is the creole and the
H is Standard French. Two varieties of Greek are likewise in a
diglossic relationship: the H, classical Greek or Katharévusa, and
the L, Dhimotiki, or demotic contemporary Greek.

The nature of diglossic language can be seen if we look more
closely at the Arabic case. Arabic is spoken over an enormous area,
from the Persian Gulf to Morocco, and contains many varieties.
The H is classical Arabic. Ferguson (1970) notes that this variety,
in its written form, has been attested in literature for a millennium
and a half, extending from pre-Islamic poetry to modern technical
journals. The L is colloquial Arabic. But this general term covers
many written varieties. There are the regional dialects which are
the mother tongues of Arab speakers. Of these, some are regional
standards: the speech of Cairo, Beirut-Damascus-Jerusalem, of
Baghdad and of the northern Moroccan cities. Below these are the
dialect continua. In other words, between classical and colloquial
are many intermediate types: 'shadings of "middle language"', as
Ferguson calls them.

An interesting feature of these four cases is that the linguistic
nature of the H and L, their respective uses, their differing prestige

the manner in which they are acquired, all interact to create
diossia and maintain it as a stable system.

Linguistic features of H and L

In each case, the H is linguistically 'very divergent' from the L.
Interestingly, the divergence is most marked in the grammar,
rather than in the lexicon or phonology. In general, the H is more
complex than the L. For example, the H may have more alternative grammatical categories and more exceptions to its rules. Stewart
(1968) represents the linguistic relationship between French and
Haitian creole in the following diagram:

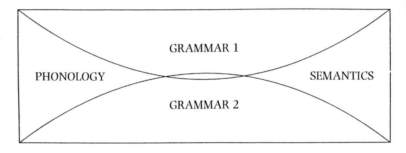

This linguistic pattern is a reflection of the social nature of diglossia.
Sound and word meanings are characteristically the two levels of
language which change and therefore diverge most rapidly. By
contrast, the grammatical core of language is more resistant to
change and evolves more slowly. Therefore, the normal pattern of
relationships between dialects is that of considerable phonological
and lexical differences and rather less grammatical ones. In diglossia, the normal pattern of divergence seems to be somewhat
reversed. The H and L grammars have evolved apart while the other
levels tend to be more alike. But consider that the H, a written
variety, has been codified and thus 'fixed' and *self-consciously elaborated* over an extended time and over a wide area, and the local colloquial variants have not. The latter are thus relatively free to
diverge. Also, since the H is *only* formally acquired, through education, those learning it must mediate it through their mother

tongues, the L. This probably would tend to make the soun
word meanings partially converge, as the H is successively relea
each generation by speakers of the evolving L. But there are s
tematic divergences in the lexicon and phonology as well. In th
lexicon, Ferguson notes, there are very often lexical pairs in the H
and L, synonyms which radically mark a text as belonging to one
variety or the other.

The social meaning of the H

As we said, the divergence between H and L is probably partly
related to the long period of standardization and codification
which the H has undergone. It is the H which has been the object
of scholarship and language management. It is the H which is the
vehicle of the major religious and literary traditions of the community. It is the H, therefore, which symbolizes the community's
historical identity and its associated values. In the Arab world, for
example, classical Arabic as the language of the Koran 'is widely
believed to constitute the actual words of God' (Ferguson, 1959).
In many cases, the very existence of the L is denied. And, indeed,
there may be an absence of books about the L or any conscious
norms in its use.

For these reasons, it is the H which has prestige. There are
usually the same judgements made on the beauty and efficacy
of the H which we noted about standardization in general. The
converse of the codification and prestige of the H is the relative
absence of these in the L. The latter, therefore, is subject to variability and diversity in a way that the former is not.

Specialization of functions

The prestige of the H, in turn, is a major factor in the functional
specialization of the two varieties. Figure 3.2 presents the characteristic uses to which H and L are put. Each variety is considered
appropriate only to certain types of situation. For example, *the H is
never used by any sector of the community for casual conversation.* It
follows that it is not used in conversations between adults and children, and that, therefore, the H is no one's mother tongue. It has a

	High	Low
Sermon in church or mosque	×	
Instruction to servants, waiters, workmen, clerks		×
Personal letter	×	
Speech in parliament, political speech	×	
University lecture	×	
Conversation with family, friends, colleagues		×
News broadcast	×	
Radio soap opera		×
Newspaper editorial, news story, caption on picture	×	
Caption on political cartoon		×
Poetry	×	
Folk literature		×

Figure 3.2 Specialization of functions of H and L in diglossia (*from Ferguson, 1959*)

distinctive pattern of acquisition which is a consequence of its functional specialization. It is largely acquired through formal education.

It is the interaction of these features which makes diglossia stable. The system which maintains it works like this. The historical prestige of the H and its current social meaning lead to its functional specialization. Simultaneously, of course, these formal and culturally significant functions reinforce its prestige and symbolic value. A variety symbolizing such values cannot appropriately be used in speaking to children. Therefore, it can only be acquired formally, along with literacy at school. Once acquired, it is used on those occasions when it is appropriate, but *not* to children, and so on. This system will last for as long as the social meaning of the H leads to functional specialization, and this is a reflection of the structure of the society itself. We noted the same kind of factors at work in Canada, maintaining societal bilingualism. It would seem, then, that to account for the stable existence of language varieties, we need to use a system of four mutually defining terms thus:

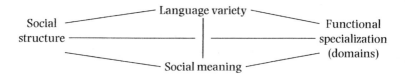

Diglossia, in Ferguson's sense, is one particular arrangemen~~t~~
varieties and relates to one particular configuration of social f~~a~~
tors. Social changes could destabilize the system: changes such a~~s~~
the competing prestige of a local nationalism, loss of belief in the
values which the H symbolizes, or loss of clearly defined domains
which must be conducted in H. In diglossic situations, there is
characteristically a sharp social stratification between an elite, who
alone have access to literacy, and therefore can learn the H, and
the bulk of the people who are only competent in L. The existence
of H, therefore, simultaneously excludes most people from participation in key social functions (politics, law, the church, education) while at the same time symbolizing the unifying values of the
society; for example, by alluding to the body of literature from the
past or from a wider 'culture area' which encodes such values.

Note the very intimate relation between social structure and
language structure. Compare diglossia, for example, with the relationship between a standard language and its dialects which we
discussed in the last chapter. Diglossia seems to be an extreme
case of standardization. Partly, this would be a reflex of the sharper
social discontinuities in diglossic situations. Accordingly, the varieties are more sharply divergent. But the H also alludes to a historical 'culture area', and the identity of the society is at least
partly defined outside itself, in space or time. The Hs are unifying
in this sense. By contrast, the Standards of modern Europe are the
linguistic side of the evolution of nation states and are the standardized 'local vernaculars' of societies. The Standards of Europe
are part of the 'nationalisms' of Europe. However, at earlier stages
in history diglossia was a characteristic European configuration.
Thus, Latin would have been the H in those countries which have
Romance vernaculars, which are modern dialects of Latin. The
allusion encoded by the H's social meaning would be the values
and identity of 'Christendom', and its continuity with the ancient
world. The situation in the Germanic, Slavic and other areas of
Europe would not have been strictly diglossic, by Ferguson's definition, but rather diglossia-like, with Latin as the H.

Consider the historical developments which destabilized this
status quo, such as the rise of nationalism, protestantism and
secular national societies. The remnants of such processes have
continued into this century. Standard languages have continued

ᴠe created out of vernaculars, symbolizing the emergent nation-ᴀɪsms of Europe. (In a moment, we will be mentioning one such standard, in Norway.) On the other hand, Latin still retains some prestige today. Its social meaning seems still to be perceived. And, indeed, it has only very recently lost a remaining functional special-ization, as the official language of the supernational Roman Cath-olic Church.

Diglossia describes only one particular configuration of variet-ies. It very closely reflects, because it is used to enact, a cluster of social properties. A typology of different linguistic repertoires, if it were to be complete, would presuppose a similar typology of soci-eties. One factor of significance has emerged from our examples, and that is social differentiation, or the degree of discontinuity or continuity between social groups. In societal bilingualism and in diglossia we found both distinct language varieties and fairly sharp social boundaries. We will now look at an example, between a standard and a regional dialect in Norway, which involves mutu-ally intelligible dialects of a language. There is much less social discontinuity and, correspondingly, much less 'separateness' of the varieties in linguistic terms. However, the four interrelated themes we diagrammed above are still involved, even in cases where the linguistic distinctions between varieties become problematic.

Code-switching

We will now take another perspective on language contact. We turn to the question of **conversational code-switching**. One of the important figures in the field, John Gumperz, defines the term as follows (Gumperz, 1982: 59):

> The juxtaposition within the same speech exchange of passages of speech belonging to two different grammatical systems or subsystems.

We are now looking at language contact from an interactional point of view. Speakers in conversational settings whose reper-toires consist of more than one variety produce stretches of speech first in one variety and then the other. This code-switching can be between participants' turns, so that one speaker speaks in one code,

but the reply comes in another. Or alternatively, any one spea
can code-switch between sentences, intersententially, or within
sentence, intrasententially. Gumperz (1982: 60) contrasts this kind
of movement between codes with diglossia. In diglossia the code
allocation is stable and the norms clearly focused. The functions
are specialized only by situation, not by participant's intended
effect. By contrast, conversational code-switching is rapid, largely
unconscious, and used for communicative effect. The switched
items are part of the same coherent stretch of speech. The codes
switched can be either recognized varieties of the same language,
or distinct languages. Code-switching is one form that language
contact takes when looked at the interpersonal level (for examples
in the context of Canadian societal bilingualism, see Poplack, 1988;
Heller, 1988a). The issues raised are of two kinds. How can we
socially explain the switching from one code to another? How are
the codes related in linguistic terms?

A very influential study of these issues was made by Blom and
Gumperz (1972, but see Trudgill, 1995a: 18). They examined the
small community of Hemnesberget in northern Norway. Its repertoire consists of two varieties of Norwegian: Bokmål, the form of
standard Norwegian current in northern Norway, and Ranamål,
the local dialect of the area. An important feature of Blom and
Gumperz's analysis of Hemnesberget is its holistic approach.
Besides studying the formal linguistic relationship of the two
varieties, a subject to which we will return in a moment, they
studied instances of code-switching in small groups and did this
in the context of a detailed analysis of the local social system. This
included the systems of values to which members of the community were oriented. Code-switching, they argued, was ultimately
explicable in terms of the values which Ranamål and Bokmål
encoded. In a community like Hemnesberget, where for all practical purposes everyone can speak both varieties, the most likely
explanation for the maintenance of distinct codes is that each
conveys particular social meanings.

There were two broad systems of values in the community. The
first, local values, were beliefs concerning the solidarity, the unique
identity and the egalitarian values of the local community. Contrasted to this were various sorts of non-local values. Thus, there

.e the beliefs associated with pan-Norwegian activities, for .ample, nationwide political, cultural and economic concerns, and the values implicit in such activities. Blom and Gumperz were able to group members of the community, not only according to occupation, descent and patterns of interaction, but also in terms of the orientation of their values.

Within the community, Ranamål and Bokmål symbolized the local and non-local values respectively. The social meanings of the two varieties were readily explicable both in terms of their historical origins, and how they were acquired. Bokmål, one of the two forms of Standard Norwegian, had first been introduced into the local area as the language of a now departed aristocracy, with its non-local and elitist values. Ranamål was indigenous in, and confined to the local community. The ways in which the two varieties are acquired parallel this historical contrast. Bokmål is acquired in school and church, where non-local values are involved, while Ranamål is acquired in the home.

In the community, then, there are contrasting systems of values. History and a pattern of acquisition associated the two linguistic varieties with those systems of values as their social meanings. The varieties can therefore be used to convey those values, or enact situations in which those values are taken for granted. In Hemnesberget, the existence of the two varieties serves to integrate the community in two directions, both locally and within the larger national society.

Situational code-switching

With such an analysis of the social meanings, the switching of an individual from one variety to the other becomes explicable. It is not random. The social meaning of the code is the link between the actual linguistic varieties, Bokmål and Ranamål, and the situations in which it is used. This meaning also connects the large-scale patterning – how the varieties are distributed within the community – with the individual's specific choice of variety. Given what we have said so far, Ranamål ought to occur in those types of situation in which local values predominate, and Bokmål ought to occur where non-local, pan-Norwegian values are most important.

We will expect **situational code-switching**. That is, the situation type will predict which variety a speaker will employ. However, in Hemnesberget, whether a speaker situationally code-switches or not further depends on the orientation of values of the particular sub-group of the community to which he or she belongs. For example, two groups, the artisans and the merchants and managers, are both strongly oriented towards local values, although with some conflict in the latter case. These groups code-switch by situation and use Bokmål, for example, in church, in school, or in speaking to an outsider, and Ranamål in local situations. Thus yet again we find the allocation of distinct linguistic varieties to distinct uses: what we have referred to earlier as 'functional specialization' or the existence of 'domains of language use'.

But since we have now introduced the dimension of the individual speaker and his choice of code, we can perhaps go further into the nature of these patterns. Since speakers regularly code-switch in the requisite situations, we might state this regularity as a causal generalization. In domain A, code A occurs; in domain B, code B occurs. On this basis, predictions could be made, deducing the occurrence of the code, given the generalization, the situation and the group membership of the speaker.

But there is a difficulty in applying this sort of explanation alone to social facts; for the collective phenomenon is made up of regularities which are individual choices. More on this later, but at this stage it must be noted that 'a type of social situation' is a complex idea, and one part of it is that the choice of the variety is part of the definition of the situation itself. This means that in choosing a given code, a speaker can be enacting an intention to *redefine* the situation in which they are participating. He or she may be saying, 'I want what we are doing to count as an instance of a given situation.' In other words, the choice of code can be *tactical*. This depends, in turn, on the larger social norm of appropriateness of variety to situation type.

A very nice example of the use of situational code-switching to redefine the situation itself is provided by Denison (1972) in his study of language variety in Sauris, Italy. In this community, three varieties have a characteristic domain allocation: the local variety of German, in the home; Friulian, the regional dialect of Italian, in semi-public places such as the local bar; and Standard Italian in church and school. Denison taped one instance, however, in which German was uncharacteristically employed in the bar. A local farmer, who was supposed to have been making cheese at the cooperative dairy, was in the bar when his wife burst in and harangued him in German for drinking when he should have been working. At one stage he briefly attempted to calm her in Friulian, but on the whole conducted the argument in German. Denison (1972: 71) interprets his utterances in Friulian (for example, '*ôôô! No stà rabiàti, capis-tu!*' – 'Oh! Don't lose your temper, d'you understand!') as an attempt to redefine the situation by language choice. This example demonstrates a number of points: that locale alone is only a component of situation; that in using German with husband-wife roles in a domestic argument, a home situation has been created in an incongruent locale; that the farmer can *use* Friulian tactically to try to recreate a situation which is congruent with the semi-public locale of the bar. Thus, he can use the possibilities of the repertoire in this context to try to evade his wife's accusations, for specific conversational purposes.

Metaphorical code-switching

Situation alone is not sufficient to account for all instances of code-switching. Blom and Gumperz describe cases of **metaphorical code-switching**. In these cases, the use of the variety alludes to the social values it encodes, but is otherwise inappropriate to the situation in which it is uttered. This is familiar in those common cases in which speakers use a local variety humorously or ironically for a rhetorical effect in a discourse otherwise uttered in a standard. There is no attempt to change the situation itself, but merely to make a comment. In Hemnesberget, speakers from groups who owed allegiance both to local and to pan-Norwegian values (for example, students at home from university), code-switched into Bokmål if topics involving non-local values were introduced. The situation of casual conversation remained otherwise unchanged and Ranamål was clearly appropriate.

Bokmål was being used in these cases to convey specific meanings related to a speaker's attitude to the topic being discussed.

The conventional social meaning is being used conversationally. So although the use seems inappropriate according to the norm of situational code-switching, it can be interpreted as meaningful against that background. In cases where this is done with communicative intent, code-switching connects the societal allocation of varieties, a society-wide fact, and individual intentionality.

The linguistics of code-switching

The notion of code-switching presupposes that there are codes to switch. The theory which we have developed thus far, which has largely originated in the studies of the anthropologists Gumperz and Dell Hymes, is a descriptive and predictive framework which goes like this. Speech communities have linguistic repertoires of varieties, each of which has a distinct social meaning. This meaning determines, and may have arisen from, the historical allocation of each variety to certain classes of situation within the society as a norm of behaviour. In general, code-switching is predictable using such a framework. However, metaphorical and tactical code-switching also occurs which is not always predictable, but is always interpretable. Note that its interpretation must be relative to the rules of appropriateness described by the theory. For a fully developed theory of this general type, see the work of Carol Myers-Scotton (1988, 1993, 1993a) and Scotton (1983).

Turning now to the issue of the linguistic relationship between codes, there have been a number of studies grappling with the complexities of the intertwining of codes when more than one is conversationally deployed (see for example Pfaff, 1976, 1979; Poplack, 1980, 1981; Berk-Seligson, 1986; Sankoff, 1971; also the readings in Milroy and Muysken, 1995).

Sankoff (1971) has pointed out difficulties in the linguistic interpretation of code-switching. There are two aspects of this problem. It is impossible to account for every switch in a text, certainly predictively and perhaps interpretatively. There is a residue of 'extremely frequent and rapid switching which, to put it bluntly, defies explanation, if by explanation one means accounting for every switch'. Secondly, there is often difficulty encountered in saying to which variety a given segment belongs. They can be so linguistically 'mixed' that it is hard to decide whether the text is an instance of variety A or variety B. Labov (1972: 189) has analysed a text in which a speaker has switched eighteen times in six lines. The italicized portions can be assigned to Standard English and the rest to the black English vernacular:

> And den like *if you miss onesies*, de *oth*uh person shoot to skelly; ef he miss, den you go again. An' *if you get in, you shoot to twosies*. An' *if you get in twosies, you go to* threesies. An' *if you miss* threesies, *then the person tha*' miss skelly shoot *the skellies* an' shoot in *the onesies*; an' *if he miss, you go* f'om threesies to foursies.

As Labov says, there is no obvious motive for switching eighteen times in such a short passage. He interprets this text as variation, not between distinct codes, but within a single system. Sankoff herself produces a fairly short text in which twenty-nine switches are identifiable between Buang, a language of New Guinea, and Neo-Melanesian, an English-based pidgin language used for specialized functions.

In all these cases, it is problematic not only to account for the intertwining of the languages, but to decide whether or not to count something as a switch. For example, are proper names in a second language to count as code-switching? Or numbers, if these are regularly drawn from only one of the codes, or official or technical terms if they are associated with only one of the cultures? – e.g. 'We went to the Syndicat d'Initiative.' Pfaff (1979: 298) notes that some writers break code-switching down into finer classifications: **code-mixing** and **code-changing**. Mixing occurs when a second language term is interposed into an utterance which remains in a first language. Changing occurs when a sentence changes from a first to a second language. Alternatively, some authors use the term 'code-mixing' to refer to all intrasentential switches, thus recognizing that the codes are both occurring in a single sentence frame. Other authors say that a sentence has a determinable **base language**, its **macro-structure**, with intrusions from the other language, its **micro-structure** (Denison, 1972: 67). But in many other cases of fluctuation, of 'frequent and rapid switching', like those mentioned above, it seems impossible to establish a base macro-structure for a stretch of speech. In the research literature, scholars are careful to establish criteria for what to count as an instance of switching, and what not.

Let us consider some other ways in which we could explain the intrusion of elements of one language into another and supplement the conversationally motivated code-switching theory with other explanations.

Proficiency. Speakers may have differing bilingual proficiency in the two codes. One or the other language may be dominant. Denison notes uncertainty about German words for activities in Italian domains. Similarly, in his study of the Norwegian language in America, Haugen noted instances of uncertainty about Norwegian words for objects from English domains. Such uncertainties would produce fluctuations in a text, which would be especially sensitive to topic. It has also been widely claimed that those with less bilingual competence concentrate on intersentential switching, rather than switching within sentences, but see Berk-Seligson (1986: 314, 327).

Language boundaries and borrowing. There may be cases in which one language is in the process of borrowing terms from another. Such words would be **incipient loans** as yet unassimilated into the sound structures of the borrowing language. This would be an especially active process in those situations in which the lending language had highly developed vocabulary in certain areas (for example, technology) in which the borrowing language was deficient. Large-scale borrowing would be convenient for talk on such topics in domains where the borrowing language was otherwise appropriate. If the loans were unassimilated, they would appear as intrusions from the lending language into a text basically in the borrowing language. One might expect the Low to be more open to borrowing terms from the High than vice versa, because of the prestige and standardization of the latter. The permeability of the boundaries between languages, how completely they are kept separate, or whether the boundaries between them are allowed to collapse without stigma, is sensitive to language attitudes and the institutional status of the languages.

In these three cases – proficiency, borrowing and interference – the relation between the codes will relate in a complex way to the nature of the social boundaries that exist in the society. Sankoff (1971) and Myers-Scotton (1988, 1993) suggest further possibilities.

Both codes are appropriate. Perhaps there are situations in which both codes are appropriate in order to convey two distinct social meanings simultaneously. If this view is correct, then any attempt to explain individual switches in a text will fail. The use of *both* codes throughout a text conveys both social meanings in that situation. Myers-Scotton (1988: 162) writes:

> any variety is indexical of the speaker's position . . . When the speaker wishes more than one social identity to be salient in the current exchange, and each identity is encoded in the particular speech community by a different linguistic variety, then those two or more codes constitute the unmarked choice . . . Each switch need have no special significance; rather it is the overall pattern of using two varieties which carries social meaning.

Relative frequencies. Sankoff further advances the hypothesis that the relative frequency of the two codes in a text may itself be determined by social and situational factors. She writes, 'it is possible to show that the extent of the use of Neo-Melanesian . . . forms a continuum which could be correlated with various social and situational variables, simply in terms of the relative proportion of Neo-Melanesian used. In terms of social stratification, for example, it seems clear that high status correlates with high frequency of use of Neo-Melanesian.'

In both these last explanations, although the fluctuation is explicable in the same social terms as code-switching in general, each individual switch or intrusion need not be explained. The mixture of the two codes is itself the realization of the speaker's intention to convey a social meaning.

An important aspect of code-switching from a linguistic point of view is the issue of whether or not there are **linguistic constraints on code-switching**. Can a speaker make any kind of switch, at any point in a sentence? Or does the structural and psychological nature of knowing and performing in two codes limit what can be switched? Early studies tended to concentrate on the social function of switching and assumed that it wasn't subject to formal constraints. But later studies by Pfaff (1976, 1979), Poplack (1980, 1981), Berk-Seligson (1986) and others have problematized this area.

Three general classes of constraints have been proposed:

1. **The equivalence constraint** says that switching only occurs where languages structurally overlap. You can't code-switch at those points where the languages are structurally different.

2. **Constituency constraints**
   A. **The high level constituent constraint** says that there is a preference for code-switching higher level items like sentences or clauses, as opposed to lower level items such as adjectives or adverbs. However, **noun switching** is an exception to this.
   B. **The constituency boundary constraint** says that switching respects the boundaries of grammatical constructions. This accounts for the preference for switching higher level items.

3. **The free morpheme constraint** says that switching cannot be at the point where a bound morpheme, one like '*un-*' or '*-ing*', that can't appear alone, joins a free morpheme, one like '*happy*' or '*run*', that can appear alone, to form words like, '*unhappy*' or '*running*'. Thus, we won't get switches like '*bavarding*', with a French stem and an English bound morpheme, meaning something like 'currently ongoing chit-chatting', unless either the stem or suffix had been integrated into the other language as a borrowing.

If something like the equivalence constraint is true, then it appears that there is an overlap of grammars in bilinguals, **L1–ISOMORPHICINTERGRAMMAR–L2**. Switching is constrained to this area of overlap. There is a 'code-switching grammar'. However, more recent work by Berk-Seligman (1986) calls into question all these constraints except the free morpheme constraint, when the languages in contact are linguistically remote. She studied the contact of Spanish and Hebrew among Sephardic Jews in Israel, those whose ancestors were expelled from Spain in the fifteenth century, and among whom Judaeo-Spanish survives. Constraints 1 and 2 did not hold, and Berk-Seligson concludes there are two separate grammars involved in code-switching.

The linguistic boundaries between codes in those cases where the codes are dialects of a language are also problematic. We saw in chapter two that dialects are not discrete entities, that the relationship between dialects is a continuum. If we look for discrete codes in situations of switching between dialects, we are not likely to find them. What we will find is a 'more or less' situation.

This is clear from Blom and Gumperz's analysis of the two codes in Hemnesberget. The community recognizes the social reality of the two distinct varieties, Ranamål and Bokmål, and it is clear that the speech community has distinct attitudes to the varieties which therefore encode contrasting social meanings. But the linguistic relationship of the two socially distinct dialects is that of a continuum.

This is particularly marked on the phonological level, the level on which sounds of language are organized. Grammatically (for example, in the system of pronouns), the two dialects have distinct and contrasting pairs. But, consider the way in which the dialects are related with respect to their sounds. Ranamål is said to have a **palatalized** series of consonants. Bokmål is said not to have this feature. What this means is that Ranamål has versions of 't', 'd', 'n', 'l' which are pronounced so that the front of the tongue also articulates with the hard surface at the front of the roof of the mouth (the hard palate) making an 'i' sound of the sort found in the pronunciation of English words like 'Kew' or 'huge'. These sounds are used to distinguish words in Ranamål, but not in Bokmål. What Blom and Gumperz found, however, was not an absolute linguistic discontinuity between the two dialects, but rather that they differed in terms of degree of palatalization on a single scale. Similarly with vowel sounds: they sometimes varied on a continuous scale between the dialects, depending on the degree to which the tongue was lowered and retracted in their pronunciation.

	Palatalization	Height and retraction of tongue in pronunciation of [ae] and [a]	
Bokmål ↑	zero	high	not retracted
continuous variation	weak	lower	some retraction
Ranamål ↓	strong	lowest	quite retracted

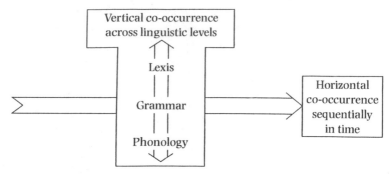

Figure 3.3 Defining a variety by co-occurrence rules

The dialects, therefore, were at different ends of a single scale with respect to each of these variable features. Blom and Gumperz discovered that, linguistically at least, the variants which were sensitive to social factors were cases of continuous variation within a single system, not of switching between two discrete and discontinuous systems. When informants seemingly code-switched, what they really did was move in varying degrees up and down continua. Informants each moved *different* distances. However, they all agreed which end of the scale marked each of the two contrasting dialects.

How is it possible, then, to conceive of the dialects as entities in linguistic terms (they are clearly entities in social terms)? We must return to our definition of any variety as a clustering together of linguistic features. Gumperz uses the term **co-occurrence rules** for cases in which one linguistic form predicts the existence of another, and in the case of dialects like Ranamål and Bokmål, we get both **horizontal** and **vertical co-occurrence**. This notion is schematized in Figure 3.3. Thus Ranamål, as an entity, is identifiable because, when speakers articulate sounds at the Ranamål end of variables, they also produce Ranamål grammar and lexis. This is vertical co-occurrence across the linguistic levels. But also, in a given utterance, if a speaker is speaking at the Ranamål end of various continua, this selects Ranamål for the next and successive linguistic items produced. This is horizontal co-occurrence as it proceeds sequentially in a text.

What, then, from the linguistic point of view, is code-switching between dialects? Labov (1972: 188) writes, 'to demonstrate that we have a true case of code-switching, it is necessary to show that the speaker moves from one consistent set of co-occurring rules to another'. But in many instances this sort of clarity will not exist. As Blom and Gumperz point out, we get degrees of shifting, sometimes a breakdown in co-occurrence rules. It is this which provides linguistic problems for the analyst who is using the conceptual framework of codes and code-switching to relate social explanations to the details of linguistic variation. It is only justified to talk of distinct codes if, in fact, co-occurrence rules define such distinct entities which also are conventionally used by speakers to implicate social meanings, relative to social norms in a speech community. But it is also the case that *single variable features* can correlate independently with social factors and also independently can encode social meanings. This is typically what happens when social boundaries are not sharp. It is to the study of such continuously varying features, and the sociolinguistic structures of which they are part, that we shall now turn.

Before doing that, though, glance back to the stanza from A. M. Klein's poem with which this chapter began. Its macro-structure is clearly English. But consider the allusive fluctuations of code within it. There are French or French-like words – '*parle*', '*vocabulaire*', '*Ecosse*' – and syntactic forms in the text. Since the two languages are distinct codes, defined by co-occurrence, and not related on a continuum, these intrusions might best be interpreted as metaphorical code-switches of some kind. Notice then how we could say that there has been a weakening of the horizontal and vertical co-occurrence rules, and hence the boundaries between the varieties. This is a witty, light poem, mock epic. Note that this is achieved by allusion to yet another variety, to the latinate syntax and vocabulary of the English epic, itself a translation-equivalent of Latin forms. The poet is intentionally creating a linguistic mix, including a pastiche of 'franglais', to actualize his meanings. This illustrates how the social meanings of whole varieties can be used and large-scale patterning related to individual acts of speech.

4 Discovering the structure in variation

'Free variation' is of course a label, not an explanation. It does not tell us where the variants came from nor why the speakers use them in differing proportions, but is rather a way of excluding such questions from the scope of immediate inquiry.

Fischer (1958)

Variability

In the last chapter, we looked at code-switching and saw that sometimes it was not plausible to account for variation as an alternation between two distinct codes. Sometimes we find instead a rapid and seemingly random fluctuation between linguistic forms. Let us make this problem concrete, so we can visualize what such variation is like. Consider words ending in the suffix '-ing', such as 'hunting' or 'working'. Very widely within the English-speaking world, people pronounce such items as either *working* or *workin'*. Sometimes the suffix is pronounced as '*-ing*'; sometimes as '*-in*'. Although from the point of view of the written word, this looks like 'dropping the g', that is not what happens. Phonetically neither form of the suffix contains [g]; the contrast is between whether the final nasal is pronounced at the back, [ɪŋ], or the front, [ɪn], of the mouth.

To imagine the variability here, let the /ɪn/ form be represented by 1 and the /ɪŋ/ form by 0. Now imagine utterances by three speakers on a given occasion where there are ten opportunities of pronouncing words which have the '-ing' suffix. The production of the two variant forms might be as follows:

Occasion 1												
Speaker A	1	1	0	0	1	0	1	1	0	0	(5 /ɪn/)	
Speaker B	0	1	0	0	1	1	0	1	0	0	(4 /ɪn/)	out of 10
Speaker C	1	0	1	0	0	0	0	0	0	0	(2 /ɪn/)	

On another occasion, however, we might find something like this:

Occasion 2												
Speaker A	1	1	1	0	1	0	1	1	1	1	(8 /ɪn/)	
Speaker B	1	1	0	0	1	0	1	1	0	0	(5 /ɪn/)	out of 10
Speaker C	1	1	0	0	1	0	1	0	0	0	(4 /ɪn/)	

This is indeed a rapid fluctuation between forms. And such variation is pervasive throughout language. We will be seeing many examples in the course of the following chapters. The problem for the linguist faced with such inconsistency is to find a structure which can explain it. To do this, both a theoretical outlook and a methodology is required, and these were first provided by William Labov who revolutionized dialect studies with the publication in 1966 of *The Social Stratification of English in New York City*. Labov's research provided a paradigm for research into variation. This chapter will be devoted to an exploration of this new methodology and its consequences.

But first, what sort of explanations of variation are superseded by this new paradigm? Earlier explanations of variation fell into two categories: namely that it is the result of **dialect mixture**, or that it is a case of **free variation**.

These explanations are implicit in two traditional approaches to language. The concept of a 'dialect' as a variety of language is, of course, a 'given' in traditional dialectology, which has as its aim the empirical study of such entities. A variety, or code, or dialect, as we saw earlier, is a 'clustering together' in terms of co-occurrence rules of linguistic features into a single coherent linguistic object. It can be given a name like 'Bokmål'. Such entities are the things that switch in code-switching. It could follow that our rapid fluctuation is simply the result of a mixing of dialects in communities and individuals. The trouble is that variability of the '-ing' kind simply does not find its origin in two distinguishable dialects that then mix. We would be postulating two distinct codes on the basis of observed fluctuation simply to explain that fluctuation as a mixture of them. But such variables fluctuate more or less independently of each other in any case. In other words, both in individuals and communities, certain features vary continuously within a single language system. We saw this with the degrees of palatalization and the height and retraction of vowels in Hemnesberget. A language seems to be a 'loose' system.

Nor can this variability be dealt with by the mainstream tradition of linguistic theorizing. We saw in chapter one how abstract a language is from the point of view of Chomsky's linguistic theory. Properties of language viewed as sets of sentences are explained by invariant rules which ultimately reflect universal features of human linguistic abilities. Variation is abstracted out in getting at the essential properties of the system. A language is viewed as an idealized 'frozen' system outside time and social space. And, as Fischer points out in the quotation that begins this chapter, 'free' variation is simply a way of excluding variability from the object of inquiry.

Labov's aim, however, is to confront the 'looseness' of the system as the data of linguistics itself, and thus to lower the degree of idealization of the object of inquiry – to study the language in use in the speech community. His initial intuition was that large-scale variation was not without pattern, but that it was socially determined. It could only be explained by social and historical factors interacting with factors within the linguistic system. One had to look for the wood in which the variation was the trees. With a sophisticated method for investigating speech within the community, consistency in the use of one variant over another in individuals, groups and contexts would be found. This is true of many 'aggregate' human phenomena, for example, in economics. Without a description in institutional or group terms, the phenomenon is invisible or incoherent viewed as individual behaviour. (Whether the group solely explains or determines the individual behaviour is another matter!)

Sociolinguistic variables

The hypothesis is that variation is socially conditioned. Although it may appear incoherent in the speech of an individual, a structure will emerge if the variation is studied socially. But in order to do this, a quantitative method is necessary. One has to be able to count the frequencies of the variants in order to compare them between individuals, groups and contexts. Therefore Labov introduced the notion of the **linguistic variable**. (If a variable can be correlated with a non-linguistic variable of social context, such as class, style, sex, or age, then it can be called a **sociolinguistic variable**.) The variable itself is written in brackets: (ing). This symbol is an abstract construct representing any given linguistic feature which can be freely realized by two or more variants, which are the **values** of the variable. Each variant has a number and these can be written inside the brackets. For example, (ing) represents the variable, and (ing-1), (ing-0) the two values of the variable. (ing-1) represents the /ɪn/ form, as in 'workin'', and (ing-0) the /ɪŋ/ as in 'working'.

$$(ing) \nearrow (ing - 1) = in' \text{ (nasal in front of mouth)}$$
$$\searrow (ing - 0) = ing \text{ (nasal at back of mouth)}$$

The next step is to count the instances of each of the values of the variable feature in the utterances in question and calculate an index. This allows the analyst to work out the quantity, for example, of the '-in'' form used, as opposed to the '-ing' form, for individuals and for groups. In the case of the variable (ing) the calculation of the index is very straightforward. It is a straight percentage of the number of '-in'' ('workin'') forms used in the total number of cases where either (ing) form is possible, thus:

$$(ing) \text{ index} = \frac{\text{number of '-in'' forms}}{\text{total number of occurrences of (ing)}} \times 100$$

We are now in a position to calculate (ing) index scores for the utterances of a given individual. This will give us a quantitative representation of variation, first for individuals and then for social groups of which they are members. Consider our hypothetical

occasions of (ing) above. On occasion 1, Speaker A produced '-in''
(pronouncing the nasal with closure at the front of his mouth)
five times out of ten. This gives an index score of fifty. On occasion
2, however, the same speaker pronounced '-in'' eight times out of
ten possible occurrences of the (ing) variable. And the score was
therefore eighty on this occasion. We can now precisely compare
individuals and individuals as between different occasions with
respect to this particular variable feature of their speech.

Sociolinguistic structures

The sociolinguistic variable is a tool which allows us next
to establish average index scores for any group or sub-group
within a larger population. People can be grouped with respect
to any social attribute which the analyst suspects is relevant, for
example, age, sex, ethnic group, education, place of residence,
socio-economic class and so on, and the average score calculated.
Similarly, if a method can be found to control features of situation,
features such as whether the utterance is relatively casual or formal, average scores for **styles** can also be arrived at. In other
words, the analyst can *correlate index scores with non-linguistic variables* for large and complex populations and reveal the 'aggregate'
structure of variation.

When this is done, the degree of structure revealed is extraordinary. Figure 4.1 shows the average (ing) index scores of
Labov's informants in his survey of the Lower East Side of New York
City according to their socio-economic class and simultaneously
correlated with the degree of formality in the style of their speech.
I shall return in a moment to the notions of 'class' and 'style' used
in this type of research. For the moment, note that the diagram
reveals a clear structure for the (ing) variable, a stratification in
the use of '-in'' versus '-ing' according to class and style, which is
not apparent in the seemingly random fluctuations in the pronunciation of any one individual in isolation. Clearly, the variation is
not 'free'. The use of the linguistic variants is socially conditioned.
As we shall see, such **sociolinguistic structures**, determined on
the dimensions of class and style, are just one significant correlation made possible by the use of quantitative methodology.

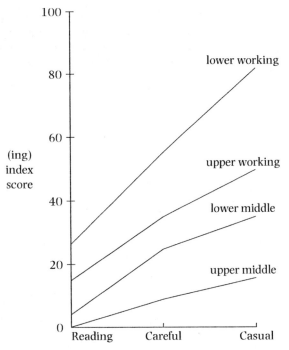

Figure 4.1 The (ing) variable in New York City (*adapted from Labov, 1972*)

Note some of the important features of Figure 4.1. The variable (ing) is stratified by class. In each style, the average index scores of the informants grouped by class form a hierarchy according to the class stratification of the society.

Simultaneously, the variable is differentiated by style. The behaviour of each class varies systematically according to whether their speech is casual, careful or reading style. Although each class has different average scores in each style, all groups **style-shift**. And each does so in the same direction. They produce higher (ing) scores in the more casual styles; the lines of the graph all rise as the degree of formality becomes less and less. And yet, as they rise, they each remain regularly stratified by class.

This kind of variable, called a **marker** by Labov, is structured two ways at once, both by a hierarchy of social status and a hierarchy of formality, or care in speech. There is clearly a connection between these two social factors. It would seem that the form produced with the highest frequency by the upper middle class in all contexts, including the most casual (the '-ing' variant), is also the form aimed at by all social classes, the more attention they pay to their speech. As Labov says (1972: 240), it would be 'difficult to interpret any signal by itself – to distinguish, for example, a casual salesman from a careful pipefitter'. This style-shifting suggests that relatively lower (ing) scores (a higher percentage of the '-ing' variant) not only characterize the speech of the highest class, but mark the standard of prestige for the community as a whole – presumably because of the social meaning of that variant. The '-ing' variant is the prestige form, at least overtly, and the '-in'' variant is stigmatized, and this seems intuitively correct.

The (ing) variable, like all the variables we will look at, also reflects a particular point in the dynamics of language change. Variability, which we see now as systematic differential frequencies in the use of the variants of a single variable, is central to the process of change. Both (ing) variants go back as far as early Middle English (Wells, 1982: 262). The literature suggests that in early modern English the presently stigmatized '-in'' variant was, in fact, the most frequent form for all social groups. Wells remarks that '-in'' was the fashionable pronunciation in eighteenth-century England, and that a folk memory of this exists in the phrase 'huntin', shootin' and fishin'', used to refer to such prestige pastimes. It was only in the late eighteenth and early nineteenth centuries that a 'spelling' pronunciation gained prestige (written '-ing' being associated with closure in the back of the mouth) and there was a prescriptive condemnation of the '-in'' form by teachers and grammarians (Labov, 1966: 395). We see here a connection between attitudes, prestige, language change and sociolinguistic structure. The (ing) variable is now stable, however, and there has been virtually no change involving this feature for nearly a hundred years. The kind of sociolinguistic structure in Figure 4.1 therefore represents the typical pattern for a *stable* variable. Thus, individual variables have histories. Other recurring types of sociolinguistic structures are diagnostic of changes taking place within the linguistic system as it interacts with social structure in complex ways. We will be interpreting some other types of sociolinguistic structures later. And we will need to do so in socio-historical terms.

Perhaps the most important point to make about Figure 4.1 is that the difference between the pronunciation of social groups is a question of *relative frequencies*, not of absolutes; similarly with the stylistic variation. Thus, both in the community as a whole and for an individual, it is *not* possible to say categorically that their speech has *only* '-in'' forms or *only* '-ing' forms. Rather, they have varying frequencies in the production of the variants which correlate with their position in society. The discovery that accent is a question of frequency of occurrence is one of the most important features of Labov's type of dialectology.

The (ing) variable occurs in almost every English-speaking community. (The exception is among English-speaking South Africans where the '-ing' form is categorical and, of course, where the social stratification is unique; Wells, 1982: 263.) That the differences are statistical can be further illustrated by looking at the variable for other groups. Thus, Labov only included adult white informants in Figure 4.1. Black informants displayed a much higher use of the '-in'' variant than did white speakers. In careful style, the average score for all white adult New York City informants was thirty-one, for all black New York City informants, sixty-two. For black informants from outside the city the average score was even higher, seventy-seven. Thus, ethnicity is also reflected in (ing) scores. And this is related to geographical differences. Northern black communities have origins in the southern states, and both whites and blacks in the South in general have higher (ing) scores, higher even than speakers of non-standard northern varieties. Thus, in the Appalachian region, Wolfram and Christian (1976: 62) found scores ranging from eighty to one hundred in casual speech. Here are the figures for six individual white informants in West Virginia:

Speaker	Age	Sex	(ing) score
1.	67	M	94.4
2.	13	M	99.1
3.	15	F	84.9
4.	42	F	96.6
5.	12	M	100.0
6.	57	M	84.4

We now have a picture of language as being variable, both individually and collectively. This variability can only be systematically investigated using quantitative methods. When this is done, we find that the variation is not 'free', but that there are patterns of distribution in the frequencies of variants conditioned by social, including stylistic, factors.

Linguistic constraints on variables

But the situation is more complex than this. Variables are usually also conditioned by internal linguistic factors. The linguistic environments of the variable, for example the set of items which precede or follow it, can affect the frequency with which one or the other variant appears. These sets of environments inside the language combine with social factors to yield the scores we observe. Such variation is termed **inherent variability**.

This can be illustrated by another variable which occurs in the speech of virtually all English speakers. This is final consonant cluster simplification or **/t,d/ deletion**.

When words end with two consonants and the second of these is /t/ or /d/, then it is possible that the final sound may be deleted. This is a phonological simplification which turns words like 'act', 'hand' or 'fist' into 'ac'', 'han'', or 'fis'':

hand → han'

But how likely is this rule to apply? How many times will it apply out of the number of times it could apply? This is conditioned both by internal linguistic and by external social factors. The rule may be said to be more or less favoured in the frequency of its application by given environments. Thus, the environments provide variable constraints on the rule. Of course, the limiting cases in such favouring or inhibiting of the application of a rule are when it always applies or never applies in a given environment. If it always applies, it is **categorical** in that environment. Environments can be ranked in the order in which they favour the rule applying.

In the case of /t,d/ deletion, the two most important linguistic constraints on the rule are listed on the right of the circle below, and some of the external social factors on the left. There are more factors (Guy, 1980), but we will limit the discussion to these.

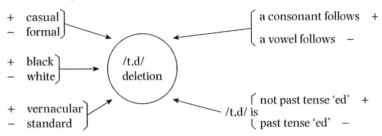

First, the internal constraints. The rule is favoured if the sound which immediately follows the /t/ or /d/ is a consonant, rather than a vowel. Thus, we are more likely to find

> post card → pos'card

than we are to hear

> last October → las' October

Secondly, the rule is favoured if the /t/ or /d/ is part of the structure of the word itself, as in 'hand', than if it has been suffixed to a verb as the past tense marker, '-ed'; for example in 'pass' becoming 'passed'. Thus, we are more likely to find

> hand grip → han' grip

than we are to hear

> passed Mary → pass' Mary

The least favoured environment is that in which we have a past tense '-ed' preceding a vowel. We are least likely to find

> rolled over → roll' over
> ripped off → rip' off

It is most important to note that all of these forms occur in the speech of *some* speakers; what we are talking about is the relative likelihood of their occurrence. These internal factors interact with external factors, which further influence whether or not the rule applies. For white standard varieties the rule is tightly constrained. It applies virtually only in the environment of a following consonant, and then usually only in casual speech. For some white vernaculars, although the environmental constraint remains the same, the frequency of application differs. Thus, Chambers and Trudgill (1980: 148) note that among speakers of a rural vernacular in northern England the rule applies about 80 per cent of the time, a frequency higher than in standard white accents. In some white non-standards, and very markedly in the black English vernacular of New York and Detroit, a following vowel also favours the rule, but less so than a following consonant. In these accents the rule may also sometimes apply when the /t/ or /d/ is the '-ed' past tense form, but is favoured when the sound is part of the structure of the word and not the suffix, 'not -ed'. Frequency also varies by social class.

So, in conditioning frequency, there are four interacting environments. In the order of how strongly they favour application of the rule, these are consonant or vowel, and 'not -ed' or 'ed'. Table 4.1 shows the effects of this interaction for a number of American varieties (Wolfram and Christian, 1976: 56). Observe that in column four, '-ed' followed by a vowel, the two weakest constraints, produce the lowest scores, but with a significant difference between white and black speakers. By contrast, the percentage of simplification is highest in column one, where the two strongest constraints favour the application of the rule. The relative difference between black and white speakers remains roughly the same, however.

Issues of method

Labov has provided us with a **quantitative paradigm** for the study of variation. But that is only the first step in the story. In the remainder of this chapter we will be examining, in turn, the following issues which arise out of this method of inquiry: *investigation, representation* and *interpretation*.

Table 4.1. *Consonant cluster simplification in some American varieties*

Language variety	1 'Not -ed', followed by consonant % simplification	2 '-ed', followed by consonant % simplification	3 'Not -ed', followed by vowel % simplification	4 '-ed', followed by vowel % simplification
Middle-class white Detroit speech	66	36	12	3
Working-class black Detroit speech	97	76	72	34
Working-class white New York City adolescent speech	67	23	19	3
Working-class white adolescent rural Georgia-Florida speech	56	16	25	10
Working-class black adolescent rural Georgia-Florida speech	88	50	72	36
Southeastern West Virginia speech	74	67	17	5

(*from Wolfram and Christian 1976: 56*)

First, how are we to *investigate* the practices of social groups and the ways individuals speak? What are the assumptions and consequences of different ways of approaching the community? This is both a practical and a theoretical matter. Second, how are we to *represent* the results of such investigations? It stands to reason that the kind of representation will influence and be influenced by the kinds of interpretations we make of what we have found. How we represent something implicitly tells us how we view it.

Third, how are we to *interpret* what we have found? Tabulations like 4.1 tell us that there is a systematic correlation between linguistic variables and social factors such as class and style. What is the significance of such findings for our understanding of the place of variation in language? How can we explain what we have found?

These three issues are deeply interrelated.

Approaching the community: assumptions

Linguists investigating actual speech are interested ultimately in individual speakers. But they are studying them also, inevitably, as members of groups. At every stage they are confronted with the classical difficulty of the individual and the group. There are individual actions and behaviour and there are practices which typify groups of individuals. It is the latter which linguists want to discover. Groups may exhibit 'emergent' properties, patterns not visible when one regards only the individual. Conversely, any given individual's behaviour may not conform to the pattern of the group.

In the course of the book we will have to refer to many different kinds of human groups – classes, ethnic groups, geographically defined communities, neighbourhoods, peer groups, age groups, social networks, families, kin groups, and the largest group, a society as a whole. These categories, of course, differ a lot among themselves. But they have some features in common which allow us to talk about them as groups in our ordinary usage. The most important point to make is that they are all human institutions, they are 'collectivities', not just 'collections' of individuals. MacDonald and Pettit (1981: 107f.) write:

The set or collection is conceptualized in such a way that A and B are the same set if and only if they have the same members. This means then that a set changes identity if it loses or gains a single member. Such a principle however does not go through with groups, for a family does not become a different entity through the birth or death of a child, a company does not mutate in the turnover of its directors, a nation does not lose its identity as one generation replaces another. The failure of the principle to apply indicates that groups are assigned by us to a different ontological category from that of the collection, an assignment that warrants describing them as collectives.

Groups have some very peculiar properties. One such is that just mentioned, which they share with physical objects; they remain the *same* entity through time even when their parts are replaced. Another is that we treat them as autonomous agents. An individual may do something, acting for a group as its agent, irrespective of his or her personal feelings – corporate agency means that the individual acts 'not in his or her own name'. We talk of 'Britain' and 'America' as autonomous agents represented by individuals' actions. Such is the power of conceptualization.

There is a large sociological literature on human groups which we cannot deal with here. However, in Figure 4.2 I have listed some of those features of human groups which will be of significance for language as we proceed. Only point 11, Groups and practices, needs explanation at this stage. A **practice** is an implicit regularity of behaviour that characterizes a group (MacDonald and Pettit, 1981: 110f.), such things, for example, as 'accepting the authority of Parliament' or 'using banking facilities properly'. A general regularity of this sort can underlie a whole range of actions. We will return to such phenomena later on. For now, consider a practice as rather like a norm or a convention such that *there is a general expectation within a group that everyone will conform with the practice*. As such, practices form a stable social background for making sense of what people do. We need to know the relevant practices of a group in order that any individual's behaviour be intelligible. This leads to point 12. The central importance for our understanding of each other, of mutual expectation, combined with the significance of group identity for individual identities (points 8 and 9), exerts **normative pressure** on individuals to do what they are expected to do.

1. *Changing membership.* A group remains the *same* group although the individuals who constitute it may change.
2. *Continuity in time.* A group remains the *same* group as it continues in time, and in spite of changes in membership.
3. *Individuals shared by different groups.* The individuals who constitute a group may *at the same time* be members of other groups.
4. *Physical discontinuity of membership.* The individuals who constitute a group need not be in physical proximity.
5. *Primary and secondary groups.* In primary groups the members are directly related in face-to-face interaction. In secondary groups the members are indirectly related, according to some wider criterion.
6. *Enduring or evanescent.* A group may endure for generations, or may be evanescent, forming for a particular purpose or circumstance and dissolving afterwards.
7. *Stratification.* Groups may be stratified relative to other groups in a hierarchy from higher to lower according to some evaluative criteria.
8. *Self-conscious significance.* Individuals can be grouped together on any criterion. Not all criteria are equally salient. The most important criterion is the self-conscious significance of the group – how it views itself as significantly different from other groups, and how solidary its members feel.
9. *Identity.* An individual's multiple group memberships make up their social identity.
10. *Reference groups.* An individual may find identity or values in those of some group of which they are not a member.
11. *Groups and practices.* Practices are regularities of behaviour which characterize groups.
12. *Normative pressures.* Pressures are exerted on a group's members to make them conform to the practices of the group.
13. *Centrality and peripherality.* Individuals may be central or peripheral members of the group.
14. *Internal structure.* Groups have different kinds of internal structure. Some are integrated, some diffuse. Some are informally organized while others are institutions, with formally specified roles and statuses.
15. *Stereotypes.* Groups may be characterized in terms of stereotypical properties and members *stigmatized* or granted *prestige* in terms of objectively false categorizations, e.g. *Blacks, immigrants, women, youths, Irish etc.* (see chapter below).

Figure 4.2 Some features of groups

A scientist normally generates their data with hypotheses already in mind. We shall see that linguists approach the community with differing assumptions about relevant groups. Different groups reveal different correlations between language and society.

But there are also three further important assumptions about practices which are made in sociolinguistic research. The first is that individuals have a **vernacular**. Labov writes (1972: 208):

> Not every style or point on the stylistic continuum is of equal interest to linguists. Some styles show irregular . . . patterns . . . In other styles, we find more systematic speech, where the fundamental relations which determine the course of linguistic evolution can be seen most clearly. This is the 'vernacular' – the style in which the minimum attention is given to the monitoring of speech. Observation of the vernacular gives us the most systematic data for our analysis of linguistic structure.

The second assumption is that individuals style-shift away from their vernaculars in situations where they are paying more attention to speech. There is a dimension of casual to formal, in which the vernacular is the most casual style.

The third assumption is what makes observation of the vernacular a problem. The very presence of the linguist, observing speech, affects the style of the speech observed. In particular, the presence of the linguist makes the speech more formal than it might otherwise be. Labov calls this **the observer's paradox**. As he puts it, how does one know whether or not the light is off inside the fridge when the door is shut?

Approaching the community: techniques

As a practical matter, the linguist must come up with solutions to these problems in order to investigate speech. There are three basic classes of techniques which have been used:

> Anonymous observation;
> The sociolinguistic interview;
> Participant observation of (a) natural groups, and
> (b) social networks.

These methods of investigation all have strengths and weaknesses. Anonymous observation side-steps the observer's paradox, since the speakers do not know they are being observed. But the linguist cannot easily identify or control either the social groups or the stylistic variation. The classic form of investigation is the interview as developed by Labov (1966). The data for sociolinguistic structures such as Figure 4.1 were obtained this way. Let us see how this was done. The hypothesis was that linguistic variables were conditioned by class and style.

Social class

Socio-economic class is one example of **stratification** within a society. To say that any group of people is stratified is to say that they can be ranked in a hierarchy, from highest to lowest, on some scale. Consider the examination results of a group of students. The students can be ranked on the scale of examination grades and thus stratified with respect to that property. Note that there has to be an evaluative dimension to this in order to establish the hierarchical ranking and thus stratify, rather than merely differentiate, the population. There has to be tacit agreement that people's relative positions can be arranged from higher to lower. The stratification of a society is constituted subjectively by its members' attitudes to themselves and to each other concerning their relative positions within a hierarchy. So stratification will be deeply tied up with **evaluation**, with prestige and stigmatization.

Within sociology there is a large literature on social class. In our ordinary use of the term 'class', we probably use it to refer to our various perceptions of people's differential access to resources and power, as well as the differing cultural practices and beliefs which represent, reflect and justify that differential access. For sociolinguistic research work, however, some way is needed to establish objectively the social class of the informants. Very often, as in Labov's work, pre-existing sociological data for the population are used. The objective measures used to establish social class were the scales of income, education and occupation. An individual's socio-economic class was established by his or her combined rank on these three scales. Using these combined criteria, a single continuum of class stratification can be established on which one can differentiate individuals as finely as the measure allows. The actual socio-economic classes used are cuts along this continuum. Labov initially divided it into ten social classes. It is important to realize, then, that social class is an abstract construct. Because of the scales chosen, it should reflect the objective stratification of society and people's subjective perceptions, whatever the deeper causes of such phenomena.

The next step for the researcher is to correlate the index scores for the linguistic variables with the social class continuum. Logically, there are a number of possible ways to do this. One possibility is to treat a set number of social classes as given, and simply work out the average score for the individuals in each of the classes. Another possibility, used in research by Pellowe and Jones (1978) on Tyneside, is to process the linguistic data first and then see how its intrinsic internal structure corresponds with combinations of social factors. A third possibility, the one used by Labov and most other researchers, is to cut the social-class continuum into social classes in such a way that it best reflects the regularities in the linguistic data.

In many cases the correlation between average index scores and social class is such that the variable exhibits **fine stratification**. This means that the average scores for each successive group, as one ascends or descends the continuum of stratification, grade into that of the group above or below it with no sharp discontinuities. Thus, no matter how finely one cuts the continuum in establishing average scores for social strata, the scores will be stratified (arranged in a hierarchy) for all styles. The usages of the classes, although different, blend into one another. The kind of stratification seems to be typical of phonological variables. It is exhibited by the (ing) variable in New York.

Other variables, by contrast, exhibit **sharp stratification**. In these cases, often syntactic variables, the average index scores seem to divide the social continuum into two, with a major discontinuity in the scores of upper and lower strata. An example of this feature is the (ing) variable in Norwich investigated by Peter Trudgill in *The Social Differentiation of English in Norwich* (1974). The Norwich (ing) scores are given in Figure 4.3. Note that, as in New York, there is a completely consistent correspondence between the stratification of linguistic scores and that of the social classes

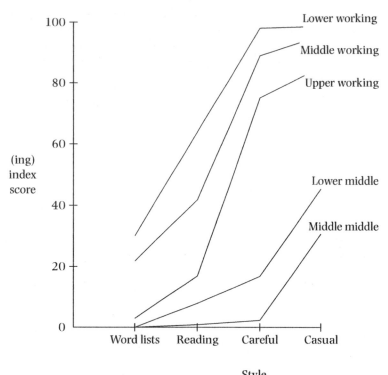

Style				
Class	*Word list*	*Reading*	*Careful*	*Casual*
I Middle middle	000	000	003	028
II Lower middle	000	010	015	042
III Upper working	005	015	074	087
IV Middle working	023	044	088	095
V Lower working	029	066	098	100

Figure 4.3 The (ing) variable in Norwich (*from Trudgill, 1974*)

in every style. I have put boxes around those pairs of figures that exhibit sharp stratification.

We noted before that the frequencies observed were *simultaneously* a reflection of the informant's style and social class. This means that an individual with a score of, say, forty-three, could be either a middle-working-class informant in reading style, or a lower-middle-class speaker in casual style. The class stratification is obscured unless some way is found to hold style constant, or for the linguist to know what style of speech is being observed. The difficulty was the observer's paradox.

Speech style

The technique which Labov used in the sociolinguistic interview is the paradigm solution to this problem. He utilized the observer's paradox itself to define a speech style, which he called **careful speech**. This is the speech elicited by the very presence of the interviewer, used as a point of reference. Any utterance in reply to the interviewer's formal questions during the interview is labelled as 'careful'. The assumption is that there are styles both more casual and more formal than this. Figure 4.4 schematizes how these styles are elicited. Careful speech is the starting point. The principle is to control the amount of attention which the informant pays to the way he or she speaks. More formal styles, those above 'careful speech' in the figure, are those which successively produce more conscious care in the informant. Thus, the context of 'reading paragraphs' of connected prose produces a **reading style**, which is itself more self-conscious than the already relatively careful speech of the responses to questions. Reading **word lists**, because it draws further attention to linguistic items and their pronunciation, is more formal again. Even more attention is paid to the act of speaking itself. **Casual style**, by contrast, is defined as those utterances made in contexts which *decrease* the amount of attention paid to the manner of speech, relative to the central reference point. The contexts are those shown beside 'casual style' in Figure 4.4. Thus, if there is seemingly a natural break in the interview (for example, the informant goes to the kitchen to get a beer, or answers the telephone, or speaks to a third party) and various **cues** are also observed, the speech uttered counts as more 'casual', closer to the vernacular, than that of straight responses to the interviewer's questions which are perceived as part of an 'interview'.

This technique defines a continuum of speech styles relative to the amount of attention the informant pays to his or her manner

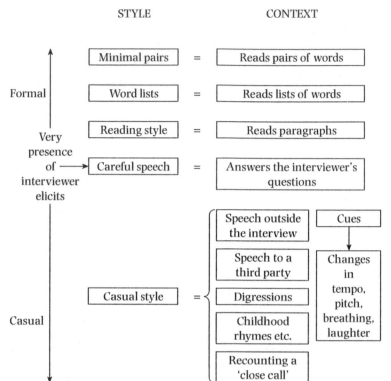

Figure 4.4 The sociolinguistic interview: styles

of speaking, and has become the standard methodology in socio-linguistic research. It is important that the contexts be defined to produce such a continuum of relative degrees of self-monitoring.

We have now seen how the two non-linguistic dimensions of sociolinguistic structures are arrived at, using the interview as the means of investigation.

What is revealed and what is obscured

There is no doubt that these regularities are significant. They reveal the large-scale structure of variability. For now, just note how in Figure 4.3 the stylistic variation is steepest for the upper working class, and the sharp discontinuities are between this class and its neighbours. The behaviour of the lower middle and upper working classes, the 'border-line' groups, figures in important interpretations of the patterns revealed by class and style stratification diagrams.

These diagrams represent *averages* for groups of speakers based on class and style. However, informants form groups on other criteria as well. Data obtained from interviews allow the linguist to get average scores for other obvious secondary group characteristics; for example, sex, age, ethnicity, locale etc. Thus, Trudgill (1974) found that women consistently had lower (ing) index scores than men. Women produced relatively more of the prestige '-ing' variants than men. The other side of this coin was that both men's speech and working-class speech were typified by relatively higher (ing) scores, more of the '-in'' variant.

A social identity is partially made up of the various large secondary groups of which the individual is a member. I am a member of a class in a stratified overall society; I am in a certain age group, of a certain sex, and so on. The averages for individuals grouped by any one of these social factors do not reveal correlations for the others. The data need analysis. The linguist has to look to the *interaction of social variables* and evaluate their relative weight in determining scores. Other factors are also buried within the correlations. The relative effects of the purely linguistic environments, such as those mentioned in our discussion of /t,d/ deletion, need to be separated out. Finally, what about the individual within the averages? An average score of forty for some group does not tell us exactly what individuals are doing. The explanation of individuals with deviant scores may tell us a great deal about the significance of the group scores. Indeed, the correlations themselves need to be interpreted. Where does the variability itself originate? If it is part of the process of language change (the assumption we made in chapter two), then how do these large-scale correlations help us to explain how language changes? We will be looking at these issues in chapters six and seven.

Sources of normative pressure

The sociolinguistic interview is not a particularly good way to observe the vernacular. (Its strength is the breadth of information it yields.) Its point of reference is the speech elicited by the presence of the interviewer and the interview situation. But the interviewer, as an 'outsider', invokes the norms of the 'outside', those normative pressures coming from the society as a whole. Note that in Figure 4.3 three of the four styles involve formality. Where reading is involved we gain access to how the individual self-consciously thinks the language ought to be pronounced. This is by definition, as it were, since those styles were set up to increase his awareness of speech. The identification of informants by social class also produces structures which give us access to the normative pressures of the society as a whole. Class involves the stratification of this largest of all groups. In Figures 4.1 (from America) and 4.3 (from England) speakers of all classes style-shift towards the forms used most frequently by the highest social class in casual speech. The upper middle classes are, it would seem, the custodians of the standard of good pronunciation. We are therefore gaining access to 'pressures from above the level of conscious awareness'. The interview reveals the normative pressure exerted by a stratified structure.

However, we will see later that there are many variables in the process of change *towards* non-standard forms and *away* from the prestige forms; for example, the Norwich (e) and the New York (oh). Paradoxically, the observed style-shifting in these cases is away from the direction of change and still towards the standard forms used by the middle classes.

It follows that there are normative pressures from other sources. Of course, any social group exercises such normative influence. One is, for example, under pressure to speak in a way appropriate to whether one is a man or a woman. But the places to look are those primary groups in which the vernacular is based; those groups based on intimate face-to-face association. The solidarity of the group exerts a normative pressure away from the values of the larger society, and towards its own vernacular culture. The identity of the individual, both given and chosen, is at the complex intersection of differing groups and their normative pressures. The intensity of these pressures will vary according to how integrated or diffuse are the structures of the groups. In large, mobile populations the pressure will be less than in those groups which are 'local' and 'vernacular' (Milroy, 1987: 178f.).

Primary groups

Access to the vernacular will clearly be gained through the study of individuals within primary groups. A number of studies, including that of Hemnesberget by Blom and Gumperz (1972), used techniques developed to do just this. What is needed is a way of obtaining large quantities of spontaneous speech in as natural a situation as possible, and still to overcome the observer's paradox. This can be done by long-term participation in and observation of 'natural' groups. Labov, Cohen, Robins and Lewis (1968) developed such a method in their study of the vernacular of black adolescent peer groups in Harlem: the Thunderbirds, the Jets and the Cobras.

After contact was established with the groups, multiple techniques were used to investigate speech. The main techniques were formal sociolinguistic interviews and the recording of group outings and group sessions. Investigation began with the Thunderbirds, and spread to the Jets and Cobras. In these last two groups participant observation was done by John Lewis, one of those interviewed in early exploratory work. The presence of an 'insider', who controlled the vernacular, helped to override the observer's paradox. Lewis rented a clubhouse and had daily contact with the Jets throughout 1966. Labov found that the group sessions yielded very natural vernacular speech. He writes, 'the setting was essentially that of a party rather than an interview, with card games, eating and drinking, singing and sounding. The effect of observation and recording was, of course, present, but the natural interaction of the group overrode all other effects' (Labov, 1972a: xviii–xix). The observer's paradox can thus be overcome by the pressures of face-to-face interaction in primary groups in natural situations.

Blom and Gumperz (1972) found the same effects. They write, 'Methodologically, self-recruitment of groups is important for two reasons. It ensures that groups are defined by locally recognized relationships and enables the investigator to predict the norms relevant to their interaction. Furthermore, the fact that particip-ants have pre-existing obligations towards each other means that, given the situation, they are likely to respond to such obligations in spite of the presence of strangers. Our tape recording and our visual observations give clear evidence that this in fact was what occurred' (Blom and Gumperz, 1972: 426–7).

In both of these studies, the speech was not viewed out of con-text. In chapter three, we discussed the social analysis made by Gumperz and Blom. Labov *et al.* (1968) used multiple methods of observation and testing. The vernacular black culture and its values and speech event types were studied. (For example, the word 'sounding' was used a moment ago; this is the New York term for exchanging ritual insults: Labov, 1972a; Mitchell-Kernan, 1972.) Systematic studies of adult black speakers and white adole-scent speakers were done. And a social analysis of the gangs was carried out. Members were categorized according to their degree of integration into the vernacular sub-culture, and index scores calculated on this basis.

Social networks

Such studies, however, are constrained in that they can only be carried out in naturally occurring groups. They are group based. An alternative approach has been developed by the Milroys and used to study the working-class vernacular in Belfast, Northern Ireland (Milroy and Milroy, 1978; Milroy, 1987).

They found it possible to begin at the other end, as it were, and base their investigation of the vernacular on the speech of individuals. The familiar quantitative method of scoring variables could be applied to an individual's **social network**, his or her face-to-face associations. Average scores for other social variables – neighbourhood, style, sex, age and so on – could be studied in relation to both individual and group network scores. This method of investigation makes assumptions: it postulates that the kinds and density of relationship which an individual has within primary groups are significant for linguistic variability; just as the interview

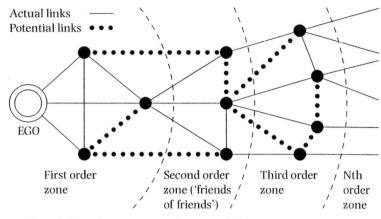

Actual links ——
Potential links • • •

EGO

First order zone / Second order zone ('friends / of friends') / Third order zone / Nth order zone

Figure 4.5 Social networks (*after Boissevain, 1974*)

methodology presupposes that the stratification of the society as a whole is significant.

A social network is a way of representing the individual's pattern of social transactions within a community. Figure 4.5 portrays an idealized social network graph. Starting at EGO, where the network is anchored, an individual's social relations with other persons are represented by lines. Some of these persons also interact with each other. All the persons who directly interact with EGO form their **first order zone**. But each of these persons interacts with further individuals who are not in touch with EGO, but who could be. These form a **second order zone**. Such people are 'friends of friends', and, in community life, serve many useful functions for EGO: the 'I can get it for you wholesale' functions. Social networks involve more than simply communication. They form the web of transactions which make up the intimate texture of daily life, and as such involve individuals in rights and obligations towards each other.

There are a number of important features which allow comparisons between networks of different types. Networks may be more or less **dense**. If the members of an individual's network are also in touch with each other independently, that network has a high **density**. In other words, a network's density is a measure of how many potential links are in fact actual links. A **cluster** is a part of a network with a high density. Networks may also be

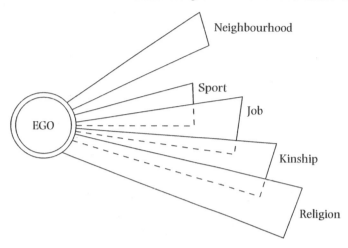

Figure 4.6 Diversity of linkages in a multiplex network (*from Boissevain, 1974*)

multiplex or **uniplex**. Multiplexity means that there is more than one transactional basis for the social relationships in the network. Figure 4.6 shows the diversity of linkages that could exist in multiplex networks. The same individuals can be simultaneously linked by kinship, employment and neighbourhood. It was the relative density and multiplexity of their networks that formed the basis of individuals' network scores.

Intuitively, the more dense and multiplex a network is, the more social cohesion one would expect. Each individual has transactions with each of the other individuals independently and in a multiplicity of ways. They are kin, who live and work together. Such networks exert a strong normative pressure on their members based on a sense of solidarity – the pressure comes from 'inside' the network. In general, high density and multiplexity, which typified the working-class communities studied in Milroy (1987), sustained non-standard norms.

The sociolinguistic research was carried on in three deprived inner city areas of Belfast: Ballymacarrett, a Protestant area of East Belfast, the Hammer, in West Belfast, also Protestant, and the Clonard, a Catholic area of West Belfast. The aim was the study of the working-class vernaculars of these territorially based communities in as natural a way as possible.

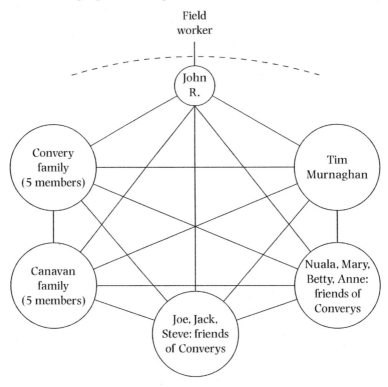

Figure 4.7 A portion of the Clonard network, showing density of 100
(*from Milroy, 1987: 58*)

Milroy gained access to the community as a participant-observer
by using the natural status of 'a friend of a friend'. She introduced
herself into the community through mutually known individuals
and entered networks 'of kith and kin'. Figure 4.7 illustrates such
a network in the Clonard. In both Labov's and Milroy's studies,
community-based norms of interaction (the important role of oral
as opposed to written verbal skills, for example) differed from 'outside' norms. Both groups, although very different, typified kinds of
urban sub-cultures with communicative norms which contrasted
with those of the wider society. We shall return to some of Milroy's
results later.

Community grammars and competence grammars

It is now time to look at questions of representation and inter-pretation. What are we to make out of our discoveries thus far? A word of caution is appropriate here. The matters raised will be difficult and controversial. Probably every point I will make in this concluding section would be disputed by some linguists. But the issues, though brain-teasing, are too important to evade.

Variability, Labov argues, is not explicable if we look only to the speech of the individual. He writes (Labov, 1972a: 124):

> we now know enough about language in its social context to realise that the grammar of the speech community is more regular and sys-tematic than the behaviour of one individual. Unless the speech pattern is studied within the overall system of the community, it will appear as a mosaic of unaccountable and sporadic variation.

The occasions of Speakers A, B and C at the beginning of this chapter allowed us to visualize how this would look. And Figures 4.1 and 4.3 showed us the regular patterns observable through the social investigation of speech. Labov is arguing for community grammars, which will represent such sociolinguistic structures. But what would be the status of such grammars?

Modern linguistics has not had to face this problem before. Since Saussure's *Course in General Linguistics* laid the foundations of the subject early this century, it has been possible to ignore vari-ation in speech. As we saw in chapter one, the aim of the linguist is to characterize 'competence'. In Saussure's terms this was **langue**, or language, viewed as a system of relations between categories, abstracted from the variation implicit in individual utterances, historical evolution of the system, or dialects. In Chomsky's terms, in order to find out 'what language is', we have to discover the universal properties of mind that make possible the acquisition of any language. A theory of language will tell us what any human being 'knows', in an abstract sense, in order to acquire a language. Since these properties of mind are biologically given, they are uni-form across the species. It is therefore possible to investigate them through the speech of any individual. This is why the variation we observe in actually heterogeneous communities or in individuals can be safely ignored. It is **performance**, or **parole**, produced by factors extraneous to competence, which varies within and between individuals.

There is a paradox here: **the Saussurean paradox**. As Bailey (1973: 35) puts it, 'competence is looked for exclusively in the individual, but variety is sought in society'. This means that to study the truly universal in language we have to look to individuals, what they intrinsically 'know'. On the other hand, if we want to explain variation within that individual (our task here), we must look to the social, as we have done. But what we discover, we are told, is not intrinsic to competence, to the universals that constitute a linguistic theory.

Let us contrast the two types of grammar. We have Chomsky's competence grammar. Such grammars have this status. They should be interpretable in psychological and, ultimately, in biological terms. By psychological, I mean in terms of the strategies of production and interpretation, of memory and so on; the sort of thing for which we can get behavioural evidence. By biological, I mean the actual neurological structures in which the knowledge is realized. For Chomsky, knowledge of language is ultimately a matter of biology. We are genetically pre-programmed to learn language: that is ultimately the locus of grammar. He argues that it is the present impossibility of directly investigating this, together with ethical considerations, that make us proceed abstractly. We investigate what any individual 'knows' via his or her judgements of grammaticality, paraphrase relations and so on.

Now contrast this with Labov's community grammar. This formalizes the quantitative patterns which are only visible when speech is investigated socially. It is a collective grammar, but not a universal one. The question then arises as to the status of the quantitative rules of which such grammars consist.

Interpreting community grammars

This is problematic. Some people working on variation believe that **variable rules**, rules that formalize in probabalistic terms frequencies such as those we observed, are psychologically real. That is to say, such rules are part of competence. They are not only the

rules of a community grammar, but are part of the intrinsic knowledge of language which any individual has.

The theory of variable rules, as a model of the quantitative patterns such as Labov and others have revealed, is an exceedingly
technical matter.

We can sketch out the basic principle. Variable rules are
constructed on the basis of the 'aggregate' data of average scores,
and observed frequencies, such as those discussed above. Then
probabilities are assigned to the various internal linguistic environments predicting, in order, the way they constrain the probability
of the rule applying in that environment. There is a prior input
probability of the rule applying, determined by the extralinguistic
factors such as class, style, ethnic group etc.

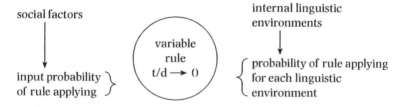

Such a device accurately predicts the observed frequencies. It is
derived from an analysis of the whole community. It therefore
states a quantitative relationship between any two informants,
such that what one speaker does is mathematically tied to what
another speaker does.

Now the problem is that it is hard to make sense of any psychological interpretation of these rules (Bickerton, 1971; Bailey, 1973;
Romaine, 1981; Sankoff, 1988a; for a discussion, see Romaine,
1982: 247f.). Bickerton argues that speakers could not conceivably
keep track of the frequencies of variables in their speech relative
to thousands of other members of the community with whom they
have never had contact. Indeed, how could such 'community
grammars' be acquired by an individual? The problem is not that
individuals apply the rule with the probabilities stated in the rule.
This, in fact, happens. There is no disputing that the rules *do*
predict the occurrences of variants. They predict them for groups
and for individuals. The problem is that in the representation the

individual probabilities are mathematically tied, the one to the other. How could individuals 'know' this, as psychological reality would demand? In brief, how could an individual 'know' a community grammar?

Any representation needs to be interpreted. The variable-rule grammar can be understood as a community grammar, and as an individual grammar. As a model of the individual it may represent what he or she knows. The individual *can* know, indeed, *must* know, the probability with which to apply the rule, because, if it is correct, he or she does as the model predicts. But as a community grammar, its claims to psychological reality are doubtful without some concept of a 'group' mind. It formalizes mathematically the quantitative relations the linguist has discovered in aggregate data. Individuals, whatever they do, simply *cannot know this* in the way the linguist does. In any case, the description simply represents the facts: it does not tell us what the connections are such that variables are mathematically related in this way in the speech of the community. There is a similar problem with mathematical modelling in any social science, for example in economics. What is required, if this is the case, is some sort of collective 'coordinative' mechanism which, coordinating what whole communities do, transmits to the individual just the information that he or she needs.

Variable rules do not tell us what this 'coordinative mechanism' is; nor why the probabilities of individuals are tied together in the way the model says. As community grammars, however, let us agree that they are not psychologically real, that there is no group competence. Competence must be universal and individual.

Autonomous social facts

Let us try again. There is another possible interpretation of community grammars. They arguably could be **autonomous social objects**. This is very much the sense in which Durkheim (1938) used the term 'social fact'. In this case, community grammars would exist in some sense independently, 'over and above' the individuals who constitute the community. No individual 'knows' such emergent properties of the group. Although speakers produce and reproduce the social pattern, it is ontologically independent of any one individual's knowledge. It seems to me that some such conception of language was involved in the notion of *langue*, before it was reinterpreted by Chomsky as grounded in biology.

Clearly, social facts exist since we are able to talk about them. They have, at least, 'expressive autonomy' (MacDonald and Pettit, 1981: 115f.). The rules of a community grammar would be social facts of this sort. But what is the status of such rules? And what kind of relationship might exist between such community grammars and the individuals who constitute the community?

Statistical statements expressing social facts such as the relationship of class, style etc. and index score (for example, the kind of information displayed in Figure 4.1), are generalizations expressing regular and significant **correlations**. That is all. They could be considered the social equivalent of empirical scientific statements of a statistical type. Given a certain input, for example, network score and sex, there is a predictable regularity in observed behaviour over a number of instances.

It is a further matter to develop an **explanatory theory or model** which might be able to give a causal account of why we observe the correlation. It would be a mistake to say that the correlation *itself* either 'caused' the speaker to perform in such a way, or 'explains' why the speaker did so. This is because we haven't explained the correlations in terms of an underlying causal mechanism which might tell us what is causing them. Hence, because of its emphasis on empirical, quantitative studies, the Labov paradigm is sometimes called **correlational sociolinguistics**. The 'community grammar' summarizes these results. It merely represents the 'social facts'. By contrast, a Chomsky grammar *does* interpret its principles and rules in terms of an underlying causal mechanism, namely innate structures of the brain which, in interaction with performance factors, causally explain the data in terms of a biological mechanism. In sociolinguistics we need instead some social or contextual mechanism with which to explain the correlational results of a community grammar and show how the individual performances representable by variable rules have come about.

The patterns of a community grammar make social facts 'visible'. The correlations are 'clues' for the interpretation of the behaviour (Sankoff, 1988: 150), 'symptoms' of as yet unexplained processes of linguistic differentiation and change. As Romaine (1982: 187) puts it, the method is a 'valuable analytic device'. However, consider that the analyst has had to *choose* what social and contextual variables to investigate and this has generated just certain kinds of facts which are considered significant. The socio-linguist may have 'had in mind' some explanatory hypotheses or intuition beforehand, which made that empirical result relevant. The variables are not selected arbitrarily, but are part of a research programme.

It would seem, however, that we now need to search for an underlying coordinating mechanism which will explain why groups do, in fact, behave with such astonishing regularity.

Waves of change revisited

In chapter two, we talked of the diffusion of linguistic changes as waves moving through both social and linguistic environments. This was illustrated in Figure 2.2. So far we have investigated variation using the correlational method. The results have been represented by variable rules, rules which represent the statist-ical structure of what a community does as it is manifested in individual behaviour. There is an alternative approach to the significance of variation, one that may throw some light on the mechanism that transmits community-wide information to indi-vidual speakers. This approach represents and interprets inherent variation in terms of the wave-like movement of change through language.

This **dynamic paradigm** has largely been due to the work of Bailey (1973) and Bickerton (1971, 1973). The issues are com-plicated and controversial and I must necessarily present them in an oversimplified way (see Fasold, 1970, 1975; Anshen, 1975; Sankoff and Rousseau, 1979; Romaine, 1982).

Let us imagine that a linguistic change is taking place. There will be two variants, X and Y, and Y is replacing X within the language. Before the change occurs, X will be categorically present in any **lect** of the language. (A lect is a minimum variety of the language which has a combination of features different from any other lect.) After the change, X will be categorically absent. And Y will then be categorically present in any lect. If variability between X and Y occurs, it will be in the transition phase between categorical X and categorical Y.

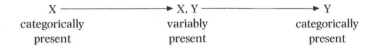

X	X, Y	Y
categorically present	variably present	categorically present

It might be easier to imagine this in a case where a variant is being lost from a language. First, it will always be present. Then, it will sometimes be present and sometimes absent; it will be variable. Finally, it will always be absent. And the reverse happens if a feature is being gained. A change from X to Y involves the loss of X, the gaining of Y, and a phase where both occur and are variable. The notion of a wave itself implies that change is not instantaneous.

The wave model traces this process. Look at Figure 4.8. In this example we can trace a change as it moves, in time, through four linguistic environments, (a), (b), (c) and (d), and through four lects. (These can be represented as four minimally different grammars.) The wave hypothesis is that the change proceeds systematically through the environments in the order represented in the diagram. Simultaneously, it moves through the lects, first lect 1, then 2, then 3, then 4. The order depends on the point of origin of the change.

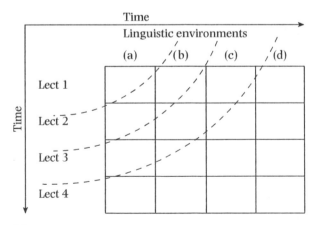

Figure 4.8

Let us look at the wave front as it moves through the environments and the grammars. The change begins at the top left-hand corner of the diagram. It originates in a specific linguistic context, and among a small group of speakers: lect 1, environment (a). The change has a definite directionality inside the grammar of lect 1. The linguistic environments can be arranged in a ranking according to the degree to which they favour the change or not. Thus, it spreads from 1 (a) to (b), (c) and (d) in this lect. In our diagram, the wave front is just reaching environment (d) in lect 1. It is virtually complete in environment (c) for this first lect.

But, simultaneously, the change is moving into the other lects. In Figure 4.8 the wave front has just reached lect 4. How far the change has gone in the environments of a lect is related to how close that lect is to lect 1, where the change originated. Thus, in lect 2, it is midway through environment (c); in lect 3, it has not yet reached environment (c); in lect 4, it is just beginning in the first environment. In each lect, in turn, it goes through the environments in the same order, but does so *later*.

We said a moment ago that variability will occur in the process of transition. This means that at the time when the wave front is moving through the cells in our diagram, the two forms will be variable and will occur with a given frequency. When the change is complete the new variant will appear 100 per cent of the time. Before it has reached a given environment or a given lect, it will appear '0' times or be categorically absent. In between, *where* and *when* it is variable, it will appear a certain percentage of the time. One would expect, then, that the frequencies will be ordered in exactly the order of environment and lect, decreasing from 100 per cent, in terms of how far they are from the point of origin. Scores of 0 will occur in environments and lects which the wave front has not reached. This would be the case at any chosen time, if the 'clock is stopped'. As time goes on, the scores for each cell will rise, preserving their relations determined by their relative distances from the origin of the wave, with new cells rising above 0 as the wave front spreads to new environments and lects, which then become variable. Cells closest to the origin will start reaching 100 per cent at these later times.

How exactly the frequencies will look depends on how, in fact, wave fronts move from cell to cell. Different views of this give different distributions of the frequencies, although we get the same direction in the rise of frequencies. If one claimed that the rate of change increased as it neared completion, then frequencies will rise more *quickly* closer to the point of origin. If one claimed that a change had to be relatively complete in one cell, before it spread to the next cells, then we would observe quite large jumps in frequencies between cells where the innovation was first appearing, and adjacent cells where it was relatively complete – rather than a gradual, smooth increase. Bickerton (1971, 1973) makes the very strong claim that, for any lect, only *one* cell may contain *both* forms (be variable) at any time. This means that the whole top left part of Figure 4.8 would be categorically 100 per cent, and the whole bottom right, categorically 0. We would observe frequencies only in a line of cells running from the top right corner to the bottom left corner of the diagram, a line at the outer edge of the wave front. On this view the group frequencies which Labov's correlational studies obtain are a 'statistical illusion', caused by working from averaged group scores. In fact, many speakers have lects which are either categorical, or only variable in one environment.

It would seem that this claim is too strong. We will take Bailey's view of the matter. Figure 4.9 shows the sort of frequencies we might expect to obtain at three relative times in Bailey's theory (Bailey, 1973: 79). Observe the regular increases in the percentages of the new variant as it approaches the point of origin, lect 1, environment (a). Observe also how the percentages of the new form increase, preserving their relations with each other, at the two later times as the change continues to work its way through the language.

Consequences of the dynamic paradigm

The Bailey wave model represents inherent variation in terms of the dynamics of the way changes move through language. This has consequences for investigation, and for the way in which variability can be interpreted.

Methodologically, it is possible to work with data from individuals. Once collected, the problem is to determine the correct order of the linguistic environments and the correct order of the grammars so that the data exhibit more or less the relations

Linguistic environments

		(a)	(b)	(c)	(d)
	Lect 1	100	90	80	20
Relative	Lect 2	90	80	20	10
time 1	Lect 3	80	20	10	
	Lect 4	20	10		

		(a)	(b)	(c)	(d)
	Lect 1	100	100	90	80
Relative	Lect 2	100	90	80	20
time 2	Lect 3	90	80	20	10
	Lect 4	80	20	10	

		(a)	(b)	(c)	(d)
	Lect 1	100	100	100	90
Relative	Lect 2	100	100	90	80
time 3	Lect 3	100	90	80	20
	Lect 4	90	80	20	10

Figure 4.9 (adapted from Bailey, 1973: 79)

displayed in our diagrams. The data are arranged implicationally
on **implicational scales**. Put simply, this means that if a feature
appears with a certain value in one cell, that **implies** that it
occurs with a predictably lower value in the next cell below or to
the right, and so on, as a result of the wave of change. We can
assign the patterns so generated to the grammars of individual
informants. The method is, at heart, linguistic, in that its concern
is with the linguistic patterning of change. The order of grammars
ought, however, to group individual speakers together in terms of
those social and geographical spaces through which the change is
working. But social factors are 'outside' the analysis of change, in
that the social groupings and styles are not used to explain the

wave front's progress, to explicate the dynamism. One advantage of working with individuals, however, is that when we observe deviant cells that break the implicational pattern (as we will), we can account for this through the idiosyncratic, personal biographies of those informants (Bickerton, 1971).

The picture of language which emerges is that of a system of related grammars, each minimally different from the next with respect to waves of change. The overall representation of language can be conceived of as a **panlectal grid**: an arrangement of possible grammars, implicationally related, for some given space and time. The variation between and within lects is thus an intrinsic part of language. Contrast this with the categorical grammars of Chomsky's view of language, in which variation is a matter of performance.

We can also contrast this panlectal, or 'polylectal' view with Labov's conception of a community grammar. In the polylectal view, the frequency with which individuals produce a given variant is understood in terms of the position of their particular lect on a wave of change. They needn't 'know' the grammars of other people's lects. This dissolves the problem of how individual speakers may be said to 'know', in Chomsky's sense of competence, a community grammar. They need not know it. The grammars of the community and of the individual are not the same. They are able to deduce the frequencies we observe without having internalized the probabilities derived from the distribution of frequency in the whole community (Bailey, 1971: 82). For any variable feature, the quantities are greater later, and lesser earlier. The frequency of one variant over another, by environment or lect, simply depends on *when* they acquired the feature.

Does this suggest that it is the waves of change that provide the 'coordinative' mechanism which relates what an individual does to the pattern observed in the whole community? In one sense, the answer must be 'yes'. It accounts for what an individual does, relative to other remote individuals, to produce the overall pattern, without the individual 'knowing' that overall pattern.

In another sense, the answer must still be 'no'. Too much is still left unexplained. Precisely what is left unexplained are the social correlations made visible by the Labov paradigm.

To conclude, it is important to be clear about the methodological claims in this section. We are not criticizing the use of statistical methods, the quantitative paradigm, in describing linguistic variation. No other approach to community wide variation is possible. The issues we have been discussing are about how to interpret and explain the quantitative results. Our main point has been that although the statistical pattern manifests itself in the variable behaviour of each individual speaker, represented by variable rules, the social correlations encoded in such rules *cannot* be said to 'causally explain' the variable performances they in fact represent. We don't know 'why' the individual performs the way they do. *But this is normal in statistical studies.* As David Sankoff writes (1988: 150):

> Macroscopic sociodemographic categories or network-level patterns of relationship do not directly affect the performance of individual speakers; implicit in any correlational study is the existence of mediating processes or intervening mechanisms which lead from extralinguistic factors, through conscious intent and/or unconscious tendencies, to actual behaviour.

The interpretative or functional issue remains to be explored after the 'correlational' results are in. Statistical method itself is neutral as to why the pattern occurs, whether it is caused psychologically or by internal structural pressures or socio-historically or is intentionally motivated and consciously (or unconsciously) meaningful for participants. Or a combination of these.

What makes it the case that individuals' utterances, remote in time and space, are 'coordinated' in such a way as to produce the large-scale pattern that quantitative studies make visible? The waves of change only reveal how individuals are socio-historically placed with respect to the transmission of the pattern of frequencies. But what is the 'coordinative mechanism' between individuals' utterances, in the first place, such that they are generating and diffusing waves of change? And this over and above any psychological or internal linguistic factors. In the rest of the book, some answers to this question will be explored. In the next chapter, however, we will look at a single variable in some detail. We will do this with an eye open for social factors in language change.

5 Rhoticity

> The generally more distinct utterance of Americans preserves a number of consonants that have begun to decay in Standard English . . . In 1913 the late Robert Bridges belaboured the English clergy for saying 'the *sawed* of the *Laud*' instead of 'the *sword* of the *Lord*' . . . The violent Anglophile, Henry James, revisiting the United States after many years in England, was so distressed by this clear sounding of *r*, that he denounced it as a 'morose grinding of the back teeth'.
>
> Mencken (1919)

The feature in question is **postvocalic** *r*. This is the *r* in words like 'guard', 'art', 'lord' and 'fourth', and at the end of words like 'floor', 'far' and 'rider'.

In line with our popular beliefs about accents, a basic dichotomy can be set up about how people pronounce words like these in English. It is often said that English speakers of English drop their *r*s, and, in contrast to this, Americans pronounce all the *r*s that appear in the written language. The accents are *r*-less and *r*-full, respectively.

Even folk perceptions are more fine-grained than this, however, and within Britain there is an awareness that Scottish, Irish and West Country accents are *r*-full. As mentioned in chapter one, for English English speakers *r*-fullness has a social meaning, not only of transatlantic English, but, at home, of both rusticity and bucolic genuineness. Accordingly, it is sometimes used to advertise such wholesome products as 'butte*r*' and 'cide*r*'. In the United States,

on the other hand, over and against a norm of *r*-full pronunciation, people think of *r*-less English principally as a feature of Southern accents, 'confederate' English as it is sometimes called, and
also of what is loosely called an 'Oxford' accent – the prestige pronunciation of southern England. As we shall see in chapter seven,
stereotypes associated with people's *attitudes* towards differing forms
of speech are themselves significant facts, and an important part
of the study of variability.

After the methodological emphasis of the last chapter, this chapter will look at some descriptive studies, and will concentrate on a
single feature, postvocalic *r*. There are reasons why this is appropriate. This sound-feature has been extensively studied in a number
of different communities on both sides of the Atlantic. The pattern
that emerges is very interesting, partly because of its scale in space
and time. The sound has been involved in a long-term pattern of
changes in many accents of English. It is currently in the process
of change in New York City and was one of the features studied by
Labov (1966). Because of the change in progress, we will find an
interestingly different sociolinguistic structure for the variable (r),
as compared to that of (ing). We will also begin to see how social
factors are inextricably involved, not only in language variation
at a given time and place, but in the diffusion of linguistic change.

Before beginning, however, a note on jargon. Wells (1982) comments on the use of 'rhotic', 'rhoticity' etc. in place of the more
straightforward '*r*-full', '*r*-fullness' etc. It seems that for some
people with *r*-less accents, the term '*r*-full' may easily be mistaken
for 'awful'. We would then be describing awful accents! Shades of
Henry James – see the quote at the beginning of the chapter!

Rhotic and non-rhotic

The situation is, of course, much more subtle and complex than
any simple dichotomy. Let us consider exactly what is meant by
saying an accent is rhotic or non-rhotic. The first point is that *r*
occurs in a number of different linguistic environments. In some
of these, it is never or very rarely dropped. Places where either all
or almost all speakers never drop *r*, are:

1. Word initial: reed, raw etc.
2. Between two vowels: arrow, borrow etc.
3. In consonant clusters before a vowel: bread, bring etc.

Because of its appearance in these positions, the sound *r* is part of the sound system of English in general. It serves to tell words apart, for example, 'raw' v. 'law', 'rum' v. 'bum', and 'drank' v. 'dank'.

When we talk of *r*-dropping in *r*-less accents, we are actually talking about its loss in *two* specific environments. What these have in common is that the *r* follows a vowel, hence the term 'postvocalic *r*'. These two environments are:

4. After a vowel: guard, board etc.
5. Word final: floor, rider etc.

The environments of *r*-dropping can be made more delicate: in terms of the class of the preceding vowel, whether the syllable is stressed or not, whether the next word begins with a vowel or a consonant, and so on.

Now there are three possibilities for an accent in relation to *r* in these latter environments. It may:

(Historical	Categorically retain *r*	(Rhotic	= *r*-full)
direction	Variably retain and drop *r*	(Variable	= has *variable* (r))
of change)	Categorically drop *r*	(Non-rhotic	= *r*-less)

These are the three phases, noted above, that occur in the process of a language change. Historically, if we look at the English language overall, the dropping of *r* is an innovation. In earlier periods, English would have been rhotic throughout. That this is the case can be readily seen if we think of the system of spelling that we have been handed down, and that was regularized in the eighteenth century. In general, though not always, the presence of *r* in the spelling tells us the positions of the historic *r*.

If we look at English today, all three of the possibilities relevant to *r* can be found. Later on, we will be concentrating on speech communities where there is a **variable (r)**. Figure 5.1 surveys the overall distribution of rhoticity, variable rhoticity and non-rhoticity among English accents (Wells, 1982). In dealing with this feature,

Rhotic	Variably rhotic	Non-rhotic
General American class of accents: midland, north central, middle Atlantic etc.	Local accents in the west of England	RP (Received Pronunciation) in England and Wales
Southern mountain accents in US, 'hill type' of speech	A few local accents in the north of England.	Local accents of the east and north of England
General Canadian	New York City	Most accents of Wales and New Zealand
	'Borderline' rhotic/non-rhotic areas in US, e.g.	
Scottish accents		Australia
Irish accents	South, eastern New England, black	South Africa
Some West Indian, e.g. Barbados	English vernacular	Black English vernacular in US
		Some parts of eastern New England
		Southern speech area in US, 'plantation' type
		Some West Indian, e.g. Trinidad

Figure 5.1 Rhoticity in the accents of English

we are talking about accents, not dialect differences. You will recall that accents differed only on the level of sound, and not necessarily on any other level. Remember also that the terms in Figure 5.1 are misleading in the way that they label accents as things, as discrete objects. In fact, we are dealing with continua, as we shall see. So Figure 5.1 is just a general guide. One point is quite clear from it, however.

Although prestige accents in Britain and North America – RP and General American respectively – provide 'polar norms' of non-rhotic and rhotic speech, there is not any simple dichotomy between the two sides of the Atlantic. Variability and the opposite categorical pronunciations are common in both societies, in particular speech communities.

How r is made

Consider, for a moment, how different to the ear an *r* sound appears in American, West Country, or Scottish speech – in these three rhotic varieties. Whether we classify an accent as rhotic or not depends solely on the presence or absence of postvocalic *r*. As we saw before, this is a part of the systematic arrangement of sounds as they function in the language, permitting speakers to tell words apart; for example, 'guard' from 'god', or 'board' from 'bawd'. However, there are also considerable variations 'beneath' this, so to speak, on the purely phonetic level. There are a number of different ways in which the sound *r* can be made with the organs of speech. The *r* sounds different depending on how it is made, and this is irrespective of whether the speaker's accent is rhotic or not. We all have *r*s in some environments.

In word-initial position, most accents make *r* in roughly the same way. In this position, it is a consonant sound, shaping the beginning of an initial syllable. Usually, the tip of the tongue is held near to, but not touching, the ridge just behind the upper teeth. The tongue tip is usually turned slightly backwards. This is called **retroflexion**. The sides of the tongue are touching the molars and there is a lateral bunching of the tongue. The air stream escapes continuously and freely out of the mouth, without friction, and the vocal chords are vibrating, giving the sound 'voice'. Bronstein (1960) points out, in connection with a common American pronunciation of this initial sound, that it can be alternatively made with the tongue-tip held low, and the central part of the tongue bunched and raised upwards and rearwards. One major difference between accents has to do with the **degree of retroflexion** in articulating the sound. Thus, RP has slight or no retroflexion, while American and West Country accents have more. Such movements produce the *r* impressions that we perceive.

There are other ways in which *r* can be pronounced. It is one of the most various of English consonants. It was originally a **trill**, a series of rapid taps by the tongue against the teeth ridge. This still occurs in some accents and some individuals in certain styles. It later became a **fricative** sound, in which audible friction can be heard in the narrowed gap between the tongue and the teeth ridge. This still occurs when *r* follows *d*, as in 'drink' in RP and other accents. Also, in RP, in the position between two vowels, for example in 'very' or 'marry', *r* is often realized as a **flap**, a single tap of the tongue-tip on the teeth ridge. We will be mentioning these various pronunciations of the same abstract *r* sound later, as they are relevant.

The English pyramid

Figure 5.1 tells us that RP is non-rhotic. This accent is the national prestige norm of England and Wales. Before looking specifically at *r*-lessness in England and Wales, we must look at how various accents are related to each other within the overall society.

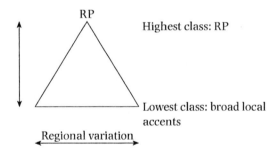

It is generally agreed that the relationship of accents to each other in England takes the form of a pyramid (Wells, 1982: 14; Hughes and Trudgill, 1979: 6). The pyramid represents two continua of variation. The base represents geographical variations, local accents. The vertical dimension represents social stratification. At the apex is RP.

It can't be emphasized enough that RP, at the top of the pyramid, is a national norm. *It is not localized.* It is distributed in the highest social classes up and down the country. At the opposite end of the social scale, at the base of the pyramid, we find the speech of the lowest classes – which is also the most highly localized pronunciation. It is the broad local accent of that area. Working-class accents vary markedly from region to region: Cockney, Scouse, Tyneside, West Midlands and so on. These can be broadly classified, of course, in larger regional terms, as southern or northern, for example. But the most localized accents are also those at the bottom end of the social scale.

The middle social strata are distributed between these two norms. In each geographical area, therefore, as we move up the social scale, speech becomes more RP-like. Conversely, as we move down the social scale pronunciation becomes less RP-like, and, at the same time, more local. We saw this situation in the Norwich (ing). In the case of this feature, consistent use of the 'ing' variant, scored as 000, represented consistent RP pronunciation. This was achieved by the middle class in two reading contexts. At the other end of the scale, the lower working class scored 100, or complete use of the 'in'' form in casual speech. Middle-class accents, therefore, can be 'mildly regional', in different parts of the country, in their approximation to the national RP norm. Style-shifting tells us also that individuals can shift towards RP on appropriate occasions.

A word about the RP accent itself. It is the accent particularly associated with BBC radio and television newsreaders and with individuals and social environments associated with the conventional establishment. It has been pointed out that, like any other accent, it is associated with and maintained by social and communication networks; in this case, however, networks directly involved in social and economic power (Milroy, 1987: 183ff. for example). Hughes and Trudgill (1979: 2f.) write:

> RP has . . . remained the accent of those in the upper reaches of the social scale, as measured by education, income and profession, or title. It is essentially the accent of those educated at public schools (which are, of course, private, and beyond the means of most parents). It is largely through these schools that the accent is perpetuated. For RP, unlike prestige accents in other countries, is not the accent of any region (except historically: its origins were in the speech of London and the surrounding area). It is quite impossible to say from his pronunciation where an RP speaker comes from.

Although RP has been extensively described in phonetic and phonological terms, there is an urgent need for empirical studies of how such overtly prestigious standards are created, maintained, and convey normative pressure. There is also internal variation and change within RP, though not on a geographical basis. Note also that the use of RP as a prestige accent must be interpreted as relative to the meaning which its use conveys in a given context. There are occasions when it would be seen as 'affected'.

The diffusion of r-lessness

It was in the eighteenth century in the south-east of England that English began to lose postvocalic *r*. Let us look at the situation geographically. If today we plot on a map of England those areas where any rhoticity still survives, as in Figure 5.2, what are we looking at? If we put ourselves at the point of origin of the change, the south and east, we are looking *outwards* to the limits of where the loss of *r* has diffused as a categorical property of all accents. This is the white area of Figure 5.2. In this area, pronunciation is *r*-less, from RP down. We are looking at the past diffusion of the change through geographical space.

But we are also, simultaneously, looking *downwards* towards the lower end of the social scale, towards the base of the pyramid. We can assume that the loss of *r* was a prestige innovation, and therefore related to the norm of higher status groups. The fact that RP is categorically non-rhotic tells us this. Therefore, those areas where rhoticity survives, since they are plotted in geographical and therefore 'local' terms, also represent the situation looking down towards the bottom of the pyramid, down the scale of social variation. We know that RP speakers are *r*-less. How far downwards through social space has the loss of *r* progressed? Figure 5.2 tells us something about this. The shaded *r*-pronouncing areas represent the accents of the informants of the *Survey of English Dialects*. These are the most conservative speakers of all – older, working-class and *rural* speakers.

The categorical area of *r*-lessness, the white area, is larger if one plots regions where *r* is observed in *urban* speech, as in Figure 5.3. We can immediately see by comparing the two maps that

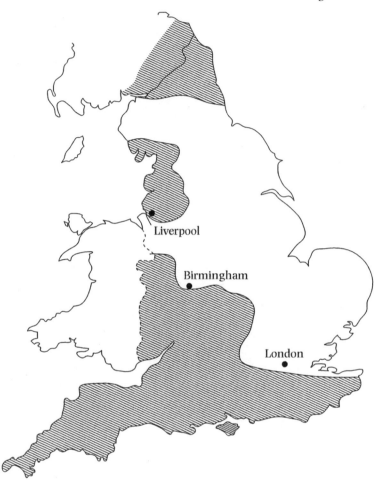

Figure 5.2 Areas (*shaded*) of England where /r/ may still occur in the speech of older, rural, working-class speakers (*from Chambers and Trudgill, 1980: 110*)

the extension of rhoticity is much shrunken. The change has diffused all the way down the social scale more widely in urban areas
than in rural ones, so that urban areas shaded in Figure 5.2 – for
example, Merseyside or Tyneside – are not shaded in Figure 5.3.
The working-class (most local) speech of these conurbations is

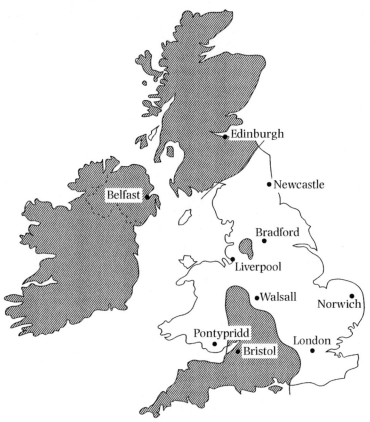

Figure 5.3 Areas (*shaded*) of Great Britain where /r/ still occurs in *urban* accents (*from Hughes and Trudgill, 1979: 33*)

non-rhotic. This suggests, as we shall see in chapter six, that urban areas act as foci in the diffusion of change. Its progress does not proceed smoothly from the point of origin.

It is possible to infer from Figures 5.2 and 5.3 that a complex wave of change has passed through geographical and social space, leading to a loss of rhoticity in most English accents. The process has gone further in the north than in the west. In the north, urban rhoticity has practically disappeared. Wells (1982: 368) says, 'The patch of residual urban rhoticity, ever shrinking under the pressure of the non-rhotic majority, now seems to be located to the north of Manchester, in places such as Rochdale and Accrington. It remains also in the country areas around Preston and in the north of the county' (Lancashire). In the west of England, by contrast, rhoticity is more widespread, even in urban centres. Thus, there is a postvocalic *r* in the speech of Bristol, with considerable retroflexion (Hughes and Trudgill, 1979: 47). The situation can be generalized in this way. The further west one goes, the more widespread is the *r*-fullness and the higher up the social scale it extends. The converse is true heading eastwards. Broad local accents are fully rhotic and this 'extends well up the social scale in cities such as Bristol, Exeter, or (to a lesser extent) Southampton. Plymouth and Bournemouth, large cities with very mixed populations, seem to have variable rhoticity or even none. Traces of variable rhoticity may be found as close to London as Reading (Berkshire)' (Wells, 1982: 341). In 'borderline' areas, *r* is clearly a variable (r).

It is also clear that we are dealing with a continuous process of loss of postvocalic *r* in England that may have lasted nearly three centuries. As Chambers and Trudgill (1980: 109) point out, the discontinuity of the rhotic areas in Figure 5.2 shows us that we are dealing with **relic areas**, where the older form has persisted in spite of the long-term spread of the '*r*-dropping' innovation. One imagines that if maps such as 5.2 and 5.3 had been drawn in the nineteenth century, the rhotic areas would have been joined together, rather than appearing as islands of *r*-full speech in a sea of *r*-lessness. The diffusion of *r*-lessness makes concrete the waves of change in social space.

Some linguistic consequences for r-less accents

When an accent loses postvocalic *r*, it has widespread ramifications throughout its sound system. We have already noted that in non-rhotic accents we get homonyms which we do not find in rhotic ones, for example 'bawd' and 'board' in RP, or 'guard' and 'god' in New York City. What happens is in fact very complex and beyond the scope of this book. So, I will briefly sketch some basic

consequences, to give an idea of what happens when *r* is lost, and
to show that changes in one sound affect other sounds.

The consequences we are going to consider apply in varying
ways to all non-rhotic accents, although RP will be the main example. One major consequence takes place in the vowels. There
is a wider range of contrastive vowel sounds in non-rhotic than
in rhotic accents. To explain why this should be so, we need to be
able to describe differing vowel sounds and how they are made.
We will have to describe vowels in dealing with variables in later
chapters in any case. Imagine the trapezium shape below as representing a cross-section of the oral cavity (i.e., the inside of the
mouth) as viewed from the side. The diagram is, of course, highly
idealized. A vowel sound is produced by the completely unob-
structed outward movement of the air-stream through this chamber, with the vocal chords vibrating. The sound quality of each
particular vowel sound is determined by the shape given to the
chamber by the position of the tongue.

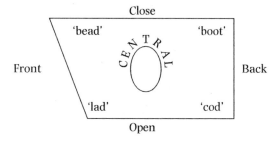

Using **vowel diagrams** like this, the vowels of a language can
be charted according to where in the mouth the highest part of
the tongue is put as the sound is made. Vowels can be front or
back and close or open. Try to observe the four peripheral vowel
sounds, indicated by the four key words in the diagram, by noting
the position of your own tongue as you make the sound. The oval
at the centre of the diagram represents the central area of the
mouth where central vowels are made. These are sounds such as
the last sound in 'the', in rapid connected speech, or the vowel in
RP 'bird' or 'fur'.

To appreciate what happens in non-rhotic accents, we should first look at how postvocalic *r* is made in accents that have it. (Above, we looked at how *r* was made in initial position.) I will follow Bronstein's (1960) analysis of General American. In general, the tongue is held in the position of a central vowel. This sound is then *r*-coloured. Either the tongue-tip is turned back towards the hard palate in retroflexion (the amount of retroflexion varies from accent to accent), or the tongue is bunched and retracted upwards, or both. This is a very vowel-like sound. Conceive of it as a constriction of a central vowel that produces an audible *r*-colour to the sound.

When *r* is dropped from an accent, the constriction disappears. The process could be thought of as the absorption of the r-coloured central sound into the preceding vowel. In cases other than word-final 'er', where we gain a syllable consisting of *only* a central vowel, the outcome for non-rhotic accents is a system of centring glides or **diphthongs**. These are vowel sounds in the course of which the tongue changes position. In centring glides the tongue ends up in the central area of the mouth. The number of distinct, centring diphthongs, and the range of positions from which they begin vary enormously both between and within non-rhotic accents. Here is the RP system (Gimson, 1962):

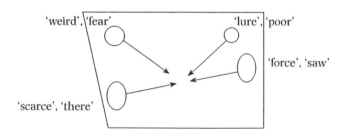

Other things also follow, with much possibility for variability. Thus, these diphthongs can become simple vowels, so that words like 'fear', 'poor', 'scarce' and 'force', especially the last two, have variants which are *not* diphthongs, but a single lengthened vowel. For most RP speakers, in fact, the 'force' sound is always a long vowel. In varieties where rhoticity *also* exists, variably, such as that of New York City, the situation can become very complex indeed.

Linking r

Another consequence of the loss of *r* is its reappearance under certain conditions. Thus, it is a common characteristic of non-rhotic accents that *r* appears in word-final position to serve as a link with a following word – but *only* when the following word begins with a vowel. Thus,

with linking r	without linking r
far away	fa . . . country
answer it	answe . . . badly
car engine	ca . . . port

Intrusive r

But the reappearance can go further than this. The *r* can appear before vowels *where there never was an historic r* and where, accordingly, there is no written *r*. This **intrusive r** is common in non-rhotic accents. Thus,

intrusive r
idea-r-of
area-r-of agreement
Shah-r-of Iran
draw-r-ing

This is a very interesting feature because of what it tells us about the rules of non-rhotic accents. It suggests that *r*-less speakers, in fact, don't 'know' which words historically end in *r*, and that therefore they do not represent final *r* in the way they 'store' these words. Therefore, for such words, the rule is not to *drop r* before a consonant, but rather to *insert r* whenever there is a following vowel. This rule applies to words where historic *r* occurred, and we observe linking *r*. But it *also* applies to similar words where there was no historic r, and we observe the so-called 'intrusive' sound. Since this tells us that the accent is fundamentally *r*-less and cannot have a 'dropping' rule in final position, it is an excellent diagnostic of *r*-lessness. In fact, intrusive *r* never occurs in rhotic accents. But it is a perfectly natural phonological process for non-rhotic accents. It follows from their rules.

In spite of this, intrusive *r* is stigmatized in Britain. Speakers of non-rhotic accents accordingly attempt to suppress it, especially inside words (as in 'drawring'). But think about how difficult this will be! In the absence of *r* in one's knowledge of the word, one has to be guided solely by the preceding vowel's class, and the *spelling*. The spelling tells us which words had *r* historically. In fact, the stigmatization is related to the existence of these final *r*s in the written language, and shows us the power of literacy in relation to notions of correctness. A standard written form in this case is a vehicle of normative pressure in terms of the prestige norm. This will ensure that intrusive *r* will tend towards lower frequencies in more careful styles. In fact, suppression usually involves suppression of linking *r* as well, or its realization by an alternative sound. This set of rules, consequences of loss of *r*, thus opens up new possibilities for variation.

Scotland: rhotic accents

A look at the map in Figure 5.3 shows that Scottish accents exhibit full-blown rhoticity; a striking contrast to English norms.

We can see in Scottish accents how vowels combine with *r* and contrast this with the centring diphthongs of *r*-less speech. The diagram below illustrates how *r* functions in rhotic accents (adapted from Wells, 1982: 408). Ideally, each set of words is distinguished by a simple vowel sound, numbered 1–9 in our diagram, plus an *r*-sound. Of course, there is much variation between

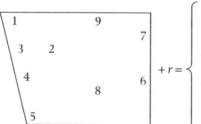

1. beer, fierce, weary,
2. stir, bird, spirit,
3. air, scarce, fairy,
4. err, pert, ferry,
5. bar, start, merry,
6. war, horse, sorry,
7. ware, hoarse, story,
8. purr, word, hurry,
9. poor, guard, jury

Scottish varieties. Thus, in general, Scottish vowels 2, 4 and 8 are kept distinct; the pronunciation of 'bird', 'pert' and 'word' are different. In popular Glasgow speech, however, 2 merges with 8, and 'bird' and 'word' rhyme, although remaining distinct from 'pert'. By contrast, in middle-class Edinburgh pronunciation all three categories are merged into a constricted central vowel, and all the words of 2, 4 and 8 rhyme. We find similar processes in General American.

Let us look now at how this systematic *r* is actually articulated in Scottish English. Nearly the full range of variants occurs. We discussed how each of these was made above. They are:

(a)   trilled *r* (popularly, rolling your *r*s)
(b)   flapped *r* (a single tap on the teeth ridge)
(c)   the frictionless continuant (described above)
(d)   *r*-lessness (newly observed by Romaine, 1978)

I noted earlier that the trill was the original form of English *r*. The literature and popular opinion suggest that this persisted in Scotland until this century as a major pronunciation (Wells, 1982; Romaine, 1978). Today, however, this sound has been largely replaced by the two middle variants, the flap and the continuant. The rolled *r* is mainly confined to special formal contexts. The latter two forms are variable, and conditioned by both linguistic and social factors. We thus have an **(r) variable**, with the flap and the continuant as its values (although the trill could be included as a third value).

Romaine (1978: 145) reports that in Edinburgh it is the continuant form which is the prestige variant. It is more frequently found in Scottish standard English, is a marker of 'polite' Edinburgh speech, and is endorsed for teaching. But both Romaine and Abercrombie had also informally observed some cases of apparently *r*-less speech in the city. This, in the context of complete Scottish rhoticity, was remarkable.

Romaine (1978) investigated this *r*-variability by studying the speech of twenty-four working-class Edinburgh schoolchildren aged from six to ten years old. Her (r) variable had the three values below. The (r) scores were the percentage of each variant observed. The study was restricted (unfortunately) to *r* in word final position.

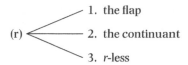

1. the flap
2. the continuant
3. *r*-less

The overall index scores for all speakers show that the flap was the most commonly used form, the continuant next, and *r*-lessness last. Although *r*-lessness did occur among Scottish schoolchildren, it did so relatively little. Remember also that it was restricted to word-final position and was most favoured by utterance-final position. The figures are

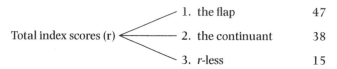

Total index scores (r)
1. the flap   47
2. the continuant   38
3. *r*-less   15

The correlations that proved really suggestive, however, only emerge when sex and style are looked at. The boys produced more of the flap, and of the *r*-less variants. In contrast, the girls produced more of the continuant than the other sounds, and had very little *r*-lessness. So, the continuant seemed to mark female speech, and the flap and non-rhoticity, male speech. The style-shifting was even more interesting. Among the ten-year-olds, when reading passages the boys shifted from the flap to *r*-lessness and the continuant, in that order. But the girls also shifted to *r*-lessness in reading style!

Romaine (1978) interprets her results in this way. There seem to be two norms at work. The Edinburgh prestige norm is the continuant. This accounts for the sex differentiation of the scores. Girls are responding more positively than boys to the prestige norm. The girls are closer to the middle-class variant. But, at the same time, there is a vernacular norm – the *r*-less innovation. The 'innovation' seems to be located among the boys. Both boys and girls also recognize the prestige of this form (a covert prestige perhaps) because they both shift towards it in reading style, although boys also shift towards the overtly prestigious continuant as well. Such patterns suggest that a change is taking place. We will return to such matters later. However, Romaine feels that the source of this *r*-lessness is separate from RP influence in Scotland. The

Scottish norm is clearly *r*-full, and, within Scotland, this is the prestige form. If the local non-rhoticity is significant, it is as a vernacular and male innovation.

Transatlantic

The rhoticity plot really thickens when we look to the other side of the water.

The map in Figure 5.4 sets out the main dialect areas of the eastern United States. The particular speech communities which we shall look at in the course of this chapter are labelled. The shaded areas show us that rhoticity is a feature of the accents in the centre of America; more specifically of the north central, central midland, middle Atlantic and mountain speech areas. Sometimes all these rhotic accents are grouped together under the label, 'General American'. They have in common the fact that they exclude those Eastern and Southern accents which are *r*-less. It is important to realize, therefore, that General American is not the same sort of thing as RP. Rather, it is a class of accents which are *geographically* defined.

So let's be geographical. It is usually said that *r*-less speech occurs in eastern New England, New York City, and in the coastal

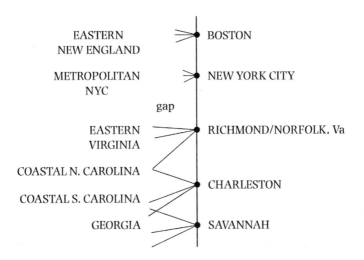

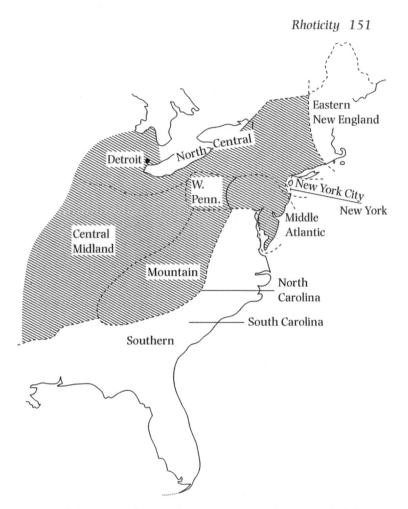

Figure 5.4 Major speech areas of eastern USA, with rhotic areas shaded

plain of the South. We can think of American *r*-lessness as radiating outwards from the major ports of the eastern seaboard. (There is a gap in the middle Atlantic region at Philadelphia.) Such a pattern is suggestive of diffusion. Thus we find the eminent American dialectologist Hans Kurath writing, 'the so-called "*r*-less" type is spreading as a prestige pronunciation from the old cultural centres within these areas, a process that in all probability has been in progress for generations' (Kurath, 1965, in Williamson and Burke, 1971: 105).

Maps like Figure 5.4 are very frustrating because they are highly idealized. This is because, as the results of research conducted for linguistic atlases, they are largely based on the geographical distribution of variants. It ought to be obvious by now that space is only one dimension against which variants can be plotted. Internal linguistic, and a multiplicity of external social dimensions condition variation – so the resulting structures are multi-dimensional. Without quantitative methods and social correlations we cannot observe these patterns. So the maps represent a static yes/no situation which hides social variation, and the processes that have happened and are happening in time.

We find another important dialectologist, Raven McDavid, who worked on the *Linguistic Atlas of the South Atlantic States* (1947), commenting,

> The conventional statement about the Southern postvocalic *r* is that it does not occur as constriction . . . The fact that in every Southern state one may find locally rooted native speakers with constriction in at least some of the words has been either overlooked or deliberately ignored.

It seems that, in fact, the feature was *variable* for at least some speakers in the *r*-less areas.

The sources of r-lessness in America

The shaded areas in Figures 5.5 and 5.6 show the distribution of rhoticity in the 1930s and 1940s in New England and South Carolina respectively. These two areas have in common the fact that *r*-lessness seems to radiate outwards from the cultural centres of Boston and Charleston.

Bernard Bloch, writing in 1939, and drawing on the records of the *Linguistic Atlas of New England*, reported the highest frequencies of *r*-pronunciation in the western part of New England. In the east, focusing on the Boston area, loss of *r* predominated. This had spread to New Hampshire and Maine. One sure sign that one is dealing with the diffusion of an innovation is the existence of

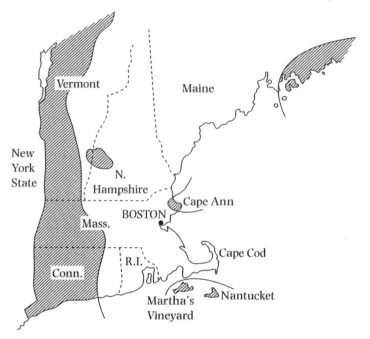

Figure 5.5 Main *r*-pronouncing areas (*shaded*) of eastern New England, circa 1930s (*after Bloch, 1939*)

discontinuous relic areas, as we noted above. Figure 5.5 shows a number of fairly self-contained communities bypassed by the spread of non-rhoticity. These included the islands off the coast. (We shall have occasion to look at one of these, Martha's Vineyard, later on.) There were signs in these relic areas and in certain parts of the boundary between the two types that younger speakers preferred the Boston pronunciation. This would indicate that loss of *r* was still spreading.

Writing in 1947, Raven McDavid argues, in a classic article, that a purely geographical account of *r*-pronunciation in South Carolina could not account for the facts of its distribution at that date. Traditional explanations of geographical data tend to be in terms of the historical pattern of settlement. Note, for example, the 'mountain' speech area in Figure 5.4. The accents of

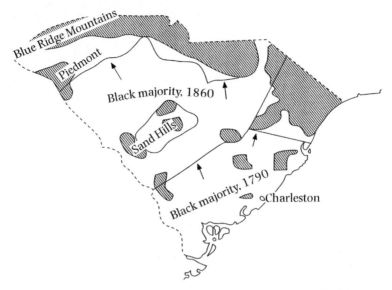

Figure 5.6 South Carolina: the spread of the plantation system. Shaded areas are those where *r* was found in 'worm', 'father', 'barn' and 'bread', circa 1940s (*after McDavid, 1947*)

the Appalachian mountains differ markedly from those of the coastal south. This can be explained in terms of the speech of the original settlers. It was Scotch-Irish (Ulster) people who first settled the mountains, and they migrated to that area from Pennsylvania. Their presence therefore explains this southward prong of rhotic midland type speech. We have a reason to divide southern speech into 'hill type' (rhotic) and 'plantation type' (non-rhotic) (Stephenson, 1977: 75).

McDavid argued that complexity of distribution in the 1940s could not be explained so simply. The coastal areas settled by speakers from England, who therefore might be expected to be both rhotic and non-rhotic, was very small compared to the extent of contemporary *r*-lessness. It was, indeed, the case that Scotch-Irish had settled the two areas where rhoticity was densest (see Figure 5.6), but both rhoticity and non-rhoticity occurred in areas where the other was expected.

This required a *social* explanation. McDavid noted that rhoticity was associated with lower levels of education, older speakers, and rural, as opposed to urban, speech. His conclusion was that, in South Carolina, *r*-pronunciation was a mark of cultural isolation. Various communities were outside the historically dominant social pattern of the state. Conversely, *r*-less speech was associated with the dominant pattern, which was the plantation system of agriculture, and the planter caste, focused on the culturally and commercially dominant city of Charleston. His argument was that *r*-lessness had diffused outwards from Charleston along with the plantation system, and had, as its social meaning, the prestige of that city and the social system of which it was the focus. Constriction had survived among 'poor white' speakers outside the system. These were people living in areas unsuitable for plantation agriculture.

Figure 5.6 shows this quite clearly, by illustrating that *r*-less areas largely coincide with those into which plantations had spread, as evidenced by black majorities in 1790 and 1860. It follows, for example, that those 'poor whites' would be those also most 'threatened' by blacks. Those most hostile to blacks would therefore be rhotic. McDavid remarks, 'It is also worthy of note that almost every lynching in South Carolina in the last twenty-five years [up to 1947] occurred in counties where field work for the *South Atlantic Atlas* has disclosed strong constriction of postvocalic *r*.'

McDavid also pointed out the close ties of the Charleston elite with England, both before and after the American revolution. The obvious question then is the relationship between the *r*-less areas of the American eastern seaboard and the southern British prestige norm. Is the source of American *r*-lessness a diffusion of the feature across the Atlantic, or were the original settlers in these coastal regions *r*-less? When did *r*-lessness gain prestige in America? Or was it a prestige form in America from the beginning?

In order to answer these questions one has to go back and ask when *r*-less pronunciation first appeared in England, and more particularly when it became the prestige form in London and southeast England. I have included a note in a separate box below summarizing some arguments people have used to try to establish these dates, because I think the methods and evidence used are intrinsically fascinating. (If we are going to look at *r*, we might as well go 'whole hog', right back to the beginnings of the variants.) For those that want to skip this, however, we can conclude that both forms very probably crossed the Atlantic as 'folk' pronunciations. But we can also say that the period at which loss of postvocalic *r* became a feature of the English prestige norm is quite late. This suggests that loss of *r* as a prestige form was, in all probability, diffused from British English to American English via the coastal centres, and from there to the hinterland, as Kurath suggested.

The Kurath-McDavid theory tells the following story. Postvocalic *r* would have come to America, at least latterly, as a variable feature. The original settlement patterns would include both rhotic and non-rhotic speakers from England, reflecting the state of the loss of *r* in the part of England from which they came. (Of course, all Scottish and Irish settlers, like those of the mountain region, would be rhotic.) On our dating, the weight of accents would be towards *r*-full speech the further back one went in time. The relic areas tell us this.

The *r*-less form acquired prestige in America, when it was adopted from Britain by the elite classes of New England and the Southern aristocracy. Kurath points out the transmission mechanism: the very close ties between these groups and southern England. The planters and merchants of the South, especially, had their children educated at the English universities or by imported English tutors, and were accepted as equals in London society. In other words, there was a single culture and a dense network of communication between the elites of New England, the South and southern England. The change then diffused downwards and outwards from the coastal centres as a new 'prestige' form. We saw how this process had worked itself out in South Carolina. But on the borderlines, the feature remained variable.

An alternative picture is presented by both Lass (1987: 282–3) and Romaine (1994: 146). They argue that first settlement played a crucial role in the distribution of rhoticity in eastern North America. Lass asserts that 'the earliest colonies are in fact non-rhotic, and seem to have been at least partly so at the time of settlement; the history suggests that rhoticity may be a kind of

The original loss of postvocalic r: a note

Early loss of r. There seems to be agreement that *r*-less speech became the standard of London speech in the late eighteenth century. But some writers have suggested earlier dates. Archibald Hill (1940) describes a loss of *r* as early as the fourteenth century. But this is in a single restricted environment: in stressed syllables before just those consonants which are made by the tongue-tip and the teeth. It looks as if *r* was assimilated to the dental sound which followed it in words like 'barn' and 'bird' at a very early period.

A second view of early loss of *r* is that of Wyld (1920) and Jesperson (1954). They argue that there was a very general 'weakening' in the pronunciation of *r* from the fifteenth century. Jesperson notes a very general movement from a trilled to a continuant *r* over a number of centuries. In the seventeenth century we find Ben Jonson writing that *r* was 'sounded firm in the beginning of the words, and more liquid in middle and ends' (1639). Wyld cites written forms like *Woseter* – Worcester, and *Dasset* – Dorset, from a sixteenth-century diarist of humble origins, Henry Machyn. Similarly, Kurath (1965) points to spellings like *libity* – liberty, and *patchis* – purchase, as evidence that some American colonists were *r*-less, even by 1700.

Wyld paints the following picture. The loss of *r* began in the east of England by the middle of the fifteenth century, especially before *s*. By the middle of the sixteenth century it had extended both to other consonants, and to the London vernacular. (The forms used by Henry Machyn are an example.) By 1650 it had diffused upwards to London society. In this case, both pronunciations would go to America, but *r*-less speech would go as a prestige form.

Eighteenth-century origins. There are reasons for thinking these dates are too early. Stephenson (1977) points out that there are three places where *r* fluctuates in rhotic accents *without indicating a general loss of the sound.* These are

1. in unstressed syllables: 'adve(r)tise', 'su(r)prise' etc.
2. before a following dental: 'ho(r)se', 'nu(r)se', 'me(r)cy' etc.
3. when two *r*s appear in the same word: 'co(r)poration', 'fa(r)ther' etc.

These are all reported in rhotic speech. And most of the evidence for early loss is based on cases like these; for example, Machyn's spellings above.

> Actual comments on *r* are more valuable, and these *do not* start appearing until the eighteenth century. We find Walker referring to London speech in 1775 and 1791. He says that in England and particularly in London words like 'bard', 'card' and 'regard', are pronounced as 'baad', 'caad' and 'regaad'. Even more revealing is Hill (1821), who writes that *r*
>
>> ought more carefully to be preserved for posterity, than can be hoped, if the provincialists of the Metropolis and their tasteless imitators are to be tolerated in such rhymes as *fawn* and *morn*, *straw* and *for*, *grass* and *farce*, etc. etc. to the end of the reader's patience.
>
>> For Hill in 1821 this is clearly a new innovation as a prestige pronunciation. *r*-lessness is thus not probably part of a prestige norm till at least late in the eighteenth century. It clearly would have been variable at this time and earlier. In this case, *r*-less speech would *not* have originally gone to America as a prestige form.

"secondary archaism" – i.e. a later import by speakers of more conservative Englishes (largely Ulster Scots or Irish . . .) . . . which had no *r*-loss at all'. The *r*-lessness of North America is original because eastern New England and the coastal areas from the Virginia tidewater as far south as the Carolinas were first settled from the south-east area of England where *r*-lessness was most advanced. Western New England and the mountainous interior were settled later by fully rhotic Scots-Irish and people from northern and western parts of Britain which would retain more *r*. Dillard (1992) is also sceptical about the claim that *r*-lessness gained its prestige from across the Atlantic.

A possible compromise view is that the Kurath-McDavid picture is correct to the extent that, if we accept a late date *r*-lessness as a prestige feature in southern England, any *r*-variability of the earliest coastal colonial English would have been at least confirmed towards continuing *r*-loss by its status in England. It would have been mobile persons of the travelled upper strata of American urban and plantation society who would have been the force behind this diffusion. Where the feature was not variable because the original settlers were Scots-Irish and where the plantation-mountain or coast-frontier cultural differences intervened, the diffusion was stopped.

There is no doubt that non-rhoticity had general prestige across the coastal south and the areas populated from it, for example, the gulf states from Alabama to East Texas. Evidence for this is the sort of hyper-*r*-lessness one sometimes finds in the Southern states, which drops *r* in places where it is not normally dropped in Britain. Some Southern accents, for example, have not only no intrusive *r*, but no linking *r*. In some non-standard varieties, *r* between two vowels, as in 'hurry', is dropped and 'Paris' can be identical to 'pass' (Wells, 1982: 544). Such features suggest attempts by successive groups to approximate to a prestige innovation, pushing the change further along.

A reversal of the pattern

Much evidence has been accumulated recently that a major change is taking place with regard to rhoticity in the *r*-less speech communities we have been discussing in the eastern United States. We have been looking at the spread of *r*-less speech focused on the coastal centres. There is evidence also of the spread of rhoticity back into these enclaves, as if two contrasting waves of preference were meeting each other.

Thus, Bloch (1939) noted that on the boundary between the two forms in western New England and in the Connecticut River valley *r*-pronunciation was becoming more general. It was spreading through western Connecticut from the rhotic areas in the north central USA. In other words, the two types were 'spreading vigorously from opposite centres': the *r*-less variant from the Boston focus, the *r*-full variant from the interior. As far as *r* was concerned, New England was not a single dialect area and the speech of many individuals was variable. When Boston was re-examined by Parslow in 1967, he found that *r* was being *widely re-introduced* even into the speech of the city. Comparison of his study with that of the Atlas survey of 1939–43, on which Bloch's analysis was based, 'demonstrates a steady progression to *r*-timbre for all regions and social levels' (Parslow, 1971: 622).

In 1947, McDavid had noted that there were some slight hints of a reversal of the trend in prestige values in South Carolina; that rhoticity, formerly associated with social peripherality, might possibly become respectable. He remarked that, even in the low country, some girls in their late teens and early twenties were sporting newly acquired *r*s. By the time of O'Cain's study of Charleston in 1972, however, *r* had *reappeared* in the city itself. McDavid and O'Cain (1977) write, 'Postvocalic *r* has advanced at a rate that surpasses almost every innovation in Charleston speech. Only aristocrats and older whites of other classes consistently approach fully *r*-less speech.' In other words, it is variable for all other groups. McDavid (1975) notes that this feature, formerly associated with Southern poor white speech, seems to have become part of the regional standard, although it is not yet used by all standard speakers.

In 1966, Levine and Crockett, in a classic piece of research, studied *r*-pronunciation in Hillsboro, North Carolina. This is a piedmont community at the western edge of the coastal plain, not far from the Virginia border. The community is at the confluence of several dialect areas and near the boundary of midland and Southern speech types. They wondered if 'inhabitants spoke some "transitional" dialect, or, instead, one or more of the nearby dialects in relatively unmixed form' (Levine and Crockett, 1966: 77).

They found *two r-pronouncing norms* within the community. But the community was not regularly stratified, from higher to lower, according to frequency of *r*-pronunciation. High-status speakers were associated *either* with the *r*-full norm, *or* the *r*-less norm. Low-status speakers fell *between* the two norms. Levine and Crockett concluded that it was the 'clarity' or 'strength' of the norm that was associated with social position. So both norms could be models of prestige speech in Hillsboro.

The interesting point here was the direction of change observed! In more formal styles of pronunciation, *r* was more frequent, and it was also more frequent among the young. There was evidence that older people, men, blue-collar workers, and those who had resided in the community longer favoured *r*-lessness. Younger speakers, women, short-term residents, and those near the top of the 'white-collar' class (but not at the top of this class) favoured rhoticity in that they conceived it to be 'correct'. All this led to the conclusion that the community was transitional, and moving towards rhoticity under the pressure of outside norms. If this is right, then rhotic General American would become the prestige norm for this community.

There is strong evidence that rhoticity in America is spreading in white speech throughout many historically *r*-less areas in the south and northeast. Agreeing with this diagnosis in 1989, Butters (1989: 37) quotes the result that *r*-lessness is gradually disappearing among Southern whites. This is an extraordinary reversal of a historic pattern.

New York City

Labov comments that a New Yorker's overt attitudes to his or her own vernacular speech patterns are extremely negative; that it is a 'sink of negative prestige'. Vernacular New York City features have been stigmatized. Consider the 'Brooklynese' stereotype of working-class New York speech. This can be the subject of humour.

> Toity doity boids sittin' on de koib, choipin' and boipin' an eatin' doity woims

> Thirty dirty birds sitting on the kerb, chirping and burping and eating dirty worms.

In fact this 'toity-toid street' diphthong has attracted such stigma that it is rapidly disappearing from the speech of the city, and now survives only among lower-class speakers. If the British reader wants to get some general idea of how the New York City vernacular sounds, he can think of Archie Bunker in *All in the Family*.

Perhaps connected with this general stigmatization is the self-contained nature of the New York City speech community. Metropolitan speech patterns do not extend further than the outer suburbs. In pure geographical terms, it is by far the smallest of the speech areas on the map in Figure 5.4. In terms of *r*-lessness, it became a non-rhotic island surrounded by rhoticity. Contrast this with the extent of the spread of 'plantation' type speech in the South. Stephenson (1977) reports *r*-less speech as characteristic of the 'cultivated' classes in much of the South. Reporting on San Antonio, Texas, Sawyer (1959) notes the variability of retroflexion.

R-less speech characterized older informants. Even here, however, r-less speech showed signs of decline. Middle-aged informants pronounced r half the time or more, and the young educated informants were fully rhotic.

Historically, New York City has followed the same pattern as the other coastal centres. An r-full area in the eighteenth century, it had become r-less by the end of the nineteenth century, under the influence of eastern New England and southern British norms. Berger (1980) also points out a strong maritime connection with the South.

Labov (1972) writes thus about the adoption of r-less speech:

> It seems to be one of our best examples of a 'change from above' – originating in the highest social group – which eventually spread to the entire speech community and became the vernacular form. Our first documented evidence for r-less pronunciation in New York City dates to the middle of the nineteenth century; Richard Norman has observed that the New York poet Frederick Cozzens rhymed 'shore' and 'pshaw' in 1856. Babbitt's study of 1896 was the first linguistic report, and it showed that the r-less speech was the regular vernacular pattern of the city. Babbitt's report as well as Linguistic Atlas interviews of the 1930s show a completely r-less dialect.

By the time of Hubbell's study in 1950 and Labov's own study in 1966, the situation had changed substantially. In the speech of any given New Yorker in the area which Labov studied, the lower east side of Manhattan, there was a great deal of apparently random fluctuation between the production of constriction and its absence. The two forms appeared to be variable. They were freely substitutable for each other in the same environments. This was true for the various instances where r would be possible during a single utterance, as well as between different utterances by the same speaker and, of course, between speakers. The speech both of individuals and of the community was inconsistent. Hubbell (1950) had assessed New Yorkers' usage as follows (quoted by Labov, 1966: 36):

> The pronunciation of a very large number of New Yorkers exhibits a pattern . . . that might most accurately be described as the complete absence of any pattern. Such speakers sometimes pronounce /r/ before

a consonant or in final position and sometimes omit it, in a thoroughly haphazard fashion.

The department stores

Labov's work in New York City includes one of the best examples of anonymous observation which we have. You will recall that this was one of the techniques of investigation mentioned in chapter four. One of the ways of overcoming the observer's paradox was to engineer a situation in which people's speech could be observed without their knowing it. Labov (1966) was able to do this in three New York City department stores. The suspicion he was working on was that rhoticity was being reintroduced into the city as a prestige feature. Labov (1966: 64) predicted: 'If any two subgroups of New York City speakers are ranked in a scale of social stratification, they will be ranked in the same order by their differential use of (r).'

The groups of speakers in question were the salespeople of three large department stores in Manhattan. Labov, using a series of quite objective criteria, ranked the stores in the following order: (1) Saks Fifth Avenue; (2) Macy's; (3) S. Klein. He argued that jobs in the three stores would be socially evaluated in the same order, if only in terms of the working conditions and relative prestige of the stores.

Now, how was he to observe the salespeople pronouncing or dropping their *r*s? The technique was both ingenious and amusing. He chose a department which was located on the fourth floor of each store, and asked salespeople, 'Excuse me, where are the–?', which would, of course, elicit, 'Fou*r*th Floo*r*', as a reply. The investigator would then lean forward and say, 'Excuse me?' This would normally cause the unwitting informant to repeat, in a more careful and emphatic way, 'Fou*r*th floo*r*.' In this way, Labov was able to get four instances of postvocalic *r*, in two contrasting styles and two linguistic environments, for each informant.

The results are below. And they are as predicted. The sales personnel, ranked according to the three stores, could also be ranked by their differential use of *r*. The overall stratification of (r) by store is Saks 62 per cent, Macy's 51 per cent, and Klein's 21 per cent of *r*s pronounced.

Saks	Macy's	S. Klein

32
30

31
20

17
4

The bottom figure in each column is the percentage of *all r*-pronunciation; the top figure is the percentage of *some r*-pronunciation (Labov, 1966: 73).

But the results were even more fine-grained than this. There was style-shifting. In each store, the amount of rhoticity was greater in the more emphatic style. And, amazingly, there was a difference in (r) scores inside the Saks store itself. On the quieter and more expensive upper floors of Saks, the percentage of all or some (r) was 74 per cent. In the hustle and bustle of the ground floor the figure was 46 per cent.

Sociolinguistic structure of (r)

Figure 5.7 displays the stratification of (r) by class and style as revealed by further sociolinguistic interviews in Labov's study of the lower east side. The (r) index score is the percentage of postvocalic *r*s used out of number of times *r could* have been used. The general shape of the diagram is familiar to us from our study of the (ing) variable in chapter four.

But the structure of the (r) variable is different. On the dimension of social class, each class is differentiated from the other. On the dimension of style, there is a clear style-shift towards more rhoticity for all social classes. This confirms that *r*-full speech is now the prestige form in New York City. The difference is that there is a **cross-over** pattern in the more formal styles. In casual speech only the upper middle class really has any significant rhoticity. However, in the more formal styles, the *r*-score for the lower middle class (classes 6–8) rapidly increases and, crossing over, is higher than that of the upper middle class (class 9) in the most formal styles.

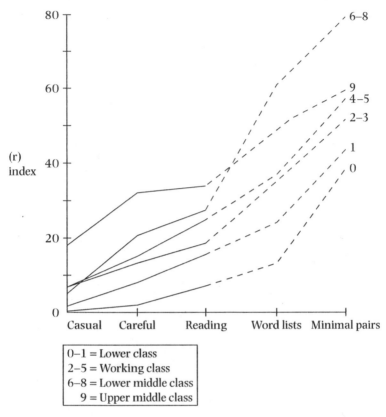

Figure 5.7 (r) in New York City (*from Labov, 1966*)

Labov calls this phenomenon **hypercorrection**. In this case, we observe hypercorrect behaviour by the lower middle class. Earlier on, when we were discussing the 'sharp stratification' of the Norwich (ing), in Figure 4.3, these 'borderline' classes also came to our attention. In the case of (ing), however, we had a stable and regular structure, without hypercorrection. We will be making generalizations about irregular structures later on. Suffice to say at this point that both hypercorrection and irregular structures are diagnostic of linguistic change in progress. In particular, hypercorrection by the lower middle class tells us in this case that a new prestige norm is entering the community.

Let us see exactly what we find out about informants in the most formal styles. Remember how these styles were defined in chapter four. They were designed to produce relatively more self-conscious attention to speech. They therefore measure, not what people's vernacular is like when they are being casual and not paying attention to how they speak, but rather what Labov (1966: 241) calls their **phonic intention**. They tell us the norms of the speakers, rather than their everyday performance. The dotted lines in Figure 5.7 represent these norms.

We can see this in a concrete way by looking at what the informants were asked to do in the more formal styles. Here is a part of a paragraph they were asked to read, which had the (r) variable concentrated in it (of course, they weren't told this).

I remember where he was run over, not far from our corner. He darted out about four feet before a car and he got hit hard etc.

The most formal style involved judgements about 'minimal pairs'. People were asked, at the *end* of the interview, whether pairs of words *sounded* the same or not; for example, 'guard–god', 'dock–dark' and 'source–sauce'. At this stage, they are most self-conscious about language, and furthest removed from the auto-matic motor-production which characterizes their vernacular. All their attention is focused on a pair of words which will not be homophones if the individual is rhotic, and will, if one isn't. What we observe, therefore, is precisely how people believe these words *ought* to be pronounced in the formal situation of an interview. It is the relative differences between the styles that matter. And, from this, it seems that *r*-fullness was the prestige norm in New York City by the early 1960s.

How rhoticity is entering New York City

Yes! The norm but not the practice. Labov's hypothesis is that rhoticity is being introduced into the New York City speech com-munity by the highest status group, more or less consciously, as a new prestige form. It replaces one borrowed norm, the *r*-less one, with a new borrowed norm, the rhotic one; and thus reverses the prestige relations (Labov, 1972: 290). In casual speech, rhoticity is really only a feature of the upper middle class. Here are the average (r) scores in casual speech by age and class:

Age	Lower	Working	Lower Middle	Upper Middle
8–19	00	01	00	48
20–29	00	00	00	35
30–39	00	00	00	32
40–49	00	06	10	18
50+	00	08	00	05

Since 00 means a complete absence of rhoticity, these figures tell us that New York City, in its everyday styles, is very largely an *r*-less community. It is only the upper middle class, who are introducing the change, who have respectable amounts of constriction.

But note how, in the upper middle class, there is a steady decrease in *r*-scores as the informants get older. We said earlier that *average* scores for classes and styles conceal significant patterns in variation on other dimensions. This is the case with *age* in New York City. Speakers over forty have much lower amounts of constriction than do their younger counterparts. Speakers over fifty have virtually none. This suggests that the change entered the city, in the upper middle classes, in the 1940s.

But notice there is no age-grading in the other classes. Rhoticity, as a practice, has not reached them. But it *has* as a norm. We can see this from hypercorrection and style-shifting. The younger

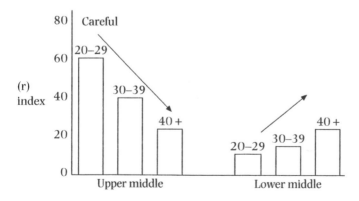

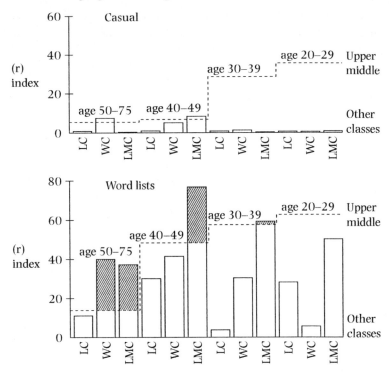

Figure 5.8 Upper middle compared to other classes by age group in two styles, New York City (*from Labov, 1966*)

upper middle class is the 'reference group' for this new norm. In fact, it is the older lower-middle-class speakers who hypercorrect; those over forty. And so, for this class, average scores rise by age because they are using the younger speakers of the class above them as their model of correct speech.

This pattern only really becomes clear if you look at the two diagrams in Figure 5.8. The dotted line in each diagram is the upper-middle-class score for each age group. In both styles, this line steps down to the left. It is clear that rhoticity is a property of younger upper-middle-class speakers. They are introducing the new form.

The columns in the two diagrams in Figure 5.8 represent the average index scores of the other classes, also for each age group.

Now look at the columns for the lower middle class in the word-list style, when they are self-conscious about how they speak. The columns cross the dotted line. The shaded part of each column represents hypercorrect speech. What is clear is that older lower-middle-class (and oldest working-class) speakers are the ones who hypercorrect. They are giving evidence, in doing so, that they accept the new norm introduced by the younger speakers of the class above them.

Labov (1972: 136f.) has tentatively suggested that this pattern serves to accelerate the process of change. By hypercorrecting, lower-middle-class speakers provide a model of the new norm for their own children. This leads to its more rapid diffusion downwards through successive classes, in successive generations.

We now have a precise picture of how an innovation may be introduced by higher-status groups into a stratified society, and a possible role for hypercorrection in its diffusion. We will be returning to these matters later. But note how, in New York City, Labov's quantitative methodology has made visible the way in which rhoticity is being reintroduced into that community. Contrast this with the frustrating and very partial accounts which we have had in the earlier part of our study of *r*; those done before or outside of the new quantitative paradigm.

Black and white

To conclude, we will look at one more variety of speech. The language of black people has been the subject of research and controversy in America since the 1960s. We will be looking at Black English in more detail in chapter six. But for the moment what can we say about *r* in black speech?

The original home of the black vernacular is on the plantations of the south. This means that black speech is historically *r*-less. So that is the norm from which we can examine black rhoticity today. We saw that there seems to be a general change in progress whereby southern white speakers are introducing *r* into their accents. Are black people participating in this change? Bailey and Maynor (1989, cited in Butters, 1989) argue, on the basis of contrasts between rates of *r*-loss among white and black children in the Brazos Valley of Texas, that the southern black community has not participated in the increasing rhoticity. For example, while black children pronounce *r* 80 per cent of the time in words like *bird*, white children do not pronounce it at all in that environment and white adults have a 69 per cent score. Southern black speech remains largely *r*-less. Bailey and Maynor deploy this data to support their argument that the difference between the speech of blacks and whites is increasing, as part of a wider debate about whether the two varieties are diverging or converging. We will examine this debate in the next chapter. For now, suffice to say that Butters (1989: 13–14) contests any notion of 'divergence' by pointing out that black speech has *always* been *r*-less (and some 'mountain-type' southern white accents have *always* been rhotic) so that any new *divergence* cannot be at issue. Nevertheless, a change *is* taking place in which blacks *appear* not to be participating. But is that true?

Butters (1989: 41f.) goes on to present evidence for the opposite. He shows that in other communities where there has been a recognized increase in white rhoticity, blacks have also become more *r*-full, but at a slower rate. We revisit Hillsboro, North Carolina, where in 1966 Levine and Crockett found increases in white *r*-pronunciation. Working in 1969–70, Anshen discovered that blacks were also becoming variably rhotic. In Wilmington, North Carolina, Butters reports that his own research revealed that younger black speakers were style-shifting towards *r* in formal contexts. We conclude that the increasing use of *r*, the new prestige norm, is also affecting black speakers in these two communities. Butters also remarks that the normative pressure appears to be coming from education. Rhoticity was being treated as 'correct' in schools; starting 'in the 1930s, Hillsboro schools began stressing the pronunciation of orthographic *r*' and this might itself produce style-shifting without effecting a real change in the vernacular. But both blacks and whites appear to be susceptible to the correction.

Let's now turn our attention further northward and look at Wolfram's 1969 study of black speech in Detroit. In contrast with New York City, *r* is not a variable feature in the pronunciation of the white community in Detroit, a city which is in the north central speech area of the USA, and, as Figure 5.4 shows, is categorically

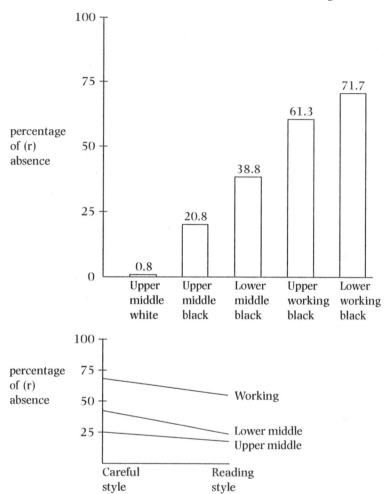

Figure 5.9 (r) absence in Detroit Negro speech, by social class (*from Wolfram, 1969*)

rhotic. However, the feature is variable for the black community in Detroit.

The top diagram in Figure 5.9 shows the percentage of times postvocalic *r* is absent in the speech of Black Detroit for four social classes. For comparison, the average score is also given for a group of upper-middle-class white speakers. Variability of *r* only really characterizes the black ethnic group. The two main groups in American society whose speech is *r*-less are whites of the coastal enclaves and speakers of the black English vernacular. These two groups are not unconnected.

In the 1960s, the majority of black Michigan residents were not born in the state. Older persons were internal migrants from *r*-less areas of the American South, and younger persons were overwhelmingly the children of recent arrivals. The parents of 53 per cent of Wolfram's informants were born in the three deep Southern states of Mississippi, Alabama and Georgia. Another 21 per cent were born in other Southern states. Thus a linguistic boundary coincident with an ethnic boundary exists in Detroit. But is is not a full explanation to say that *r*-lessness among Detroit blacks was caused by the movement of people who speak a non-rhotic vernacular into a northern city in which the basic pattern is rhotic. As Wolfram (1969: 25) points out, 'One of the most important factors accounting for speech behaviour in the Detroit Negro population is racial isolation. Patterns of Northern segregation are a main source for transforming many Southern speech characteristics into ethnic and class patterns of speech in Northern cities.' In fact, class, sex, age and racial isolation interact in complex ways. The migration of black people into inner cities in the north – the inner city of Detroit has very high densities of black people as a percentage of the population – has led to the emergence of a 'uniform caste dialect – the black English vernacular of Harlem and other inner cities' (Labov, 1972: 299). Labov sees this as part of a general tendency connected with worldwide urbanization in the past several centuries: the transformation of local dialects into language varieties defined in terms of stratification. Innovations emerge that reflect the processes of urbanization.

These processes can lead to vernacular innovations away from the norm of the 'host' community. But with respect to *r*, the degree of convergence in Detroit seemed to depend on class differences within the black community. The contact was complicated. And there were signs that the black working-class vernacular wasn't changing towards white norms. Wolfram's study showed that within the black community *r* reflects social class differences among blacks. Figure 5.9 shows the stratification of r absence by social class. Each class increases its amount of rhoticity as one moves up the social scale. The bottom diagram in Figure 5.9 shows the style-shift between careful and reading styles. We see that this is also in the direction of rhoticity, but no hypercorrection is visible. Wolfram's data on age, which show no age-grading for r, suggest that working-class adults are persistently retaining a non-rhotic Southern norm (Wolfram, 1969: 118). However, the picture that emerges for r in terms of class and style is one in which, for the black middle class at any rate, there has been an acceptance of the norm of General American. Clearly what has happened is that the pronunciation of the host community has become the form with *overt* prestige within the black ethnic group's upper strata.

There are signs of linguistic adaptation in Detroit between middle-class blacks and white rhoticity. Presumably these are the most socially mobile black people, those who have the most diverse and intensive linguistic contact with whites.

We find evidence of the importance of such contact if we look at black r pronunciation in two northeast cities, Philadelphia and New York. Myhill (1988) studied postvocalic r in the black vernacular of Philadelphia. As in Detroit, white speech in that city is rhotic (with the interesting exception of working-class ethnic Italians). Myhill found that there was an increasing convergence between black and white speech. Blacks were becoming increasingly rhotic depending on their relationship to the white speech community. Those with 'more white friends' *versus* 'fewer white friends' or 'more white lovers' *versus* 'as many black as white lovers' had significantly less r-lessness. Commenting on this research, Butters (1989: 46) writes that 'the original /r/ deletion rule of Blacks in Philadelphia . . . has been modified in the direction of r-retention practices of the national standard and local Philadelphia white vernacular'.

Butters takes the interesting further step of comparing Philadelphia with Labov's results for blacks in New York. As we saw, the New York vernacular is largely r-less. Accordingly, New York black speakers maintain a much higher degree of r-lessness than those in Philadelphia. He uses this to reinforce Labov's point that linguistic traits are the result of real face-to-face contact, not the standard norms experienced in school or the mass media. In New York, public middle class norms would be largely rhotic. But in New York, r-less blacks would have little opportunity of face to face contact with a 'dominating' r-full white norm compared to the experience of blacks in Philadelphia. The key fact is a convergence of black speech to the rhotic norm in Philadelphia. And this convergence depends on the degree of contact between blacks and whites. So it is not the case, nationwide, that blacks are not participating in an increase of rhoticity. But they are doing so at a slower pace, depending on the 'dominating' dialect of each city and the opportunities of black contact with it.

Specificity of explanations

Our sketch of rhoticity has been on a very wide canvas. We have looked at the diffusion of the loss of postvocalic *r*, and the gain of postvocalic *r*, in many speech communities: from Charleston, to Edinburgh, to eighteenth-century London, to postwar New York. The inescapable effects of social factors in the diffusion of linguistic change were clearly visible.

One reason why it is possible to study *r* so widely is that the innovations we have looked at have characteristically been introduced by the highest status groups in the community. This was the first sort of normative pressure we discussed in the last chapter, and is a reflex of stratification as characteristic social structure. The processes involved are analogous, on the level of the single variable feature, to those involved in standardization, as discussed in chapter two. In the next chapter, we shall see that social stratification and its concomitant stratification of styles are just one social dimension relevant to linguistic variation.

Even more important is the way in which *r* must be explained differently in different communities. In England, *r*-lessness is the prestige norm. In New York City, *r*-fullness is being introduced by the highest ranked social group from outside the community. In Edinburgh, *r*-less speech has appeared in one sex, in one social and one age group. That looks like a vernacular innovation, which probably will not spread because of the prestige rhotic norm of Edinburgh English. There seems to have been a reversal in the fortunes of *r* as a variable in the speech of coastal South Carolina. How could this be explained? If a new prestige norm has replaced an older one, we could look for the way institutions create and sustain prestige norms. For example, in England, how is RP maintained as the prestige norm? The system of stratification is probably central to this; and the control of large-scale institutions by the upper strata of society, including education, public culture, state institutions and the media. But could *that* apply to *r*-less speech in Charleston? McDavid (1975) argues instead that the profound postwar changes in Southern society, including a great increase in educational and economic opportunity for the formerly disadvantaged, has led to upward mobility by rhotic whites. Such people have modified the Charleston standard. If this is true, it would be an example of a change introduced by a lower strata of society.

Whatever the case, this explanation will clearly not do for either New York City or Detroit. The point, then, is that postvocalic *r* is a *different* sociolinguistic variable in each of these communities. The rhoticity or otherwise of speech means something different in different speech communities.

6 At the intersection of social factors

> Thereupon those who had been presented with the head answered. 'Your majesty, an elephant is just like a pot,' and those who had only observed the ear replied, 'An elephant is just like a winnowing basket.' Those who had been presented with the tusk said that it was a plough share. Those who knew only the trunk said it was a plough. 'The body', said they, 'is a granary: the foot, a pillar: the back, a mortar: its tail, a pestle.'
>
> *Some Sayings of the Buddha*
> (tr. F. L. Woodward, 1973)

When we introduced sociolinguistic variables it was mainly in relation to the two interconnected social factors of class and style. This is important but somewhat misleading, since it highlights only one particular sociolinguistic structure. It quickly became obvious that other social variables also reveal patterns in linguistic variability which are significant. An index score, whether individual or averaged for primary or secondary groups, is at the intersection of social factors.

In this chapter, we will look at some of these factors in turn and try to see how they intersect in particular cases. The main factors are: (1) geographical space; (2) stratification; (3) social networks; (4) sex; (5) ethnicity; (6) age. These are woven together in a very subtle and complex way in a speech community. They interact differently for different variables. Using quantitative methods to study correlations with one social factor makes the pattern partially visible. Like the blind people in the quotation above, we see only a bit of the elephant and can easily misinterpret that bit. The aim, of course, is to view each sociolinguistic structure as evidence for a theory of how language structure and change must, in part, be explained in terms of social structure and change. We will look at that issue in chapter seven.

Spatial diffusion

I remarked earlier that 'where one lived' was a social characteristic of people which affected their use of language. The study of the way in which linguistic variants were geographically distributed was very much the province of traditional dialect geography. That this is important can be seen from the very clear evidence of spatial diffusion which we observed in connection with *r*; for example, in Figures 5.2, 5.3, 5.5 and 5.6. The use of quantitative methodology can make the study of spatial distribution of variants more exact and rigorous.

We can illustrate some of the possibilities by looking at a proposal by Trudgill (1974a, 1983) for the application of some of the techniques of modern geography to the study of the diffusion of linguistic variants. Trudgill adapted the methodology of the Swedish geographer Hägerstrand to the examination of the spatial diffusion of a linguistic innovation in the Brunlanes peninsula, Norway. The study was meant to be mainly illustrative of what might be possible if the notion of a linguistic variable is joined with sophistication in geographical method.

In the Brunlanes area, the variable studied was the vowel (ae). This has to do with the relative height of the vowel. Evidence suggested that the pronunciation of the sound was in the process of being 'lowered', or pronounced more openly, so that it was variable within and between the communities of the peninsula.

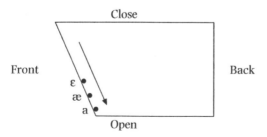

The score of 000 marked a consistently high pronunciation and a score of 400 indicated a consistently low pronunciation. The higher an informant's score, the further the change towards 'lowering' had gone in his or her speech.

The relative height of the vowel is a gradient, or 'more or less' phenomenon. The individual score for each informant is a measure of where, more close or more open, (ae) is pronounced. We have seen how average scores were determined for categories such as class and style. But how can this be done for space?

The method is to find out the quantitative relationship between two spaces of equal magnitude. One divides into a series of equally sized cells the geographical space through which one is trying to observe some innovation moving. For each cell, the percentage of times the new innovation appears, out of the total number of times the variable occurs overall, is calculated, giving the ratio of new to old for each cell. Then, by comparing any two cells, it is possible to measure precisely the increase or decrease of new cases as opposed to old for the two spaces. At a point in time, a relatively higher score for a cell suggests that the innovation is further advanced in that space. At the same point in time, a relatively lower score for a cell suggests that the innovation is less advanced in that space.

One could imagine how this method might, for example, be used to measure the spread of non-rhotic pronunciation through geographical space. If (r) index scores were the percentage of *r*s used out of the total number of possible postvocalic *r*s, then a lower score would represent an increase in *r*-less speech. To apply the method, the space in question (say the West Country of England) would have to be divided into cells of equal magnitude. Using Labov's techniques, an average index score would then be calculated for each cell. The result, for that point in time, would tell us precisely how *r*-lessness was distributed in space for that region. Relative increases or decreases, if they followed regular patterns, would allow us to infer from which and to which areas *r*-lessness was spreading, if it was. Maps, such as those in Figures 5.2 and 5.3, would thus present much more information for interpretation. In fact, they would be the spatial equivalent of the sociolinguistic structure diagrams – with space instead of class and style as the social variable. As Trudgill (1974a: 223) points out, spatial cells are the equivalent of Labov's social class cells.

The immediate interest is spatial diffusion of change. Häger-strand suggested that this ultimately depends on the 'sender's network of interpersonal contacts and that the configuration of this network is primarily dependent on various barriers' (Trudgill, 1974a: 223). Social barriers have the same effect as physical barriers. We mentioned this notion when discussing the differentiation of varieties in chapter two: that the boundaries between dialects will be along lines of weakness in communication networks (Bloomfield, 1933: 328). It is also possible that social networks may be useful here. Changes will spread from individual to individual along networks. Clustering, density and multiplexity will facilitate diffusion within a group. But weak network links between groups will slow down the process.

The sheer geographical distance between people will itself have an effect on diffusion. If everything else is equal, people who live close together are likely to be similar in their adoption of the innovation, as opposed to those who live further apart. In the theory, this is called the **neighbourhood effect**.

But patterns of communication are clearly not dependent only upon spatial proximity. Changes diffuse more rapidly between urban areas which are in close contact than they do between those centres and their respective closer rural areas. Changes can 'jump' between these **central places**. And then they will spread out from such foci to the intervening hinterlands later. Both these effects were observed in Brunlanes.

Trudgill's first step was to impose a grid of cells on a map of the Brunlanes peninsula to divide it into spaces of equal magnitude. Figure 6.1 shows how this looks. Average (ae) index scores were then calculated for cells in a profile from east to west. This is represented by the dotted lines between the centres of Larvik and Hamna. Figure 6.2 represents the average index scores for the cells through which the dotted line passes as it crosses the peninsula.

Remember that higher scores represent relatively low vowel height, and that this 'lowering' is the direction of the change we are studying. The lowest vowels are to be found in the urban communities. The highest variants are in the rural areas most remote

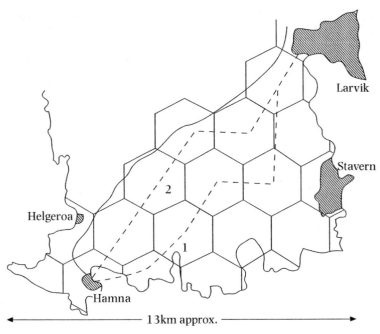

Figure 6.1 Grid imposed on Brunlanes peninsula, Norway (*from Trudgill, 1974a*)

from these centres, gradually increasing the further one gets from the centres of influence. Trudgill suggests that the linguistic change is radiating from Larvik, spreading by the 'neighbourhood effect' to the surrounding area. It has 'jumped' to Hamna, a central place, and is also radiating from that secondary centre. The next step is to represent scores on maps which will graphically display the dynamics of diffusion.

Space and time

The profile in Figure 6.2 gives us the spatial pattern at one time. But an innovation diffuses through space in time. At progressively later times, a change will not only be more widely diffused, but will also be more advanced in its purely linguistic development. In the case of Brunlanes, the scores will be higher later, as the

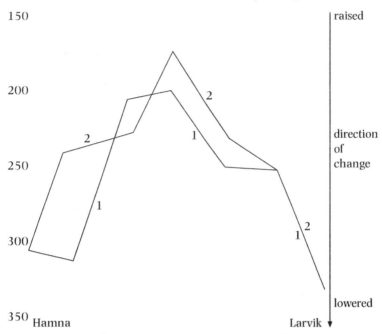

Figure 6.2 Average (ae) index scores from east to west. The numbers 1 and 2 represent the routes of the profiles marked by the dotted lines in Figure 6.1 (*from Trudgill, 1974a*)

'lowering' of the vowel develops. As we shall see in more detail in the next chapter, on the assumption that a change is in progress, lower scores ought to characterize *older* speakers, and higher scores ought to characterize *younger* speakers. We saw such age grading in (r) in New York in chapter five.

But this will be in systematic relationship with the spaces through which the change is diffusing. Although the young ought to be most advanced in each space, we ought also to preserve both the *relative* differences in age in every space and the *relative* differences between the spaces, depending on how far the change has gone in each one.

Figure 6.3 shows that this is the case on the Brunlanes peninsula. Average (ae) index scores for each cell by age group have been worked out, and isoglosses drawn which reflect these average

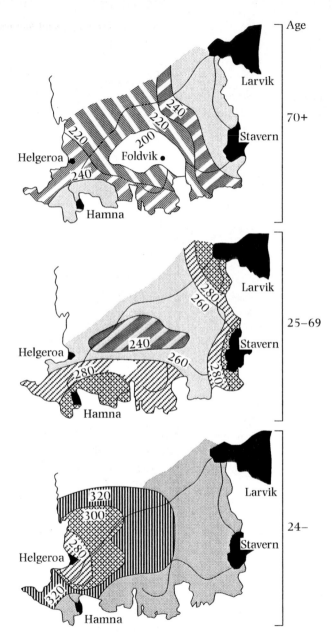

Figure 6.3 Brunlanes (ae) by age (*from Trudgill, 1974a*)

scores. The top map shows the scores for those aged seventy and over, the middle map for those aged twenty-five to sixty-nine, and the bottom map for those aged twenty-four and younger. The scores clearly increase by age group for all spaces, with younger speakers having higher scores, and therefore 'lowered' (ae) variants. For Larvik's neighbourhood the scores are 240+ at seventy and over, 280+ at twenty-five to sixty-nine, and 320+ for twenty-four and younger. But spatial differentials are preserved. Thus Larvik is always ahead of Helgeroa in the innovation for each age group. Increasing scores also spread out further from the 'central places' into their 'neighbourhoods' for each successively younger age group.

The nature of change tells us that the highest scores (the most 'lowered' vowel heights) will be for the younger speakers in a relatively larger area in the neighbourhood of the place where the change began. As predicted, the highest scores are for the under twenty-fives in a large neighbourhood around Larvik. The lowest scores ought to be for the oldest speakers at the place which the change reached last – a place at the outer limits of the neighbourhoods of the central places. The top map, in fact, does show the lowest average scores for the oldest speakers, those aged seventy and over, in the intermediate area north of Foldvik. The origin of the 'lowering' at Larvik, its spread to its neighbourhood, its 'jump' to Hamna and its diffusion from there are all made clear by the application of quantitative methods to the study of the diffusion of this change.

Trudgill's research is illustrative of the possibilities. Processes such as these were clearly taking place during the spread of *r*-lessness and *r*-fullness in the speech communities we looked at in chapter five.

There have also been attempts to determine whether spatial weaknesses in networks of communication do correlate with isogloss bundles. Labov (1974) was concerned to see if this traditional hypothesis, that language differentiation was caused by relatively less communication between rather than within groups, could be empirically corroborated.

There is a major isogloss bundle that runs east to west across Pennsylvania, separating its northern tier of counties from the rest of the state. It reflects differences both in vocabulary and pronunciation. The usual assumption is that what most affects people's vernacular speech are face-to-face contacts with other people. (Passive contact through the media etc. probably serves to transmit norms 'from above', and therefore principally affects attitudes rather than practices.) It follows from this assumption that if we could measure the daily density of travel between the residents of different areas, we would also have a rough measure of the amount of communication between the areas. In the USA, up to 90 per cent of inter-city passenger traffic is by road.

Accordingly, Labov calculated the number of primary highways crossing the east-west dialect boundary from north to south. There were 2.2 crossings per hundred miles. But this needs to be compared with the number of north-south crossings of east-west lines up and down the state to see if it is a low or a high figure. Imaginary lines were drawn on the map east to west at thirty-mile intervals, and the number of north-south crossings per hundred miles was calculated. In fact, the dialect boundary *was* in a trough of north-south links. This converged with data about traffic flows. Using traffic-flow maps he was able to show that there was also a trough in average daily traffic flows roughly at the point where the isogloss passes through the state. Similar results were obtained for many, but not all, major dialect boundaries in the eastern states.

The exceptions are crucial. For example, we noted before how small and stable the New York City speech area was in geographical terms, compared to that of other cities. It is almost 'the prototype of a concentrated metropolis', in Labov's words. Yet the average daily traffic flows in and out of New York City are very large indeed, over fifty times greater than the Pennsylvania isogloss. This means that density of communication and weaknesses in lines of communication *alone* cannot account for the diffusion of innovations – although it might have some validity in accounting for broad regional differentiation.

We have seen that the distribution of variants is spatially structured in relation to change through time; that there are 'city effects' and 'neighbourhood effects', and that lines of communication are significant, but not definitively so. Changes diffuse to and from 'places' in a patterned way.

Social stratification

In variables like (ing) and (r) we observed scores stratified by class and style. These two social variables were clearly interdependent. The variable was simultaneously structured on both dimensions. The shifts of style that occurred in the more formal contexts are towards the variant used most frequently by the highest class in casual speech. This is a reflex of social stratification.

When informants are most consciously aware of their speech and 'phonic intention' can be observed, we can talk about variants being produced under **pressure from above**. The word 'above' here is being used in the sense of 'above' the level of conscious awareness. People are aware of the normative pressure being brought to bear on them, for example, in terms of the overt prestige or stigma of a variant, notions of correctness, and so on. As we shall see, however, there is also the opposite case. Normative pressures can affect people's speech without them being aware of it. It is below the level of consciousness, and hence termed **pressure from below** – pressure to conform to norms of which people are not self-consciously aware, in response, as Labov puts it (1972: 123), 'to social motivations which are relatively obscure'.

Now notice how we can map these two kinds of normative pressure on to social stratification. Pressure from above, that of which people are aware, has also come from above in the social sense. It has typically been an awareness of what is overtly treated as having prestige or stigma in the society. These 'society-wide' normative pressures have been associated with the higher ranked social strata, although all strata may consciously accept them. We saw how the design of the classic sociolinguistic interview revealed, through style-shifting, the connection between overt prestige, conscious norms and the practice of the upper middle class. Conversely, the non-standard stigmatized variant was characteristically the practice of the lower strata in casual speech. Style and class interact to reveal this conscious, evaluative stratification of the variants.

But there is a possible source of confusion here. The connections just described seem to be a matter of fact, but they are not necessary connections. There is no reason why 'pressures from above', conscious awareness of a norm, could not be exerted on behalf of a non-standard variant. People would attach overt prestige to the vernacular, and judge the use of standard forms negatively. Judgements of 'affectation' are of this type. More characteristically, it is 'pressure from below', without conscious awareness of the norm, that attaches a hidden **covert prestige** to the vernacular. But we must be careful not to assume that all conscious norms and overt prestige are by definition generated from the top down, as it were, and then generalized throughout the overall society. There are both conscious and unconscious pressures acting on all strata. Linguistic innovation can emerge at any point in the social system, and eventually become overtly prestigious.

The distinctions we have just made can be clarified by the diagram below. Solid arrows show the links between strata and normative pressures which seem to reflect the system of stratification. The dotted arrows show the other possibilities. Stratification involves both differentiation and ranking from higher to lower. Talcott Parsons, for example, sees the process of differentiation producing stratification, as different social roles are associated with different statuses within the social system. The ranking is the source of the differing evaluations we find, which presumably serve to *integrate* this kind of social organization. Stratification characterizes complex societies, which are highly differentiated. Urban industrial societies exhibit *class* stratification. One of the trends observable in the modern period has been the relative decline of rural speech varieties. In urban melting-pots these have been transformed and there has emerged variation that reflects the overall system of urban class stratification and the social attitudes that serve to sustain it.

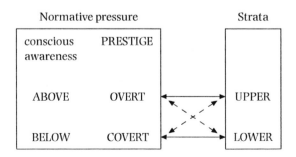

We can make a useful distinction here, borrowed from the socio-logist Ferdinant Toennies, between *gemeinschaft* and *gesellschaft* types of society. The former type is based on community, and the latter on more impersonal relationships. Community, as a form of social organization, is based on stable personal relationships, for example systems of kinship. In the latter type of society, by con-trast, relationships are characteristically mediated through institu-tions. People relate to each other in a fundamentally different and more impersonal way. When we look at language variation in terms of a *class-style* structure, we are observing the *gesellschaft*-type pattern that reflects the large-scale organization of our soci-ety. The *prestige–stigma* axis reflects the evaluative dimension of this structure.

A number of basic kinds of such sociolinguistic structures have been discovered. Four recurring types are illustrated in Figure 6.4.

Sociolinguistic indicators. Sometimes a variable is stratified by class but hardly at all by style. There is no significant shift in average index scores between casual and formal styles. Such variables are called **indicators**. The variable (aː) in Norwich provides us with an example of this type. Its sociolinguistic structure is illustrated in Figure 6.4a (Trudgill, 1974: 98).

This variable has to do with the relative fronting or backing of the vowel in such words as 'after', 'cart' and 'path'. In Norwich, this is variable between a relatively back vowel of the RP type and a very front vowel characteristic of the local vernacular. A high score (200) represents the fronted local variant while a low score (000) represents the back RP type of pronunciation.

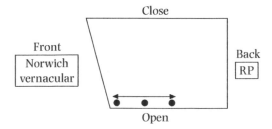

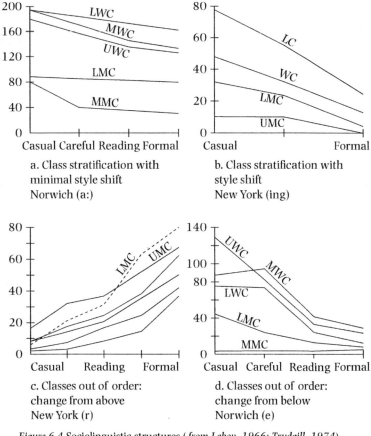

Figure 6.4 Sociolinguistic structures (*from Labov, 1966; Trudgill, 1974*)

On the basis of the regular sociolinguistic structures discussed earlier, we should be able to predict style-shifting towards the RP norm in more formal styles due to pressure from above. However, a look at Figure 6.4a will show that (aː) does not do this. Thus we observe, in this type of variable, class stratification with only minimal stylistic stratification. The two dimensions are separable. This is particularly noticeable in the working-class scores for (aː). Trudgill (1974: 98) writes:

> We can interpret this as indicating that although WC speech is charac-
> terised by a pronunciation of this variable that is significantly different

from that of MC, little attention is directed towards this difference in the Norwich speech community.

We shall return to the whys and wherefores of this in a moment.

Sociolinguistic markers. The other three diagrams in Figure 6.4 all exhibit stylistic stratification as well as social stratification. Such variables are called **markers**. These three diagrams represent recurring types of markers.

Figure 6.4b returns us to the (ing) variable in New York City. In contrast to Norwich (aː) the slope of the lines for all classes shows clear style-shifting. Although the classes remain stratified in the same order for all styles, each one's average index score slopes regularly towards the most formal styles. The question is, why are the structures of this type different from structures of the first 'indicator' type? Why are style and class separated in the first, but not in the second?

Trudgill's analysis of the (aː) variable in Norwich gives us an answer. The Norwich (aː) does not seem to be subject to any of the normative pressures from above which shape pronunciations towards standard forms. Trudgill (1974: 98f.) gives a number of reasons for the lack of style-shift in (aː).

First, the fronted variant is not stigmatized in Norwich, nor is it overtly stereotyped as an object of humour. It is not corrected in educational institutions. It would seem, then, that although the classes are stratified with respect to (aː), there is little correction towards the RP variant. Trudgill notes that overtly stigmatized forms are quite often those that deviate from a spelling pronunciation, as popularly conceived. Thus, people are consciously taught not to 'drop' their 'h's, 't's and 'g's. In this case, the vowel position cannot be conceived of in those terms. So, in contrast to '*in*'', a front (aː) does not attract stigma.

Second, the (aː) variable is not involved in linguistic change. Trudgill argues that speakers will be more self-consciously aware of variables which are in the process of change, if only because within the group people of different ages will pronounce the form differently. Attention will be drawn to the conflicting forms co-existing within the same social group. From this, we can conclude that *sociolinguistic indicators represent variables which are not in the process of change.* So we can have

+class –style –stigma –change

as represented by Norwich (aː) and diagrams like Figure 6.4a.

Does this mean that contrasting diagrams which exhibit style-shifting indicate that the variable is involved in a linguistic change? Not at all. We can get both stigmatization and style-shift (as in New York (ing)) in a variable which is *not* undergoing change. You will recall that we termed (ing) a 'stable sociolinguistic marker'. Chambers and Trudgill (1980: 83ff.) point out that, in fact, the following combinations occur for sociolinguistic markers:

$$+ \text{class} \ + \text{style} \begin{cases} + \text{stigma} \ - \text{change} \\ - \text{stigma} \ + \text{change} \\ - \text{stigma} \ - \text{change} \end{cases}$$

This last category is different from the others, in that style-shift without stigma or change can be accounted for by phonological features of the variable which make speakers aware of the contrast between the variant forms. We can say, in general, that stylistic stratification, and the self-conscious awareness of language it indicates, can be produced by either stigmatization or change or both. It follows that a sociolinguistic marker by itself is not diagnostic of a linguistic change in progress. It is a necessary but not a sufficient condition for change.

Diagrams c and d in Figure 6.4 represent markers that *are* diagnostic of linguistic change. In both cases this can be corroborated by the age-grading of the index scores. These types of structure have in common that social classes are 'out of order' in relation to their index scores.

Prestige innovation. Figure 6.4c represents the by now familiar pattern of the (r) variable in New York City. The contrast with a marker such as Figure 6.4b is very clear. The slope of style-shifting is accentuated for a 'borderline' class. We observe hypercorrection by the lower middle class, represented by the dotted line in the diagram.

This third common pattern is characteristic of a linguistic change taking place within a speech community under pressure from above. (Recall that the new prestige norm of rhoticity was being introduced to New York by younger members of the upper middle class.) By contrast, the first pattern usually represents a stable situation; and the second may or may not involve change.

We saw how hypercorrection from above worked to accelerate the diffusion of an innovation through the class system. Let us now look rather more deeply at this phenomenon. Why should the second highest ranked class behave in this way?

The standard answer to this question is that this group is in the most vulnerable and potentially mobile position in the system of class stratification. Because of this, such people are also the most sensitive to the social significance of prestige and stigmatized variants, and therefore most susceptible to pressure from above in their speech. This becomes obvious when they are consciously exercising control over their speech in the more formal styles.

We saw above that the role of the lower middle class was *not* to originate the innovation, but to be the driving force in its diffusion. Hypercorrection accelerated the spread of a linguistic change. Now we see that hypercorrection is driven by the linguistic insecurity of this, the second highest status group. We should look at this more closely.

Labov (1966) studied his informants' reports of their own usage. On the whole, New Yorkers were very inaccurate in their reports of how they spoke. They consistently over-reported the prestige forms of pronunciation. Labov considered that when speakers report their own usage, they are in fact reporting norms of correctness. This works in the following way (Labov, 1966: 455):

> It appears that most New Yorkers have acquired a set of governing norms which they use in the audio-monitoring of their own speech . . . the process of stylistic variation . . . is governed by the degree of audio-monitoring which is superimposed upon the motor-controlled patterns of native speech. The audio-monitoring norm is the form which is perceived by the speaker himself as he speaks. He does not hear the actual sound he produces, but the norm which he imposes.

Pressure from above produces a cleavage between vernacular pattern and superimposed norm because the norm arises outside the speaker's own group and is transmitted to him or her through notions of correctness. The degree of over-reporting will measure this cleavage and the strength of the externally imposed norm.

And just as the degree of hypercorrection was greatest in the second highest status group, the same tendency appeared in its reports of its own usage. For some variables, the lower middle class over-reported the use of the prestige variant more than the other classes.

There were more overt indications of this linguistic insecurity. **A linguistic insecurity index** was worked out by measuring the difference between how informants reported that they *actually* pronounced certain diagnostic words, and how they said that they believed those same words *should* be pronounced. This, in fact, measures people's willingness to admit to the 'badness' of their own accents – and nothing could measure insecurity more profoundly. On this measure, the lower middle class turned out to be the most linguistically insecure. Some informants roundly condemned their own kind of speech as rendering persons who spoke *that* way unsuitable for prestige occupations.

Social mobility was also related to hypercorrection. Labov (1967) investigated this relationship. Four types of social mobility were distinguished: *upward, steady, downward* and *up and down.* These were based on the present social level of the informant's occupation, compared to the occupational status of his or her father, and their own first employment. The ranking of occupations into four levels followed the practice of the Census Bureau. Upward mobility was largely a feature of the middle classes, and, to a lesser degree, of the upper section of the working class. Of Labov's informants, the consistently most upwardly mobile group was the lower middle class. (For later, it is important to note that the *steady* type was most marked in the working class.)

It was upwardly mobile groups that showed the pattern of hypercorrection in the use of *r*. Upwardly mobile members of the lower middle class and of the upper stratum of the working class went beyond upper-middle-class scores in formal styles. It was upward mobility, even more than class membership, that characterized the hypercorrecting groups.

This suggests that those who are upwardly mobile are more likely to adopt those exterior norms which are prestigious throughout the community. This is in contrast with stable groups, who are less likely to be subject to normative pressures from outside. For upwardly mobile people, the group just above them in the scale of stratification acts as a 'reference group' for norms of pronunciation. Downwardly mobile people were found not to be influenced by normative pressure from above, and stable groups were governed by their own norms, balanced in behaviour by a recognition of external norms. As we saw, the acceptance of an external norm which differs from one's own vernacular also leads to insecurity. So upward mobility and insecurity converge on those on the 'borderline' between the working and upper middle classes, and generate hypercorrect linguistic patterns.

Labov (1967: 74) sees linguistic behaviour, then, as governed by such normative pressures and the values they encode. These operate irrespective of contact and this shows us again that we cannot account for linguistic boundaries simply in terms of lines of weakness in communication networks. Rather, it is the system of norms that is at work.

Vernacular innovation. Now let us look at a contrasting situation, in which the classes are again 'out of order', that is, a linguistic change is occurring; but this time the change and its spread are from below in the system of social stratification. This pattern occurs in the Norwich (e) variable studied by Trudgill (1974). It is illustrated in Figure 6.4d.

The Norwich (e) represents the progressive centralizing of the vowel sound in words such as *tell*, *well*, *bell* before an *l*, and in words like *better* and *metal*. The front variant of this variable is the same vowel as in RP. The other variants fall along a continuum in which the tongue is retracted and lowered from the RP position. The vernacular vowel is centralized and lowered so that in extreme

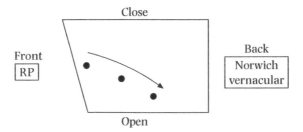

Norwich pronunciation *hell* is identical with *hull* (Chambers and Trudgill, 1980: 94). Index scores are calculated for (e) along this continuum so that 000 represents a totally RP pronunciation and 200 a totally vernacular pronunciation. The higher the index score, the more non-standard is the pronunciation.

Now look at the average index scores for Norwich (e) by class and style. Figure 6.4d shows the familiar pattern in some ways. The middle middle class approximates most closely to the prestige RP norm in all styles. With average scores ranging from 000 to 003, this is a virtually consistent RP pronunciation. All other classes style-shift towards this norm in more formal styles. Note the sharp rightward slope of the lines in the diagram. We see, therefore, that the whole community is aware of this larger norm. But otherwise the pattern is quite different from what we have come to expect. Look at the figures for each class in casual style:

Social Classes	Casual
Middle Middle	002
Lower Middle	042
Upper Working	127
Middle Working	087
Lower Working	077

The classes are strikingly 'out of order' at the working-class end of the social scale. The score for the lower working class is immediately below that of the lower middle class. That means that in any given style of speech those at the very bottom end of the social hierarchy, the lower working class, have less non-standard centralization, pronounce (e) more closely to the RP norm than do other members of the working class. Note also that in casual speech the upper working class centralizes its pronunciation more than the middle of the working class. In short, within the working class as a whole, the upper, middle and lower parts are in the exact opposite order to that expected in terms of the prestige RP norm. The upper parts of the working class diverge most from the standard.

Trudgill interprets this pattern as a linguistic innovation originating in the upper part of the working class in Norwich; an innovation *away from* the RP norm. Norwich (e) is becoming more centralized. In this case, the working-class 'borderline' is leading the process of change. The other 'borderline' class, the lower middle class, is also participating in the change, and so is the lower working class. The upper middle class alone seems insulated from centralization. In fact, a look at Figure 6.4d shows a virtually flat line for this class. It is clear that innovation in the upper working class is also serving as a norm for other parts of the working class. See how the middle working class 'crosses over' the upper working class in more formal styles, and increases its centralization.

In chapter four, I mentioned varying sources of normative pressure. In this data we are witnessing covert prestige driving a linguistic change. Contrasting with what the overall society overtly recognizes as the norm and what is portrayed by the direction of style-shifting (which is consistently towards RP), the actual direction of this change is away from the standard. Clearly, working-class speech also has prestige. But we cannot reach it through the concept of formality, the degree of self-conscious attention to speech. This only gives us access to those forms which people overtly believe are 'correct', those that have the prestige of overt institutional support which we noted in discussing 'standardization' earlier on. They are the forms learned through contact with the larger structures of society – in school, at work, in church or the media – and connected with the written standard. It is these forms of which people approve when overtly asked. *But the positive social significance of vernacular speech resides in the community and culture of its speakers.* This will often diverge from superimposed norms. Although overtly 'stigmatized', its actual 'social meaning' may be positive from the point of view of those to whom it is the vernacular, and deeply tied up with their identity.

Thus, we can see normative pressures affecting people from two directions. Both of these can drive linguistic innovation and its diffusion within the system of stratification. By 'pressure from below' we mean both 'below' in the class hierarchy and 'below' in the sense of not affected by the norms that govern conscious audio-monitoring of basic motor patterns. Far from 'pressure from above' smoothing out language variation, in city after city vernacular

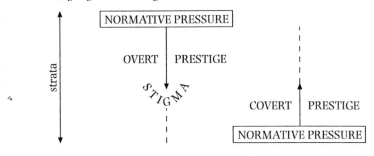

innovations originate and spread. The vernacular is extremely alive. It finds its sources in the *gemeinschaft*, or community type of social life.

Social networks

In chapter four we saw that vernacular speech, the speech of working-class communities, could be studied using the notion of the individual's social network. Informally, an individual's social network simply is that network of relationships in which he or she is embedded and that makes up the texture of daily life. It must be emphasized that this provides us with a radically different perspective from that of an analysis based on secondary group membership. For one thing, the methodology has universal application. As we saw, stratification applies only to one type of society. But everyone lives within a social network irrespective of the type of larger society. By using networks, we can get a picture of the individual within the local community.

We can see how different kinds of networks both make up and are affected by the social conditions in the community. And language variation can be observed in the actual patterns of relationship where the vernacular emerges and is used. In principle, social networks could be studied in any strata. However, our concern here will be the Milroys' study of the working-class vernacular in three Belfast communities (Milroy and Milroy, 1978; Milroy, 1987; Milroy and Margrain, 1980). We are now going 'inside' the large-scale social groups that have preoccupied us thus far. The aim is to gain insight into the dynamics of non-standard speech.

The Milroy studies revealed a very complex interweaving of local community, sex, age and, most important, the relative density and multiplexity (see page 118 above) of social networks in relation to linguistic scores. The relation of these factors was different for different variables, and yet reflected regular processes within and between the three communities.

A Belfast variable

We will look at the interpretation of one variable feature. The communities studied were Ballymacarrett, in East Belfast, and Hammer and Clonard in West Belfast.

One of the most interesting variables was (a), the vowel sound in words such as *man*. The middle-class norm in Belfast for this sound locates it in the lower front area of the mouth. Working-class Belfast speech is currently in the process of *backing* this sound – the tongue moves back and is raised and the lips are rounded. (In other words, the vowel in *man* sounds somewhat like that in the RP pronunciation of the word *father*.) There is a linguistic change in progress in the direction *away* from the middle-class norm. The index scores in Figure 6.5a indicate the degree of backing in the pronunciation of (a) in the three communities by age, sex and style. The higher scores indicate a greater tendency to back the vowel.

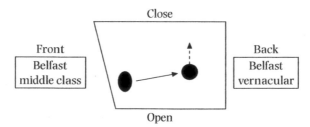

Now let us look at the three communities. We shall see that the relative density and multiplexity of their networks and specific sex and age clusters within each community are important in interpreting results. All three are inner city working-class communities which suffer from a high level of social malaise, indicated by

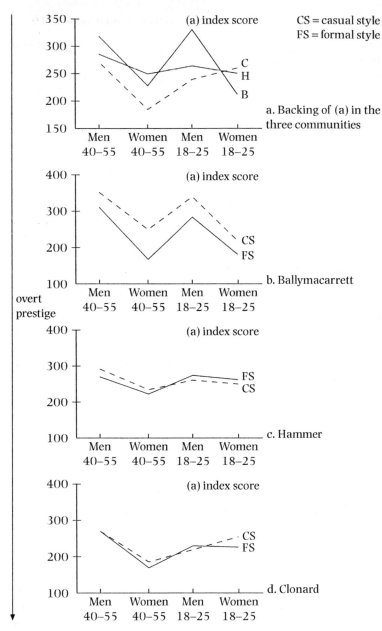

Figure 6.5 The (a) variable in Belfast (*from Milroy and Milroy, 1978*)

'unemployment, sickness, juvenile crime, illegitimacy and premature death from disease' (Milroy, 1987: 72). Although all three areas are poor and of low status, the intensity of the problems is worse in West Belfast, in Hammer and Clonard, than in the east, where Ballymacarrett is located.

Ballymacarrett. Ballymacarrett is the most cohesive of the communities. It is a very old, ethnically Protestant, industrial settlement with very dense and multiplex networks based on kin. One factor which sets it apart from Hammer and Clonard is the availability of employment in the local shipyard. The men can work where they live. All the male Ballymacarrett informants had been connected with the shipyard at one time or another. This had produced a very strong territorial element in the local male culture – boys and men tended to restrict their activities to the Ballymacarrett area. Ballymacarrett women, however, were much less territorial and most women worked outside the area. The stability of local male employment was the most important single factor in making Ballymacarrett the area with the most dense and multiplex networks.

The other two communities, by contrast, suffered from a lack of local male employment.

Hammer. The Hammer, a Protestant area, had been extensively redeveloped and a large part of its population dispersed to other nearby areas. But Hammer people still based their recreational and daily interaction on the old neighbourhood. However, the disruption to social networks caused by the dispersal of the population served to make the social networks of the Hammer less dense and multiplex than those of Ballymacarrett.

Clonard. The Clonard was the only Catholic area studied. In Belfast, ethnicity is cast in terms of Protestant and Catholic, and these labels also serve to rank communities in terms of status. As a Catholic area, the Clonard had the lowest status of the three communities. It also had the worst levels of male unemployment. Only two of the Clonard men whose networks were studied were employed. This lack of local opportunity made the Clonard men less territorial than the men of Ballymacarrett. Consequently, the male social networks were less dense and multiplex. By contrast, the Clonard women were almost all employed.

Against this background, let us now try to interpret the linguistic facts in Figure 6.5. Recall that the (a) variable measures the tendency to 'back' the vowel and that, since the middle-class Belfast norm is a front pronunciation, the more a speaker backs the vowel, the more it deviates from the standard and towards the vernacular. I will treat the diagrams in turn.

6.5a   The first diagram shows the backing of (a) in the three communities. *In general, the scores are stratified according to the density and multiplexity of the social networks in the areas.* Ballymacarrett, the most cohesive working-class community, has the most vernacular pronunciations, especially among the men, and the Clonard the least vernacular pronunciation. The degree of backing of the vowel roughly reflects the degree of cohesion in the community. But the situation has many subtleties.

6.5b   The second diagram displays the distribution of the scores by age and sex, in casual and formal styles, for the Ballymacarrett area alone. Of particular importance is the sharp sex stratification. The men 'back' the vowels more in both styles, while the women approximate more closely to the middle-class norms. Ballymacarrett has the most dense and multiplex networks found. Milroy (1987: 79f.) argues that density of network goes with polarization of sexual roles. It is the men in Ballymacarrett, with local employment, who form the most dense and multiplex network found. The women's personal networks are 'measurably and significantly less dense than the men's'. The nature of the networks and the linguistic scores by sex correlate in this community. Presumably, the women of Ballymacarrett have *less normative pressure from local patterns of interaction than do the men, and a wider experience of the 'outside', and this is reflected in their scores.*

6.5c   The remaining diagrams give the results for the Hammer
6.5d   and the Clonard. The most striking contrast with Ballymacarrett is that there is relatively little sex differentiation of the scores in these two areas. This reflects the fact
that only Ballymacarrett has the traditional structure of a
working-class community with local employment, dense
networks and clearly demarcated sex roles. In the case of
the Hammer, the collapse of social networks and the mobility of the inhabitants have levelled out the sex differences
in network density and multiplexity. In the Clonard, this
effect is due to the extensive male unemployment. There
remains one extremely important result. In diagrams a
and d, it is clear that the *younger Clonard women* 'cross
over' and have unexpectedly high linguistic scores. The
women aged from eighteen to twenty-five in the Clonard
who were interviewed formed a single localized cluster.
As a group, their networks were the most dense and multiplex in west Belfast. That is, the network structure of the
young women in Clonard was denser and more multiplex
than that of the men, reversing the Ballymacarrett pattern. The high linguistic scores of the young women in the
Clonard correlated with their high network density and
multiplexity.

   The (a) variable in Belfast is a case of linguistic innovation away
from middle-class norms. The innovation began within the most
socially stable and most highly ranked of the working-class communities, Ballymacarrett, and is most advanced among the men
there. They form a very dense and multiplex network, based on
local employment and its consequent territoriality. The norms of
the other two lower ranked communities are paradoxically closer
to those of the middle classes. The 'backing' innovation is spreading
to the Hammer and Clonard. In particular it is being introduced
into the Clonard by its young women. This is striking because it is
a non-standard innovation. What these points of innovation and
diffusion have in common is homogeneity and tight social cohesion.
The individuals at these points have the highest degree of integration, in terms of their interactions, into close-knit communities

which thus exert strong normative pressure. Overt 'society-wide' norms exercise less influence in these circumstances.

What we can say, in general, is that the strength of social networks serves as a norm enforcement mechanism. It stands to reason that in primary groups, where there is dense and varied face-to-face interaction, people will have a powerful normative effect on each other. Normative pressures are focused, rather than diffuse (Milroy, 1987: 178f.). A strong sense of group identity and solidarity generates cultural focusing, and this results in both the clarity of the linguistic norms of the group (as opposed to other groups) and a pressure to conform as an expression of individual identity.

In linguistic terms, a high degree of social cohesion sustains and reinforces the vernacular. If that cohesion weakens or breaks down – for example, as a result of urban renewal and dispersion – then norms become more diffuse. Weakening of network strength opens the way for normative pressures from outside the group, normally the society-wide norms of overt prestige, to have a greater effect. This is exactly what we observed when we looked at Labov's research into social mobility. Recall that it was the upwardly mobile strata who hypercorrected – who seemingly were most subject to pressure from above. Mobility thus relates to diffuseness of norms. Individuals fall in varying ways between normative pressures, and where and how they fall depends on their social networks.

But this leaves us with a paradox with respect to the innovative backing of (a) by the men of Ballymacarrett. As the group with the strongest social networks they will experience the greatest normative pressure. Thus they ought to be conservative. But we have seen that they are also leading something new, the backing innovation. We also just said that it was *weaker* network strength that led to the introduction of new norms from *outside* a group. And, in fact, the (a) backing did originate 'outside' Belfast in the rural Scots-Irish dialect area of adjacent North County Down. How was this most dense and multiplex group of working-class men able to be the leading edge in this change (Milroy and Milroy, 1985, 1992)? So we haven't yet got the complete story with respect to linguistic innovation. We shall return to this below.

We should not assume, however, that strength of social networks, and focused norms, are features only of working-class community

and vernacular. We saw in chapter three the importance of residential segregation and clearly defined domains in the maintenance of separate languages. Milroy (1987: 180) argues that
close-knit networks and consequent focusing can occur in any
strata. In British society focusing in fact characterizes the highest
and lowest classes. The argument here is that it is from dense and
multiplex social networks at the upper edge of society that the
highly focused RP norm emerges and is sustained (Milroy and
Milroy, 1992: 17). To this degree, it is like any vernacular. But,
unlike the others, it is also legitimated by the overall ideology of
the society – by, for example, its notions of status and mobility. It
is institutionalized and thus becomes a society-wide force.

Sex and gender

Next we will look at sexual differentiation. Like social networks,
work on this variable has been important in calling into question
the primacy of stratification in the older sociolinguistic research.
Work on women's language and a feminist critique of methodology have developed a great deal in the last fifteen years (Coates,
1993; Cameron, 1985, 1990; Cameron and Coates, 1988).

It is customary to distinguish between sex and gender. The
category of sex is taken to refer to differences between females
and males which are based on biology. By contrast, 'gender' is a
sociological category. It characterizes the socio-cultural features
of identity which make up the contrast between 'masculine' and
'feminine', in being 'men' and 'women' in a given society. Genders
have histories, so one can talk about the category 'woman' in
different historical epochs and cultures. People are socialized into
gender characteristics, not born with them. Above and beyond
any sex differences as regards speech, for example in pitch due to
the length of the vocal chords, language varies according to gender, and therefore has a role in this aspect of social identity. Gender maps on to sex. But the relationship is not as obvious as one
might first think. In the unmarked case, the feminine is female,
but the possibility exists of all sorts of interplay between the categories, and the relation changes with age. There are many kinds
of girls and women. It is usually argued that speech differences

between men and women are gender, not sex, characteristics. But there are exceptions to this view. Chambers (1995: 132f.) argues that women display superior verbal abilities, and this may be a biological difference between the sexes.

We shall look at linguistic variables of the kind which are familiar. There is a central issue that has arisen with regard to sex/gender differentiation in study after study.

The typical pattern

There is a typical pattern whereby women's scores approximate more closely to the standard prestige variant than do men's. Figure 6.6 reveals this patterning for two widely separated examples: (r) absence in Detroit and the (ing) variable in Norwich. Women have more *r* in Detroit and more of the prestige form of (ing) in Norwich than men, for all classes. Coates (1993) marshals results that show that women use more prestige forms than men. She cites studies of variables from Glasgow, West Wirral (near Liverpool) and Sydney, Australia, as well as Norwich, and Romaine's study in Edinburgh. Recall that gender differentiation was the single most important factor in the speech of the Edinburgh schoolchildren. And it was the girls who favoured the more prestigious continuant form. By contrast, the boys were more oriented to the vernacular. In New York, Labov reported that it was the women among the lower middle class who were the most linguistically insecure and style shifted towards the prestige norms most sharply. All these results support the typical pattern.

By every measure, women consistently achieve scores closer to the standard, to the form which has overt prestige and is enforced, according to Labov, by normative pressure from above. But why this is so is not at all clear! The result is clear, the explanation problematical. The attempts at explanation have been useful in revealing issues in sociolinguistic theory (Coates and Cameron, 1988).

The first kind of explanation is in terms of status. It is found in early studies such as Labov (1972) and especially Trudgill (1974: 94). In status explanations, the typical pattern is explained in terms of the subordinate role of women in the society. It is a reflex of

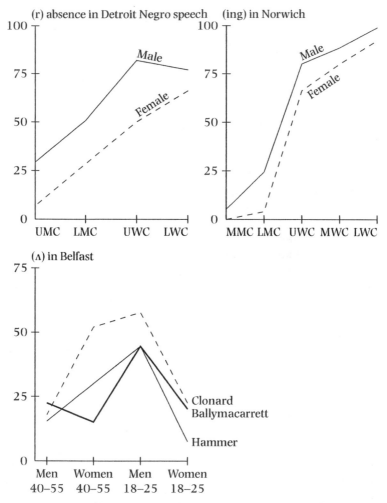

Figure 6.6 Sex differences in speech (*from Wolfram, 1969; Trudgill, 1974; and Milroy and Milroy, 1978*)

women's powerlessness. Social status in western industrial society mainly depends on a person's occupation. Adult men commonly have direct access to these sources of social status. Women as a group are excluded from this direct validation. The theory is that this leads to a heightened sensitivity to the *symbolic* markers of status, among which are the prestige variants in speech. Thus, women are more linguistically status conscious, more susceptible to 'pressure from above' than are men. This interpretation is corroborated in Trudgill's Norwich study by the tendency of women to **over-report**; that is, to claim that they are using more of the standard forms than they actually are. This is a nice symptom of normative pressure 'from above'. On the other hand, men tended to **under-report**. This is the opposite case of claiming to use more vernacular forms than they actually do. There are other explanations which account for the pattern in terms of women's relative powerlessness; but these see it not so much as a matter of symbolic compensation for status deficit, but as a positive strategy deployed in conversation to gain advantage. For example, Deuchar (1988: 27f.) motivates women's choice of variant in terms of politeness (see below, chapter eight). Women could be choosing the prestige variant to enhance the social attributes they project, and hence the social identity claimed in specific interactions. They can do this and still be polite because they are *in fact* relatively powerless and routinely play themselves down in order to enhance and protect the identities of others. The fact that women are not threatening permits them to enhance their identities with 'power' speech. This also enlarges the linguistic repertoire available and hence is socially useful for a gender otherwise economically disadvantaged. Elyan *et al.* (1978) studied informants' perception of RP speaking women in Lancashire. The accent itself conveys very positive social information about attributes like competence and intelligence (but not 'warmth' or 'reliability', see below chapter eight). The surprising result was that 'The female RP accent is the voice of perceived androgyny.' The voices were perceived *at the same time as more feminine and more masculine* than the local northern accent. *This is a very useful social meaning because it extends the individual's repertoire of behaviour.* In both these cases, we have a motivation for the intentional use of prestige variants which might explain the typical pattern. It is not just a consequence of the compensatory status consciousness of those without status.

However, these accounts are operating in a world defined by social stratification, with the standard at the metaphorical top and the vernacular at the metaphorical bottom. Looking at gender within this model of research foregrounds differences only with respect to these dimensions. The way the question is worded, the women's scores are viewed as *anomalous*. They are more standard than one would expect on the basis of class alone. And more standard than men's speech. This central issue in studying women's speech is generated by a paradigm of research based on a certain model of stratification. And the question posed by the result shows that women's speech is viewed as 'marked', an anomaly requiring special explanation.

Before going any further, it is worth pointing out that a number of scholars have more broadly criticized how social class has been used in sociolinguistics (Rickford, 1986; Milroy and Milroy, 1992: 1–5 and see below). Early sociolinguistic surveys relied on previous sociological social class constructs and simply adapted them without question (Labov, 1966; Trudgill, 1974). The measures used to determine class were 'objective'; for example, income, occupation, place of residence and so on. But people have argued that class may also have an important 'subjective' dimension in terms of values, etc. The models of class used have relied on the importance of occupation. Trudgill (1974: 36–7) notes the overriding importance of occupational position as a measure of social class in industrial societies. But such 'objective' measures make class problematic with respect to women. Often it has been the occupation of husband or father (and 'his' income) that figures in the assignment of class to women, if they are not independently employed. Thus, many women were assigned to classes only with respect to men. More recently, it has been suggested that the traditional family and the relation of class and occupation may be changing in ways that might affect the measurement of class. In post-industrial societies there is widespread male unemployment, much more female employment outside the home and an increasing number of people who live alone, are divorced, or single parents. Less than half the population live in traditional families.

There is no doubt however that given the design of the research, the results obtained are indisputable. But we could re-phrase the questions! Instead of viewing women's scores as anomolous, we could ask, 'Why are men's index scores lower than one would expect from their position in the class system?' The 'sexist' problematization of the results is obvious if one puts it this way. Coates (1993: 81) makes the interpretative issue more precise. The groups that deviate most in the *direction* of the preferences that one would expect solely on the basis of their class are middle-class men and working-class women. The former tend more towards vernacular scores than their class affiliation would predict. The latter score higher than their class as a whole. By contrast, working-class men and middle-class women are most extreme in line with their class positions. These groups don't seem to be in a position of conflict as between class and prestige. Put this way, the results offer no evidence that women as a gender are more sensitive to the social significance of linguistic variables *per se* than men as a gender.

One possibility is that men are more sensitive to what was earlier termed 'covert prestige' or 'pressure from below'. (We will be criticizing these notions shortly.) Trudgill (1974: 94) attempted to explain this by aligning masculinity with working-class values. The vernacular had connotations of masculinity which accrued to it by virtue of the perceived roughness and toughness of working-class life. The trouble with this is that it excludes women from any other values of working-class life (locality, solidarity) which might be associated with vernacular speech. It makes the vernacular a colony of the male. And it is hard to see that the symbolism of *machismo* masculinity by itself might mean enough to upwardly mobile or upper-middle-class men to produce a general lowering of their scores.

Milroy and Milroy (1993) proposed another account of the problem of the typical pattern. The forms preferred by women bore prestige, not because of the fact that they were used by the highest strata, but *because* they were used by women. The origin of prestige wasn't class, but gender. One can interpret this in terms of an ideology of the feminine (stereotypes of civilization, gentleness, gentility etc.) which is the *source* of prestige in society. Each class of men would aspire in different ways to this 'civilized' feminine form of life and reject the overtly stigmatized ideology of the masculine. The effectiveness of such a hypothesis would depend on how it explained patterns of change for each variable.

Networks and the typical pattern

We will now see if this typical pattern can be related to the complex way in which sex is interwoven with the other variables in Belfast. It was characteristic of many Belfast variables that women's scores tended to follow the vernacular less closely than did those of men (Milroy, 1987: 112f.). But this interacted with age, network structure and neighbourhood. It was also explicable in terms of social network.

We can take Ballymacarrett as typical of the sex pattern in a working-class community. Recall that in Figure 6.5b women's scores were closer to the prestige norm than were men's for the variable (a). The bottom diagram in Figure 6.6 shows index scores for another variable. This is (ʌ), which represents a lowered and backed variant of the sound in a small set of words like '*pull*', '*took*', '*shook*' and '*foot*'. (In other words, in this community, the vowel is pronounced somewhat like the RP vowel in the words *hut* and *shut*.) The index score is the percentage of this lower variant in such words, as opposed to a raised and centralized alternant. The lower form is stigmatized in Belfast, so lower scores signify the prestige variant. As we would expect, Ballymacarrett women in both age groups have lower scores in Figure 6.6 than do their men. For both (a) and (ʌ) the typical sex pattern can be observed in this community.

But Ballymacarrett is also typical of the way sex roles are handled in working-class communities in general. Milroy points out, as we said above, that dense and multiplex networks foster sex-role differentiation. Quoting Bott (1971), Milroy (1987: 135) points out that the kinds of social networks which people have determine the way that they divide up responsibility for tasks within marriage and, in general, how independent they are of each other. The idea is that dense and multiplex social networks contracted before marriage enforce group norms even after marriage, and so there is marital segregation – sharp differences between men and women – in communities with such networks. We saw that Ballymacarrett was the most dense and multiplex of the communities studied.

This separation of the sexes is sustained by the local male employment in the shipyards and the territoriality of Ballymacarrett.

Within this sexual role specialization, men's social networks are more dense and multiplex than women's. There was enhanced male solidarity. By contrast, the women had lower network scores. And they also worked outside the local community.

So we have an explanation for the gender differentiation based on social networks and sex role differentiation in *micro* social structure. In communities of this type, men are relatively more integrated into social networks which act as norm enforcement mechanisms for the vernacular. Women are relatively less integrated and therefore under relatively less normative pressure. At the same time, women have more contacts outside the community. Taken together, these suggest that women are under less peer pressure to conform to vernacular norms and have alternative models which may be of social value. Therefore, the typical pattern may not be a result of a positive preference for the overtly prestigious norm of the standard, or a flight from male vernacular values. Rather, it may be the result of the experience of more variation and hence less focused norms, less normative pressure, and the exploitation of variation for communicative purposes in ways similar to those suggested by Deuchar and Elyan above. Chambers (1995: 125–6) puts this as a generalization: 'In societies where gender roles are sharply differentiated such that one gender has wider social contacts and greater geographical range, the speech of the less circumscribed gender will include more variants of the contiguous social groups.'

Female innovation

We now have an explanation of the typical pattern of gender differentiation in terms of density and multiplexity of social networks and sex role differentiation. One test of this sort of explanation would be if we can find a situation where sex differences in network strength differ from the norm and this corresponds to a reversal in the linguistic behaviour of men and women. Gender differences would be predicted by differences in *micro* social structure. (Of course, these will also relate to *macro* processes going on in the society like patterns of unemployment, social mobility etc., see below.) This is exactly what we find in the Clonard.

The sex differentiation in the Clonard is the most interesting of all. In a community with the lowest network density and multiplexity of the three due to high male unemployment, it was younger women who had introduced the backing of (a) into the community. The young Clonard women formed a very dense and multiplex cluster – they worked together and spent their leisure time together. In fact, the shape of their social life was of a kind that would, in a more typical community, characterize younger male groups. They had the highest network scores of any sub-group. (By contrast, young Ballymacarrett women had the lowest network scores of any sub-group.) Milroy (1987: 144) writes:

> very dense, multiplex networks are associated particularly with men living in working class communities of a traditional kind, with a locally-based homogeneous form of employment. More specifically, network structures in the three areas . . . seem likely to co-vary to some extent with factors like the stability of the area and availability of male employment locally. The men in Ballymacarrett lived in conditions particularly likely to favour the formation of dense, multiplex networks and polarization of the sexes. Conversely, the young women in the Clonard contrast with the men in being fully employed, and have developed the solidary relationships of the kind usually associated with *men* of the same age.

So this group of women has introduced a vernacular innovation, the backing of (a), originally associated with men in Ballymacarrett, into the Clonard.

Now let us look at the variable (ʌ) in Figure 6.6. We saw how in Belfast as a whole it is the higher, central variant which has overt prestige, and the lower, backed variant which carries overt stigma. But this is not so in terms of *vernacular* prestige. The lower, backed (ʌ) has conscious vernacular prestige – 'it is almost *prescribed* amongst adolescent and other close-knit male peer groups' (Milroy and Milroy, 1978: 26). This would seem to be an example of pressure from above being overtly exerted in favour of a non-standard within a specific sub-group. A variant which is overtly stigmatized in the wider society nevertheless has overt prestige in the sub-group.

These norms are reflected in the bottom diagram in Figure 6.6. Older men seem to favour the standard variant in all the communities. Women in Hammer and Ballymacarrett and the younger women in the Clonard also favour the form with society-wide prestige. But younger men and *older women* in the Clonard have high percentages of the vernacular form. The conclusion is that just as today's young women have introduced the backing of (a) into the Clonard from a higher-status community outside, so when today's older women were younger they had done the same thing with (ʌ).

For these variables, Clonard women do not follow the typical pattern. Other studies, by Trudgill (1972) and Chambers and Trudgill (1980: 99), also suggest that younger women are sensitive to covert prestige and non-standard forms. We saw in Edinburgh that there was some shifting to the boys' vernacular among girls in reading style.

Our conclusion with respect to gender and linguistic variation is complex and cautious. The typical pattern isn't inevitable. It gains its *visibility* because it forced its way into attention as a consequence of the stratification model employed in early *macro*-social or *gesellschaft* research. Neither is it an inevitable result of any *intrinsic* female conservatism or sensitivity to status, overt prestige or pressure from above. Rather, it is a reflex of gender differentiation at the *micro*-social or network level which results in different kinds of exposure to norms, with different degrees of normative pressure, for women and men. It is possible that the greater diversity available to women might be deployed strategically in conversation, to convey social meanings (see 'code-switching' above for a similar phenomenon). Given that gender differentiation is the result of such social factors, if the other sex were put into a similar social situation, similar results might be expected (everything else being equal). It is possible, as Chambers suggests, that there might be sex differences to do with verbal ability, but it would be very hard to distinguish that from socially motivated differentiation in skills. Finally, it would be interesting to compare network results from middle-class professional couples where one or the other or both partners worked with respect to gender differentiation.

Class and social network have been highlighted in this section, but clearly gender differentiation interacts in complex ways with the other social factors. There is now a considerable body of multi-disciplinary research on many other important issues to do with gender and language: for example, gender differences in conversational interaction; the representation of women and how gender is discursively constructed; the role of language in social-ization into the genders; the hypothesis of men's possession of language itself (see Spender, 1985); the role of 'sexist' assumptions throughout linguistics (see Cameron, 1985; Mills, 1995; Coates, 1993). Unfortunately, these issues are outside our purview.

Ethnicity

Perhaps **ethnicity** is the hardest to define of all the large-scale social variables used in sociolinguistics (Edwards, 1985; Fishman, 1989). People in western industrial societies tend to think of eth-nic groups as **minority ethnic groups** within a larger host soci-ety; for example, immigrant groups like Italians in Toronto, Jews in New York, West Indians in London, Koreans in Los Angeles or Asians in Bradford. But ethnic affiliation is a *general* aspect of social space. Dominant host ethnicities like the English, French, Germans or Great Russians are also labels for ethnic identities. If an ethnicity is expressed politically in (the demand for) its own autonomous institutions in a state as an ethnic 'homeland', we can speak of **nationalism**. As we saw in Quebec, ethnicity can be symbolized by language. Dominant ethnicities often have developed autonomous standard languages parallel to their ethnic autonomy. They feel they 'own' their language. But an ethnic group need not be *very* nationalistic (e.g. the Welsh) or be dis-tinguished by an autonomous language (e.g. the 'Scots-Irish' or 'Ulster Protestants').

So what is ethnicity? It is a category similiar to gender. That is, it is a shared socio-historical construct based on a putative his-torical experience which is the genealogy of a 'people'. Internally, it acts as a focus for 'we-feeling' and solidarity. Externally, the ethnic identity of a group can be stereotyped by other groups. It can be created and utilized to represent the 'other' to those outside it. It inexorably involves a dialectic of identity between groups. Ethnic identity depends on narratives of the unique history of the group; sometimes also a myth of biological distinctiveness or **race**, claims of shared descent or kinship, usually a geographical homeland and defining culture, especially a religion. In one sense, ethnicity is benign. It is about human diversity. But it is also a dangerous social space because it is about 'us' over and against some 'them'. This can lead to paranoid ethnicity (we are victims) or conversely, supremicist ethnicity (we are better than them). **Racialism** is the ideology of ethnic difference deployed to the disadvantage of the 'other', especially when the differences are imagined to be biologically based. Linguistic variants, either *inter-* or *intra-*language, correlate with this complex of attitudes and practices.

We will look at two examples, both of minorities in American society. Martha Laferriere studied ethnicity and linguistic variation in Boston, Massachusetts. She noted how ethnic minorities formed subcultures with traits and organizations which 'provide the **cultural force** to transmit the particular groups esteemed, educational, occupational and linguistic values' (1979: 615). She studied the (or) variable. This has to do with the relative height of the vowel in words like '*form*', '*short*' and '*horse*'. The lower variant characterized the Boston vernacular while the more close variant characterized a standard pronunciation. For vernacular speakers, using the lower variant, the word '*short*' would rhyme with '*shot*'.

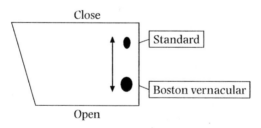

In the Boston study, ethnic group was found to correlate with the percentage of the lower variant found. (The significance of ethnic group was not surprising since this was also a major factor for the variables in Labov's New York research.) In Boston, speakers aged over sixty, in all three of the ethnic groups studied, almost exclusively used the vernacular form. It seemed that the standard variant had entered ethnic speech as an alternative way of pronouncing words of this type. A variable feature had been created for speakers under sixty. Clearly a linguistic change was

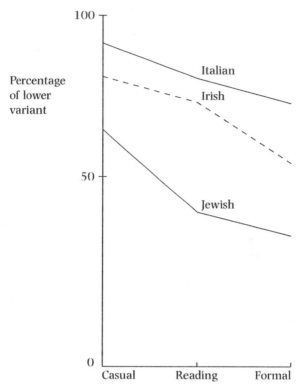

Figure 6.7 Variation by ethnic group in Boston (*from Laferriere, 1979*)

occurring. The ethnic groups differed in their treatment of this
new prestige variant. Figure 6.7 displays the percentages of the
lower vernacular variant for the three ethnic groups.

Laferriere advanced the hypothesis that the change was proceeding through the ethnic groups in the following way. In the
first stage, some members of an ethnic group acquire, mainly as a
by-product of education, a positive knowledge of the norms of the
wider community. They know that the vernacular is stigmatized
but it remains their active, automatic form of speech. People in
this position ought to be very sensitive to the stylistic significance
of the variants, and style-shift in an extreme way. In stage two,
this knowledge is transmitted to some younger speakers in their

ethnic group. These make the prestige variant their 'active' automatic form. In the final stage, acceptance of the new standard becomes generalized among the younger speakers of the ethnic group. At this stage, for speakers in this ethnic group the older vernacular form is both stigmatized and perceived as representing those other ethnic groups who have not yet begun to participate in the change.

A study of educational levels and age, and the utilization of the stylistic significance of the variants, led to the conclusion that the Jewish ethnic group had completed all three stages of the change. By contrast, the Irish group was at the second stage, and for the Italians stage one was just beginning. The fact that only *older* Jewish speakers utilized the stylistic distinctiveness of the variants, although the Jewish group had the most standard scores overall, suggested that the change was most advanced in this group. The Irish were the only group where there was a systematic relationship between the years of education a speaker had and his proclivity to use the variants stylistically. For these speakers, education had brought with it an awareness that the variants were respectively prestigious and stigmatized. The Italian group was only beginning to be aware of the stylistic significance of the variants. For example, those Italians with the highest education were those that style-shifted the least.

This pattern, if correct, illustrates how movement 'outside' the networks of a group (in this case an ethnic group) can be the means by which pressure from above can be introduced into the group. Education was the means of transmission of norms in this example. Ethnic groups are important because the members of each group stand in different relationship to the variants, both in terms of the frequencies used, and in the perception of their social meaning. The groups evaluated the vernacular variant differently. There was a measurably weaker stigma attached to it by Irish and Italian speakers. Laferriere hypothesizes that this form will remain variable; the change will not reach a completion in the universal acceptance of the standard form. The 'cultural force' of the ethnic group will preserve the vernacular variant, because it has also come to be a symbol of ethnic identity.

Black English vernacular

Black Englishes are ethnic dialects which are strikingly different from standard English. The reasons for this are historical. I have outlined some current issues about the origins and relations of black and white vernaculars in the USA in the box on pages 218–19. One must be cautious about speaking of any *one* black English for there are many. There are the standard African 'new Englishes' discussed in chapter two. But the name 'Black English' refers to Caribbean creoles, black British English and the non-standard vernaculars spoken by black people in the United States. There has recently been important work on black English in Britain (Edwards, 1986; Sebba, 1993). Black British English is the result of a 'contact situation' which, beginning in the 1950s, brought Caribbean creoles into contact with British varieties in the United Kingdom. Edwards studied the creole, called 'patois' by its speakers, with respect to young people of West Indian descent. She found that its use related to the degree of integration into the black community, level of education and attitudes to whites. As in the Milroy studies, degree of integration served as a norm enforcement mechanism.

In mainland America, not only are there the non-standard black vernaculars of the south, the source of black speech in the north (see chapter five, page 172), but there are the new black vernaculars of the northern inner cities. Labov began his investigation into this ethnic dialect of the inner city in the study of pre-adolescent and adolescent gangs in Harlem (Labov, 1972a; Labov *et al.*, 1968). He originally labelled this street speech **Black English Vernacular** or **BEV** for short, although this term is now widely used for all non-standard black speech. He noted that **BEV** was a vital and innovative urban vernacular highly resistant to 'pressure from above'. Labov (1972: 299f.) says, 'in the larger ghetto areas, we find black speakers participating in a very different set of changes bearing no direct relation to the characteristic pattern of the white community'. But this view of divergence has recently been challenged, as pointed out in the 'issues box'. It is important to note though that new vernaculars are being created around the world as people leave hinterlands and flood into cities.

Issues in Black English: a note

Why should there be divergence between black and white ethnic vernaculars in the United States? This is rooted in the historical circumstances in which Black English originated.

The creole hypothesis. By the 1980s the consensus was that Black English Vernacular began as a contact language of the sort described in chapter two. Under the historical conditions of slavery, people of diverse African mother tongues were thrown together with limited access to a single superordinate variety, English. These are precisely the conditions for pidginization and creolization. Hence, contemporary black vernacular began life as a creole (Labov, 1972a, 1982; Dillard, 1972; Rickford, 1977; Bailey, 1965; Stewart, 1967). Stewart writes:

> the Negro slaves who constituted the field labor force on North American plantations . . . spoke a variety of English which was in fact a true creole language – differing markedly in grammatical structure from those English dialects which were brought directly from Great Britain . . . and, although this creole English subsequently underwent modification in the direction of the more prestigious British-derived dialects, the merging process was neither instantaneous nor uniform. Indeed, the nonstandard speech of present day American Negros still seems to exhibit structural traces of a creole predecessor, and this is probably a reason why it is in some ways more deviant from standard English than is non-standard speech of even the most uneducated American whites.

Decreolization. So there is linguistic evidence that black vernacular was once more like the creoles of the Caribbean. And there is a true creole, **Gullah**, spoken in the coastal regions of Georgia and South Carolina, which also has many African features. Creoles in the Caribbean and elsewhere vary along a **creole continuum** from the most deeply creole, the **basilect**, to middle varieties, **mesolects**, to more standard-like dialects, the **acrolect**. It is hypothesized that this continuum is the result of **decreolization**. Through contact and over time there are complicated but regular linguistic processes by which creoles converge towards the standard language.

White and black vernacular contact. One factor that originally caused problems for the creole hypothesis was the fact that black and white vernaculars in the American south share many features. Traditional dialectologists argued for non-creole origins in the non-standard white dialects. But the relation of black and white vernaculars in the south is complex and there is evidence of black influence on white speech as well as white influence on black speech. This accounts for some of the similarities (Labov, 1982: 175–6, 192).

Convergence versus Divergence. If we accept creole origins and subsequent decreolization, then it follows that over time black and white varieties are **converging**. But Labov has long argued that urban BEV is something new (1972: 299). More recently he has argued that black and white varieties are **diverging**. In Labov's studies in Philadelphia, blacks are the *only* group not participating in a general sound change in progress. Bailey and Maynor (1986) have marshalled a number of features which they claim are evidence for divergence. For example, they point out that southern blacks are not participating in the increase in *r*-full pronunciation among southern whites. They also claim that the specialized aspectual meaning of invariant 'be' before verb + -*ing* is an innovation. Bailey argues that if at first black and white speech converged, up to about 1915, since then it has diverged. One inference is that this is due today to increasing black racial isolation in the inner cities.

The most careful and comprehensive survey of the issue to date, Butters 1989 (also see Spears' 1992 review), suggests that a strong view of divergence is incorrect and the evidence is at best inconclusive, illustrating mild convergence in many cases. Consider the survey of black *r* in chapter five, where even in Philadelphia, we see convergence of black to white norms. The issue remains unresolved and of methodological importance (Wald, 1995). Perhaps both processes are going on at the same time with respect to different variables in different black sub-communities, interacting with other social factors.

Here we shall simply examine three well-known features of all varieties of black vernacular speech in the USA. All three involve forms of the word 'be'. The first is the use of **invariant be** to refer to characteristics of events in time. Such meanings are termed **aspects** of the system of the verb. The second feature is also aspectual. It is the strongly stressed use of 'been', which we can write as BIN, mimicking its pronunciation. These two features are chosen because they demonstrate the linguistic distance between black and white vernaculars. The third feature is the variable deletion of 'be' in many environments. This feature illustrates the systematic relation between the dialects.

First, the invariant 'be'. This is the use of the auxiliary verb 'be' before a noun in the -*ing* form in sentences such as 1 and 2.

1. This woman *be* wait*in*' on the bus.
2. He always *be* try*in*' to catch up.

This use is interpreted as referring to the shape of the event in time. Either the event is habitual, occurring over and over again, as in 2, or it refers to duration over an indefinite period of time. Use of this form doesn't occur significantly in southern white vernaculars. And it has become a conscious prestige marker of urban black youth (Butters, 1989). Bailey and Maynor (1986) regard the increasing use of this form with this meaning as an innovation which is a sign of black-white divergence. But Rickford (1977) plausibly argues for creole origins with examples. Black vernacular is very rich in such ways of distinguishing events in time, making contrasts which differ from other dialects. The aspectual stressed BIN is another example of this. Sentences 3 and 4 illustrate this form.

3. I *BIN* know you you know.
4. She *BIN* married.

BIN signifies that the event began in the remote past. It only implies 'completion of the event' with some verbs, and does not do so in our examples. Thus, 3 means 'I have known you for a long time, and still do' (Rickford, 1977: 206) and 4 means that she was married in the remote past *and still is*. Labov (1982: 191) reports experiments where whites systematically misunderstand sentences like 4, mistakenly taking them to imply that she is *not* still married. These aspectual distinctions are not available in either standard or white non-standard varieties of English.

Let us now turn to the deletion of 'be'. At first glance, this appears to be a BEV feature that is very different from standard. But as we shall see, the rule deleting 'be' is systematically and closely related to the rules of standard and other dialects. There are four possibilities with regard to the copula in English: the full variant; the contracted variant (captured by the apostrophe in writing); the deleted variant typifying BEV; and the invariant 'be', just discussed. The first three can be illustrated:

Full variant	Contracted variant	Deleted variant
She is real nice	*She's real nice*	*She real nice*
She is a nurse	*She's a nurse*	*She a nurse*
Some say you are going to die	*Some say you're gonna die*	*Some say you gonna die*

This variable is one in which superficially there is a real discontinuity between white and black communities. Only black English permits deletion. But the situation is more subtle than that. Figure 6.8 displays Wolfram's analysis of the percentage of contracted and deleted forms for the black social classes in Detroit and the white upper-middle-class group. Out of the total number of possibilities for 'doing something' to *be*, whether contraction or deletion, all the groups are roughly the same. That is, they all have roughly the same percentages of full forms. And this includes the white group.

The crucial factor for the black groups is the ratio of deleted to contracted forms. The white group uses no deleted forms at all, as expected. But the relative percentage of deletions for the black groups increases as one moves downward through the social classes, relative to the number of contractions, until it reaches 56.9 per cent deletion and 25.0 per cent contraction in members of the black lower working class. As was the case with (r), the black middle classes, under pressure from above, have adopted the white norm of contraction and delete very little. Style-shifting

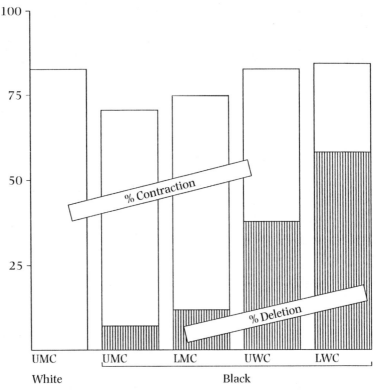

Figure 6.8 'Be' in Detroit Negro speech (*after Wolfram, 1969*)

is in the direction of contraction, testifying to its overt prestige. Conversely, the black working-class vernacular is characterized by deletion.

But to return to the question of the apparently sharp linguistic discontinuity between the ethnic groups: it is true that the white groups in Detroit never delete, but the varieties are in a systematic, structured relation to one another. Black and white treatments can be covered under a single rule. Both groups can optionally reduce the full form of the copula in certain specific environments – these are practically the same for either variety. In the standard, the form can only be contracted. *And wherever it can be contracted in the standard it can be either contracted or deleted in the vernacular.* The reduction process is carried one step further – but it is still part of the same process.

There is a great deal more that could be said about 'be' and many other features of black English. I have only scratched the surface. There are serious educational and political issues involved when dialects diverge in ways that could disadvantage the dialect speaker. Black English, and non-standards generally, are often the target of stereotyped perceptions which denigrate their speakers. We saw in chapter two that such attitudes are fostered by standardization itself. Such prejudice combined with ignorance about dialects among teachers can affect perception of children's intelligence or educational progress, for example in writing or spelling. Labov (1982) reports on the 'Black English trial' in Ann Arbor, Michigan, in which concerned black parents sued a school on the grounds that its lack of linguistic recognition of BEV had led to disastrous educational outcomes for their children. Edwards (1984) discusses such issues from a British angle. But BEV and creoles in Britain have also increasingly been a force in popular culture, especially in music, and have prestige in youth culture. For the linguistics of BEV, the reader is referred to the literature, especially Butters (1989), Dillard (1972), Labov (1972a, 1982), Fasold (1969, 1972) and Wolfram (1971, 1974).

Age

In the course of these chapters it has become obvious that age interacts with other social variables in complex ways. We saw, for example, the age-grading effect in (r) in New York which allowed us to say that a linguistic change was taking place. We saw the preference of younger male speakers in Belfast for the vernacular (ʌ) variant, and the role of younger Clonard women in spreading the (a) innovation.

There is a recurring pattern in which scores of younger speakers are closer to the vernacular, and away from overt prestige norms. If one wants to observe the most extreme forms of vernacular speech, the place to look is among male adolescent 'peer groups'. For example, Labov's (1972a) study of the peer groups in Harlem found higher percentages of copula-deletion than among adult blacks.

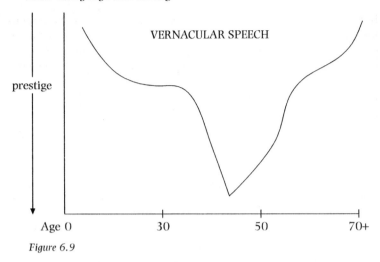

Figure 6.9

The peer groups, close-knit clusters in social network terms, differed also between each other. Peer groups of young people exert great normative pressure on each other, and are correspondingly less susceptible to society-wide norms conveyed to them by the institutions of the adult and outside world, for example, in schools. When this is reinforced by ethnicity, one gets a strikingly different dialect such as the black English vernacular.

The normal pattern of age differentiation, when a variable is not in the process of change, has roughly the shape illustrated above. We can explain this diagram in terms of the pressures of different sorts of norms for different age groups. It is those in the middle age groups, those who are working and who are contacting other groups and other society-wide values, whose social identity must deal with pressure from 'outside'. Lives become more 'public' at the middle period.

The relationship between age and variation also depends on the way in which accent is acquired and made part of 'automatic' motor production. It is this automatic speech that is an individual's vernacular. It contrasts with the speech that occurs when people exercise conscious control of their pronunciation in formal styles. At different ages individuals are subject to different normative pressures.

It is the normative pressures that affect them when their vernacular is being acquired that are crucial. Of course, later circumstances can lead people to adapt their accents. We will be discussing linguistic accommodation in the next chapter. But from the point of view of the linguistic system itself, and from the point of view of that system changing, it is the continuum of vernaculars in time and social space that is significant. Self-conscious speech reflects the conflict and interaction of norms. We saw how hypercorrection transmits pressures from above to a younger generation, providing a model which is more 'standard' than parents' vernacular, and thus accelerating linguistic change.

One basic fact is that, as far as accent is concerned, children speak more like their peers than like their parents. There is controversy about the mechanism by which the vernacular accent is acquired. Labov (1972) distinguishes three stages. In stage one, ages two to three, the child has its first experience of language. At this stage the relevant social network is the child's immediate family. In stage two, ages four to thirteen, the basic vernacular accent is created. The most important normative pressure at this stage is the social network of peers. But hypercorrection shows us that parental speech interacts with this as a model. The accent an individual acquires at this stage depends on his or her network structure. Individuals on the periphery of clusters are subject to different, more diffuse and less focused norms, and accordingly deviate within their age group. In stage three, ages fourteen to seventeen, the evaluative norms of the wider community are acquired, and somewhat later, at age sixteen plus, the production of prestige forms begins. The networks operating at this stage are also very important for enforcing norms. In general, the structure is less tight-knit than the peer group. But we saw above how different network structures played a key role in the relative importance of vernacular and society-wide norms. These latter norms exert their greatest pressure during the working ages, and taper off again in favour of the vernacular over the age of fifty.

We have seen that if a linguistic change is taking place in the pronunciation of a variable, this is reflected in the average score by age. As each generation acquires its vernacular, the average score of that age group is further along the direction of the change

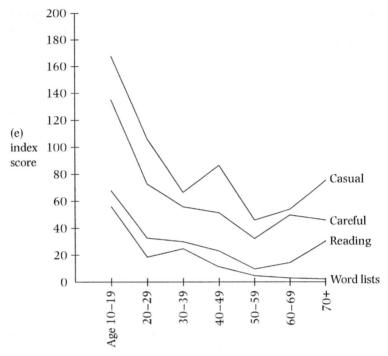

Figure 6.10 Norwich (e) by age and style (*from Chambers and Trudgill, 1980*)

than that of the immediately preceding generation. Each successive generation, having acquired the form later, will have gone
further than the last; so, in general, younger speakers will be more
advanced, and older speakers less advanced with respect to the
change. This is observable as age-grading when age is plotted
against average index scores. Normally, youngest speakers are most
advanced in the change, although this is not always so.

Figure 6.10 shows such a pattern for Norwich (e). You will
recall that this involved a vernacular innovation of centralizing
the vowel sound in words like '*bell*' and '*tell*'. Higher scores signified
a greater degree of centralization. Note the significant increases in
the degree of centralization for speakers under thirty, but especially
in the unconscious casual style, which most closely reveals the

basic form of the vernacular. We will be looking at this kind of pattern in the next chapter when we study the problem of language change.

Conflict, social class and social network

Two of the most important factors are social class, primarily associated with Labov's methodology, and social network, employed by the Milroys. In this section we will ask how these two might be related.

Each method both reveals and obscures. This is because it is only oriented to a single dimension of social space. Labov's use of class and style has a 'consensual' outlook. The standard norm unconsciously unites a large 'speech community' although it originates in the upper middle class and the overt prestige that relates to power. This presents a **status oriented model** of linguistic stratification. Although results can be studied with respect to other factors, the model is blind to the fact that the assignment of individuals to classes with respect to gender may be problematic. And it also takes no account of ethnicity or network type. Therefore, this model cannot explain the anomaly noted above – why are vernaculars so dynamic? The notion of 'covert prestige' and 'pressure from below' was introduced to deal with this. Although attitude studies, hypercorrection, style-shifting and over-reporting are all evidence of the domination of the superordinate class-based norms, we also find innovations *away from* the standard towards the vernacular. And sometimes *conscious prestige* is attached to vernacular speech.

The antidote to the status oriented model of a normatively unified speech community has been to look to smaller scale social structure, and find support for the vernacular in social networks. The powerful norm enforcement effects of network strength have provided a contrasting **solidarity oriented model** mainly based in urban working-class or ethnic groups. This provides a countervailing force to the dominant norms of the larger society. Aware of prestige norms from above, it has its own prestige norms.

This fractures the notion of a society unified with respect to prestige, into one where there is a recognition of potentially conflicting sources of valuation. The network and class models align social factors and language variety in the following way:

network	class
solidarity	**status**
norm enforcement	**normative consensus**
vernacular	**standard**
working class	**upper middle class**

There are other possible analyses of social class. Labov's model of class is under-theorized. It presupposes a 'consensual' community unified within a system of differentiation which stratifies people in terms of education, income and occupation and therefore access to power and prestige. An alternative model could presuppose conflict, not consensus. It was Marx who made class a sociological category. In a Marxist picture there is a basic conflict of class interest deriving from different relations to the means of production. This will shape and, in more recent analyses be shaped by, ideology; the practice (**praxis**) of the cultural superstructure which is unconsciously motivated by class interests. From this point of view standardization is 'ideological' in a deeper sense than merely aiming at an 'ideal' (see chapter two). As we saw, it is imposed by the **ideological state apparatus**, institutions of education and law (Althusser, 1977). The prestige of the standard rationalizes the class interests of its 'owners'; it is a form of cultural capital (Dittmar *et al.*, 1988). But it is 'imaginatively misrecognized' as the correct or true form of the language and symbol of a unified people.

Use of the standard will be a *site of unconscious ideological conflict* between the norm of the standard and norms of less powerful groupings: ethnic minorities, immigrants, aboriginal peoples, women, adolescent peer groups, deprived rural 'folk' communities, religious sects, traditional working-class communities, etc. Studies of attitudes reveal these conflicts in which people are **alienated** from their own practices. Conceptually, Voloshinov's influential *Marxism and the Philosophy of Language* (1973; in fact, possibly written by M. Bakhtin) rejected the notion of a linguistic sign as a unity, but claimed that all signs were ideological, had an 'inner dialectic quality' and were fundamentally **multi-accentual**, representing within themselves these conflicting social meanings and forces. Such a model would present a better picture of black vernacular innovation, anomalous attitudes, working-class 'covert prestige' (which isn't always covert) and so on. And we could highlight the idea of the standard as having social and economic value in a linguistic market, so that switching might be motivated socio-economically, but without unambivalent acceptance of evaluative norms depending on the situation. We saw above how something as subtle as unconscious linguistic androgyny could be very useful to a woman RP speaker.

If we turn to social networks we find that their use in research has been skewed towards results that are listed in the left hand column above. Social network studies have demonstrated the existence of strong networks which support the vernacular among the urban working class. But just as the usual model of class orients it towards a 'top down' consensus, this use of network orients it towards a 'bottom up' fragmented, perspective on society. But class and network are not incompatible models and recently efforts have been made to theoretically connect them.

Milroy and Milroy (1992) relate social network and social class through the concept of **network strength**. A network is strong if it is dense and multiplex. It is weak if the relationships are not dense – the members of an individual network do not relate to each other – and are uniplex; that is, people are known on only one basis. However, weak networks tend to be wider. They consist of multiple weak ties, instead of fewer dense and multiplex ones. (They are therefore much harder to study.) Now, relative network strength can apply to individuals or to groups. The working-class communities studied in Belfast were on the whole characterized by strong networks. The picture of social structure that emerges is of groups having **strong networks** with strong norm enforcement which are resistant to outside pressure. This leads to a potential fragmentation of society. However, there are other groups and individuals with **weak networks**. Such people transmit outside influences. They provide the bridges between the dense groups. This produces a social configuration with strong, relatively impervious nodes connected by weak networks.

Milroy and Milroy (1992) use the concept of weak network to relate network to class. We gain explanatory insight if we can align network types with social classes. They agree that the traditional urban working class is typified by locally based, strong networks. *By contrast the middle classes are characterized by weak networks.* Therefore, the middle classes are much more susceptible to normative influence from outside and are in contact with more people on a more diverse basis who will provide those influences. The Milroys also find they can align differences in network strength with different 'ways of life', which is another way of viewing class differences (Milroy and Milroy, 1992: 19f.). As we shall see in the next chapter, network strength has consequences for linguistic innovation. We have already seen with respect to black postvocalic *r* that degree of contact with whites and integration into the black community correlated with convergence in Philadelphia. In Detroit, assuming that middle-class blacks had looser social networks could account for their acceptance of the rhotic white norm. We also discovered above that women had relatively less dense and multiplex scores. That is, women had *weaker* networks. Now we see that this would align women as a gender with 'outside' influences and more 'middle-class' norms. Women as a group share relatively weaker network strength with the middle class as a group.

Let us now return to the paradox of the Belfast (a) which we left on page 202. The Ballymacarrett men introduced the innovative backing of this vowel. This was paradoxical because their network strength ought to have made them resistant to outside influences. It turns out that they are leading in this change *not* because of their network strength, but because (a) is not strongly correlated with the men's network structure, and therefore *escapes* the normative pressure of their network. But that is an issue for the next chapter.

Figure 6.11 illustrates some of the points we have been making in this section. Instead of one model, we now have two integrated

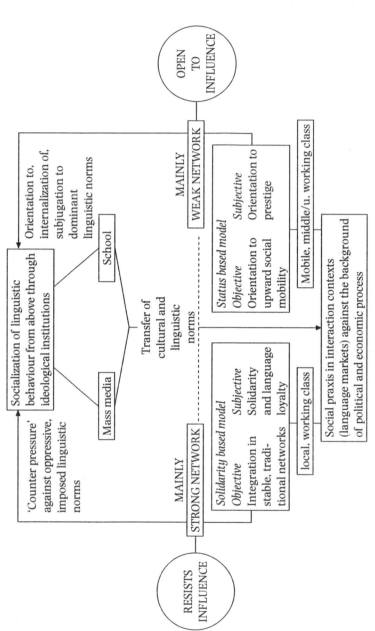

Figure 6.11 Network strength, solidarity, status and class *(adapted from Dittmar, Schlobinski and Wachs, 1988)*

models which bring together network and class. The 'solidarity' model of the network and the 'status' model of class can be integrated by aligning network strength and class. Later on, we shall see the general importance of exactly these two dimensions in other aspects of sociolinguistic study.

7 Change, meaning and acts of identity

> There is the element of habit, custom, tradition, the element of the past, and the element of innovation, of the moment, in which the future is being born. When you speak you fuse these elements in verbal creation, the outcome of your language and your personality.
>
> Firth (1950)

Variability and change

A language system is always in the process of change. The study of such change is the province of **historical linguistics**, a separate branch of the study of language (see, for example, Aitchison, 1991). The role of this chapter will be, not to discuss language change in all its complexity, but to examine the role that social factors play in the process of change.

As we have already seen, linguistic theory has approached language in an idealized way. It has been characterized as governed by a homogeneous system of rules. The historical and social dimensions of language, including its use to make utterances in context, are not in general admitted as primary data for a linguistic theory, because the aim of that theory (as we saw with Chomsky) is to specify just those universal psychological principles that define what *any* natural language is. The regularities looked for are very abstract, and sets of sentences, with variability omitted, will do as the data for such an enterprise.

The idealization is a 'convenient fiction' of the sort used in any science. The fiction is that it is possible to make statements about 'a state of the language', as if time were frozen, and with all the heterogeneity and inherent variability smoothed out. But we have seen in the last few chapters the actual extent of the variability within a language. Each linguistic variable is a statement that for some linguistic category, for example the front vowel found in some classes of words, there is a continuum of alternative forms which appears. Individuals and groups have different frequencies, starting with categorical presence or absence, of one alternative as opposed to the other.

As we saw in chapter four, a stage of variability is a necessary condition for a linguistic change. In some cases, therefore, we observe systematic heterogeneity because a change is taking place. Recall the Bailey wave model. The distribution of the variants was systematic in terms of the purely linguistic environments through which a change was moving. Linguistic environments could be ranked according to how they favoured one form over the other. The distribution of the variants was also systematic in terms of lects. In different people's grammars the change had reached different stages depending on their remoteness from its point of origin. So the systematic nature of linguistic heterogeneity reflects different points in the direction of linguistic change.

Linguistic change can be viewed as change in the rule system of a language. For example, rules can be added to or lost from a language. They can be reordered or simplified. An innovation, a new specific change, may appear and then propagate until it entirely replaces the earlier rule. While this process is occurring, the rule is likely to be variable because, within both the individual and the group, older and newer forms co-exist. In order to fully explain why such dynamic processes take place within a language, one must consider both *internal* and *external* factors. Internally, the rules of language are interdependent. A change in one rule will always have complicated effects upon other rules. Innovations may appear and be driven, not by pressures from outside language, but by interaction with another change in some related rule, rather like a chain reaction. Such processes are psychological. Psychological pressure, whether it be pressure towards simplifying the overall system, or producing symmetry or equilibrium within it, or in order to facilitate production and comprehension, can cause change. The process by which language is acquired by each generation in turn also causes change to occur in a systematic way. So explanations of some language change can be found internally to language itself (see Aitchison, 1991: chs. 9–10; Labov, 1994)

It is such internal factors that account for why linguistic environments can be ranked in the order in which they favour one variant over another in the wave model. For example, an item is always produced or perceived in the context of neighbouring items. Some neighbouring items favour one variant more than another for purely psychological or physiological reasons.

But these internal factors only offer a partial explanation of the systematic fluctuation between forms. (There is always some 'noise' or non-systematic random fluctuation as well.) Internal factors always interact with external causes of change. These are social and situational factors. Variation is only fully systematic when viewed in relation to social context. We have seen the correlations between sociolinguistic variables and a number of intersecting social factors: class, age, sex, social network characteristics, ethnicity and spatial distribution. One reason why groups which are established on these bases may differ in their index scores for a variable is that they may each stand in a different relationship to the linguistic change that the variable is undergoing. Our aim now is to try to make more explicit how the mechanism of change works, and how social groups and their values figure in it.

Nineteenth-century historical linguistics had not used quantitative social science methods and therefore was not able to empirically or systematically study ongoing transitions between successive 'states of the language'. With the advent of quantitative techniques it became feasible to revitalize historical linguistics through the empirical study of language change as it was happening in social contexts. A programme for such research was outlined by Weinreich, Labov and Herzog (1968) and revisited by Labov (1982a). Labov's long-term research remains true to this project (see, for example, Labov, 1994 and its promised companion volumes).

The classic early study of linguistic change in progress is Labov's research on the island of Martha's Vineyard, Massachusetts, three miles off the southern coast of Cape Cod. We came across this area earlier, as a 'relic area' or 'speech island' which still preserved constriction over and against the *r*-lessness of eastern New England (see Figure 5.5). Martha's Vineyard will provide our main example of the mechanism of change in progress, because of its relative clarity and simplicity.

Weinreich, Labov and Herzog (1968: 183–7) set out the task for a comprehensive theory of language change in terms of five separate problems, of which four will concern us here, namely:

1. *The transition problem.* What is the route by which a linguistic state has evolved from an earlier linguistic state? Can this route be traced?

2. *The embedding problem.* Can the linguistic and social conditions in which this change has been embedded be found? The variable which is changing is correlated with dimensions of social context. Equally important, it is also correlated with factors internal to the linguistic system, the linguistic structures and functions in which it is embedded.

3. *The evaluation problem.* What subjective factors of speakers and hearers correlate with the observed change in the variable? What do the forms involved in the change 'socially mean' to the speakers, consciously or unconsciously? And how does this relate to the process of change, if it does?

4. *The actuation problem.* Finally, why has this particular change taken place here and now? What originally began and then diffused this innovation regarding this particular linguistic feature at this time as opposed to other linguistic features or the same feature in other languages or at other times?

The fifth problem is that of proposing *general constraints on possible changes and conditions for change.* This would be the goal of a general theory of language change and would involve constraints and conditions on both internal and external factors. Since we are looking only at social factors, it is beyond our scope (but see Lass, 1980; Labov, 1994).

Besides the above, there are other general presuppositions of a theory of language change. One of these is the **uniformitarian hypothesis** that language change is always governed by the same principles everywhere and at all times. This is perhaps more problematic than it first appears since historical change in general doesn't seem to be governed by general constraints and conditions. Think of the socio-historical process of 'standardization' discussed in chapter two. It could be said that particular 'standard language' *versus* 'dialect' *versus* 'accent' configurations – French, German, Spanish, Italian, Russian, English, each of a slightly different shape from the other – that have emerged in western and central Europe since the fifteenth century are a 'one-off' phenomenon, unique to the literate class-based nation states of that time and place. We may not find *exactly* that kind of standardization occurring again because the historical conditions won't be exactly replicated, although the post-colonial new Englishes, the turning of pidgins and creoles into standards, the introduction of written forms for vernaculars are related phenomena. These are the twenty-first century equivalents to the construction of European National Languages in previous times. In this case, factors involved in standards (Figure 2.6), factors such as 'codification', 'language planning and legislation', 'canonical written texts', 'symbolic value regarding ethnicity and statehood' etc. should be regarded as separate linguistic processes which will interact in *new* ways (for a view with this flavour, see LePage and Tabouret-Keller, 1985).

Be that as it may, answers to the first four questions will frame how we can study language change in an empirical way. It is to this we now turn with an eye to the specific role of social factors.

Real and apparent time

The distinction between **real** and **apparent time** provides a solution to the temporal transition problem. Any change entails at least one difference in what is the same thing (a linguistic variable) at, at least, two successive points in real time. Real time is calendar time. Imagine that a linguistic change has been occurring in the period between 1890 and 1950. The solid arrow in Figure 7.1 represents the sixty years in real time between the two dates. If we are examining some feature which we think has changed in this time, one avenue open to us is to consult a study conducted earlier in real time, say 1900, if one exists. If the feature differs

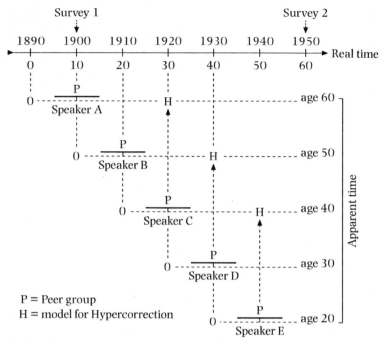

Figure 7.1 Real and apparent time in language change

between the two surveys, then we can conclude that a change has occurred in the interim.

But we can also observe the change in another way. Earlier on, I remarked that a linguistic change in progress would be reflected in the age-grading of index scores. (Although the normal pattern for the age-grading of a linguistic change in progress is a correlation between chronological age and index score, with the youngest speakers being most advanced as regards the change, there are exceptions to this pattern.) How this happens is made explicit in Figure 7.1. Each generation acquires both its basic motor-controlled vernacular and its evaluative norms between the ages of four and seventeen. This means that if we look at a feature now, at Survey 2, the accent of each age group will reflect the state of the feature at the time when they acquired it. Those who are sixty years old in 1950 will have acquired the feature in the span of years around 1900, and so on for each successively younger generation, until we reach those who are twenty years old and who only acquired their accents in the preceding decade. The sixty-year-old informant ought to have a score about the same as that recorded in Survey 1, fifty years earlier. And, if a linguistic change is occurring, each successively younger generation should 'freeze' the feature at successive points along the direction of change. The current age-grading of the scores therefore presents the direction of change 'frozen' in apparent time. (If a change is not occurring we get the alternative pattern mentioned earlier with younger and older speakers having similar scores.) The distribution of scores in apparent time corroborates observation in real time and allows us to trace the stages of change.

In terms of what may be going on *inside* the language, the Bailey wave model gives us a solution to the linguistic transition problem. In Figures 4.8 and 4.9 we saw how the frequencies of one variant over another were implicationally related from cell to cell, as the wave of change moved through linguistic environments and lects. So our progressively younger speakers in Figure 7.1 will, in each generation, have more cells in which the change has gone to completion, or has high frequency. This will produce higher scores in younger speakers.

To say that a linguistic change is taking place is to say that the movement to categoricality is increasing as time goes on. Why should frequencies increase as the speakers in Figure 7.1 get younger? After all, are not the older speakers nearer to the beginning of change; thus, according to Figures 4.8 and 4.9, should they not have gone further towards its completion and have higher scores?

The answer to this question has to be in terms of the *relative* stability of the motor-controlled vernacular of most individuals throughout their lifetime. The speech of an individual can change stylistically, but that is when the underlying vernacular is consciously or unconsciously overridden. There are regular age-effects, which we have seen before, caused by the varying normative pressures of different ages. There also can be a certain amount of adaptive change to new norms in the course of a lifetime. But these patterns are not sufficient to speed up the change in an individual's vernacular to the extent that it becomes anything like the change that occurs between generations. So for long-term changes in the vernacular, the change is visible in apparent time, as age-grading.

The question then is, why should younger speakers acquire a variable feature with a higher frequency, and in more linguistic environments, than the variable has in the speech of those older speakers from whom they acquired it? We can refer back for two possible answers. The first is hypercorrection. The **H**s in Figure 7.1 show us the locus of hypercorrect models in the older generation's more formal styles. These can be internalized as casual norms by younger speakers. The second is the normative pressure of the peer group; the principal factor in the acquisition of accent. The peer group (**P** in Figure 7.1) enforces the innovative form with frequencies higher than those of the older speakers who provide the model, as a distinguishing feature of its own identity.

Speakers A to E in Figure 7.1 are the *same group* of people persisting in time. The change is moving through this group. Other groups will participate in the change, beginning at later times.

Centralization on Martha's Vineyard

Labov studied the centralization of (aw) in Martha's Vineyard. This sound is a diphthong. That is, it involves a gliding change from one vowel position to another.

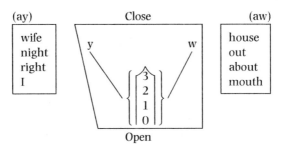

In the case of (aw), the glide is towards the upper back part of the mouth, in words like '*house*', '*out*' and '*mouth*'. However, the first part of the diphthong was variable. It could be very 'open', represented as 0 in the diagram, or very centralized, represented as 3 in the diagram. (Centralization means that the first part of the diphthong, the a, becomes somewhat like the schwa at the end of *sofa*.) The variable (aw) represented the degree of centralization in the first part of the diphthong, with 3.00 marking completely centralized, and 0.00 marking a completely open pronunciation. There was another parallel variable (ay) in which the first part of the diphthong in words like '*wife*' and '*night*' also varied between centralized and open. In this case the glide was towards the upper front of the mouth. So we find (aw) embedded in a system of upgliding diphthongs. The long-term process within the English language since the sixteenth and seventeenth centuries has been towards the lowering of both of these sounds. In the mainland USA, both sounds are in general pronounced in the lowered form. However, on Martha's Vineyard it appears that this historic pattern has been reversed. Labov found increasing centralization of both sounds.

Figure 7.2 presents the index scores by age group in both real and apparent time. The top row shows the results of the 1933 *Linguistic Atlas of New England* survey. At this date the (aw) variable showed virtually no centralization. The (ay) variable showed moderate centralization. Historically, this might be expected. The 'lowering' process had already occurred. In the case of (aw) it was complete. With regard to (ay) Martha's Vineyard was a relic area, preserving the older form, just as with rhoticity.

Now look at the 1961 distribution of index scores in apparent time. It is most striking how the average scores for both (aw) and (ay) increase regularly at each successive age level. This regular increase in centralization is even more striking when the individual scores of a critical subgroup, a social network of descendants of original settlers, are examined. This provides clear evidence of transition in the direction of increasing centralization. Note also that although (ay) begins with more centralization, and although this process continues, (aw) passes (ay) in degree of centralization for younger speakers. Transition from 'lowered' to 'centralized' can thus be clearly traced.

Real time 1933–61

		(aw)	(ay)
1933	Linguistic Atlas of New England	0.06	moderate
1961	Average scores for age levels		
	75+	0.22	0.25
	61–74	0.37	0.35
	46–60	0.44	0.62
	31–45	0.88	0.81

Apparent time 1961

1961	Speakers in a critical subgroup		(aw)
	Mr H.H., Sr	aged 92	0.10
	Mrs S.H.	aged 87	0.20
	Mr E.M.	aged 83	0.52
	Mr H.H., Jr	aged 60	1.18
	Mr D.P.	aged 57	1.11
	Mr P.N.	aged 52	1.31
	Mr E.P.	aged 31	2.11

Figure 7.2 Increase of centralization of (aw) in real and apparent time, Martha's Vineyard (*after Labov, 1963, 1972*)

Embedding and evaluation

How is this process of centralization embedded in both the linguistic and social structure of the community? I have attempted to schematize the main points of Labov's solutions to the embedding and evaluation problems in Figure 7.3. The island's permanent population consists of three main ethnic groups: the Yankees, descendants of the original settlers; the Indians, the remnant of the island's aboriginal inhabitants who are few in number and concentrated on Gay Head, a remote headland; and the Portuguese who are the most recent incomers, having only been established on the island for a few generations. Geographically, Martha's Vineyard

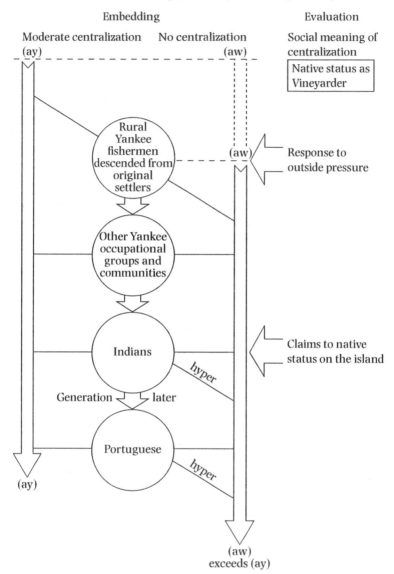

Figure 7.3 Interaction of social and linguistic factors in centralization of (aw) and (ay), Martha's Vineyard

can be divided into Up-Island, which is rural and of which Gay Head forms the tip, and Down-Island, where the main towns are located.

The general embedding pattern for the change can be seen in Figure 7.3. The innovation began Up-Island among the Chilmark fishermen, rural Yankee descendants of the original settlers. This group had the highest centralization scores. The initial change began in (ay) which had retained some centralization over and against the historic lowering of the sound on the mainland. From the Chilmark fishermen centralization of (ay) spread to the rest of the Yankee community.

This change in (ay) affected the symmetrical upgliding (aw). Here the purely internal linguistic embedding had an effect. The (aw) variable also began to increase in centralization, following along slightly behind the (ay).

From the Yankee community, the change spread to the adjacent Indian group. After the lapse of a generation, diffusion continued to the Portuguese. These latter two ethnic groups hypercorrect in the case of (aw), and the centralization of that variable is greater than that of (ay). Portuguese and Indian informants had higher index scores for (aw) than for (ay), although this was not true of the Yankee group.

The task now is to elucidate this pattern in terms of the social and evaluative context. Because of economic change, the traditional way of life and social fabric of Martha's Vineyard were under considerable strain. The original economy of the island, based on whaling, commercial fishing and agriculture, had declined and had been largely replaced by a service economy based on tourism. In season, the native islanders were vastly outnumbered by 'summer people' from the mainland. Much of the island was being alienated from its permanent inhabitants by outsiders. For the Yankee group particularly, who felt that it was *their* island, this provided a major challenge to their social identity.

Labov found a close correlation between degree of centralization and a positive attitude to Martha's Vineyard. Each ethnic group on the island was challenged in terms of identity, and their treatment of the variable reflected their response to that challenge. The original centralization had begun with the rural Chilmark fishermen. As a 'reference group' they would represent island **indigenousness** most naturally – given their descent and traditional occupation. *Through their usage, centralization encodes the social meaning, 'native status as an islander'.*

Their increase in centralization, contrasting as it does with the lower variants of the mainland, was a response to the challenge to identity provided by the summer people and the tourist economy. From the original 'reference group', centralization had spread to the rest of the Yankee ethnic group to the degree that their attitudes coincided with the social meaning of the variable. For the Indians and Portuguese, the claim was different; it was to be accepted as having equal status as islanders with the Yankees.

The point of central importance here is that the external social force driving the change is mediated through the social meaning of centralization.

Social factors can effect variable features because certain variants encode meanings. They get these meanings because they are originally associated with some subgroup who provide a link between a complex of attitudes and a particular linguistic variant.

On Martha's Vineyard, those who began the change, the Chilmark fishermen, were differentiated by their traditional occupation, their rural provenance and their Yankee ethnicity. Given the historical context, this subgroup typifies island identity and thus, within the context of language heterogeneity, variants which they use can potentially encode a complex of attitudes to the island. Under pressure, such subgroups respond below the level of conscious awareness by developing such a variant more fully in the direction which encodes the social meaning. The form spreads to the rest of the group, and successive generations further the change.

It is the social meaning of the form, its encoding of attitudes, that diffuses the change to other groups within the community. The form is employed symbolically by other groups, each in response to its own social circumstances. It is at this point that variants spread or not, depending on whether the social meaning invokes a positive or negative response in other groups.

The role of internal factors must also be taken into account. Given structural pressures inside the language, some changes take place solely due to the effect of other prior changes. In other words, not all variation in itself is socially significant. On Martha's Vineyard, the centralization of (aw) was, in the first place, a response to the centralization of (ay).

Other groups who adopt the change later can respond *both* to the original change and to other variables which have begun changing due to structural pressure. The social meaning is now encoded by these latter variables as well as by the original change. In Martha's Vineyard, the concomitant variable (aw) has been driven even further along in the direction of the change than (ay). Labov calls this process the **recycling** of the change by successive groups. It is this which accounts for very high scores for (aw) among the Indians and Portuguese on Martha's Vineyard.

Subjective evaluation of the variables

The complex of attitudes which links society and linguistic forms can be explored independently. On Martha's Vineyard, Labov found a high correlation between centralization and attitudes towards the island. Islanders were divided into those who expressed positive, negative or neutral feelings about Martha's Vineyard (Labov, 1963: 306).

Persons		(ay)	(aw)
40	Positive	63	62
19	Neutral	32	42
6	Negative	09	08

Correlation between such attitudes and index scores is sharper than for any more objective social category. Labov found this very fine-grained indeed. Scores even correlated with the specific intentions and life histories of individuals.

One of those with the highest degree of centralization, for example, was the son of a Chilmark lobsterman. He was a university graduate who had returned to the island after having tried and rejected mainland life. Among high school students, too, Labov found a significant relationship between index scores and whether or not individuals intended to leave the island and seek educational and career opportunities elsewhere. The very significant and detailed relationship between centralization and orientation to Martha's Vineyard suggests that it is the social symbolism of this linguistic feature which best explains its change.

We shall return to the question of attitudes in a moment.

The stages of a sound change

Let us now step back and take a broader view of the stages of a linguistic change. Figure 7.4 represents some of the basic stages proposed by Labov (1972) and which we have observed on Martha's Vineyard. Some points about how changes begin need further clarification.

Basic heterogeneity

Heterogeneity is the normal state of a language. At any given point in time many features are variable. As we saw, a change from one form to another necessarily involves a phase in which there is a fluctuation between the two forms. But although variation is a necessary condition for change, it is not a sufficient condition. Much of the pervasive fluctuation in language is not diagnostic of a change in progress.

But the various types of 'inherent variability' in the language system are usually the result of earlier change, concomitant pressure as the result of a change elsewhere in the system, factors of production and perception, contact between languages or varieties, or the requirements of communication in context. What *may* change is selected from this pervasive fluctuation. Thus, in Martha's Vineyard the centralization of the diphthongs emerged from their *previous* lowering which created a contrast between a conservative island variant, (ay), and a lower mainland diphthong. The reintroduction of r as a linguistic change in New York City emerged from its *previous* loss. In some cases, earlier changes and the effects they have on other sounds in the system of distinctive sounds seem to

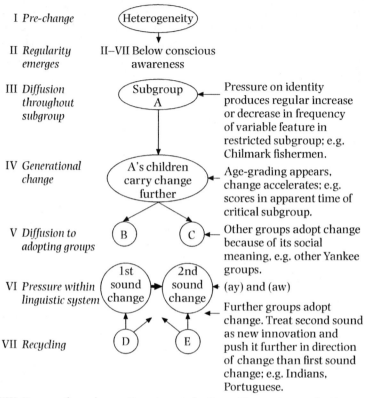

I *Pre-change* — Heterogeneity

II *Regularity emerges* — II–VII Below conscious awareness

III *Diffusion throughout subgroup* — Subgroup A — Pressure on identity produces regular increase or decrease in frequency of variable feature in restricted subgroup; e.g. Chilmark fishermen.

IV *Generational change* — A's children carry change further — Age-grading appears, change accelerates; e.g. scores in apparent time of critical subgroup.

V *Diffusion to adopting groups* — B C — Other groups adopt change because of its social meaning, e.g. other Yankee groups.

VI *Pressure within linguistic system* — 1st sound change → 2nd sound change — (ay) and (aw)

VII *Recycling* — D E — Further groups adopt change. Treat second sound as new innovation and push it further in direction of change than first sound change; e.g. Indians, Portuguese.

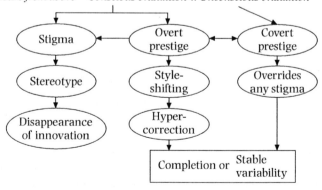

VIII *Pressure from above = Conscious evaluation v. Unconscious evaluation*

Stigma — Overt prestige — Covert prestige

Stereotype — Style-shifting — Overrides any stigma

Disappearance of innovation — Hyper-correction

Completion or Stable variability

Figure 7.4 The stages of a sound change

rotate vowels around the mouth over a long period of time (Labov, 1974: 225ff., for an example of this).

Let us look at some cases of variability which are the regular result of linguistic processes. Remember that a variable consists of two or more alternative ways of doing the *same* thing. 'Inherent' variability occurs when the conditioning of the alternants is at least partially attributable to factors within the language itself. For example, in any language a sound which is systematically the same is regularly pronounced in different ways in different environments. This is called **allophonic variation** and is a basic structural property of any language. We had an example of this kind of variation in chapter five, when we noted how the /r/ sound is made in different ways in different positions. In RP, /r/ was **realized** as a continuant in initial position, a fricative after *d* as in '*drink*', and a flap between two vowels, at least for some speakers. One finds the same kind of conditioned variation when dealing with meaning-bearing grammatical items.

Consider the category **plural**. This category is realized in different ways in different kinds of word. The following words have plurals which are pronounced differently: *dog-z, cat-s, horse-iz, men, sheep, children* and so on. Yet the same grammatical distinction is being made. This variability is 'inherent' because it is conditioned by the linguistic environment of the item in question. The first three variants of plural, for example, are conditioned by the way in which the last sound in the word to which it is attached is pronounced. Sounds are regularly **assimilated** to adjacent sounds in casual speech. Hence, the *n* of *in* is made on the back of the teeth in *in the*, but further back on the teeth ridge in *in heaven*; or *n* becomes *m* in *ten men* to give us *tem men* when we are speaking quickly. The simplification of the final consonant cluster in t/d deletion which we studied in chapter four was favoured, you will recall, by a following consonant as opposed to a vowel.

Some variability, on the other hand, appears random. It has been argued that **phonetic drift** can account for sound change (Hockett, 1958). Drift is the product of scatter in the pronunciation of a sound around a 'target' at which people are aiming. The 'targets' at which speakers aim in making a sound are internal models of the distribution of the sound. These are based on what they hear

A note on pervasive variability

Lexical

Most of the variation we have considered is at the phonological level of language. However, variation is also pervasive at other higher levels of language structure, for example, **lexically** and **syntactically**. On the lexical level, **synonyms** – words that mean the same thing – are variables. Often, such synonyms differ in formality, for example, *eat-dine* (see Geertz, 1960). Some are dialectical variants, for example, *lift-elevator, hood-bonnet*, and so on. Others stand in more complex relations to context, for example, technical terms (*urinate-pee-piss*) and terms of address. Consider the implications of addressing someone by their title alone, title and last name, first name alone, last name alone or multiple names (Brown and Ford, 1964; Brown and Gilman, 1960). The partial nature of synonymy is a function of the differing social meanings within a set of terms which are otherwise 'cognitively' synonymous.

Syntactic

Syntax is the level of language in which words are put together to make sentences. Variability is also pervasive at this level. Inherent variability is the case where the linguistic environment affects which of the alternative forms will appear, or appear with a certain frequency. We find inherent variability in the case of **contraction and deletion of the copula** and in the **rules of negation**, discussed earlier. Thus, contraction and deletion of the copula is most favoured when a noun phrase follows *be*, and least favoured when a verb in the '*-ing*' form or the 'future' verb *gonna* ('going to') follows *be*. Both of these constructions also vary in terms of social group, and are therefore dialectical variants (see Labov, 1972a: chs. 3 and 4; Baugh, 1980).

Sentence relatedness

Perhaps the most pervasive and most significant variability in the linguistic system is termed **sentence relatedness**, or sometimes **stylistic variation**. This occurs when two or more stable grammatical structures can be used to 'say the same thing' – i.e. be true or false under the same conditions. Sentences and phrases which are related in this way are **conventional paraphrases** of each other. This phenomenon is a central property of syntactic structure and involves most constructions in Standard English. Here are nine examples:

1 (Dative)   The vicar gave a book to the saint → The vicar gave the saint a book.

2 (Passive)   The vicar killed the shark → The shark was killed by the vicar.

3 (Extraposition) That he killed the shark surprised us → It surprised us that he killed the shark.

4 (Dislocation) left   My mother was a saint → My mother, she was a saint.

        right My mother was a saint → She was a saint, my mother.

5 (Topicalization) I like that sort of music → That sort of music I like.

6 (Adverb preposing) The car started yesterday → Yesterday the car started.

7 (Though movement) Though it's big, it's not dangerous → Big though it is, it's not dangerous.

8 (Cleft)   The vicar is clever → It's the vicar who is clever.

9 (Pseudo-cleft) The vicar loves good food → What the vicar loves is good food.

Variables of this kind are difficult to study using quantitative methodology, primarily due to low frequencies of occurrence (Labov, 1972: 247; Romaine, 1982: 29f.; Sankoff, 1974). However, explanation of such variants' potential for use in contexts of speech is an important part of the study of the pervasive variability of language. Some syntactic structures also form implicational scales of the sort we saw in chapter four. This suggests that variation on this level also plays a part in linguistic change. We shall return to these matters in chapter eleven (see page 454).

in the speech of others and their monitoring of their own speech. Such 'targets' drift because of the only approximate nature of the hits. These produce changes in a speaker's 'expectation distribution' through time. The drifting may not be in a determinate direction. Nevertheless, according to Hockett, it constitutes sound change.

Orderly differentiation

However, the type of pervasive fluctuation which we have looked at does *not* in itself constitute a change in the language. Rather, it provides the 'material' out of which a change can be unconsciously established, or **actuated**. For a change to have happened, it is not enough for an individual's speech to vary in a new way. Other speakers must interactively share the change in the variable in a consistent way. In other words, it must take on a regular change of frequency in a determinate direction within a group before we can actually speak of a 'change' occurring. The point is made by Weinreich, Labov and Herzog (1968: 187):

Linguistic change is not to be identified with random drift proceeding from inherent variation in speech. Linguistic change begins when the generalisation of a particular alternation in a given subgroup of the speech community assumes direction and takes on the character of orderly differentiation.

On this view, a change cannot really be usefully distinguished from its diffusion. It has diffused, has become a joint feature of those in some subgroup, by the time we can use the word 'change' to describe it at all – a process which, if not checked, would lead to the replacement of one variant by another in a variety of language. (Say we observed a change like this in the speech of only one individual: that would not be language change.)

To illustrate the relationship between fluctuations of the sort just described and change, reflect on the original loss of *r* as discussed in chapter five. We saw reports of very early but environmentally restricted loss of *r*, before dental consonants, and particularly before *s* (e.g. '*horse*'). This looks like a case of assimilation. There were other specific environments in which *r* is or has been lost within otherwise fully rhotic accents. One was in unstressed syllables; another was a kind of **dissimilation** that occurred when there was more than one *r* in a word. Each of these are cases of regular phonological processes – they can be given a recognizable physical or psychological account.

We argued then that the observation of such variation in rhotic accents is not in itself evidence for a general loss of *r*. It could be that this variability might become the beginnings of a linguistic change. It has the 'potential' of a change because (in restricted circumstances) there is more than one way of doing the same thing. But if it *is* a pre-change state of the language, we could only know that retrospectively. It is a case of inherent variation which is not necessarily involved in change.

Similarly, the earlier change in English allophones of *r* in postvocalic position, which might have been from trill, to fricative, to continuant (the 'weakening' of *r*), would 'set the stage' for loss of *r*, but doesn't necessarily mean that *r*-dropping will follow.

Actuation: why and where?

But why should change begin? Why should variability take on the character of an orderly differentiation in a group? The answer for Martha's Vineyard is quite clear: it is because of the social significance of the two ends of the articulatory scale. The relatively centralized end of the scale stands for 'native status as a Vineyarder'; the relatively open end of the scale, its opposite. As Labov (1980: 262) writes: 'The functions of language reflected in these sound changes cannot be limited to the communication of referential information. We are clearly dealing with the emblematic function of phonetic differentiation: the identification of a particular way of speaking with the norms of a local community.' The argument, then, is that the origin/spread of change is due to the 'social meaning' attached to a variant within a subgroup – and the emergence of a new 'norm' of pronunciation, as part of the system of norms which constitute and identify that group, and govern its practices.

There are other 'why' questions that follow! Why should a subgroup generate a new norm of pronunciation? More specifically, what motivates specific individuals to innovate and who are they? This is the 'activation problem' described above.

There are some inquiries into this problem. Labov (1980) makes certain suggestions and these have been criticized and developed by Milroy and Milroy (1985, 1992) and James Milroy (1992).

Labov on actuation. Labov (1972: 178) suggests that actuation can be motivated within a group when its *separate identity is subject to some sort of internal or external pressure.* Linguistic norms are central to identity and stress on identity within a community could lead to problems with norms or openness to normative change. This certainly seemed to be the case for each successive innovating subgroup within Martha's Vineyard.

In terms of social stratification, Labov's evidence suggests that in systematic changes the highest and lowest classes lag behind. *The groups who innovate are the classes centrally placed on the hierarchy,* the upper-working and lower-middle classes (Labov, 1980: 235f.). The reasons for this may differ for these two strata, as we saw before, but the middle part of the class hierarchy may be particularly susceptible to new norms.

Finally, Labov tentatively goes on to propose more precisely those who lead in linguistic change. He does this in terms of *a particular type of individual who innovates because of the shape of their communication networks.* He writes (Labov, 1980: 261):

> It appears that the speakers who are most advanced in the sound change are those with the highest status in their local community . . . But the communication networks provide additional information, discriminating among those of comparable status. The most advanced speakers are the persons with the largest numbers of local contacts within the neighbourhood, yet who have at the same time the highest proportion of their acquaintances outside the neighbourhood. Thus we have a portrait of individuals with the highest local prestige who are responsive to a somewhat broader form of prestige at the next level of social communication.

It is such individuals who lead in local, i.e. vernacular, change as opposed to changes in the direction of the standard originating in the upper middle class.

Milroy and Milroy on actuation. More recently James and Lesley Milroy have developed a more comprehensive theory of innovation based on social networks. It offers a critique and reinterpretation of Labov's suggestions.

In chapter six (page 229), we drew the distinction between strong and weak social networks. Drawing on the views of the sociologist Granovetter, Milroy and Milroy argue that weak network ties foster innovation and are the conduits by which cultural influences move between more tightly knit groups. A multiplicity of uniplex, one function, ties with outsiders, repeated over and over again, fosters innovation. James Milroy (1992: 181) refers to a report by Trudgill that an innovation among Norwich teenagers was probably the result of repeated weak links. Norwich teenagers were adopting the London merger between the dental and labio-dental fricatives, so that *thin* becomes *fin*, and Trudgill speculates that this innovation was transmitted by tourists and football sup-porters. Likewise, in Belfast, there are many 'weak' links *between* the closely knit working-class communities.

By contrast, strong networks would foster conservatism and resistance to outside influences; 'no strong tie can be a bridge' (Milroy and Milroy, 1985: 365). Multiplex networks mean that individuals are repeatedly interacting with the *same people* who are also interacting with each other. The relationships will be more 'friendships' than mere 'acquaintanceship'. They will be complex, confiding and intense. (Reflect for a moment on the social net-works portrayed in soap operas like *Eastenders* or *Coronation Street*. If the networks were weak, the narrative structure of such pro-grammes wouldn't work.) This is why network strength is such a powerful norm enforcement mechanism, oriented to solidarity as social meaning. However, both the opportunity to receive and the ability to employ new norms representing 'outsider' values are greatly reduced and resisted within a strong network.

The hypothesis that weak networks foster innovation is cor-roborated by a curious result involving the changing Belfast vari-ables (a) and (e). In chapter six, we examined the innovative backing of (a) and pointed out that this was most advanced among the men of Ballymacarrett. We noted as a paradox how a subgroup with the greatest network strength could lead in this innovation. The answer turns out to be that the new 'backed' variant is *not closely correlated with network structure*. For (a), choice of variant is less correlated with their network structure for men than it is for women. And it is the men, not the women, who are leading in the change. The converse is true for (e), where it is the women who are leading the change. The conclusion is that a group can lead an innovation only if the choice of the new variant is relatively less significant as a **network marker**. Speakers of a vernacular who have strong network ties can only innovate if the innovation isn't a prominent feature of their networks. That is, for the feature in question the connection between language and network has been weakened. Because of this, the new feature has slipped through the mesh of solidarity oriented norms. It isn't symptomatic of being a member of the group.

However, a further issue arises. How did the innovation enter the closely knit group in the first place? If innovation initially arises in individuals with weak networks, that means it arises in people who are 'marginal' to dense groups. How can an innovation originate with such peripheral people and end up at the heart of strong networks? The solution lies in the separation of the roles of **innovator** and **early adopter**. Innovators are marginal. Through repeated but less intense contact with 'outsiders' they transmit new variants into the tightly knit groups. But then innovation is taken up by core members of the group, after percolating around the periphery becoming familiar and available, by the 'early adopters'. These in turn become models for less innovative members. But there must be some motivation for the early adopters accepting the new variant. As J. Milroy (1992: 182) writes, 'Ultimately, for an innovation to be adopted, it seems that the adopters must believe that some benefit to themselves and/or their group will come about.' It is at this point that pressure on identity, even if it is negotiating relations with changes happening outside, may come into play.

Milroy and Milroy's position allows them to reinterpret Labov's latter two suggestions described above. The fact that innovations originate in the middle groups of society and not at its highest or lowest strata follows from the relation of innovation and network strength. Weak networks characterize the middle classes (see Figure 6.11). However, Labov's profile of the 'innovating individual' is criticized in terms of social network theory. Such an individual is impossible in network terms. No one individual could at the same time be characterized by both network strength and network weakness, with a dense and multiplex and a non-dense and uniplex network structure, subject to normative pressure and relatively free of it. J. Milroy (1992: 183) suggests that Labov has conflated the innovator and the early adopter roles into a single figure, although in fact he has recognized the position of early adopters within communication networks. These are the core members who are in touch with marginal figures and who are initially motivated to find the new variant worthwhile.

Norms and change in norms

A language change involves a change in norms. We have used the words 'norm', 'normative pressure' etc. freely so far, but without trying to be precise about what we mean. We have said that the norms we are referring to are norms of pronunciation at which speakers aim in producing the variants of a variable feature, and an interpretation of the variants in terms of their social meaning. The norm is also what makes it possible to say that centralization encodes local identity. So, a norm has two sides.

We should explore this more fully. Within sociology, 'norm' is a crucial idea. In general, a norm is said to be a **rule**, or a **standard**, for an action. (The term comes from the Latin, *norma*, 'a carpenter's square', according to the *Oxford English Dictionary*.) Williams (1968) writes, 'A norm . . . is not a statistical average of actual behaviour but rather a cultural (shared) definition of desirable behaviour.' So when we are talking about a norm in relation to a sociolinguistic variable, we are not talking about the actual frequencies speakers produce, but rather the intersubjective group standard, or the rule, that guides or motivates the act of its production. Note that this rule, being intersubjective, coordinates the individuals who constitute the group. It may do so, definitively, if the rule in question guides a practice that defines the group. If the norm is effective, we will 'observe a marked regularity of social acts in recurrent situations of a particular kind' (Williams, 1968). The regularity of the frequencies we have observed in sociolinguistic variables is not now the object of our study, but rather the norms, rules or standard that led speakers to use such frequencies.

Why should an action need a standard to which people are expected to conform? In terms of 'desirability', it is usually said that norms are legitimated by *values* and *beliefs*. Behind every norm is a value. We have already seen one such value in Martha's

Vineyard: that of local identity, and the beliefs intertwined with considering that of value.

But there is another reason why actions are governed by norms or standards. The norm in fact makes it possible to understand what act it is – to interpret the act as of a certain kind, and not of another kind. So, for example, centralization as opposed to non-centralization can be reliably interpreted as conveying that the speaker is positively oriented to Martha's Vineyard (everything else being equal). The norm, or rule, is what makes it possible to interpret the action as conveying what it does. It says, do *this* in this context, and anyone who knows the rule will find what you are doing intelligible; in this case, 'speaking with a certain accent' and therefore 'claiming a certain identity' in relation to the hearer. Without this norm, the frequencies would be uninterpretable in this way. Within the community where the rule is known, it creates intelligible action, and governs mutual expectation in interaction. Such norms or rules make *possible* a social life which is constituted by actions, because they *constitute* the very actions themselves (Parsons, 1951: 11; Searle, 1969; Winch, 1958).

We have now detached the observed frequencies with which a variant occurs from the norm which governs that pattern by making it convey something about the values of the community. But there is no reason why the norm should specify actual frequency level as the action to be interpreted. The rule itself can be put in invariant terms (LePage, 1980). All that is required is that, in any given context, the speaker produce a high or low enough relative frequency so that his or her action can be interpreted one way or the other. The norm can simply be put thus: centralization will convey local identity, openness will not. That is, the norm may be categorical although the actual performance it governs is not. In a context, the frequencies required to convey the distinction will only approach the norm in a rough way, sufficient in that instance to convey the social meaning. This accounts for why accents or dialects are perceived or, at least, talked about categorically, although their linguistic nature is statistical. Conversely, of course, the 'more or less' nature of the variable means that frequencies can be adjusted to convey very 'fine-tuned' degrees of identity.

Given what we have said about norms, we can reconsider the notions of normative pressure, focusing, diffuseness etc. In LePage's view, we are motivated in our linguistic behaviour such that 'we create our "rules" so as to resemble as closely as possible those of the group or groups with which from time to time we wish to identify' (LePage, 1980: 15; also LePage and Tabouret-Keller, 1985). LePage uses a cinematic metaphor. We **project** the model norms on to the social screen and bring these into **focus** with those of others.

Network strength can be related to these ideas. Focusing will be easier in densely knit groups of kin and neighbourhood. With network strength we would get clear models, normative clarity reflecting consensual, solidary values and beliefs. In such cases social identity could be felt as relatively unproblematic, as in traditional 'working-class' or 'ethnic' neighbourhoods. And deviation from norms would be incorrigibly communicative within the group. But such 'in groupings' fragment the larger society and are vulnerable both to external stresses outside its control and social conflict, e.g. unemployment due to economic change, decline of income, marginalization and alienation from power, defensiveness and traditionalism, xenophobic paranoia and prejudice etc. (The vernacular can be viewed through either utopian or dystopian lenses – the positive and negative sides of 'solidarity' are respectively pride of identity and cultivation of tradition *or* inward looking prejudice, unadaptability and exclusiveness.)

Weak networks are in some ways more interesting but more difficult to study (Milroy and Milroy, 1992: 9). When networks are weak, individuals are open to multiple, perhaps conflicting, normative models from different sources. And norms may be unclear and diffuse. It follows that identity can be at once more problematic, even fragmented, but possibly also more open, richer and innovative. Since weak networks empirically characterize the middle classes (as a matter of fact), this structure of norms can be related to its innovative role. The nature of normative change may historically alter as the structure of societies changes through 'embourgeoisement', identities suffer new pressures and rates of innovation accelerate. And weak networks may also be 'status or power-oriented'. It is possible, as Dittmar, Schlobinski and Wachs (1988) point out, that normative pressures from dominant culture and legitimate language may predominate where solidarity based structures are weak. People may be more oriented to prestige and upward mobility. Hence models for focusing and projection may derive from the institutional prestige norms of school or media.

What we have been doing is relating network type and social class configurations to the range of normative models and options they make available for focusing and projection. The contrast between the ideal antithetical types, strong network/solidarity oriented/highest and lowest classes, *versus* weak network/power-status oriented/middle classes and their respective norms is a matter of degree. Just as the concept of network or normative strength is a more or less affair. But it is clear that historically different social configurations relate to norms differently. They will also be subject to stress on identity in different ways.

It follows from what we have said *that language change must necessarily involve normative change.* Milroy (1987: 187) notes that 'focusing – the formation of a recognizable set of linguistic norms – is in itself an aspect of linguistic change'. Consider now three sets of circumstances in which Williams (1968) suggests normative change is likely to occur:

> A demand for norms is likely to arise from persons who find their interactions confusing or vaguely defined; for this reason, unstructured situations often create a pressure for the development of new norms. Enduring social conflicts, when not of too great an intensity, also generate new norms, developed out of negotiation, compromise, mediation . . . Another major source of new norms lies in collective reaction to shared 'strain' experienced in relation to old norms.

We have seen language change emerging also under such conditions. Milroy (1987) postulates the break-up of social networks as a situation of change, and we have seen that social mobility is associated with hypercorrection. In Canada, we saw social conflict leading to new norms in the allocation of English and French; and, conversely, the importance of clarity of norms in terms of 'domain' for language maintenance. Finally, we saw the reaction to 'strain' in Martha's Vineyard. Labov (1980: 263) suggests that the entrance of new ethnic groups into a community also motivates diversification in language. This would be a situation of 'strain' to older norms, as each group, including the new entrants, redefines its identity and relative position within the larger society.

Attitudes to language: matched guises

In connection with Martha's Vineyard, we saw that it was possible to explore informants' attitudes to linguistic variables. In doing this we are trying to discover the content of the 'social meaning' of the contrasting variants. This is the same thing as finding out what their use conveys in context. Remember that it is by following the norm or rule in the use of the variant that the speaker conveys this meaning. So, in exploring the complex of attitudes to a variant, we are also exploring the norms which govern its use.

The most important research into the evaluation of speech has been done by social psychologists. Pioneering studies were conducted into language and inter-ethnic attitudes in Canada by Wallace Lambert and his associates at McGill University in Montreal. The methodology developed by Lambert (1967) has been applied to the study of attitudes to language in the USA, Britain and elsewhere. For surveys of social psychological research into language, see Ryan and Giles (1982), Giles (1977, 1994), Fraser and Scherer (1982), Giles and Coupland (1991) and Giles and Robinson (1990).

The central research method evolved by Lambert is the **matched-guise** technique. The problem is to elicit from informants only their reactions to the form of speech, for example to a particular accent, not to the content or to any of the expressive features of speech that mark individuals or vary with situations. What we are after is not 'what people say', but merely reactions to 'how they say it' with regard to certain features of the language they use.

The matched-guise technique employs a single speaker but in two or more 'guises'. This speaker produces the same utterances, first in the 'guise' of one language or accent, and then in the 'guise' of another. The subjects, who are unaware that the different forms are produced by a single speaker, respond not to any individual feature of the speaker's voice, or the text, which remains constant, but only to the language or accent he or she is employing. Using this technique, responses solely to code can be studied.

Empirical studies have produced three kinds of findings. First, it has been found that accents vary in terms of perceived status. Secondly, and even more interestingly, the accent or language used signals a **stereotype** of a certain kind of personality. And thirdly, *speakers' attitudes to language are more regular and uniform than the actual usage within the community.*

We can illustrate the first point by some British findings. When we investigated the pattern of variation for British variables earlier, it was clear that style-shifting, when it occurred, was always in the direction of the prestige norm of Received Pronunciation, or RP. In the more formal styles, when speakers came under greater 'pressure from above', because they were more self-conscious about their speech, the frequencies moved towards the RP norm. This was true even when the direction of change was towards the non-standard. Clearly, this pressure reflects a speaker's perception of the relative status of accents, and this can provide pressures which affect change.

Howard Giles (1970, 1971) found that accents in Britain could be arranged in a continuum of relative prestige. For example, thirteen accents were presented to 177 South Welsh and Somerset schoolchildren using the matched-guise technique. The informants rated the thirteen 'guises' both in terms of the prestige of the speaker and aesthetically, in terms of the pleasantness of the voice. The children were of two age groups: twelve and seventeen years old. They were unaware that they were listening to a single speaker.

The prestige of RP was confirmed. The rating of accents, in general, placed RP first on the continuum of prestige. Birmingham-, Cockney- and Indian-accented English came at the bottom of the scale, with the first having least prestige. In the middle were foreign-accented English (North American, French and German), then the various 'national' accents within the British Isles (South Welsh, Irish) and, last, various English regional accents (Northern, Somerset). The least prestige attached to the speech of the industrial towns.

There were important age differences. The younger informants, at twelve years of age, did not on the whole conform as closely to the above pattern as did the seventeen-year-olds. The younger speakers exhibited more **accent loyalty** to their own South Welsh and Somerset varieties. Unlike the seventeen-year-olds, the younger speakers 'unrealistically' attributed high prestige and pleasantness to 'accents identical to their own'. Both age groups in both areas exhibited some loyalty to speech 'like their own' but they still ranked the named local accent inferior to RP. There was evidence too that male and working-class informants had more accent loyalty than female and middle-class ones. This latter result is presumably the attitudinal correlate of the linguistic patterns with regard to class and sex which we discussed earlier.

Subjective evaluation in New York

Labov (1966) adopted similar techniques in order to study attitudes, not to whole accents or languages, but to individual variables in New York City. The voices of speakers were arranged on a tape recording so that they would be heard reading sentences of a text in three ways: one in which there was no occurrence of the (r) variable at all; one in which *r* was used consistently; and one in which *r* was used inconsistently. This provided both *r*-less and *r*-full 'guises' for the same speaker.

A scale of occupations was presented to informants. The occupations were ranked in order of prestige: television personality, executive secretary, receptionist, switchboard operator, salesgirl, factory worker, and 'none of these'. They were asked to imagine themselves as a personnel manager and to rate voices on the tape according to suitability for jobs on the scale.

Using the differences between the judgements the informants made about the job suitability of the *same* speaker in the three 'guises', Labov calculated the percentages of **(r)-positive** and **(r)-negative** responses. Positive responses were those in which rhoticity signalled suitability for a higher ranking job. When (r)-positive responses were plotted against age, as in Figure 7.5, the results showed the remarkable uniformity mentioned earlier. For speakers aged between eighteen and thirty-nine (r)-positive

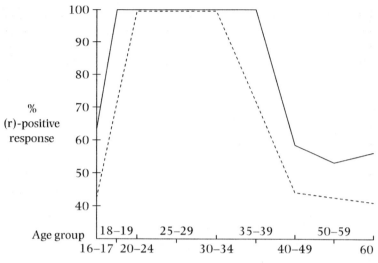

Figure 7.5 Subjective evaluation of (r) in New York City by age group

responses equalled 100 per cent for all social classes. This is more uniform than the actual index scores. That is, there is far more social agreement in evaluation of the variable within the community than there is in members' actual performance. Recall that in casual style, no class achieved an average *r*-score of more than 20 per cent. This uniformity is in all likelihood because by studying the evaluation of speech, rather than its production, we have gained access to the norms which govern the social meanings of the variants. The norm appears to be uniform in the community.

Note also the age distribution of a positive orientation to *r*. Sensitivity to the feature begins at the period when the wider norms of the society are internalized and corroborates Giles's findings. It then drops off abruptly at around age forty, which is evidence that this (*r*)-positive norm is a fairly recent introduction. As we saw in chapter five, there is a similar age stratification in actual index scores.

The uniformity of attitudes to (r) reflects the pressure exerted overtly by its social meaning: the fact that it encodes high status within the community. Such norms, because they reflect the uniform knowledge of what it 'means' to speak in a certain way, reflect the **communicative competence** a member must have in order to interpret the social significance of speech. An outsider, faced with the variation in r in New York City, would not know what it means. For this reason, and because of their uniformity, norms provide a better definition of a 'speech community' than does actual performance.

The above investigation revealed the subjective dimension of the overt prestige of a variant. We saw earlier, however, evidence for the existence of 'covert' prestige, the sort of social meanings attached to non-standard or overtly stigmatized forms. This is harder to study directly than overt prestige, since by definition people do not usually reveal positive orientations towards non-standard forms when questioned about their attitudes. The evidence for its existence tends to be indirect. However, Labov (1972) also sought to explore covert prestige in his subjective evaluation test. The 'job suitability' question clearly gives access to overt norms. But Labov also asked: 'If the speaker was in a street fight, how likely would he be to come out on top?' and 'If you knew the speaker for a long time, how likely would he be to become a good friend of yours?' The 'fight' question produced the opposite response to the 'job' question. Speakers of non-standard and stigmatized variants are 'tougher' than speakers of prestige variants. Answers to the 'friend' question were extremely interesting, and provide some direct evidence of the solidarity function of the vernacular. Informants of the lower working class produced the same scores for 'friendship' as for 'toughness'. Those who would be most likely to win in a street fight would also be most likely to become friends with informants from the lowest strata. Conversely, for the upper-working- and middle-class informants, the parallelism was between 'friendship' and 'job suitability'. The confirmation of both covert and overt attitudes to variables reflects the two types of social structure we discussed in chapter six: overt prestige being a function of the impersonal, stratified dimension, and covert prestige that of the network or community structure. It is significant that the same linguistic form can convey meanings which refer to *both* kinds of structure. Thus, in one context, a use of non-standard forms could convey group identification. In another context, the same forms might convey low status in terms of social stratification.

Social stereotypes

These results also suggest that attitudes to language involve more than merely the attribution of relative perceived status. Listeners also typically make judgements about the speaker's personality from the way he or she speaks. The research by social psychologists has shown that linguistic forms, whether accents or whole languages, seem systematically to elicit perceptions of the personality of the speaker as a representative of a type. These take the form of stereotypes of a 'typical' member of a group. Investigations of such group evaluations coded in speech usually employ the matched-guise technique. Listeners are asked to evaluate a speaker in various 'guises' using adjectives which express personality judgements. For example, Lambert's (1967) judges were asked to evaluate 'guises' with respect to the following traits:

Competence	Personal integrity	Social attractiveness
intelligence	dependability	sociability
ambition	sincerity	likeability
self-confidence	character	entertainingness
leadership	conscientiousness	sense of humour
courage	kindness	affectionateness

(Other categories used are religiousness, good looks and height.)

Simplifying the often subtle results of this research, it seems to be the case in general that guises involving prestige forms, such as RP, elicit high ratings in terms of competence. Vernacular forms, by contrast, are more favourably regarded in terms of personal integrity and social attractiveness. These contrasting evaluations, the features of personality emphasized in the stereotype, seem to reflect the two social relationships of **power** and **solidarity**, just as did the 'job-friend-fight' continuum in Labov's investigation. Informants seem willing to grant status-related attributes, such as leadership, intelligence and ambition, to stereotypes of personality elicited by superordinate linguistic guises. This leads to unfavourable

attitudes with respect to 'own group'. But solidarity-related attributes – kindness, sincerity, and so on – are part of the perceived
personality encoded in vernacular speech. What is important for
our purposes, however, is that 'social meanings' related to variability in a speech community are complex, involving stereotypes
and a number of alternative norms of interpretation, each of which
puts pressure of a different kind upon a speaker in terms of the
meaning of 'what he or she does'.

Power and solidarity

We have said that the subjective evaluation of variants is patterned in terms of two dimensions. We will explore this further.

Giles and Ryan (1982) argue that informants' evaluation of
speech varies according to the **situation** in which it is used. And
it varies in a principled way. In Figure 7.6 situation types are
classified according to two dimensions: first, the degree to which
they are status-stressing or solidarity-stressing; and secondly, the
degree to which they are group-centred or person-centred. Prototype situations for the combinations of types from each axis are
given. Linguistic variations tend to elicit the evaluations listed
under 'Rating dimensions' if the situation is of the type defined by
the two dimensions which form the sides of that quarter of the
diagram. For example, in a situation which is both status-stressing
and person-centred, the relevant evaluations would be in terms of
the competence, expertise etc. conveyed by the speaker's accent
or variety. On the other hand, in a situation which is solidarity-
stressing and group-centred, the evaluations of the speaker would
be in terms of their perceived ingroup solidarity, belief similarity (to
the hearer) and group pride etc. These evaluations are everyday
inferences, in terms of stereotypes, which we make from the 'social
meanings' conveyed by how people speak.

We can exemplify how these dimensions might work. Say that
we have a sociolinguistic variable (a), with two variants. One variant is in the direction of the standard, S, and the other in the
direction of the vernacular, V. S has overt prestige, and V has
covert prestige.

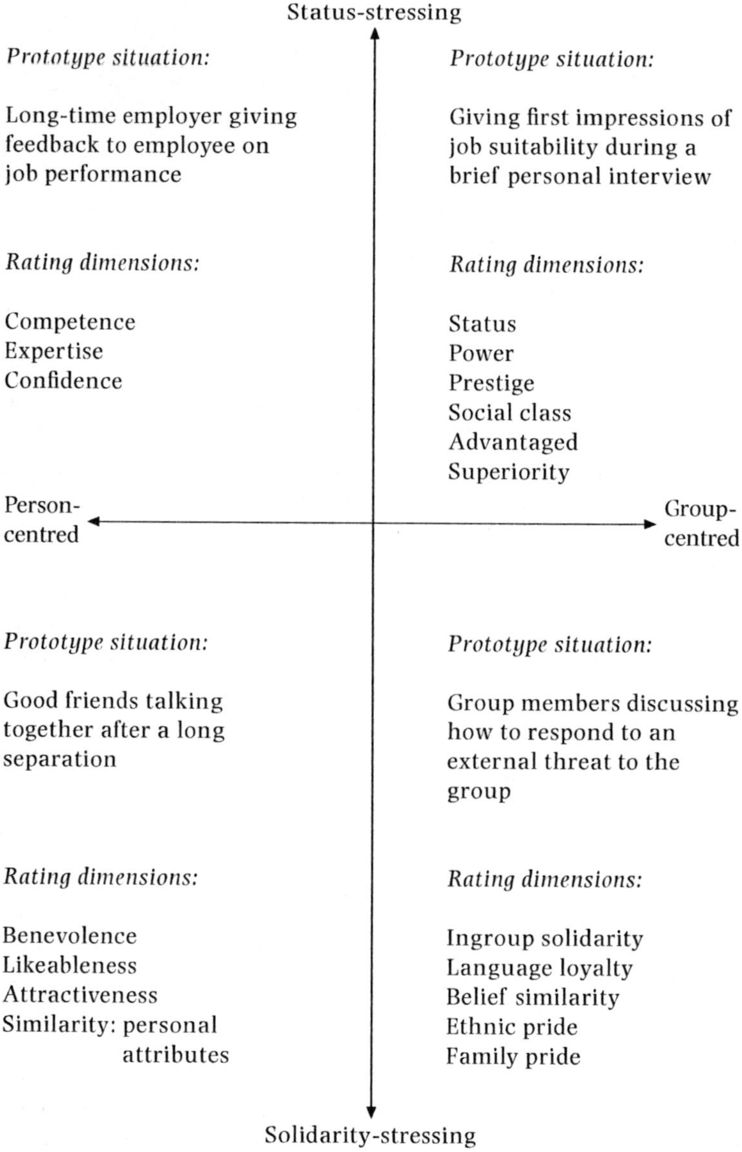

Status-stressing

Prototype situation:

Long-time employer giving
feedback to employee on
job performance

Prototype situation:

Giving first impressions of
job suitability during a
brief personal interview

Rating dimensions:

Competence
Expertise
Confidence

Rating dimensions:

Status
Power
Prestige
Social class
Advantaged
Superiority

Person-centred ←——————————→ Group-centred

Prototype situation:

Good friends talking
together after a long
separation

Prototype situation:

Group members discussing
how to respond to an
external threat to the
group

Rating dimensions:

Benevolence
Likeableness
Attractiveness
Similarity: personal
            attributes

Rating dimensions:

Ingroup solidarity
Language loyalty
Belief similarity
Ethnic pride
Family pride

Solidarity-stressing

Figure 7.6 Perceived language attitude situations and evaluative ratings vary
along two dimensions (*from Giles and Ryan, 1982*)

We would predict that in a status-stressing and group-centred situation – for example, in giving a first impression of job suitability during a brief personal interview – the use of S would elicit positive responses on evaluative dimensions such as prestige, social superiority, status etc., and the use of V would elicit negative responses on these dimensions. This is the sort of thing Labov (1966) found in measuring subjective reactions to *r* in terms of 'job suitability'. By contrast, if the situation were solidarity-stressing and group-centred, the *use of the same forms* would produce positive ratings for V in terms of solidarity, loyalty, pride etc., and negative ratings for S on these evaluative dimensions.

There are some very important points to consider here. The obvious one is the way in which people respond to a variant. *What it conveys depends on the situation of use.* It conveys a part of the stereotypical picture of a social group. The second point is that these responses follow from the social meaning of the variants of the variable. The argument goes like this. Because of the norm in the community, the variant at one end of the scale conveys *identity with* one social group and the set of social values that are believed to typify that group. Conversely, because of the norm in the community, the variant at the other end of the scale conveys *identity with* another social group and the set of social values that it typifies. The norm or rule is the shared knowledge that these connections obtain in the community and that therefore the use of one form or the other in varying degrees will convey these identifications. We have a complex of attitudes to these different *groups* within the society, and the values they represent. If linguistic forms convey *identity with* such groups, it follows that they will also elicit, depending on the situation, aspects of our stereotypical attitudes to these groups. For example, to hear people use a form like our own in a solidarity-stressing and person-centred situation will make us perceive them as positively benevolent, likeable and attractive, and similar to us in personal attributes. The stereotypes reveal attitudes to groups, which become attitudes to language, because of the normative connection between variants and group identity. The norm says that the variant 'stands for' the group.

The third point is that in the types of society we have been discussing, these identifications tend to be interpreted in terms of the two basic dimensions of power and solidarity. Presumably this is because the relationships we enact normally place participants in two ways: whether they are members of the same group or not, and all that that entails for their relationship; and whether they are of equal status or not and all that that entails. Much politeness phenomenon is involved in negotiating these relationships using language (Brown and Levinson, 1987; Brown and Ford, 1961; Brown and Gilman, 1960; see below page 292). But why should relationships be placed on *these* two dimensions? An answer could be that these are the fundamental dimensions in which our society is structured and which we have seen all along: institutionalized and therefore impersonal hierarchy, and social network or community. In social network terms, weak *versus* strong networks. In relational terms, power and solidarity.

The fourth point is that, to the degree that one can adjust the frequency of one form over the other, individuals can place themselves in relation to these meanings, according to the situation. We saw this in the phenomenon of style-shifting. The sociolinguistic interview, and especially when informants were asked to read within it, is probably best viewed as a status-stressing and person-centred situation. In such cases, increases in the frequency of the prestige variant regularly occur. In terms of Figure 7.6, these will convey the degree of the speaker's identification with superordinate groups in the society and their values, and lead to a positive evaluation of the speaker's social competence, expertise and confidence. That is what the speaker is attempting to convey.

The individual and variation

The individual speaker lives in a multi-dimensional set of relationships to various groups in society. Therefore, an individual speaks subject to a multiplicity of conflicting pressures mediated by the social symbolism of the variants. An **idiolect**, those features peculiar to an individual's 'lect', reflects each person's unique position in relation to the structural heterogeneity of a changing language but also the normative pressures, strong or weak, exerted on them by the various symbolisms available to them. The speaker is 'between norms' to a greater or lesser degree. From social networks come pressures deriving from solidarity. From other social loci come other norms, including those made legitimate by the institutions of the society at large and deriving from power/status. Utterances will be interpretable in the light of these norms – for example, the social affiliation or social status, the gender or age identity, being claimed by the use of variables.

Lames

There is strong evidence that an individual's unique index score reflects their own particular personal relationship to these norms. We saw on Martha's Vineyard how fine-tuned were index scores to personal attitude and biography. Milroy (1987: 131f.) found also that individual linguistic variability strongly correlated with degree of integration into local social networks. For example, of two individuals, Hannah McK. and Paula C., the latter approximated more closely to the vernacular. This was not explicable in terms of any objective social attribute, but in terms of Hannah's isolation, relative to Paula, within the community. Similarly, Labov (1972: 255f.) noted that individuals on the periphery of the adolescent peer groups in Harlem, called **lames** in the vernacular, differed significantly in speech from core members of the gang. In the case of lames, weakened pressure from the peer group could in fact open the way to a more positive orientation towards the institutional norms of the wider society. This is similar to the relationship established by Milroy between group cohesion, measured by network density and multiplexity, and adhesion to the vernacular norm and its symbolism of solidarity. Disruption of networks, or the less dense and more uniplex networks characteristic of middleclass life, could lead to the opposite effect.

Accommodation theory

Social psychologists have recently been developing a paradigm of research based on the notion that speakers modify their speech in interactions with respect to listeners, by becoming more like the listener or less like the listener. In other words, people's speech can come together, or **converge**, in interactions, or alternatively, their speech may **diverge**. The aim of **accommodation theory** is to understand the processes underlying these phenomena.

We have not time here to survey the literature in this field (Giles, 1980; Thakerar, Giles and Cheshire, 1982; Giles, 1994). In general, linguistic convergence is normally taken to reflect a group's perhaps unconscious wish for mutual identification. That is, it is expressive of a wish for approval and solidarity. On the other hand, linguistic divergence (or the maintenance of a speaker's own speech pattern) will occur when speakers, 'either (a) define the encounter in intergroup terms and desire positive ingroup identity, or (b) wish to dissociate personally from another inter-individual encounter (both identity-maintenance functions)' (Thakerar, Giles and Cheshire, 1982: 248).

In other words, two of the principal factors behind accommodation involve identity – either its maintenance as *distinct* from that of the recipient, or a wish to be seen as *similar* to the recipient and hence win social approval. It has been shown, for example, that convergence produces positive reactions in hearers. The situation is made very complex, however, because psychological convergence and divergence (what people subjectively believe they are doing) is not in a simple relationship to objective linguistic convergence and divergence. People may converge towards what they 'believe' to be the norms of another's speech, without this being objectively the case (Thakerar, Giles and Cheshire, 1982).

Nevertheless, in accommodation theory we see individual speech shifting in relation to perceived norms, and to enact social relationships. This area of research may be extremely important in connection with the mechanisms of diffusion of change and maintenance of differences, because it views them on the level of interaction.

Acts of identity

An individual is 'socially placed with respect to norms'. This varies with social position and network structure. The manner in which what is said is pronounced conveys social meanings about the speaker and their relation to both hearer and larger social structure. The fact that speech is systematically and incorrigibly meaningful in 'identity' terms at the level of sound is demonstrated by the social psychological research. It is the system of norms of contrasting pronunciations that makes this possible. It does this by establishing a connection between variants of a variable and identity in terms of ideal reference groups. The variant becomes a 'phonetic icon or emblem'. A speech community could be viewed as a system of such possible norms reflecting its various possible social identities and their stereotypical meanings, on to which variables can be mapped.

Now an utterance is also an action. Given the framework of norms, each utterance is also what LePage (1980; also Lepage and Tabouret-Keller, 1985) has called an **act of identity**. We saw earlier how LePage argues that people create their linguistic rules to resemble those of the groups with which they wish to identify. He writes (1980: 14):

> Each speech act is an announcement: 'to this extent I wish to be thought of as my own man, to this extent like A, to this extent like B, to this extent like C . . .' and so on, where A, B, and C – and myself, and their properties, are the speaker's own constructs.

That is, A, B and C can be viewed as idealized models constructed by projection and focusing from the speech of relevant groups. From the variability experienced, the individual constructs invariant models, the norms described above. Individual speech will be '*a variable mix of idealized invariant norms*'. Depending on network type and social position, there are constraints on constructing models: difficulty in identifying model groups, strength of motivation with respect to the cost/benefit of 'being like' a group, ability to modify speech patterns and so on.

However, by introducing the 'meaningfulness' of utterances on this dimension, we have introduced the possibility of intentional action, in claiming identity, into issues of variability. Variability can thus be integrated, using the notion of norms, into the analysis of language as social action. People can convey specific messages about identity. Since specific messages are being conveyed about claimed identity, we have also linked variability to the notion of communication. One issue is how much of such communication is intentionally controlled. Clearly much of this sort of meaning is below the level of conscious intent – it is a claim to identity of a more primordial kind. In this respect it is similar to and part of the way people project their social identities more generally, for example their **social faces**, images of a standard socially accredited sort, used by Brown and Levinson in their theory of politeness (Brown and Levinson, 1987; Goffman, 1955). We will consider this again in chapter eleven. However, we turn to issues of utterances as action and intentional communication in the next part of the book.

To conclude, let us return to the question of the 'coordinative mechanism' that puzzled us at the end of chapter four. How was it that speakers who had never contacted each other could produce frequencies that were related in such a precise and regular way over a whole community? It was noted then that there must be some mechanism which transmits statistical information to individual behaviour, intentional or non-intentional. *However, we can now propose that the 'coordinative mechanism', that which makes countless 'acts of identity' exhibit statistical structure, is the norms and their associated meanings which make such actions communicatively intelligible.*

8 The discourse of social life

> Here the term 'language-*game*' is meant to bring into promin-
> ence the fact that the *speaking* of language is part of an activity,
> or a form of life.
>
> Wittgenstein (1953)

In this chapter we switch gears and leave higher level sociolinguistic patterns. For the next few chapters, we are going to examine how speakers and hearers use language in the context of
everyday discourses. At the end of the book, we will circle around
and connect these two kinds of study.

One of the first points to make is that an utterance, in the traditional sense of someone speaking, is something people *do*. Arguably, the most basic instance of 'doing' with language is in face to
face context. Lyons (1977) terms this **the canonical situation
of utterance** and describes it as 'one-one, or one-many, signalling in the phonic medium along the vocal-auditory channel, with
all the participants present in the same actual situation able to see
one another and to perceive the associated non-vocal paralinguistic
features of their utterances, and each assuming the role of sender
and receiver in turn' (Lyons, 1977: 637). Although this is just one
type of context of situation for language use (see below), there is
evidence from the very form of language that it is perhaps basic in
that language evolved within it. It is also the home of such terms
as conversation, dialogue and utterance.

We'll begin this chapter by examining some features of utterances in this conversational context. Consider the above quotation

from Wittgenstein. To utter is to perform an activity. If it is an activity, it is a constituent of an event. And, as such, it is the verbal constituent of a type of event, a token of a social situation, for example casual conversation with a friend. In this case the verbal aspect of the social situation, 'casual conversation', is criterial for the very situation to occur. But virtually all social events have both verbal and non-verbal constituents woven together in varying proportions. (We can use the word 'discourse' in an everyday sense to refer to this verbal aspect of events.) This verbal aspect has certain basic properties which mirror the structure of social events in general. Consider a largely non-verbal example such as a tennis match. This has participants who have roles and associated activities specified by the fact that they are playing tennis. The participants take turns. Their actions are coordinated. We have names for the things they do when they hit or miss the ball. Similarly, utterances are activities in discourse. People bat the conversation backwards and forwards like the participants in a game of tennis.

Activities and rules

Once we have said that utterances are activities, we must immediately return to the question of norms or rules. **Social actions** are essentially rule-related behaviour. When people *do* something, for example vote or make a conversational move or play tennis, the identification of their behaviour *as* that activity – as an intelligible instance of that social practice – is a function of the rules to which the behaviour conforms. The rule in fact states the criterial regularity in the observable public behaviour. In a context, if the act of 'voting' is to be successfully accomplished, then the voter must do such and such (and other conditions must also usually be satisfied). Following the rules makes the activity *count as* an activity of a certain kind. The behaviour becomes also a sign conveying the information that this doing such and such is an instance of such and such an action in this context, by virtue of the social rule. The use of the words 'count as' draws our attention to the fact that action is not mere behaviour, but is meaningful to one competent in a culture.

One way to think of a culture is as a system of such rules which constitute social activities and thus make them intelligible for competent members. The view of social action as 'meaningful' because 'rule-following' which I have presented here is roughly that of Peter Winch (1958) which itself grew out of the later philosophy of Wittgenstein. But it has also been a central strand in both sociological and anthropological thought (for a discussion, see Ryan, 1970: ch. 6; Giddens, 1976; and Wilson, 1970). From this perspective, the task of the social scientist is the explication of the rules or norms which constitute social activities. A word of warning is in order, however. To say that the meaningfulness of actions depends on their being statable in terms of rules – the rules that constitute the actions of a culture – is not to make the psychological claim that participants are consciously following, or being guided by, such rules. In his analysis of rule-following and the famous 'antiprivate language argument' Wittgenstein is marshalling evidence against such a mentalistic picture of rules (Wittgenstein, 1953: sections 185–315). Indeed, he sees rules as necessarily public, socially accessible, and grounded in communities of agreement with respect to our behaviour (for problems as regards rules, see Martin, 1987: ch. 7).

Language is the paradigm case of meaningful human action; and it is the language-like nature of activities in general that is the starting point of Winch's arguments. (Indeed, impressed by this one can talk by analogy of the grammar or logic of actions.) In most events linguistic and non-linguistic acts are seamlessly interwoven in a communicative and expressive texture and are mutually interdependent for their interpretation.

A cooperative activity

The canonical situation of utterance is that of conversation. Let's look at some of the regularities involved. To converse is a cooperative activity. Just as it takes two to tango or play tennis, it takes (at least) two people to have a conversation. And, as if they were dancing together, people engaged in conversation are successfully doing something together; mutually accomplishing the creation of a social event, 'the conversation' itself. Think of the simple matter of taking turns. How is it that the participants speak one at a time for the most part, with very little overlap? How does one know when it is one's turn, or go about getting a chance to speak? How does one know 'what one is supposed to say'?

The fundamental aim of this conversational cooperation is for each participant to achieve the understanding of what the other intends to convey. In other words, to communicate. But for people jointly to perform this activity, they have to be able to assume also about each other that they are behaving in regular ways. Such norms in conversation are of two kinds. They govern both the practical machinery of conversation itself, such as **turn-taking**, and they tell us how utterances should normally be interpreted in the specific kinds of contexts in which we find ourselves and which the utterances themselves at least partially constitute. They are essential tacit assumptions about conversation and context which we can assume our interlocutors share (at least in our own speech community) and which are necessary to **gloss** what the other person is doing. They enable one to say to oneself, 'It's my turn to speak' or 'She's ready to close the conversation' or 'In this situation, that can't be a real question.'

The social organization of conversation has been studied extensively in an approach to sociology which is termed **ethnomethodology**. I will explain the term later, but first we will look at some of its relevant results.

Openings

Emanuel Schegloff in his important article, 'Sequencing in Conversational Openings' (1968), studied the problem of how participants achieve coordinated entry into a conversational exchange. Conversation has a basic structure *ab, ab, ab,* in which participants a and b speak successively in turns. The question is how they begin to 'lock' themselves into such a structure. How do you begin to engage someone in talk and guarantee yourself a further turn later? How does one begin to create this conversational social relationship?

Schegloff studied this in the **openings** of telephone conversations. His research was carried out by analysing the tape-recorded telephone calls to and from the complaints desk of the police department in an American city. Although the data was very specific, Schegloff's aim was to find the deeper structural generalizations underlying the openings of conversations. I have summarized his conclusions in Figure 8.1.

Schegloff found that the basic structure of such openings could be generalized into what he called **summons-answer sequences**, which were 'a general way that participants initiate a conversation, provide a coordinated entry to interaction and establish that they are available to interact'.

To account for his data, Schegloff had to view the ringing of the telephone as an integral part of the exchange, a **summons**. Note that in this case, an act which conveys a participant's intentions, the summons, is realized by a bell ringing. Although in other situations we often summon someone verbally, this example shows that communicative acts need not always be expressed in words. Schegloff interpreted the first words actually spoken in the exchange, those of the answerer, as an **answer** to the summons. These two form what is called an **adjacency pair**. Faced with a summons, the answerer is under a conversational obligation to respond (on the pain of certain inferences being made by the summoner, as we shall see later). Note that the answer can be one of a range of possibilities, such as 'Hello', or 'Yes', or the answerer's telephone number, or some other means of identification. When one thinks about it, it is odd that the answerer, and not the caller, speaks first, since the answerer does not know to whom he or she is speaking, and is not the participant wanting to initiate an exchange. Viewing the ring as a nonlinguistic realization of a caller's summoning act solves this problem.

What happens next is clever. The answerer must respond in order to complete this summons-answer sequence successfully. And Schegloff found that he or she characteristically does so with a rising question intonation. Thus, the answer can also be construed as a **question**, a case of an utterance realizing more than one act. So now the original summoner has been questioned and is under the obligation to provide an answer to that question. He or she must produce the second part of a **question-answer** adjacency pair, and, furthermore, the original answerer is obliged to listen to this answer.

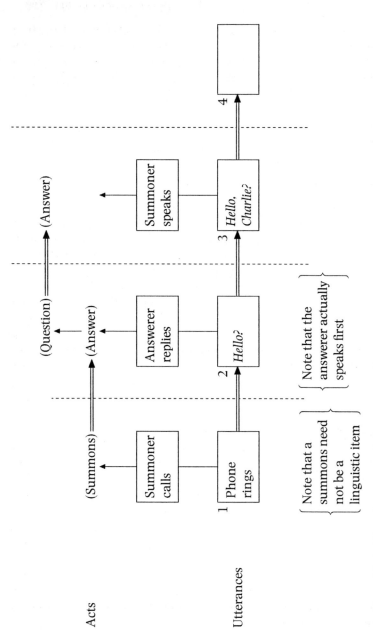

Acts

Utterances

(Summons)	(Answer) (Question)	(Answer)	
Summoner calls	Answerer replies	Summoner speaks	
1 Phone rings	2 Hello?	3 Hello, Charlie?	4

$\left\{ \begin{array}{l} \text{Note that a} \\ \text{summons need} \\ \text{not be a} \\ \text{linguistic item} \end{array} \right\}$

$\left\{ \begin{array}{l} \text{Note that the} \\ \text{answerer actually} \\ \text{speaks first} \end{array} \right\}$

Figure 8.1 Coordinated entry to a telephone conversation

Thus, by mutually following the conventions involved, the summoner has been guaranteed turn 3. Then he or she is entitled to raise the first **topic** of conversation following the general rule that those who initiate conversations have this right, and the original answerer is obliged to listen. In short, the structure which Schegloff discovered cooperatively 'locks' the participants into a conversational social relationship in which they have strong obligations to each other by virtue of the conventions governing conversation itself. These conventions make smooth coordinated openings possible.

Adjacency pairs

It can be seen that the notion of adjacency pairs is crucial to the working of openings. This notion originated in the work of Harvey Sacks, and Schegloff himself, on sequencing rules in conversation. The adjacency pair is a set of two adjacently positioned utterances, by different speakers, closely related to each other in a specific way. We have already seen two examples – the summons-answer and the question-answer sequences. Other examples in the literature are: a **greeting** and its **return of greeting**; an **offer** and its **acceptance** or **refusal**; a **thanks** and its **acknowledgment**; an **apology** and its **acceptance**; a **complaint** and its two sorts of replies, a **diminisher** or a **sympathizer**; a **challenge** and its **rejection**; and a **compliment** and its **acceptance** or **rejection**. It is clear that these types are little institutions, coordinated pairs of communicative acts. Many acts, then, conventionally require replies of specific kinds and put the hearer under a conversational obligation to provide them.

Adjacency pairs have the following properties. Their crucial feature is what Sacks calls '**the conditional relevance**' of the second part on the first, and the '**sequential implicitiveness**' of the first on the second. Basically this means that when the first part is produced, the next turn has an expected interpretation projected on it. Therefore, whatever is produced second will be specifically interpreted as an act of the kind required by the first part. Questions demand answers, for example, or greetings require greetings in return.

We assume that an interpretation of the second utterance as a relevant reply to the first must be calculable from the two utterances, and we will ransack the background information in order to be able to construe the second utterance in the appropriate relation to the first. We are now talking about very powerful conversational constraints on how we are to construe utterances which come immediately after, for example, a summons, a question or a greeting. This power can be seen from the notion of **official absence**. Say, for example, I am ringing you on the telephone and there is no answer. In fact, nothing has happened at all between the successive rings of the telephone, the series of summonses which I have uttered. But this nothing is not nothing. The silence *will* be interpreted. I conclude that either you are out, or otherwise unavailable to interact. Sacks writes, 'If there is no answer, then inferences are warranted in the culture.' Think of how we interpret the official absence of a reply to a greeting we have just issued. The kindest inference which is warranted is that our acquaintance did not see or hear our greeting. Similarly, consider the case of the officially absent answer to a question. The convention of adjacency pairs generates these inferences.

Why should pairs of acts of this type characterize the close-ordering of conversation? What sort of 'work' has to be done by participants that is reflected in adjacency pairs? Remember that we are studying '*inter-action*'. As the form of the word itself suggests, we are dealing with the normal coordination of actions as a mutual accomplishment of participants. The rules are conventions which *enable* this accomplishment. One thing that adjacency pairs provide for is that, when the first pair part has been uttered, a future event – the next pair part – is guaranteed to occur (or to be officially absent) as a reply. A future turn by the current hearer is therefore to this degree controlled by the speaker; a 'projection' of a future event is made by the utterances of the first pair part. The current hearer's next turn will be expected to be relevant, so the utterance of the speaker at this turn 'projects' just what the *other* participant's utterance is required to be relevant to. Against this expectation, deviations can be interpreted, and thus can convey specific meanings. The absence of a reply, or the particular form a reply takes, is communicative over and against the norm established by the adjacency pair structure. Any act that flouts normative expectations is 'meaningful', as we shall see later.

Another accomplishment enabled by this close-ordering is described by Schegloff and Sacks (1973; in Turner, 1974: 240):

> What two utterances, produced by different speakers, can do that one utterance cannot do is: by an adjacently positioned second, a speaker can show that he understood what a prior aimed at, and that he is willing to go along with that. Also, by virtue of the occurrence of an adjacently produced second, the doer of a first can see that what he intended was indeed understood, and that it was or was not accepted. Also, of course, a second can assert his failure to understand, or disagreement, and inspection of a second by a first can allow the first speaker to see that while the second thought he understood, indeed he misunderstood. It is then through the use of adjacent positioning that appreciations, failures, correctings, etc., can be themselves understandably attempted.

There are other important features of adjacency structure. Once the successful accomplishment of a pair is 'brought off' by the participants, some pairs are then **repeatable** and some are **non-repeatable**. Of course, if a speaker judges that a second pair part has not been achieved at all according to rule – if the current hearer's next turn is *not* construable in such a way as it can be said that it occurred at all – then the first act can be **reinstated**. For example, if someone clearly did not hear my greeting, or did not understand that I was making a request, then I can reinstate my greeting or request. But once an exchange of greetings has been accomplished to the mutual satisfaction of the participants, it cannot be repeated in the same interaction. This 'mutual satisfaction' rider which I have included on the rule can, of course, cause 'trouble' in those cases where participants differ in their view of what counts as successful accomplishment of the pair. Other kinds of pairs can be repeated as a matter of course. Thus, the successful bringing off of a question-answer sequence allows the questioner to pose further questions. So we sometimes observe a conversational organization composed of a chaining together of question-answer adjacency pairs:

Q-A, Q-A, Q-A, etc.

The use of such repeatable rules is one way of structuring an overall conversation. We shall see later, however, that what superficially appears to be a question and its answer is not always or even usually a question. It may look like a question, for example, if it is an interrogative form, but at the same time it may be realizing other acts. In such cases, conversational reasons for the use of a repeatable adjacency structure may be to provide a superficial way of organizing speaker control over successive turns, or to introduce new topics, or simultaneously to do other kinds of 'work' in the discourse.

Also, in those cases of adjacency pairs where there are alternatives for a pair part, one of these may be **preferred** to the other in most circumstances. Alternatives are normally available in second pair parts, as replies to first pair parts. For example, in the class of acts which attempt to get the hearer to do something, there are two types of reply, compliance or refusal. Similarly, in supportive actions, such as invitations, compliments and so on, the first pair part may be either accepted or rejected. In general, it is the compliance and the acceptance which are preferred outcomes, and the refusals and rejections which are less preferred, by *both* participants. In the figures which follow, I have marked preferred alternatives with an asterisk.

Schegloff (1979: 49) points out that this preference can project the influence of an intended, but not yet performed, adjacency pair 'backwards' to a turn, before the first pair part is actually uttered. A speaker may attempt to pre-empt a dispreferred outcome (or guarantee a preferred one) by use of a **pre-sequence**, which is mutually understood to preface a later turn. A clear example of such a construal is the **pre-invitation**, as in the following:

(pre-invitation)	1. Are you doing anything tonight?
	2. Not really – no.
(invitation)	3. How about we go to the show?
(acceptance)	4. OK.

The first pair part, 3, will be placed or not in the speaker's next turn, depending on the reply, 2, to the pre-invitation, 1. From another point of view, what we are observing here is also the 'forwards' projection of the pre-sequence. The form of the later adjacency pair is conditional on the outcome of the earlier one. We will see such 'projection' later on when we look at closing sequences.

Adjacency pairs: compliment responses

Adjacency pairs are on the whole not as simple as the notion first appears. Let us look at one sequence in more detail. This is the pair compliment and compliment response (Pomerantz, 1978). Three main points will emerge. First, that the relation between the first and second acts is *dynamic*; it is not merely a question of recognizing a compliment, and responding with a fixed type of reply. The second pair part is, in fact, an 'outcome point' where what is uttered becomes *intelligible as a reply* because both participants know the rules involved. The adjacency pair is more a norm of interpretation than it is a list of appropriate utterances. Although certain words do recur in adjacency pairs of the more institutional types and certain words are conventional, in fact it is how the words are interpreted that is important. Second, many pairs enable solutions to conversational *problems*. Third, the pair parts may be doing more than one thing at the same time. In Pomerantz's terms, compliment replies are subject to multiple constraints.

This last point first. Pomerantz argues that there are three systems of constraints which govern the action of replying to a compliment. Two of these exist because the utterance of a compliment can be viewed as simultaneously two different types of action. Characteristically, these require different kinds of replies. The action types and their appropriate replies are illustrated in Figure 8.2.

A compliment is a **supportive action**, akin to 'offers', 'gifts' and 'congratulations', which sequentially implies an acceptance or rejection as second pair part. At the same time, a compliment is also what Pomerantz terms an **assessment action**, which sequentially implies agreement or disagreement as a second pair part. This latter type of act presumably includes all those acts, like 'stating' discussed above, in which the speaker in uttering a proposition also intends the utterance to count as an undertaking that the utterance is true. It is this truth claim that makes agreement or disagreement a relevant reply. Other assessment actions would

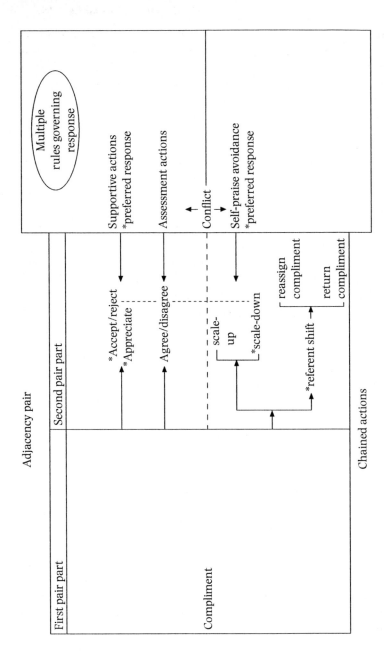

Figure 8.2 Compliment responses (*after Pomerantz, 1978*)

include 'remarks', 'assertions', 'statements' etc. Now think about compliments from this point of view. An utterance which is to count as a compliment must also convey, in some way, that the proposition on which the hearer is being complimented is *true*. In the examples below this undertaking is explicit. Characteristically, therefore, such utterances perform the two types of acts simultaneously. *An utterance is a complex of related actions.* This property will concern us again in chapters ten and eleven.

As we said, each type sequentially implies different classes of reply. As a supportive act, the rule is that hearers either accept or reject the compliment. But the rule goes further than this. There is a 'preferred' response, namely acceptance, particularly by means of an appreciation token, such as 'thank you'. There is an affiliation between acceptance (supportive actions) and agreement (assessment actions). This means that a compliment can also be accepted through the expression of agreement with its content. This is a secondary way of accepting compliments. Sequentially, if both positive replies occur they do so in the order, accept and agree. Pomerantz (1978: 84ff.) gives the following examples:

1. Why, it's the loveliest record I ever heard. And the organ –
2. Well, thank you.

1. Oh, it was just beautiful.
2. Well, thank you + Uh, I thought it was quite nice . . .

Because of the affiliation of accept/agree and reject/disagree, just as one can accept through agreement, one can reject a compliment through disagreement with the truth of its content (Pomerantz, 1978: 87):

1. (You) did a great job cleaning up the house.
2. Well, I guess you haven't seen the kids' room.

Interestingly, this is the preferred method of rejecting a compliment. This is because it avoids *explicit* rejection, which is the dispreferred response to supportive actions. The preference for explicitness in acceptance leads to the preference for inexplicitness in rejection.

Politeness

But a third norm complicates the picture. Although acceptance is the preferred outcome of the adjacency pair, the prevalent empirical response to compliments is disagreement and rejection. How could this be? Pomerantz invokes a third rule to account for this: **self-praise avoidance**. Participants should, at least conventionally, avoid assenting to enhancements of their own status/prestige. Therefore, one who has received a compliment has a problem of conflicting norms. Stated categorically, he or she should accept the supportive action and the truth of the speaker's assessment with a token of appreciation. On the other hand, one should avoid agreement with a proposition to which his or her assent will count as self-praise. To disagree, however, threatens both parties. It repudiates both the complimenter's supportive act and his or her competence in uttering the truth, and, for the hearer, it involves an act of self-deprecation. Compliment response, therefore, is problematic.

This is reflected in the solutions which exhibit an 'in-between-ness' in attempting to resolve the conflict. Remember, earlier we saw a similar 'in-between-ness' in that, for a given phonological variable, an individual was *between* norms. The outcome was the statistical positioning of the 'act of identity' in relation to the various norms. Note, however, that identity claims always imply relationship claims relative to some hearer, on the dimensions of status and solidarity. Presumably to receive a compliment is status-enhancing and simultaneously an expression of solidarity. Self-deprecation in a response is status-reducing, and therefore expresses solidarity in return. A speaker may 'scale down' an agreement following an acceptance. To do so exhibits features of *both* agreement and disagreement (Pomerantz, 1978: 95):

Compliment	1. She's a fox (of the hearer's new bride).
Agree 'scaled down'	2. Yeh, she's a pretty girl.

But, given the problematic nature of responses, why should one compliment anyone at all? Clearly, in the terms we have been discussing, the speaker is following *another* politeness rule such that he or she should express solidarity with and enhance the status of the interlocutor where possible. To compliment (congratulate, offer, praise etc.) does this.

However, there are two dangers in complimenting. One we have already seen. By enhancing their status, it puts the hearers on the spot. If they agree, they both commit self-praise and weaken solidarity by virtue of accepting this enhanced prestige. The other danger involves the complimenter. Although complimenting someone *does* express solidarity towards them, it often does so at the price of obtruding rather badly into that area of the personal that is the possession of every 'other'. To compliment necessarily involves making public an assessment, albeit a favourable one, of the 'other'. This is presumptuous and can be potentially an enactment of a power asymmetry in favour of the complimenter. Imagine a compliment issued by an employer, for example, to an employee. This danger is inherent in enacting the norm of expressing solidarity through the means of compliments (praise, offers etc.). The complimenter must obtrude to do so.

Conventionally, the 'scaled-down' agreement as a response is beautifully 'poised' between the potential inferences generated by the conflicting rules. The receiver of the compliment accepts it, with reservations, by agreeing with the assessment, also with reservations. He or she thus accepts, and does not repudiate, the other's supportive expression of solidarity and *returns* it by partially rejecting any enhanced prestige/status that might accrue by virtue of being praised. At the same time, the receiver restores the privacy of his or her 'area of the personal' by partially disagreeing with the assessment. This reduces the status of the complimenter and restores symmetry of power. Any 'presumptiveness' is repaired. Ironing out any possible asymmetry of power itself enacts solidarity and lets the complimenter know that the compliment was taken and accepted according to that norm. The problem is resolved and the adjacency pair 'brought off'.

Once symmetry is assured and intent cleared up, the complimenter sometimes reasserts his or her position; 2 above is followed by 3: 'Oh, she's gorgeous.'

Agreement which is 'scaled down' typically follows compliments which do not directly refer to the hearer. In the example above,

the referent was the hearer's new bride. Usually, a more overt disagreement follows a compliment that directly refers to its recipient.
For example (Pomerantz, 1978: 98):

1.   Well, we'll haftuh *frame* that.
2.   Yee – *Uh*ghh, it's not worth fra(hh)mi(h)ing.
3.   W'*sure* it is.

Sometimes disagreements do not completely counter-assert the
proposition but rather qualify the compliment:

1.   You brought – like a *ton* of things.
2.   *Just* a few little things.

Presumably, when compliments directly refer to their recipients,
the danger to both participants' status is more overt, as opposed to
less direct compliments. Overt disagreement, correspondingly, is
both more self-deprecatory and has a greater effect on the possible
'presumptive' status on the complimenter. When the status problem is thus resolved, the mutual accomplishment of a compliment-
response pair can be interpreted as the expression, acceptance and
return of solidarity.

Another solution to the problem is to reassign the compliment
elsewhere, or return a compliment to the original speaker.

So far, then, we have demonstrated that much more is involved
in adjacency pairs than the simple occurrence of two acts in
sequence. In general, it seems that close ordering is a framework
of expectations which can be used for the solution of problems in
the enacting of relationships. The adjacency structure in this sense
enables, and is a resource for, coordination of actions. In the above
examples, *the participants are negotiating their relationship.* Now just
what is the best outcome for them? What, in general, are people
trying to 'bring off' together in a compliment-response pair?

We expect that the speaker ought to be intending to reinforce
or establish solidarity by 'building up' the socially accredited identity of the hearer, doing something good to him or her. Given this,
the hearer ought to accept the offer and in so doing make the
solidarity mutual. In this light of this norm, the prevalence of rejection in compliments is only *ritual* rejection. The response is not
really rejecting the compliment. The conflict of norms produces

indirect rejections as responses (disagreements, reference shifts etc.) but in fact the preferred response of acceptance is being accomplished on another level. The preference for acceptance is what generates this interpretation.

Of course, when we use the word 'preference' here we are talking about a social rule. At this point, we ought to distinguish between two uses of the word rule, which up to now we have conflated. Most of the rules we have talked about so far have been rules which one must follow in order that what one is doing can count as *that* kind of action at all. They make what one is doing intelligible as an action of a certain kind. If one does not know, or follow, the rule, the action will not count as doing *that*. The adjacency-pair rules are of this type. The rule is simply that the second pair part, produced on the completion of the first pair part, will count as a reply to it. The necessary condition of a reply is that it be a reply to something. On the assumption that this rule holds, not following it will be communicative, witness the notion of 'official absence' of a reply. The rule is both **constitutive** of the act and our means of interpreting what people do. The second sense of rule, by contrast, is its **regulative** aspect. Such a rule stipulates that an act 'ought' to be performed or avoided. Constitutive rules are logically prior to regulative ones; for example, one has to know what counts as murder in order to be able to obey the rule which says not to murder. Many constitutive rules are also regulatively interpreted. So participants 'ought' to cooperate in adjacency pairs by producing the second pair part. But within this conversational obligation are more specific regulative constraints. Participants 'ought' to produce preferred alternatives and hence work towards preferred outcomes in 'bringing off' the pair. Failure to accomplish the pair in this *way* will also warrant inferences and be communicative. Preferences, therefore, are regulative aspects of language use – the 'ought' aspect.

This helps us to understand something more of the possible force of normative pressures. The largest part of this pressure has to do with the requirement that one follows the rule or norm simply in order to convey the meanings one intends and be understood. This is the enabling aspect of rules. A participant follows rules under this aspect because it is *rational* to do so. When the rule is also interpreted regulatively by the community, then a moral, legal, aesthetic etc. pressure is also exerted by the group and its judgements. The two aspects are not only connected by the priority of the enabling aspect, but by the incorrigible communicativeness of real or apparent violations under both aspects. The interpretations differ as between aspects, however. Under the constitutive aspect we ask what the participant intended to convey in acting that way. Note how this assumes both rationality and the 'taken-for-granted' nature of the rule. Under the 'regulative' aspect, besides the first kind of interpretative activity, there is also a judgement of the act in moral, legal, aesthetic etc. terms. The normative pressure exerted through language usually has this regulative aspect. In extreme cases it can take the form of language legislation. More often it has the form of prescription regarding correctness or aesthetics. But it pervades the interpretation of every speech act under the heading of **politeness**. We have already seen that the use of variants is expressive of power (relative status) and solidarity (degree of social distance).

Let us see what kinds of generalizations can be made about the politeness phenomenon. Arguably, it can be derived from the notion of **face** as this is used in the analysis of 'face-to-face' interaction by Erving Goffman (1955, 1967). For Goffman, a participant's face is the image of him or herself in terms of approved social attributes. In an encounter, a participant claims a face which is 'lodged in mutual appraisal' between him or herself and the other participants. All the participants are responsible for maintaining their own and each other's faces cooperatively in the course of the interaction. This responsibility leads to a pair of related rules: the **rule of self-respect**, wherein participants must stand guard over their own face, and the **rule of considerateness**, wherein they must go to certain lengths to respect the face of others. Participants cooperate to try to make sure that neither themselves nor others are defaced, out of face, or in the wrong face.

This is evident in **repairs**. Repairs occur when there is some source of 'trouble' in a conversation. The trouble need not be a mistake. It can be any of a range of difficulties. For example, a hearer may not have heard or understood some remark, or a speaker may not be able to remember a name, or find the right word for what he or she wants to say. Schegloff, Jefferson and Sacks (1977) show that conversation is so organized that there is a preference for **self-repair** over **other-repair** in dealing with such troubles.

In a major study of politeness, Brown and Levinson (1987) distinguish between negative and positive face. The former is, 'the basic claim to territories, personal preserves, rights to non-distraction – i.e., to freedom of action and freedom from imposition'. The latter is, 'the positive consistent self-image or "personality" (crucially including the desire that this self image be appreciated and approved of) claimed by interactants'. These two aspects of face can be framed in terms of participants' wants, to be unimpeded in action, and to be desirable at least to some others. Many activities are intrinsically face-threatening. Earlier we saw the face-threatening aspects of compliments to their recipients. Although compliments enhance positive face, they threaten the hearer's negative face because they predicate some desire towards the hearer and/or his or her goods. This limits the hearer's actions because, in response to this imposition, he or she feels impelled to self-effacement (Brown and Levinson, 1987).

Participants adopt **strategies of politeness** in order to avoid or minimize face-threatening activities. There are positive strategies, such as claiming common ground or fulfilling the hearer's wants. (Issuing compliments to someone might be an example of this latter aim.) There are negative strategies, aimed at the hearer's negative face, such as avoiding overt coercion, not making assumptions, being direct about one's intentions and so on. A particular linguistic form in itself is not usually polite or impolite, rather its politeness has to do with how it is interpreted relative to the available strategies and the context. For example, what is polite or impolite to a particular participant is relative to the dimensions of power (relative status) and solidarity (social distance) claimed and granted in the faces which have been accredited in the encounter. What actually threatens face, and therefore motivates choice of strategy, for example, depends on relative status and intimacy. To receive a compliment from a superior differs from receiving one from an intimate. In general, in modern Western societies, the preference seems to be to mask status differences (which threatens hearer's negative face) and reinforce solidarity (which enhances hearer's positive face). The particular preferences we have noted – acceptance, agreement, self-correction etc. – would seem to reflect this. Keep in mind as well the ritual nature of these meanings. Politeness interpretations decode just one dimension of the complex of activities done in the performance of an utterance.

Identification

So far we have seen that interaction between participants is dynamic (involving the continuing negotiation and mutual definition of their relationship), coordinative, oriented to problem-solving, and enabled by conventions. Another problem for participants is that of the achievement of mutual recognition, that is, to identify to whom you are talking from the resources available. Schegloff (1979) analyses this aspect of the organization of conversation.

Usually, identification is accomplished in what Schegloff terms the **pre-opening** sequence, and among acquaintances this is achieved through 'inspectables' – very simply, by what people look and sound like. The preferred method of identification involves the minimum use of recognitional resources. The basic resource is self-reference by the use of one's name, but the resources a speaker provides are **recipient-designed**; that is, they give just the amount of information the speaker believes the hearer requires to identify him or her, and in the appropriate form. The preference is to achieve mutual recognition with less than the basic resource, by appearance and/or a minimal sample of voice, and to do so immediately and without problems.

Schegloff (1979: 50) writes, 'This is a specification, in the domain of reference to persons, of the general recipient design preference: don't tell the recipient what you ought to suppose he already knows; use it. This principle builds in a preference for "oversuppose and undertell".' Again, a preference reflects a general politeness strategy – in this case, one oriented to the hearer's positive face. To set things up so that a hearer will identify you with minimal resources also conveys, and can allow the hearer to infer, that you suppose that he or she and you are solidary. Conversely, there are dangers in this assumption of 'common ground' or 'intimacy', since it obtrudes on the speaker's negative face. The

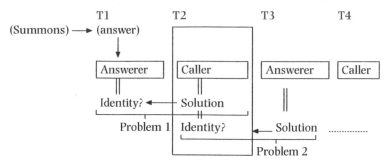

Figure 8.3 The problem of identification (*after Schegloff, 1979*)

hearer's freedom is limited by the assumption that he or she can identify the speaker from minimal resources. Consequently, if there is doubt, the speaker can 'undersuppose and overtell'. This switches strategy to one of negative politeness. By 'being direct', any threat is removed to the hearer's negative face.

Identification becomes particularly problematic when visual cues are unavailable and there is no pre-opening sequence. So let us confine ourselves to such a case: the opening of telephone conversations. Schegloff's analysis is very complex and subtle. Here I can only summarize a few of its main points.

There are *two* identification problems, that of the caller in identifying the answerer, and that of the answerer in identifying the caller. Figure 8.3 shows the locus of each problem. 'Identity?' marks the point where the resource is provided. 'Solution' marks the turn where, as preferred, the earliest resolution of the problem can be accomplished. Turn 2 is the most problematic. At this point the caller (who knows who he or she intended to call) ought to achieve recognition of the answerer and, at the same time, provide just the right resource for the answerer successfully to recognize him or her. This is accomplished at the same time as other adjacency pairs, which appear to be the main business of the conversation. Earlier, we saw that the answerer's first turn, T, was an answer to a summons. Next we commonly observe an exchange of greetings:

Answerer	1. H'llo?	(answer to summons)
Caller	2. hHi.	(greeting)
Answerer	3. Hi:?	(greeting)

Schegloff points out that these utterances are at the same time acts which invite and give recognition. Again we see that the same utterance is used to perform a complex of acts. Schegloff (1979: 35) describes this:

> The doing of an initial greeting in second turn has two aspects at least. First, it is the first part of a basic sequential unit we call an adjacency pair . . . its recipient properly responds with a second greeting, or greeting return. Second, it is a claim to have recognized the answerer and a claim to have the answerer recognize the caller. These two aspects of the caller's initial 'Hi' are intertwined. A first greeting having been done, a second greeting is what should relevantly occupy the next turn. But as the first greeting displays recognition, so will a second greeting; it will thus do more than complete the greeting exchange, it will stand as a claim that the answerer has reciprocally recognized the caller.

There is strong evidence that this is what is going on. The second greeting may be withheld, if recognition has not been achieved:

Answerer	1. Hello?	(answer to summons)
Caller	2. Hello, Charles.	(greeting)
pause	(0.2)	
Caller	This is Yolk.	
Answerer	3. Oh, *hello*, Yolk.	(greeting)

The second part is officially absent (note the pause). The silence conveys that the caller has not been recognized. He or she, therefore, provides a further resource over and above the minimum voice sample. Since this is dispreferred, the recognition, when it comes, is in the form of 'the big hello' and is accompanied by an 'Oh' which signifies 'success now'.

Schegloff has isolated a number of solutions to the identification problem. Let us just look at one more very interesting type. In some cases, the caller's first turn consists of the answerer's (presumed) name pronounced with an interrogative or quasi-interrogative intonation. Fox example:

Answerer	1. Hello.
Caller	2. Connie?
Answerer	3. Yeah. Joanie.

Schegloff (1979: 50ff.) argues that the use of this intonation conveys that the caller doubts that merely a minimal sample of his voice will be sufficient for the answerer successfully to identify him or her. It is a form of presequence designed to pre-empt the dispreferred result of not being identifiable from such a sample. It conveys that the speaker recognizes the danger, to him or herself, of oversupposition. The display of doubt in fact provides a turn for the answerer to confirm that he or she *does* recognize the caller. This happens in the example above. The answerer, as requested, does confirm that mutual recognition has been achieved. Another common reply is for the answerer to utter the first pair part of a new adjacency pair in turn 3, for example: 'Oh, hi. How are you?' This signals that the problem of identification has been solved, and that the conversation may proceed.

Turn-taking

Another problem for conversation organization is that of the orderly allocation of turns to speak among the participants. The rules for coordinating turns in casual conversation were explored by Sacks, Schegloff and Jefferson (1974). In Figure 8.4 I have designed a machine which displays the main points of their analysis.

The machine starts at those points in the current speaker's turn where it is relevant for the floor to be taken by someone else. These **transition relevance points** are the boundaries of linguistic items such as sentences, clauses, phrases and even, in some cases, words. The participants, knowing the structure of such items, can collectively project each construction to its formal conclusion and therefore foresee those points at which a change of speaker is possible. If I am uttering a sentence, say a grammatical interrogative, all the participants will know the places where that construction could be considered completed.

At each transition relevance point, a number of things can happen. The current speaker can select the next speaker. If this happens, the party selected has the right and the obligation to speak. There are a number of ways in which the current speaker can select a successor. Remember that the adjacency pair creates

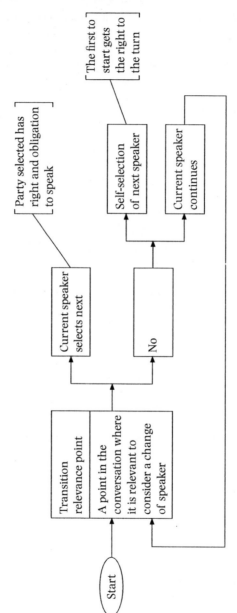

Figure 8.4 The organization of turn-taking in conversation

an *interpersonal* conversational obligation. Thus, by issuing a particular first pair part, for example a question, I can oblige the participant to whom the question is addressed to reply (on pain of warranted inferences caused by its official absence) and thus select him or her as the next speaker. This is a common mode of current speaker selection. Recent research has also shown that paralinguistic factors, such as the use of the eyes and features of intonation, are used to mark both the coming ends of turns and the selection of the next speaker.

But the current speaker need not select the next speaker. In this case, self-selection of the next speaker may occur. Other participants may attempt to take the next turn at a transition relevance point, since the speaker has not selected anyone. The rule is that the first to start gets the right to the turn. This is called the **pressure rule**, since those who want to speak will attempt to 'get in first' at those points where self-selection is permitted, and this pressure tends to close the gaps between turns. Finally, of course, the current speaker may continue (he or she may have to if no one else selects themselves) and the system returns to start again at the next transition relevance point.

Closings

Appropriately, let us conclude our look at the organization of conversation by examining the work of Schegloff and Sacks called 'Opening Up Closings' (1973). A moment's reflection will reveal that a conversation cannot be closed simply by a **terminal exchange** such as, A: 'Bye bye'; B: 'See you around', appearing out of the blue. One cannot simply say goodbye and walk away from interaction. The problem is how to recognize an utterance as the first part of a termination adjacency pair. If it is recognized as this, then the hearer can reply with the second part (his or her own 'goodbye') which shows that he or she does recognize that this is a terminal exchange and agrees that the conversation should now end. When this terminal exchange is successfully completed, then the silence which follows will be interpreted not as the official absence of anything, but just as nothing. The silence after a conversation.

Schegloff and Sacks argue that this problem is solved by preparing the way for the terminal exchange, so that when its first pair part appears it is expected and readily identifiable. A conversation, they argue, has a **closing section**, which has to do with the organization of **topics** of conversation. A conversation has a topical organization. Another part of its machinery, therefore, must make it possible for the participants to raise and develop those topics they wish, and also to allow for the efficient introduction of new topics. A feature of the closing section of conversations, according to Schegloff and Sacks, is for both participants to signal that they have nothing further which they wish to raise. They do this by, in effect, 'passing' a turn. Thus exchanges like the following occur:

A: Well . . .
B: OK, then . . .

A conveys that he or she has nothing further to mention and simultaneously gives B a chance to introduce a further 'mentionable'. B, in reply, conveys that he or she also has nothing further to mention. Since this is now agreed, the stage is set for the terminal exchange and it will be possible to recognize the first part of it when it appears. Conversational acts like the above are termed by Schegloff and Sacks as **pre-closings**.

It is clear from the above that ethnomethodology is concerned with the explanation of the methods (hence its name) that we employ in constituting our everyday social life. Talk, conversation, is a central, commonplace, cooperative activity. It is clearly *ordered by convention.* But exactly how do people 'gloss', that is, understand, the meaning of the activities of everyday life? What is the structure of their practical reasoning? This will reveal the very fabric of assumptions that underly social life and make it possible. For discussions of ethnomethodology see Garfinkel (1967), Turner (1974), Atkinson and Heritage (1984), Sharrock and Anderson (1986) and Boden and Zimmerman (1991).

For us, ethnomethodological research, based on rich data, has demonstrated that *the organization of talk itself is a social institution.* We have seen 'metaconversational' speech acts proposed such as 'replies', 'repairs', 'bringing up a topic' and 'pre-closing', and the phenomenon of the sequencing of successive pairs of acts by different participants. It is clear, then, that part of what participants intend to convey in their utterances will be about the conversation itself. And, therefore, the rules organizing conversation itself will figure crucially in the understanding of what an utterance means.

Ethnography of communication: speech events

This chapter has shown us so far that utterances are activities and that activities are constituted by participants behaving in regular ways which can be stated as norms or rules. More specifically, we have seen that one kind of everyday verbal interaction, conversation, has a rich organization and that participants also communicate with each other about how their conversation is organized and is unfolding.

But each of these utterances is performed in some social context, inescapably so. This is true of any kind of action. Therefore, equally inescapably, we must ask how the non-verbal aspects of social context figure in relation to the activity of speaking.

We will have more to say about how context figures in utterance interpretation in chapter nine. For now we want to consider two things. First, can we develop analytic frameworks which will allow us to describe and understand how social contexts relate to texts of any kind, including utterances in conversation? And second, since any human action if intelligible as an action is in conformity to a rule, do the rules for certain kinds of social situations specify the performance of certain speech acts as 'constitutive' of those situations?

One approach to the study of language in context finds its origins in social anthropology, particularly in the work of John Gumperz (1982 and references therein) and Dell Hymes (1962, 1964, 1972, 1977). This approach to language and context is termed **the ethnography of communication** (there are good accounts in the above, but see also Saville-Troike, 1982). We have already seen this anthropological approach at work in the analysis of code-switching in Hemnesberget by Blom and Gumperz in chapter three. It is worth reminding ourselves at this point how academic subjects, disciplines and subdisciplines have a history and a social dynamic of their own. One aspect of this is the development of specialisms and methodologies, which emerge in social networks and institutions, focus on individuals or issues, perhaps, and then dissolve or develop. We saw above how ethnomethodology, a school of American sociology, associated with particular scholars like Garfinkel, Sacks and Schegloff, developed for its own reasons detailed empirical descriptions of the structure of spoken conversation. This is sometimes absorbed into linguistics and melded with many other approaches, such as the ethnography of communication, under the heading of 'conversation analysis' (see Levinson, 1983: ch. 6). This is simply to say that language in social context has been studied from many different perspectives by differing groupings of scholars. Sometimes, as in the case of the ethnography of communication, the approach was first disseminated by collections of articles, for example, Gumperz and Hymes (1964), *The Ethnography of Communication*; Hymes (1964), *Language in Culture and Society*; Gumperz and Hymes (1972), *Directions in Sociolinguistics*. Such collections manifest the scholarly network creating the 'problematic' or 'methodology', and provide models for further study. Sometimes, conferences and learned societies assist in the same dissemination. These points draw attention to the social and historical context of the situational study of language. This also accounts for the very diverse and sometimes fragmentary nature of what we have to say in this area.

One of the roles of the anthropologist Dell Hymes (1962, 1964, 1972) has been programmatic, outlining the directions and methods of the new area. Hymes has discussed various components which must be included in a full ethnographic description of the act of speaking. He organizes these under the letters SPEAKING as an aid to memory, as shown in Figure 8.5. Note how this framework of situational categories, a **context of situation**, constrains some of the more general features of interaction we have looked at. For example, particular contexts will specify certain speech acts and adjacency sequences (A, act sequences). Particular outcomes – for example, a 'verdict', a 'sale' or a 'diagnosis' – will be normatively expected to be mutually accomplished (E, ends). Turn-taking may be specified in relation to particular roles – for example, a

S	situation	1. Setting or locale 2. Scene or situation	The *setting or locale* is local and concrete; the place and time. The *scene or situation* is abstract, a recurring institution, a type of social occasion like 'a committee meeting'.
P	participants	3. Speaker 4. Addressor 5. Hearer, or audience 6. Addressee	Whom the act is addressed to, and who it is uttered by, are significant. In various situations, participants are allocated *communication roles* by the culture, for example, 'a chairman', 'a therapist', 'a patient', 'a client', 'a teacher', 'a pupil', 'an interviewee'.
E	ends	7. Purposes – Outcomes 8. Purposes – Goals	Some speech events have conventional outcomes, for example, 'a diagnosis', 'a sale' or 'a verdict'. These, as well as individual goals, are significant.
A	act sequences	9. Message form 10. Message content	Topics of conversation and particular 'ways of speaking'. In a culture, certain linguistic forms are conventional for certain types of talk. Certain adjacency pairs typical for certain speech events, e.g., a political interview.
K	key	11. Key	Tone, manner or spirit of the act, mock or serious.
I	instrumentalities	12. Channel or mode of discourse	Spoken, written, written but read aloud, recited etc.
		13. Forms of speech	The dialect, accent or other variety of language in which the act is uttered.
N	norms	14. Norms of interpretation	Interpretation that would be normally expected for the speech event in question.
		15. Norms of interaction	Interpretation in relation to the conventions of conversation itself, turn-taking etc.
G	genres	16. Genres	Categories such as poem, myth, tale, riddle, lecture, commercial, editorial etc.

Figure 8.5 Components of speaking (*after Hymes, 1972*)

teacher and a pupil, or a doctor and a patient (P, participants). Context of situation provides a grid which can be placed on the empirical data of speech so that it can be ethnographically described. (A framework such as this is similar to that employed in the theory of register which we shall examine below.)

Another notion employed by Hymes (1972) is that of the **speech event**. We need to distinguish speech events from both **situations** and **settings**. We'll be looking at situations below, so just an introductory word at this stage. The social actions of a culture enact recurring situations. Situations are not the same as settings. Settings are what the word implies; the actual physical setting of the act, a classroom or a church or Leicester Square. But a situation is more abstract. It is a recurring institution in a society, a 'form of life', in which actions are intelligible and meaningful. The difference is that between a 'religious service', a situation which could be enacted anywhere, and a 'church', as a setting specially set aside for religious services.

Now language may or may not figure in a situation. By contrast a speech event as an ethnographic category is one which focuses on speech itself. Hymes (1972: 56) writes that a speech event is 'restricted to activities, or aspects of activities, that are directly governed by rules or norms for the use of speech'. We have names for some such events: 'interview', 'lecture', 'quiz', 'conversation', 'press conference', 'negotiation', 'trial' etc. Caution is in order here. Some of our traditional or folk labels may be confusing. For example, is 'an argument' a type of speech event, or a genre of talk similar to 'teasing', or 'sarcasm', which could cut across speech event types? A mutual recognition of the speech event type, which participants assume they are sharing, is crucial to the reasoning involved in construing utterances. It is part of the background information to be taken into account if what one utters is to be relevant to the preceding utterances, and to the continuing purposes of the conversation.

How to enter a Yakan house

Some illustrations are perhaps in order. There are excellent anthropological descriptions of speech events. See, for example,

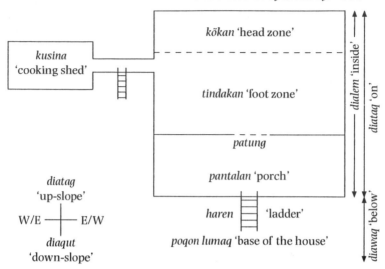

Figure 8.6 Yakan house settings (*from Frake, 1975*)

Bauman and Sherzer (1974), Sanches and Blount (1975), or Frake (1980). We will look at a study by Frake (1975) 'How to Enter a Yakan House' which analyses the rules for entering houses among the Yakan, a Moslem people of the Philippines.

The typical layout of a Yakan house, with each part labelled with its Yakan word, is displayed in Figure 8.6. The house is a setting with a limited number of conceptually distinct locales, for example, the 'porch' and the 'head zone'. (The wall opposite the doorway is the sleeping area of the residents.) Various parts of the house can be the settings for a wide variety of different social situations. For example, the 'porch' is where 'conferences', 'negotiations' and 'litigations' are held. (For these speech events, see Frake, 1969.) The 'head zone' is where rituals are held. Thus, a setting within the house does not uniquely determine one situation, but various situations are appropriate to particular settings.

The organization of the house, and the language used to describe it, are such that they define a definite sequence of settings which must be followed in gaining entry. Frake (1975: 30) arranges these in order of a progressively deeper penetration into the resident's private space. We can follow this progression in Figure 8.6.

1. From 'vicinity' to 'at'.
2. From 'below' to 'on'.
3. From 'on' to 'inside'.
4. From 'foot zone' to 'head zone'.

We will examine a very particular speech event enacted between *a householder* (H) and *an outsider* (O) which enables the latter to enter the house under the auspices of the former. The householder is one of a class of persons who has legal 'free access' to the house. Outsiders are all those who can only enter the house at the invitation of the householders. The rules we are going to consider do not apply to everyone, nor on all occasions. For example, if a prior invitation has been issued for some occasion, the entry of the outsider is a foregone conclusion, and only a general call of 'approach' is appropriate. There are other persons and circumstances when the rules of entry are suspended. However, whenever there is some 'uncertainty' about whether or not an outsider will enter the house, when choice is available to participants, then a house-entering speech event takes place.

There are rules for 'making a pass' or 'approaching' a house in the first place, always initiated by the outsider. These are complex and form a kind of pre-entering sequence. We will pick up the sequence of events at the stage where the outsider is 'below' the house at the base of the ladder in Figure 8.6. Frake points out that moving to this position is the functional equivalent of a knock on the door in our society. Like the telephone ringing, it is a summons, and puts the hearer under the obligation to respond. The Yakan sequence at this point is Schegloff's 'summons-answer' adjacency pair (Frake, 1975: 32). The answer takes the form of a 'customary question' or *addat magtilewin*. (Recall the question intonation in the telephone answer pair part.) This utterance could be an answer to the summons, a greeting and/or a question. In other contexts, which Frake describes, the 'customary question' is taken as a greeting and, if returned, the sequence of exchange of greetings is accomplished. In this context, however, the utterance is not to be interpreted as a greeting, but rather as an answer to the nonverbal summons. Since it is a question, an answer is expected. This enables householder and outsider to 'lock in' and begin the speech event proper. Note how the specific context of situation was crucial for the interpretation of the 'customary question'.

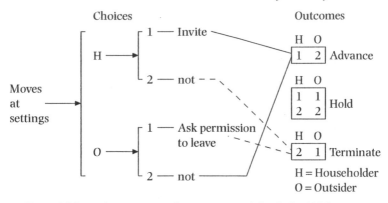

Figure 8.7 Invitation-permission language game (*after Frake, 1975*)

The main body of the speech event has the following form. The householder is only permitted to issue or not issue invitations to the outsider to progress to the next setting. Invitations for each setting have a different form. The outsider, on the other hand, is only permitted *to ask for permission to leave or not*. He or she can never go deeper into the house without an invitation, and can never withdraw from a setting without asking permission and receiving it. The householder, on the other hand, cannot end the event but has control over who can enter each of the settings.

Frake (1975: 31) notes the 'game-like' nature of the event. At each setting, each participant has two choices of action. The outcomes are the joint result of what each participant does. The way the rules work is illustrated in Figure 8.7. Possible outcomes are *advance* to the next setting (for example, from 'below' to 'on'), *terminate* the interaction, or *hold*. The condition for 'advance' is met when the householder invites and the outsider does not ask for permission to leave. The condition for 'terminate' is met when the outsider asks for permission to leave and the householder does not invite. The 'hold' conditions obtain when both participants do the same thing: either both perform 1, or both perform 2, in which case play remains at the same setting. The regulative aspect of these normative rules is the social obligation for the householder to 'render attention' to the outsider and for the outsider to 'display respect' in return. The simple system of rules in Figure 8.7 underlies what is superficially a rich variety of different routines.

A notion which has been implicit throughout this chapter can now usefully be made explicit. This is Wittgenstein's concept of a **language game**, alluded to in the quotation that begins the chapter (Wittgenstein, 1953; Kenny, 1973). This notion captures, by analogy, both the game-like character and the *doing* nature of language in use. In another analogy, language is a set of tools of diverse kinds, used for diverse purposes. (The game analogy by the way does not refer to the 'non-serious' nature of games, but rather the game-like properties of the calculi which characterize linguistic regularities.)

Acts of speaking, or using language, function only in the context of other linguistic and non-linguistic activities. In the quote that begins the chapter, the non-language activities are termed **forms of life**, and it is always as an integral part of such social activities that the game-like, rule-governed procedures of language use are found. Wittgenstein uses the phrase 'language game' vaguely but suggestively to refer to the way individual words are deployed, uses of sentences in speech acts (see chapter ten), and more broadly to refer to larger scale and other kinds of linguistic practices; the act of referring, for example, or performing a measurement. In this suggestive way, every figure in this chapter thus far has been illustrating the rules of a different language game. It is clear that one cannot play a game unless one's activities are in conformity with the rules that make the game possible. The Yakan example illustrates these points very clearly. It would be impossible to perform or construe the utterances without an understanding of the non-verbal activities – the forms of life – which the linguistic procedures – the language game – at least partially constitute.

The concept of register

Wittgenstein's notions of language games and their forms of life are philosophical tools for exploring the nature of meaning. By contrast, the concept of **register**, mainly associated with the socio-functional linguistics of M. A. K. Halliday, provides a framework for the detailed interpretative study of how language is used in situations. We have another methodology which we can compare to the anthropologists' ethnographic descriptions, for example, those of Gumperz, Hymes and Frake.

Register variation is the systematic variation of language according to its functioning in contexts of situation: it is variation according to use, rather than user. The notion has undergone considerable development since its origins (Halliday *et al.*, 1964; Gregory, 1967; Halliday, 1978; Gregory and Carroll, 1978; Ghadessay, 1993. The functional and contextual approach has its origin in the linguistics of J. R. Firth, 1957).

This kind of sociolinguistic variation is well illustrated by the texts in Figure 8.8. One characteristic of register is how obvious it is. Registers are immediately recognizable. And one is also struck by how peculiar and diverse are the actual patterns of grammar and lexis in real texts in various registers when compared to the internalized ideal of Standard English. Associated with the Standard is a plain style of written prose which is taken as the written norm. This norm is in fact a feature of registers only in some narrow range of social situations – that is obvious from our sample in Figure 8.8.

The reader is invited to identify the situations illustrated by the register samples; prayer, a dictionary entry, and so on. Each one is integral to and diagnostic of a 'form of life'. One startling aspect of register is how small a sample is sufficient to recognize the situation type. Often just a word or two will do. Consider, for example, the form of a diary entry. 'Tuesday. Did shop. Went to music. Enjoyed *that* a lot.' To deepen our study we must ask exactly what sort of social practice is involved in the situation of 'keeping a diary'. Can we explicate the meaning of this practice in social context? Further, how is the practice implemented in terms of register, the particular pattern of linguistic forms used? For example, does the absence of a subject in the clauses have a function and carry a social/contextual meaning? Note that this feature is every bit as noteworthy as any dialect variant, and equally ungrammatical from the point of view of the Standard grammar, which says that every English main clause, which isn't imperative, must have a subject.

It is worth remarking that the whole first part of this chapter reported investigations into the organizational properties of one register, that of spontaneous conversational dialogue. We can ask

Sample of Register Variation

1. Eternal God, Who dost call all men into unity with Thy Son, Jesus Christ our Lord, we pray Thee to pour Thy spirit upon the students of all nations, that they may consecrate themselves to Thy service; that being joined together by their common faith and obedience, they may come more perfectly to love and understand one another, that the world may know that Thou didst send Thy Son to be the Saviour and the Lord of all men; through the same Jesus Christ our Lord Who with Thee and the Holy Spirit liveth and reigneth one God world without end. Amen. (Prayer published for the Universal Day of Prayer for Students, 15 February 1953.)

    reprinted from R. Quirk, *The Use of English*

2. **A:** ⌈which (unintelligible)
    B: ⌊**this** after a full day's work
    A: yeah
    B: I think th-that's **fantastic**⌈I'm sorry I wasn't **there**
    A: ⌊I think its (unintelligible)
    A: and . . . um and they're utterly **charming** you know Crystal and Sean are utterly charming . . and so . . in the eh . . his comments the next morning were
    B: there wasn't much to it
    A: yeah . . that . . . and . . (1.5 sec pause) . . . **why**. n **earth** is was Crystal dressed like **that** and I said ⌈like what
    B: ⌊how was she
    dressed (laughs)
    A: and he said **baring** her midrift . . in **this** weather . . (2.0 sec pause) . . and I said I tho . . I thought she looked rather nice . . and she was **wearing** . . cause Crystal . . uh . . is what a **delight** Crystal's is that she wears clothes . . which . . like **nobody** else . . you know she's **entirely** individual and she **picks** things . . well she's **just** . . **extraordinary**

    Spontaneous Conversational Dialogue
    ⌈Represents overlap

3. Friday 20th November – 8pm
    TOBIAS ON SWING STREET
    Norwich Sports Village

'One of the best tap dancers of 'em all' (Time Out). Tobias
Tak presents a brilliant fusion of live jazz music, rhythm tap
dancing and songs straight out of Betty Boop and the heyday
of Basie/Ellington. In a wobbly street with a drunken lamp-
post lit by a crazy moon, Tak and famous hoofer, Jeanefer
Jean-Charles, do the Lindy Hop (Jitterbug), Crazy Shimmie,
Eccentric Snake-Hips, The Sand (real sand!) *et al.* to the
Boogie-Woogie, Blues, Swing, Be-Bop *et al.*; ivories tickled by
Maurice Horhut.

TICKETS: £7. Concs. £5

Sponsored by Broadland District Council

Norwich Arts Centre programme, November 1992

4. Within these Regulations, the following terminology shall apply:

> *Credit*: a measure of the amount of work attached to each
> unit of study completed successfully by a candidate. Candid-
> ates are required to accumulate credit by compliance with
> the appropriate Regulations and may not normally proceed
> or qualify for the award of a degree without accumulation
> of an appropriate number of credits.
> *Unit*: a discrete block of study specified in the Course Cata-
> logue and carrying a number of credits.

Programme of Study
> A degree course shall normally be of six or eight semesters'
> duration, shall comprise such units as may fulfil the credit
> requirements of the appropriate programme of study as set
> out in the Course Catalogue and as prescribed by the Board
> of the School responsible for the course.

Draft Regulations, 1992, University of East Anglia

5. Bear (bē°r), *sb*[1] Forms: I bers, 2–7 bere, (beore, 1 bore, 4 beeyr,
5 barre, beer, 6 *Sc.* beir, 6–7 beare, 7 bare), 7-bear. [OE. *bera*
= OHG. *bero, pero*, MHG. *ber*, mod.G. bär, MDu. *bere*, Du. *beer*:-
OTent. **beron-*, The ON. *björn*:-**bern-oz* seems to be an extended
form. Supposed by Fick to be cogn. with L. *ferus* wild, as if '*the*
wild beast' of northern nations]
I. 1. *A heavily-built, thick-furred plantigrade quadruped, of the
genus* Ursus; *belonging to the* Carnivora, *but having teeth partly
adapted to a vegetable diet.*

Oxford English Dictionary

Figure 8.8 Registers

the same deeper questions about its function or functions in situations and society. Has conversation a special role in defining persons, or what we take as reality, or as a 'social glue' (see Berger and Luckman, 1971)? As noted above, some scholars have argued that face to face dialogue in the spoken mode, the 'canonical situation of utterance', has a special status since language evolved in that situation (Lyons, 1977: 637–8). In the next chapter we shall study a theory of intentional communication that is characteristic of this face to face situation type. One value of register study is to make us aware of how diverse are the patterns of language in use, and correspondingly how narrow is the popular norm of written Standard language.

Social semiotics: Halliday's sociolinguistics

Halliday (1978) entitled one of his later collections of essays, *Language As Social Semiotic*. In this text, he embeds his theory of register in a comprehensive sociolinguistic theory of language. I have schematized the main features of this theory in Figure 8.9. Don't be put off by the apparent size and complexity of this diagram. It is the result of the very comprehensiveness of Halliday's system, which attempts to relate the details of actual **text** (bottom of diagram) to their ultimate function in the whole **social system** (top of diagram). It is this which is the strength of the approach and the reason for its usefulness in textual description and analysis. Halliday's type of sociolinguistic interpretation of text has been widely influential in applied linguistics, including stylistics, the linguistic study of literature (see Halliday, 1973, 1978; Fowler, 1986; Birch and O'Toole, 1988).

The only way to persuasively elucidate this approach is through an example. First I will sketch out the system by explaining Figure 8.9, and then I will illustrate the method by interpreting the 'prayer' text from Figure 8.8 in some detail.

Let us begin with the top and the bottom of Figure 8.9. *We will ultimately be able to interpret a text in terms of the social system.* Text is not only a material tokening of written or spoken language, the words on the page. It is also dynamic. Halliday (1978) calls text, 'the linguistic form of social interaction', and a 'semantic process'

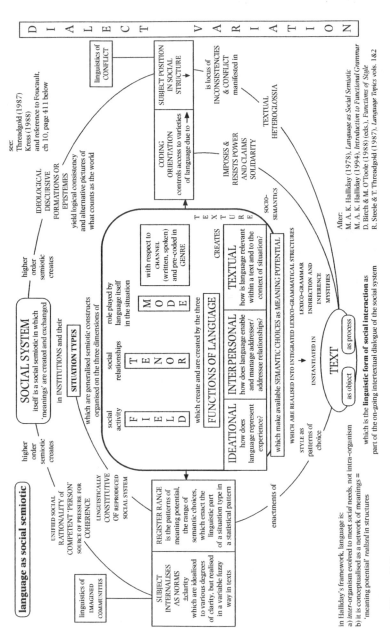

language as social semiotic

linguistics of IMAGINED COMMUNITIES

SUBJECT INTERNALISES AS NORMS ±clarity
which are idealised to various degrees of clarity, but realised in a variable fuzzy way in texts

UNIFIED SOCIAL RATIONALITY of COMPETENT 'PERSON' SOURCE OF PRESSURE FOR COHERENCE

LINGUISTICALLY CONSTITUTIVE OF REPRODUCED SOCIAL SYSTEM

SOCIAL SYSTEM
itself is a social semiotic in which 'meanings' are created and exchanged in INSTITUTIONS and their

higher order semiotic creates

SITUATION TYPES
which are generalised semiotic constructs organised on the three dimensions of

social activity	social relationships	role played by language itself in the situation
F I E L D	T E N O R	M O D E
		with respect to channel (written, spoken) and pre-coded in GENRE

which create and are created by the three

FUNCTIONS OF LANGUAGE

| **IDEATIONAL** how does language represent experience? | **INTERPERSONAL** how does language enable and manage addresser/addressee relationships? | **TEXTUAL** how is language relevant within a text and to the context of situation? |

which make available SEMANTIC CHOICES as MEANING POTENTIAL

CREATES

LEXICO-GRAMMATICAL STRUCTURES
INDIRECTION AND INFERENCE
MYSTIFIES

WHICH ARE REALISED INTO INTEGRATED LEXICO-GRAMMATICAL STRUCTURES

STYLE as patterns of choice

INSTANTIATED IN

TEXT as object / as process

which is the **linguistic form of social interaction** as part of the on-going intertextual dialogue of the social system

enactments of

REGISTER RANGE is the patterns of meaning potential, the range of semantic choices, which enact the linguistic part of a situation type in a statistical pattern

higher order semiotic creates

higher order semiotic creates

IDEOLOGICAL DISCURSIVE FORMATIONS OR EPISTEMES
yield logical consistency and alternative pictures of what counts as the world

see:
Threadgold (1987)
Kress (1988)
and reference to Foucault,
ch 10, page 411 below

linguistics of CONFLICT

SUBJECT POSITION IN SOCIAL STRUCTURE
is locus of INCONSISTENCIES & CONFLICT manifested in

CODING ORIENTATION controls access to varieties of language due to ↑

IMPOSES & RESISTS POWER AND CLAIMS SOLIDARITY

TEXTUAL HETEROGLOSSIA

SOCIO-SEMANTICS

T E X T U R E

D I A L E C T V A R I A T I O N

in Halliday's framework, language is:
a) *inter*-organism evolved to meet *social* needs, not intra-organism
b) it is conceptualised as a network of meanings =
'meaning potential' *realised* in structures

After:
M. A. K. Halliday (1978), *Language as Social Semiotic*,
M. A. K. Halliday (1994), *Introduction to Functional Grammar*
D. Birch & M. O'Toole (1988) (eds.), *Functions of Style*
R. Steele & T. Threadgold (1987), *Language Topics* vols. 1&2

Figure 8.9

of making and exchanging meanings. Text is 'the operational unit of language'. It is important to see the significance of this. For example, consider that in this perspective each occasion when I consult *The Oxford English Dictionary* is actually a social interaction between me and the source of that text. The act of 'consulting' is as real a social interaction as any conversation. On further reflection, it is clear that the larger scale social activity that is going on – the meaning of my consultation in the culture or social system – is the standardisation of English. This results in my spelling the word I am looking up exactly as prescribed by the dictionary I consult. As we saw, there is no real latitude in my behaviour in the case of spelling – the text act – the operational unit of language – has real social consequences in creating linguistic uniformity. The social process of standardization discussed in chapter two is actually realized daily in millions of diverse text interactions like this, 'looking up' an authoritative spelling of the word in English.

To turn to the top of the diagram Figure 8.9. For Halliday, a social system or culture is essentially a complex of semiotic systems. That means that a social system is the meaningfulness or signification of its signs; it is the locus where meanings are produced and exchanged in actions and in artifacts. Human beings transform aspects of the substantial world, including their own behaviour, into systems of signs with meanings, that make it and them intelligible. This is one sense in which language is reality-creating.

Semiotics or **semiology** is that science, proposed by Saussure (1915/1959: 16), which 'studies the life of signs within society'. For Halliday a social system consists of the multiplicity of its codes, which are generated in and function to produce and reproduce the meanings of social behaviour, including texts. Thus all semiotic study must be contextual and explicate how texts and codes function to produce a social system. In classical semiotic studies of culture there are codes of dress, of the body itself, of music, art, architecture, food, and so on. Language is the unifying global system – or meta-system – because it is the only one that acts as an interpreter (an 'interpretant' or 'signified') of its own signs and all the other sign systems ('systems of signifiers') (see Barthes, 1967; Eco, 1976; Hawkes, 1977: ch. 4). A distinguishing feature of

Halliday's social semiotics is this emphasis on the socio-historical and contextual nature of the sign as opposed to the more abstract Saussurean conception (see Hodge and Kress, 1988).

Looking just below the social system in Figure 8.9 we come to the category of **situation types**. These are the social institutions mentioned earlier, such as 'lectures', 'trials', 'casual conversations', 'football matches', 'school assemblies' etc. We can now view these as semiotic constructs in that they form a system of contrasting meaningful classes of social events constituted from the material of human interaction. And the role of language itself varies from one situation type to another. In some situations, for example, in tennis matches, language figures in scoring or umpires' judgements or in the media commentary, but non-verbal activities *make* the game. In other situations, for example, a job interview, a university examination, or a casual conversation, language activity is itself the central constituting behaviour. We can now ask in what kind of situation type would our prayer text in Figure 8.8 occur.

Halliday argues that we can analyse situation types in terms of three dimensions which are salient to the way language functions in situations. In Figure 8.9, these are represented by the three boxes labelled **field, tenor** and **mode**. We will characterize each of these in turn. The **field** signifies the ongoing social activity carried on by the text. For many texts, this is a new way of looking at language. For example, what sort of social activity do we perform when we pray, or write up a scientific experiment, or sit an exam? And how is this activity realized by the language used, the linguistic choices we make? Or to put this the other way around – what resources does the English language make available for us to be able to pray? This latter way of putting things is more impersonal. The linguistic field is given by a culture and speech community. We could write a social history of the register of prayer, and its concomitant social activity. This latter characterization also allows us to see a language as providing 'meaning potentials' for its speakers. It gives us the linguistic way to 'mean' whatever we 'mean' when we perform the activity of praying.

The term **tenor** refers to that aspect of situations which involves particular role relationships between participants, both social and conversational. It is the interpersonal aspect of situations.

Finally, the **mode** has two aspects. First, it describes the relation to the medium: written, spoken, and so on. We have seen above just how profound the influence of writing is on our conception of language. On the other hand, mode also describes the **genre** of the text. Genre is a subtle idea. Genre means that a great deal of the linguistic form of a text is generically pre-specified or laid down beforehand – 'pre-coded' as Halliday puts it. This pre-coding *enables* the field and tenor of every instance of a text in that register. For example, the precise linguistic form of a prayer in English is laid down by its genre, so when following those norms, we automatically are enabled to enter into the activities and relationships of which 'praying' consists. In this way, via situations, the culture or social semiotic hands down the significances which inform our activities. The interpretation of these 'meanings' relates to the overall social system and both its **context of culture** and **discourses** (see Figure 8.9). These higher level categories describe more general patterns in the culture or social system, those that underlie many different situation types, and which have long and complex histories. Examples would be the higher level semiotics of gender and sexuality, or the semiotics of individualism and the modern concept of a person. Similarly, discourses in this model would be features of broad semiotic-cultural movements; for example, the general features of bureaucratic language in all its varieties of register. (As we shall see, the term 'discourse' alludes to the thought of the historian of ideas, Michel Foucault.) Hopefully, we would be able to relate general features of the linguistic form of texts to changes in a culture. For example, Halliday and others have described the development of a 'nominal' style of English and suggested that the enrichment of linguistic resources of taxonomy and classification is a prerequisite of the practice and world-view of modern science.

The last features of Figure 8.9 can only be dealt with in summary fashion because they are more technical. Reading downwards in the diagram we come to Halliday's proposal that language has evolved to serve three major functions which are part of every situation, the **ideational** or the representation of experience, the **interpersonal** or the relation of addressor and addressee, and the **textual**, the linkage of linguistic forms with each other and with situations. These three functions reflect the three semiotic dimensions of situations, field, tenor and mode. Halliday's basic view is that the vocabulary and grammar present all the potential meanings needed to perform these functions. The very shape of the grammatical structure is simply a meaning resource from which we must choose to create texts. This allows a more precise definition of register (see Figure 8.9) as a 'blocked out range' or 'set of options' in meaning, which statistically are chosen according to the historically given norm of the genre (in mode) to perform the activity of the field and enact the social relations involved, also using the given channel, written or spoken. Register, then, is a pattern of 'meaning potential'.

Note that the diagram linking text and situation takes the form of a circle. It is precisely the range of **meaning potential** which is the register, that, when chosen by individual subjects, constitutes and reproduces the situation in the social system which is the origin of those very meanings. Meaning is super-personally or socially given – it is *always already there* – from the point of view of the individual, but only because each individual is already constrained to opt to use it that way. From the point of view of our individual interpretation of a text, we can only achieve understanding because we already know the situations and their meanings which have been acquired by understanding texts in that way. This circular relation between text and situation, speaker or interpreter and context in Figure 8.9, is one aspect or version of the famous **hermeneutic circle**. This is a problem of interpretation which will arise again in chapter nine.

Exemplification: a prayer

We will end this chapter with a register analysis of the prayer in Figure 8.8, reproduced here for convenience.

Eternal God, Who dost call all men into unity with Thy Son, Jesus Christ our Lord, we pray Thee to pour Thy spirit upon the students of all nations, that they may consecrate themselves to Thy service; that being joined together by their common faith and obedience, they may come more perfectly to love and understand one another, that the world may know that Thou didst send Thy Son to be the Saviour and the Lord of all men; through the same Jesus Christ our Lord Who with Thee and the Holy Spirit liveth and reigneth one God world without end. Amen.

Prayer published for the Universal Day of Prayer for Students, 15 February 1953. Reprinted from R. Quirk, *The Use of English.*

The most obvious features, of course, are the archaisms, the third person singular forms of verbs, *dost, liveth, reigneth*; inflected second person pronouns, *thou* (nominative), *thee* (accusative and oblique), *thy* (genitive). Also noteworthy are the specialized religious vocabulary *faith, pray, consecrate, more perfectly, love*; formulae such as *liveth and reigneth one God world without end*; and the characteristic syntactic patterns such as *we pray thee* instead of *we pray to thee*, and the specialized use of *that* to mean 'in order that'. When read aloud the text also seems to demand a highly characteristic intonation. On the analogy of the social meaning of variables in accents studied above, all these features together imply a 'social meaning' characteristic of religious situations. They also allude to other historical texts, pre-eminently the *King James Version* and *The Book of Common Prayer*. This encodes a distancing and monumentalizing effect. All these features of prayer symbolize that the text is performing a practice which is far removed from everyday situations and also has a public institutional aspect (compare to the languages of law or bureaucracy). This is why there is an outcry when a reform of religious language is attempted.

One of the dangers of register study is simply to catalogue such features of texts. But the social semiotic theory allows us to probe much deeper. Note, first of all, that the very term 'prayer' is ambiguous. On the one hand, a prayer is a genre of text – I could give someone a copy of a prayer. One the other hand, prayer is something performed, which can be described by the verb, *pray*. Praying is something participants *do* in situations, and the field and tenor provide an analytical frame for considering this practice.

Consider the prayer text. What sort of social activity does it involve? What are the social relationships involved? How is it produced and consumed? A text simply can't stand on its own. We have to imaginatively reconstruct a context of situation for it. Many are possible. Let's focus on one common situation type where people pray, that of a School Assembly. (This draws our attention to the fact that although there is but one word 'prayer', there are many distinct kinds of prayer.) Now consider how praying might fit into an Assembly. Let's look at this from the point of view of the tenor and its dynamic role relations. It is immediately clear that the simple pair, addressor–addressee, will not do. One possible network of relationships is:

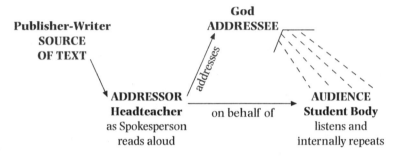

In this example, the headteacher reads aloud a written text which was produced for this purpose by an anonymous institutional source. In what sense, then, can the headteacher's role be that of an origin of some intended communication? Rather, he or she seems to be acting as a spokesperson, publicly intoning the text – that is 'praying' – for a participating audience of a special captive sort. The law actually requires textual activity of this sort. So what are the pupils supposed to be doing? There are a number of variations on this situation. Equipped with copies of the text, they may be reading it aloud along with the teacher. Or, the teacher may be leaving gaps after each phrase, in which the pupils are expected to repeat the words. Alternatively, they may simply appear to silently witness the headteacher praying. But that would be absurd! Presumably a special sort of 'listening' is socially prescribed in which each pupil is expected to somehow mentally attend to the words in a way which makes them also silently pray. (This posits a social control of the contents of consciousness, in which the outer at that very moment structures the inner. But that is a general phenomenon.) The headteacher's social role as 'Head' is mapped on to the communicative role of spokesperson in addressing the deity on behalf of the pupils. The pupils are also praying, but *via* the spokesperson. The 'we' or exclusive plural marks this, that is part of its function.

But the tenor involves more than this, and the relationship is very elaborately precoded into the very grammar. The subject and main verb of the sentence are, 'we pray'. Why do we find the complex phrase *Eternal God, Who dost call all men into unity with Thy Son, Jesus Christ our Lord*, preceding the subject pronoun 'we'?

This structure involves a vocative noun phrase *Eternal God*, intonationally marked off from the subject and preceding it. Such vocative phrases are used to make explicit, catch the attention of, or otherwise address the hearer.

The text and the headteacher are thus engaging in dialogue, using language to address God, a metaphysical entity. The vocative phrase is qualified by a non-restrictive or appositive relative clause which glosses it, and this is followed by another appositive phrase, *Jesus Christ* which glosses *Thy Son*, and the former is further glossed with another appositive phrase, *our Lord*. Grammatically, a complex interpersonal theme – the address to God – is chosen. It is not enough to say that such constructions are part of the genre, e.g. *Our Father, Who art in Heaven; Hail Mary, full of grace*. What is the function of such an elaborate construction? Furthermore, the content seems informationally empty. Surely God already knows that 'he has called all men into unity' with his son, so he hardly needs to be informed of this. Rather, the sheer quantity of the address, its copiousness, serves to add weight to God, to honour him. This is exactly the same use found in the elaborate titles and addresses made to secular power. Its origins appear to be in the Latin titles of antiquity. Indeed, the generic origins of English religious language are in translations from Latin. There are two points here: first, that the form of address and its 'social meaning' are very ancient, going back to Roman times, and measuring asymmetry of power in weight of linguistic titles; second, that secular and religious power use the same forms.

The interpersonal structure of the prayer continues with:

'WE PRAY THEE / TO DO X / IN ORDER THAT'
performative   infinitive   'that'

As evidenced by the use of the verb *pray*, this is the very heart of the prayer. And it is the point at which the interpersonal meets the field, the social activity, and how it is represented in language. The verb *pray* in this use is performative (see chapter ten below, page 379). When properly uttered it actually 'performs' the action of praying; in one sense of prayer. Here, the activity seems to be one of 'entreating', 'begging' – an extremely power asymmetric form of requesting, a 'very humble' request of someone to do something; '*thee*', '*to pour*', with pouring being a typical part of an ancient system of religious metaphors of spirit and grace.

The structure continues with a complex series of *that*-clauses specifying the reason for the request, and the outcome of its being granted. In this case, the outcome is essentially one of *unity* among *the students of all nations*. We won't analyse this in detail, but the spiritual outcome is embodied in the lexical and grammatical choices in fine detail, for example by the reciprocal construction.

> they may consecrate themselves
> (they) being joined together
> their common faith and obedience
> they may come more perfectly
> (they) love and (they) understand one another.

The question arises as to who 'they' are in relation to the actual participants in our example. If 'they' has as antecedent *the students of all nations*, and if the prayer is being performed – at least in surrogate – by students, then 'we' is also included in 'they'. And, if the prayer is performed by students everywhere, in these performances, as in its collective inner utterance by our pupils, *it enacts the very unity, under and because of God, that it prays for*. That is, this prayer seeks *solidarity*, and at the same time, enacts solidarity.

Our analysis reveals two social semiotic dimensions which allow us to understand the text. These are the familiar dimensions of power and solidarity, which we found functioning earlier with respect to politeness and address terms (chapter seven, page 267). *In fact the prayer text provides a model of social order, of solidarity engendered because of a superordinate unifying power, which at the same time it ceremonially reproduces as textual activity.* And we can explain details of linguistic choice, the use of 'we' instead of 'I' for example, in terms of this social semiotic. The school assembly enacts very well this model of power and solidarity. Indeed, one imagines the very architecture and forms of social arrangement in the assembly hall as interpretable in the same terms.

Such a text, both in genre and as activity, is highly authoritarian or **monologic**. The text itself admits only one voice, and does not interrogate, undermine or doubt itself. That is, it isn't **dialogic**, building into itself alternative voices. In our imagined situation, public dissent isn't possible during the headteacher's performance without invoking a response from authority. The commonest form of dissent would be a hidden opting out of the inner replication of the text, by being bored, blank, silly, or thinking of something else. (In fact this is probably the normal state of affairs in school assemblies.) Note also that conversation, as studied in the first part of this chapter, is by definition dialogic, involving more than one voice.

To conclude, it is important to note that this social interpretation of the prayer is not something of which participants would be aware. They could not be said to be intentionally communicating the content of our social analysis. So language socially functions in ways that *can* transcend intention and communication. We will return to this issue in chapter ten. But in the next chapter we will develop a theory of intentional communication.

9 Communication, words and world

> Verbal communication involves both code and inferential processes.
>
> Sperber and Wilson (1995)

Limits of semantics

Consider the following utterances:

1. Brenda: I'm pregnant . . . and it's your fault.
2. Brenda: I told you to be careful . . .
3. Arthur: How do you know?
4. Brenda: I'm twelve days late.
5. Arthur: How do you know it's mine?
6. Brenda: I ain't done owt like that with Jack for a couple of months or more.
7. Arthur: Well, have yet tried owt? Took owt I mean?
8. Brenda: Yes, took pills but they didn't work.

If we reflect on the semantics – the meanings of the words and sentences taken by themselves – it is clear that such meanings fall far short of what is required to comprehend either what the participants are intending to convey or how the utterances connect with one another to form a coherent text.

The sentence and word meanings of a language are the **coded** part of what a sentence conveys when uttered. Such coded meanings are connected to the sounds by convention and conveyed in any occasion of use. Now look at sentence 4: 'I'm twelve days late.' What is encoded by the semantic structure of this sentence? All Brenda literally says is that she is late by twelve days. Resolving the expressions that depend on the context of utterance we can paraphrase the coded meaning of 4 as: 'Brenda is now, at the moment of speech, twelve days after the due or customary time.' As it stands, the content of this sentence isn't adequate for us to know what she is trying to convey. Ignoring context, Brenda could be telling Arthur that she is twelve days late with an essay or a gas payment. It appears that coded meaning, the semantics of the language, underdetermines what the speaker is actually intending to convey. This is pervasive in utterances for a multiplicity of reasons. For example, in 3, the linguistic form representing what Brenda is supposed to 'know' has undergone ellipsis. The content is incomplete.

But of course we do comprehend the utterances. The point is that the coded meanings of the sentence are not alone sufficient to determine the proposition expressed in its utterances. We do comprehend that in uttering sentence 4 Brenda is conveying that 'the onset of her period' is late. But that is only the first step. We also discern that she intends to convey not only this, but to communicate to Arthur that this is how she knows that she is pregnant – that is how 4 is relevant as an answer to his question 3. But to understand both steps we have to go beyond the coded meaning of 4 and, employing both immediate **context** and **background information**, infer both the actual proposition she expresses and any further propositions she intends to communicate. The conclusion we come to is that quoted from Sperber and Wilson (1995: 3) which introduces this chapter: 'verbal communication involves both code and inferential processes'.

It is useful to idealize this in terms of stages. First, we are presented with an utterance of a linguistic item which only gives us a skeletal coded meaning, or **logical form**. This is all that the language system *per se* gives us, simply the first input to the process of communication. (J. Fodor, 1983, argues that language itself is an 'input system', autonomous and insulated from general processes of inference and background information. Sperber and Wilson, 1995, accept Fodor's 'modularity of mind' hypothesis mentioned in chapter one.)

In the second stage, this skeletal representation is enriched through inference to yield the actual proposition that the speaker is using the sentence to express. But this inferencing process is itself simultaneously sensitive to a third stage. In this final stage the hearer infers the informative intent of the speaker, that which the speaker intends to communicate. The speaker intends the very recognition that he or she was trying to communicate this message to be the cause of the hearer's understanding of the speaker's meaning, of what they particularly wanted to convey (for this intentional theory of **speaker meaning**, see Grice, 1957; Schiffer, 1972). These intentionally communicated propositions can and most often do differ from the proposition expressed. They are not overtly expressed. Instead they are **contextually implied** or **implicated** employing contextual and background information (Grice, 1975).

We can informally illustrate the three proposed stages using Brenda's utterance 4:

STAGE 1   The coded meaning of the sentence uttered.
          'I'm twelve days late.'

> *Speaker is, as she speaks, twelve days after the due or customary time.*

STAGE 2   Proposition actually expressed by the utterance of this sentence in this context.

> *Speaker's period did not commence at the due time, loosely, within a twenty-four hour period, either eleven or twelve days prior to now.*

STAGE 3   Further proposition(s) which speaker intends hearer to recognize that she intends to be inferred in this context and thus communicated from speaker to hearer.

> *The non-commencement of speaker's period at the due time is how she knows she is pregnant and is the evidence for the truth of 'I'm pregnant.'*

The inferences involved in stages 2 and 3 are relative to both general background information and this specific context, so

A: Background information
> *If a woman misses a period, then she is probably pregnant. (If no other explanation is available.) The later a period is, the more likely it is that it will be missed altogether.*

B: **Context**

> *Arthur has questioned in sentence 3 what warrant Brenda has for believing she is pregnant is true, as stated in sentence 1.*

Note in passing that I've already made another interpretative decision in this account. I've excluded the alternative that Arthur's question was about how she knew it was his fault. In this chapter we shall study intentional communication and the processes of inference it involves in terms of a new and influential approach, **relevance theory** developed by Sperber and Wilson (1995). It presents a complex picture and we shall have to deal with the issues in a simplified way. Much of the discussion will also have a philosophical flavour, inescapable when dealing with such issues as inference. However, since both context and knowledge of the world are involved, this is an area where social and contextual factors are needed to explain language use. It is therefore part of the study of language and society as we have defined it in chapter one. Ultimately, we will be able to link communication to the issue of 'social meaning' in chapter eleven.

Dictionary versus encyclopedia

We have distinguished between the coded meanings that constitute the semantic structure of a language and the background information required for utterance comprehension. The job of semantics is to theorize the former and there are disputes about how this should be done. We shall have to simplify here.

For our purposes, we can get at the coded meaning of a sentence by isolating what it **analytically entails**, that is, what other sentences follow from it as a matter of definition or semantic necessity. For example, if 'X is pregnant' is true, sentences such as 'X is female' and 'X is adult' and 'X has a foetus inside her body' and 'X is going to have a baby' appear to be also true. This is because they are definitions of, and therefore synonymous with, the original sentence. There is a problem with this example to which we shall return later.

The surest test for analytic entailment is its opposite, **contra-diction**. This occurs when we both assert the original sentence, and at the same time deny its 'meaning', one of its entailments, e.g.

> X is pregnant but X isn't female
> X is pregnant but X hasn't got a foetus inside her body.

If the response is 'that's impossible because of what the word "pregnant" means', we know that we are dealing with an analytic entailment.

One can see how entailment and contradiction give access to our intuitions about the meaning of words and sentences. Consider the predicate 'is at fault'. This entails that some state of affairs is bad and that badness is the responsibility of the subject. Thus it would be contradictory to say that Y is X's fault, but X is not responsible for Y; or that Y is X's fault, but Y isn't bad. This is the kind of meaning that appears in a **lexicon** or mental dictionary, capturing the meanings of words as they are coded by convention on to the sounds of a given language.

A dictionary can represent such meanings using **meaning postulates** which specify the meaning relation between predicates as an analytic entailment, for example:

> X is at fault with respect to Y → X is responsible for Y.
> entails

Or the same relationship can be represented in a single **analytic statement**:

> If X is at fault with respect to Y, then X is responsible for Y.

This is the sort of coded meaning, accessible from the mental dictionary and constituting semantic knowledge of English, involved in the first stage of comprehension described above. Now consider what Arthur knows and can conclude when he comprehends the literal meaning of Brenda's remark 'it's your fault', by virtue of his knowledge of English alone. Since he has the above meaning postulate in his lexicon, he can draw the following inference by substituting himself for X and 'Brenda's pregnancy' for Y:

Meaning Postulate from Lexicon	1.	If X is at fault with respect to Y, then X is responsible for Y.
	2.	Arthur is at fault with respect to Brenda's pregnancy.
Conclusion	3.	Arthur is responsible for Brenda's pregnancy.

This **deductive** argument would be formally or logically valid – the conclusion follows necessarily from the premisses – no matter what predicates appeared in the premisses. But in this case, since a truth of meaning drawn from the lexicon is included as the first premiss, the semantic necessity of this definition is passed down, as it were, in the inference from 2 to 3, since deduction always preserves truth. Such arguments are **demonstratively valid**. Sperber and Wilson (1995: ch. 2) claim that our central processors are equipped with a **deductive device** capable of demonstrative inference. We have seen what happens when dictionary definitions figure in inferences involving this device. In Arthur's case, he can conclude on 'coded' semantic grounds alone that Brenda believes he is responsible for her 'bad' pregnancy.

But, as suggested above, such semantic content by itself is not sufficient to account for utterance comprehension or the coherence of a text. This requires access to background information. Semantic content alone does not tell us how Arthur is responsible for her pregnancy or how his carefulness might be related to her pregnancy. The connection between these is taken for granted as part of participants' knowledge of the world. Consider what we know about how intercourse causes pregnancy and how that causal story links to birth control precautions. Other items of background brought to this text involve the relation between pregnancy and menstruation such that a missed period after intercourse could be a sign of pregnancy, that pregnancy is bad for Brenda because she is married to someone other than Arthur, that pregnancies can be terminated, and so on. Note also that such information is structured. The assumptions involved are linked together in a 'scientifically primitive' common-sense or folk theory of pregnancy and related concepts.

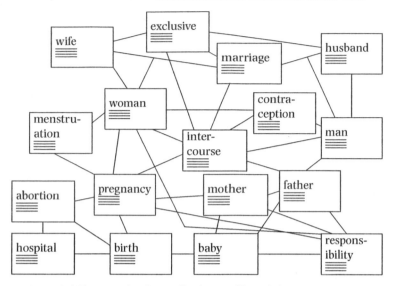

Figure 9.1 The interrelatedness of background knowledge

The point is that background information is interconnected inferentially in large-scale structures of knowledge. Items from this larger structure, not part of the meanings of the words and sentences used in our example, are somehow implicated in context, when the language is actually being used (see below). Figure 9.1 is suggestive of the conceptual areas that, interconnected together, make up some sort of large-scale structure of our folk knowledge in this area of experience.

This is the sort of information which we would expect to find, not in a dictionary, but in an **encyclopedia**, a mental storehouse of background knowledge. Each word in Figure 9.1 represents a **conceptual address**. The lines under each address suggest what we know in each area and the lines between boxes ('files', 'data bases') represent inferential connections between each set of propositions. A chunk of such a network covering a given domain could be termed a **belief system**.

The sheer size of what an individual knows, believes or assumes is breathtaking. Just consider what one has to know in order to do everyday things like driving a car, going shopping, or eating in a restaurant. The same knowledge is accessed in understanding utterances about such activities as in performing the acts themselves (Schank and Abelson, 1977; Garfinkel, 1967). Some knowledge is very basic and general, for example, things that seem indubitably true about how the physical world works. Other beliefs are weaker, although widely assented to. We also know a lot about people. We know the practices of our community – how to buy and sell, work and play and so forth – in the most minute detail. Among these are the norms for conversational organization and speech events of the sort discussed in chapter eight. We also command the **intentional** vocabulary of 'folk' psychology used to interpret human actions, both verbal and non-verbal, and human artifacts (Dennett, 1979, 1987). This is the mentalistic idiom of belief, desire, motive, intention and other **propositional attitudes**, plausibly ascribed to others and in terms of which they are conceived as 'persons', that is, competent, rational social agents whose actions we can explain in intentional terms (see chapters ten and eleven below). We also know about participants' biographies developed through their use in interactions with one another in the face of common experiences.

Background knowledge

The propositions of the mental encyclopedia are commonly referred to as 'background knowledge' or 'mutual' or 'shared knowledge'. The terms 'knowledge' and 'mutual' are both problematic. Let us examine some items of information we noted above.

A. If X misses a period and X has had intercourse since her immediately previous period, then it is possible, indeed highly probable, that X is pregnant.

B. If X is married to Z and if X is pregnant and if Y caused X to be pregnant and Y ≠ Z, then it is possible, indeed highly probable, that X considers her pregnancy bad.

C. If X and Y had intercourse and X ovulates and (other premises) then it is possible that Y could cause X to become pregnant.

D. If Y caused X to become pregnant, then it is possible, indeed almost certain, that X and Y had intercourse.

Now consider what happens when encyclopedic information like this is employed by the deductive device to construct an argument.

Background Knowledge from Encyclopedia	1.	If X misses a period and X has had intercourse since her immediately previous period, then it is highly probable that X is pregnant.
	2.	Brenda has missed a period.
	3.	Brenda implies that intercourse has occurred since her immediately previous period.
	4.	Brenda is very probably pregnant.

As a demonstrative inference, this deduction is as formally valid as the earlier one we performed. The conclusion again follows necessarily from the premisses just as in the first example. The difference this time is that 1 is not true by definition and doesn't come from the dictionary, but the encyclopedia. If it is true, it is a fact about the world, not a matter of meaning. (Such truths are called **synthetic**.) The formally valid deductive argument transmits to the conclusion exactly the degree of empirical uncertainty found in the premisses. If it is only probably the case that 1, then the conclusion, 4, is only probably true to the same degree. So Arthur can conclude that Brenda is probably pregnant with the same degree of confidence with which he accepts the premiss 1, and Brenda's claim 2. The information A–D was chosen to illustrate different degrees of empirical uncertainty in encyclopedic information. The point is to contrast the necessary truth of analytic statements, which are true as a matter of definition, with the degrees of uncertainty of synthetic statements, which are true or false depending on the facts.

This uncertainty makes the term 'background knowledge' less than apt. Knowledge is not the same as belief (Hintikka, 1962). For example, if I know something, I also believe it is the case. But, if I believe something is the case, I do not necessarily know that it is true. My belief could be wrong and have to be revised. I can believe something that is actually false. Belief is a wider term than knowledge (which is sometimes described as warranted true belief). So knowledge is too strong a term for the background information used in comprehension, since it only admits actually true propositions to this process, and this is incorrect. For this and other reasons Sperber and Wilson (1995: 2) use the term **assumption** with respect to conceptual representations of the sort that are employed in encyclopedia entries. Assumptions are 'thoughts treated by the individual as representations of the actual world' and this includes 'not only facts, but also dubious and false assumptions presented as factual'. Assumptions can also be held with various degrees of strength, depending on the evidence that supports them, and their past utility on comprehension. (In what follows, however, I will use the terms 'assumption' and 'belief' more or less interchangeably.)

The assumptions that fill our encyclopedias are empirical and are established non-demonstratively. As such, they are not necessary truths but admit of degrees of uncertainty. Such beliefs about the world, although crucial for utterance comprehension, are not part of language itself. Rather they are used in our central processing system. More on this later. For now, we should note that how people come to believe what they do – the 'fixation of belief' – is quite mysterious. So we don't clearly understand how encyclopedic information is established. For one class of beliefs, those that make up science, philosophy of science has much to say. But the status of garden variety folk theories, the sort of information that fills everyone's mental encyclopedia, is problematic. One possibility is the classical form of learning from experience; reasoning inductively to new information on the basis of recurring patterns of observed facts. Alternatively, beliefs may be established through creative hypothesis-formation and subsequent testing. Or in some cases not based on any rational justification at all.

Context and mutuality

The next issue is how background information becomes mutually available to participants in a context.

But what is a context? In the first instance, of course, we think of immediate features of the situation in which speech is uttered. These are such things as time and place, the speech roles of the participants (who is speaker and who is hearer), and the utterances preceding and following in the conversational chain. All these are part of context. But context is broader and more abstract than this.

In an inferential theory of interpretation, we can view context as the set of premisses employed by the deductive device in interpreting the utterance. Any information put into the device to interpret an utterance will be part of the context of that utterance. Of course, this often includes the immediately or more remotely preceding utterances, but in principle any encyclopedic information can be employed. A context is 'a psychological construct. A subset of the hearer's assumptions about the world' (Sperber and Wilson, 1995: 15). Other theorists have employed such notions as **commitment slate** to characterize the role of beliefs that form the context in ongoing interpretation (Hamblin, 1971; Gazdar, 1981).

If context is the subset of background information employed by the deductive device in interpretation, then the question arises whether this information need be mutually known beforehand. **Mutual knowledge** is information which is shared and is *known* to be shared between speaker and hearer. And it seems natural to suppose that a speaker's communicative task would be more reliably accomplished if the speaker knew that the hearer already knew the exact pieces of background information that made up the context for what he or she intended to convey. Indeed, the correct background information is arguably a *sine qua non* for successful inferential communication. (For discussions of 'mutual knowledge', 'shared knowledge', 'common ground', see Lewis, 1969; Schiffer, 1972; Stalnaker, 1978; Kartunen and Peters, 1979; and Bach and Harnish, 1979.)

However, as mentioned above, the notion of mutual knowledge is problematic. It is difficult to determine how it could be established and it may not be necessary for a theory of inferential communication in any case.

How could participants establish they have mutual knowledge of some specific piece of encyclopedic information? Remember that 'knowledge' – that what is known of the other person is in fact true – is a very strong requirement. Furthermore, the participant has to know what the other participant knows and also know that the other participant knows that the first participant knows etc., in order for the knowledge to be mutual. There is potentially infinite regress. Attempts have been made to resolve this by providing rational grounds for mutual knowledge (Lewis, 1969: 52ff.; Clark and Marshall, 1981).

Alternatively, Sperber and Wilson (1995) deal with the problem of mutual knowledge, by arguing that it is not in fact required for communication. Instead, they develop a notion of **mutual manifestness**, which is sufficient to deal with intentional communication, but which is weaker than mutual knowledge. A fact is manifest if an individual is 'capable at that time of representing it mentally and accepting its representation as true or probably true' (Sperber and Wilson, 1995: 39). What is manifest includes not only what one is actually aware of – one's actual assumptions – but all those other assumptions which could be inferred given what one already assumes. And these assumptions may be either true or false. Furthermore, the manifestness of an assumption is a matter of degree. So an assumption can be more or less strongly or weakly manifest. Given the above, mutual manifestness is much easier to establish than mutual knowledge. It arises when it is itself manifest to participants that they share the same manifest assumptions. Since this is the case, a speaker can assume that a hearer may be *capable* of representing some information – that it is manifest to the latter albeit weakly – even if the speaker thinks that the hearer has not explicitly entertained it beforehand. It is manifest to the speaker that the hearer can and will employ it in construing the utterance, of it becoming more manifest to the hearer as the best way of comprehending what is said. I need not 'know beforehand' why becoming pregnant is considered bad by Brenda. I am quite capable of constructing a story if I must in order to understand her. Thus the requirement of prior mutual knowledge is dissolved.

Contextual effects

We can now begin to consider the inferential processes involved in comprehending an utterance. It is necessary to do this in a fairly simplified way. Consider this exchange:

A: She's pregnant.
B: Yes, she'll be going to hospital soon.

There is no coded semantic connection between the two remarks. Sentences which contain the word 'hospital' do not entail anything about having babies as a matter of semantic necessity. Therefore inferences will have to be drawn to see how B's utterance connects to the context of A's. And encyclopedic information will have to be accessed to do this, information which connects the entries for 'pregnant' and 'hospital' in the context of this conversation. Clark (1977: 413) terms the inferential connection of utterances in this way **bridging inferences**. Since such inferences are not a matter of semantic necessity, but involve context, they are termed **contextual implications** or **implicatures** (see below and Grice, 1975). We can derive the following implicature for our example:

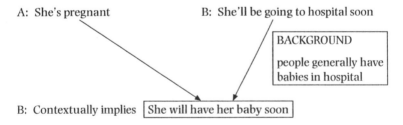

This inference is made by the deductive device. The premisses are the new context of B's remark, the already given context of A's remark, and a single piece of encyclopedic information. From these, we can infer the piece of new information that 'She will have her baby soon.' (Both the third premiss and the conclusion are implicatures in this context.) If this particular inference is to be made, it is also required that no alternative piece of background or contextual information be more strongly manifest in this context. This must be the most **accessible context**, and mutually manifest thus forming the participants' shared **cognitive environment**. For example, if it was strongly manifest to A that it was mutually manifest that she (call her Brenda) was not anywhere near term, then this particular inference would not be made.

The contextual implications which are derived thus vary in terms of the contextual and background information which is most accessible to serve as premises. For example, if the most accessible context was that Brenda always had a problem with dangerously high blood pressure in her pregnancies, and was not near term, then the following implication might be the informative intent of B's utterance.

B: She'll be going into hospital soon.

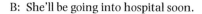

> BACKGROUND
>
> People are generally taken into hospital during pregnancy if there are medical complications, such as dangerously high blood pressure.
>
> Brenda has a history of dangerously high blood pressure during previous pregnancies.

B: Contextually implies

> Brenda will probably soon have dangerously high blood pressure again

So far we have treated each remark as implicating only one 'unsaid' piece of information, the sole point of B's remark. (Other premises in the complex chain of arguments may be implicated, but they are not the point of the remark.) However, the number of contextual implications also varies depending on how much contextual and background information is brought to bear. As a thought experiment, try expanding the accessible context of the exchange. For example, imagine that it was strongly mutually manifest that both A and B had been implicitly competing as to which of them was the closer friend of the pregnant woman. With this expanded context as a premiss, B's utterance might be said to implicate further information and have a more complex point.

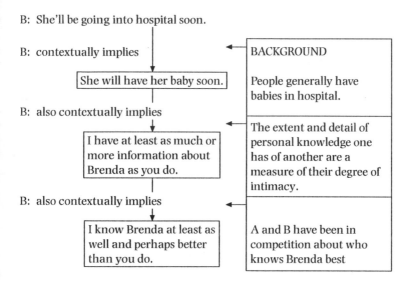

B: She'll be going into hospital soon.

B: contextually implies

She will have her baby soon.

B: also contextually implies

I have at least as much or more information about Brenda as you do.

B: also contextually implies

I know Brenda at least as well and perhaps better than you do.

BACKGROUND

People generally have babies in hospital.

The extent and detail of personal knowledge one has of another are a measure of their degree of intimacy.

A and B have been in competition about who knows Brenda best

Note that this argument could be constructed even if, indeed, especially if, A already knew that Brenda was near term. Alternative arguments, with alternative premisses and conclusions, are easily derivable if we expand or change the context and background assumptions. For example, in a context where 'time flies' has been a topic of conversation, and it is mutually manifest that Brenda has just announced her pregnancy, the nine months before her delivery might be considered relatively 'soon' and the point of the remark therefore, 'before we know it, that day will be upon us – an illustration of how time flies'.

In general, the more processing, the more contextual implications, where processing includes expanding the contextual and background assumptions in order to obtain more premisses for the construction of arguments by the deductive device. Alternatively, if such processing work failed to yield adequate implications and neither did further expansions then it would seem that the utterance had no point, or at least its point was very obscure or vague.

Sperber and Wilson (1995: 108ff.) introduce the notion of **contextual effects** to describe how implications such as the above effect the cognitive state of the hearer. One effect is to *add* previously unentertained new assumptions. For example, that Brenda is near term is added to A's encyclopedia as manifest new information and so are all its consequences. It carries the degree of credibility that A attaches to B as a source, and this determines the strength of the new assumption. But this is only one kind of contextual effect. If an implied assumption was already held by the hearer it will become more strongly manifest and may be *strengthened*, that is more strongly held. Alternatively, if the new information contradicts previous assumptions, the old assumptions may be *cancelled*. Such effects ramify throughout the system since assumptions which are entailed by affected assumptions are also affected, and any of these may have some evidential role in our pattern of beliefs. Such are the possible contextual effects of any remark that we process.

Relevance and communication

Sperber and Wilson (1995) argue that it is degree of relevance that guides how speakers in communicative situations formulate their utterances in order that hearers will understand the intended message, symbolised as {I}. It is precisely this discernment of what the speaker intended that constitutes communication.

We must first consider exactly what it is for something to be 'relevant' within relevance theory. As Levinson (1989: 467) points out, the concept of relevance that Sperber and Wilson propose does not conform obviously to our pre-theoretical notion of relevance. For Sperber and Wilson, any perceptual stimulus, verbal or non-verbal, is relevant in a context to the degree that its contextual effects – new beliefs, strengthening or cancellation of old beliefs – are *large* and the processing effort required to produce those effects is *small*.

Degree of relevance

EFFECTS	EFFORT
large number of contextual effects	effort required to produce effects is *small*

It is argued that the maximization of relevance is a general principle which governs cognitive activity. (In the 1995 edition this is called the 'First Principle of Relevance' (260).) This includes utterance comprehension, but only as a special case of verbal stimuli. Let's first consider a non-verbal behavioural stimulus. I observe a friend carrying suitcases and walking hurriedly down a street which I know leads to the railway station. This stimulus is relevant to me if the assumptions it makes manifest are relevant to me. In this case, the phenomenon of 'my hurrying acquaintance' is relevant since I obtain contextual effects as I put in the effort to maximize its relevance. He is hurrying to catch a train; he is leaving the city; he is going home this weekend; I thought that he was staying here but I was wrong. This contextual impact has a relatively low processing cost. I only have to access encyclopedic information about local geography, suitcases and travel, my friend's residential arrangements, all readily accessible. The same scene might have very low relevance if the figure was just a noticeable stranger, but more if I were looking for the station myself in a strange city, even more if my friend had agreed to repay me five pounds tomorrow. A contrasting situation is **ostensive commun-ication**. In this case, through catching my eye and moving his suitcase, he manifestly is intentionally attempting to perform those very movements in such a way that relevance is achieved by my thinking that he was performing them *in order that* I recognize his **communicative intent** and thus infer his **informative intent**, the intended message {**I**} – 'I can't stop. I'm rushing to catch a train. Sorry.' The miracle is that *nothing has been said.*

Relevance as defined is a ratio or 'trade off' between two fac-tors: the amount of informational impact on the processor and the amount of cognitive effort required to achieve it. Relevance can therefore be attained in different ways. On the one hand, a stimulus may have relatively few effects achieved at little cost. On the other, an equal degree of relevance might be achieved if the effects are great but achieved with a commensurate increase in effort. A very relevant stimulus has major effects paid for relatively cheaply. Something very irrelevant yields few and unsatisfactory effects, no matter how unreasonably great the processing cost becomes.

Relevance thus defined is the key to Sperber and Wilson's theory of communication. In this situation, the communicator must first provide the 'ostensive' stimulus; one that is relevant only if it is manifest that the actor intended the perceiver to recognize that it was done with the intention of being recognized as such – to communicate its intention to communicate. This is the intention to make it manifest to the hearer that the speaker intends to communicate something. That achieved, the stimulus also must provide what is sufficient for the hearer to derive the specific intended message **{I}**, the content of the communication.

The central issue thus becomes exactly how the speaker conveys just **{I}**, the intended contextual effects, and not something else; and how the hearer arrives at **{I}**, and not something else.

This is achieved by the **principle of relevance** (Sperber and Wilson, 1986: 158; called the 'Second Principle of Relevance' in the 1995 edition (260)). This is,

> Every act of ostensive communication communicates the presumption of its own optimal relevance.

The speaker therefore communicates in the very act of communicating that both optimal results and processing are guaranteed, namely,

Optimal relevance

EFFECTS	EFFORT
Will be 'adequate' to make the effort worthwhile, given communicator's abilities and preferences	Will be 'minimized', i.e., those effects will be achieved in the most relevant way possible

When we say that the stimulus is optimally relevant we mean that it achieves the best possible balance between maximizing effects and minimizing effort (Sperber and Wilson, 1995: 144). And every act of ostensive communication also communicates this presumption.

How the theory works becomes clearer if we illustrate it with our example of B's utterance. We can see both the 'ostensive' part and the 'inferential' part of communication. Faced with the ostensive utterance stimulus, 'She'll be going into hospital soon', and therefore being aware that it is intended to be, first, communicative, and, second, that B intends to convey some information {I}, I also automatically can presume that B's remark is optimally relevant. I *construct* a context, consisting of a set of assumptions, and from those premisses deduce contextual effects. Since it has been conveyed that the effort required to produce the 'intended' effects will be minimized, I go first to the most accessible context, namely, my previous remark and the single piece of background information, 'people generally have babies in hospital'. This yields an argument concluding: 'She will have her baby soon', which effects my present assumptions. For example, it might add a new assumption. If that contextual effect is 'adequate' given my knowledge of B, I stop and since it was achieved with least cost, I can conclude that that was {I}, the speaker's message. If it was, then the communication was successful. But that first effect might not have been 'adequate', for example, in the case where I already assumed she was near term and knew that B was able to also know that fact, this was merely somewhat strengthened. In this case, I would add premisses, expanding the context, and increasing my effort, until worthwhile effects were achieved. In this way I might conclude with a more complex interpretation of {I}, as in the 'blood pressure', 'competition' or 'time flies' examples; at a higher cost for the richer, more adequate effect aimed at by B.

We now have an answer to the question of how the hearer constructs just the right context to deduce what the speaker intended to convey. Both participants automatically behave to optimize relevance; achieve maximization in a communicative context. And this leads the hearer, or observer in the case of my friend non-verbally signalling with his suitcase, to find the context which simultaneously maximizes informational effect while minimizing processing cost. *And it is exactly that context that yields conclusions which the speaker communicates, intends that the hearer/observer should infer.*

This principle governs the inferential stages 2 and 3 illustrated above. There we claimed that the very proposition expressed was under-determined by the 'coded' or semantic meaning. The actual proposition expressed by the utterance – the 'content' of what is said – is itself constructed in such a way that it will serve as a premiss in whatever argument gives an outcome which is optimally relevant.

Criticisms of relevance theory

Relevance theory is the first fully developed, comprehensive theory of interpretation and communication, and is the 'best theory we have got' in this area. Nevertheless, there are some criticisms which have been made of the theory. There is a tangle of problems, some of which seem quite fundamental (see Levinson, 1989 and also the critical commentaries in *Behavioral and Brain Sciences* 10, 1989).

1. *The cognitive science problem.* Sperber and Wilson consider relevance theory as part of **cognitive science** and therefore espouse its assumptions. In particular, they endorse the position of Fodor's *The Modularity of Mind* (1983) with some crucial differences, one being that the deductive device alone constitutes central processing. One assumption of mainstream cognitive psychology is that the mental operations it proposes to perform functions within the mind are describable as **effective procedures**. That means they can be broken down into a series of completely explicit steps which are represented as operations performed on symbols. Any process thus represented is computable by the mind/brain. This makes this kind of psychology empirical, that is refutable and therefore scientific, because explicit predictions can be made about behavioural input and output for any proposed mental mechanism. The underlying analogy is that 'the mind is a computer'. In principle, the proposed psychological processes, formalized as operations on mental representations, ought to be programmable in a com-

putational simulacrum of what the mind/brain does. And this would have inputs and outputs replicating human behaviour. In a strong sense, such a theory would be 'psychologically real' (see Johnson-Laird, 1993).

If relevance theory accepts a **formalist** position, then it is open to attack as regards inexplicitness with respect to the cognitive operations it proposes. Although the theory as it stands is only programmatic, if it could be shown that it isn't formalizable in principle (not just in practice) then the theory would fail as a cognitive theory. And, after all, it claims that relevance is the principle guiding all cognition.

The centrality of the deductive device isn't the problem. Deductive inference can be fully formalized, and this is proposed in relevance theory. (Sperber and Wilson also propose that their deductive device can be constrained so as not to generate an infinite number of trivial inferences and this has been disputed: Gazdar and Good, 1982; Sperber and Wilson, 1982, 1995.) In the first instance, the problem would appear to be how the device also might compute the degree of relevance of its activities.

We can ask if it is psychologically plausible that the mind calculates in real time the ratio between a precise number of contextual effects (additions, strengthenings, cancellations) and the computational effort (number of steps?) involved in deriving them for a context. Presumably, in the theory the mind doesn't also have to explicitly compute and then compare degrees of relevance achievable from alternative competing contexts. If it did, the computations involved would be absurdly implausible. And when would the testing stop? Furthermore, as Levinson (1989) points out, there would be no guarantee that there would be a unique optimally relevant solution to the equation. Also, remember the vagueness of our interpretation of Doreen's remarks in chapter one.

The reply to this is that the mind *doesn't* have to compare because the deductive device simply uses the most accessible context *first* and only extends this if the effects aren't adequate. It only stops extending its search to less accessible contexts when its effort, by definition now the *least* effort, yields adequate results. So a lot hinges on the hierarchy of accessible contexts and the 'most accessible context', We *can't* say that this is chosen to maximize relevance, because that would both imply a testing of alternatives and involve us in a circularity. We would need to know the degree of relevance that context will yield before we actually choose it and calculate its effort/effect ratio – its degree of relevance. The mind then can't be said to search for a context which maximizes relevance. Rather it simply churns through a 'given' hierarchy of contexts in order of accessibility until it is satisfied. It *does* appear that the mental device would have to perform the complex quantitative calculations required to measure contextual effects on encyclopedic assumptions, while simultaneously keeping track of its computational costs in doing so, however that might be quantified. It also needs a 'measure of adequacy', a number at which to stop for a given situation, since more effects can always be obtained by more processing. The device has to perform these calculations or it would have no way of recognising degrees of relevance, or knowing when to stop.

Sperber and Wilson (1995: 129ff.) recognize the problem and claim that the mind does not in fact compute relevance, nor is degree of relevance internally represented. Nowhere in the mind is anything quantitative represented. Instead, there may be broadly comparative 'yes or no' judgements of a rough and ready kind accomplished through the mental monitoring of 'physio-chemical changes' at the neurological level. Thus, relevance isn't calculated by the mind at all. Rather, it is a reflex of unknown physical processes in the brain. But the implications of such a claim are unclear. Does the psychological description at this crucial point simply consist of a box labelled 'the monitor' which in some unknown way simply says 'yes' or 'no' when optimal relevance is reached? If so, the theory doesn't explicitly tell us anything we don't already intuitively know from a subjective point of view. More crucially, a cognitive psychology theorizes the mind as a system of representations upon which computations are performed. If relevance *cannot* be formulated in these terms, it cannot be a psychological phenomenon. Therefore, relevance theory – in spite of its mentalistic terminology – is not within the cognitive science paradigm and is not empirical in the way such theories can be. A possible reply to this would be to point out the problems of a 'formalist' requirement in cognitive science (see Boden, 1988: 225ff.). Another way forward is to examine the possibilities of alternative computational models (see the end of the chapter for one alternative).

In summary, relevance theory appears to be saying that there is a property of the unknown neurological mechanisms which process physical stimuli such that at the more abstract representational level relevance theory is correct. However, it then says that there are no explicit procedures of (unconscious) mental computation corresponding to these unknown underlying physical mechanisms at the higher mental level at which theory operates. In the context of cognitive science, this is puzzling. We must remember not to 'reify' the mental level; it is after all only an *abstract* functional characterization of brain activity (see Chomsky, 1980: 5; 1986: 23). But in our case, it is claimed that there is no explicit abstract mental representation of the function, only the unknown brain activity. There is therefore *no* explicit psychological theory in the cognitive science sense.

2. *The problem of circularity and irrefutability.* We may look for the theory to be empirical in an alternative way. It may make correct predictions about hearers' interpretations and speakers' intentions in terms of their reports about their intuitions on these matters. The data are thus reports of interpretations that participants introspect they have made or would have made. Sperber and Wilson point out that their theory predicts that the optimally relevant and therefore correct interpretation is the first subjectively adequate one that the hearer arrives at, because of the 'least effort' part of the definition. (Of course, this will depend on how the speaker and hearer interpret the situation/context they are in.) There is a whiff of circularity here and a problem of how any predicted interpretation could be refuted. For example, given my assessment of the context – from a study of a video recording – I might predict that B's utterance intended to convey 'She will have her baby soon' and that A will report that construal; it is adequate and costs little. But B might say, 'No, I intended to convey that I know Brenda at least as well as A does', and A might agree that this is how it was taken. But relevance theory is not refuted by this report. The theorist simply provides the context of assumptions necessary to make this outcome subjectively adequate at least cost and says this must have been the context A and B employed. And

similarly for *any* reported interpretation. Given this, it appears that the theory can only give *post facto* explications. Any outcome can be shown to have been optimally relevant. The only way to prevent this is to overtly agree to fix accessible contexts and processing effort for the informants beforehand. (Of course this can't be done quantitatively!) However, if we did do this, we would be in effect just prescribing their deductions. If they reason according to our logical laws, they could only report that which we have preordained as optimally relevant – and that is circular. In fact, it is the famous hermeneutic circle referred to in chapter eight. One needs to know the context to interpret a text and one needs to interpret the text to determine the relevant context.

3. *Hypothesis formation and the frame problem.* This is related to another serious issue. The problem is how participants arrive at just the correct context for the intended message, that which yields optimal relevance. Sperber and Wilson suggest that this is an automatic process which results from the quest for relevance. The context of an utterance is a set of assumptions put into the deductive device from various sources, namely, using our example:

1. The assumptions already in the device from processing the immediately preceding utterance.

2. The assumptions accessed during the conversation and held in short-term memory.

3. The assumptions manifest and mutually manifest in the physical environment ranked in degree of strength of manifestness. Presumably the assumptions employed in 1 and 2 are manifest.

4. The assumptions in the encyclopedia accessed because they are in the entries for concepts 1–3 above and those in the utterance itself, in our case, the entries for *Brenda, pregnancy, hospital* and *A's and B's biographies*, among others.

The processing of any utterance begins with an initial context as defined by 1. The hearer thus begins with the semantic, coded content of the new utterance, plus this initial context, and works from there. The initial context can be expanded from the sources 2–4. From these, assumptions are put into the deductive device to serve as premisses and implicatures are deduced. The problem is to construct just the right context; to choose assumptions as premisses which give the conclusion that the speaker intended.

The fundamental issue is whether or not this search for the correct context can be accomplished by a procedure that can be made explicit. Or, instead, does it involve the little understood processes of non-demonstrative inference mentioned earlier? Sperber and Wilson clearly suggest the former view.

Let us focus our critique on source 4, assumptions accessed from the encyclopedia. Sperber and Wilson argue that the encyclopedia has enough structure (see below) that a clearly defined hierarchy of accessible assumptions, and hence contexts, is available to be searched in a definite order. Not only are entries for concepts organized in chunks, but each assumption has a degree of strength which is a measure of how often it has been successfully employed in the past. Therefore, we access the entries for *Brenda, pregnancy, hospital* etc. and their assumptions and add these to the context in the order of their strength. This procedure is also a prerequisite for degree of processing 'effort' to be defined. The process continues through the chunks and sub-chunks of the entries according to degree of strength until the conclusions drawn yield adequate effects, as required by the principle of relevance. At that moment, least effort, the effort required to achieve those effects, has been simultaneously reached.

The difficulty is that many people simply do not believe that the correct context can be arrived at in this way. The evidence available to the hearer doesn't direct them to the 'correct' context in such a mechanical way. We hit what is called **the frame problem** – an explosion of potentially salient background information in all the domains, (for a discussion, see Haugeland, 1985: 203ff.; Dennett, 1984; there is a discussion of the frame problem as it applies to relevance theory in *Behavioral and Brain Sciences* 19, 1996). Consider the enormous number of incredibly detailed things we tacitly believe just about *hospitals* – many trivial, many not. The frame problem concerns how this mass of irrelevant information can be ruled out and never looked at. Presumably in other contexts in the past, bits of this information have been employed, maybe frequently, and many pieces of information which are strongly assumed may be irrelevant in this case, as compared to other things of equal strength.

One could argue that a potential context can be constructed from any assumption that B hypothesizes that A will be able to retrieve. But B actually has to form a hypothesis about this, and A also has to hypothesize, on the basis of past experience, which assumptions B probably believed A would access – in this immediate situation. This allows A to 'jump' directly to the correct context.

B has said, 'Yes, she'll be going to hospital soon.' Why couldn't B be suggesting that Brenda will soon need both A's and B's support, perhaps in the form of rides and other encouragements? Brenda seems to distrust medicine, lives in the country and has no car. The hospital is anyway awkward to get to. Alternatively, perhaps B is just being polite by claiming 'common ground' – saying 'I know', in a way that not only fills in the turn appropriately but demonstrates the mutuality of the information. At the same time, B may be thinking that this new mutuality will bring A and B together for the first time in some mutual interest, instead of their competitive bickering, and wants A to entertain this thought. She knows Brenda would want this, as well as their support. There is no reason to think the assumptions required to derive these effects would be organized in a hierarchy of strengths based on past use, or would be especially 'manifest' in the physical environment or this conversation. But the new polite tone will nevertheless convey the intended thought. It is worth mentioning politeness (Brown and Levinson, 1987) as a phenomenon whose requirements must enter into the calculation of the effects of each and every conversational utterance as a special obligatory contextual dimension. Politeness effects will presumably interact with more 'cognitive' aspects in determining each context for adequacy of relevance, and one can imagine limiting cases where relevance is achieved almost solely by politeness.

The process of understanding is creative precisely because the conversational context is open. Past uses of an assumption and the strength with which it is held don't guarantee it is useful this time. A relevance theorist might reply that the assumptions *must* have had the strength, and manifestness, required to deliver the correct context in which effort achieved effect, but this leads us back into the circularity discussed above.

The alternative view is that deduction alone, even interacting with the structure of the encyclopedia, is not sufficient to mechanically provide the correct context (for example, see McDermott, 1987). Instead participants must proceed by some inductive process of hypothesis formation, or 'inference to the best explanation'. Relevance theory offers no account of these. Arguably, the way in which hypotheses are formed – the 'eureka factor' – is mysterious. Let's say there is no algorithm, no mechanical procedure, for forming correct hypotheses. In this case, we can't have an explicit account of how the right background information gets into the deductive device. (Fodor's 1983 picture of the 'central processing' module assigns it precisely these mysterious functions.) Possibly, we employ a multiplicity of inductive strategies in an *ad hoc* way in forming hypotheses in everyday life. In any case, there is no formal function that could predict hypotheses as premises for a theory, given data. Theories are underdetermined by data. Therefore, we have no 'science' of theory formation. This is simply another way of saying that nature doesn't dictate to us a single correct way to explain it. And neither does everyday human behaviour, including utterances.

The above considerations if true again suggest (see *cognitive science problem* above) that relevance theory as it stands is not an empirical psychological theory. Faced with this, how may we proceed? One possibility would be to consider non-demonstrative inference more carefully. A philosopher like Dennett argues that there are indeed **heuristic** programs which, although not giving 100 per cent results, provide a computational level model of this kind of human thought (Dennett, 1996: 210–12 and ch. 15). Could heuristic principles, perhaps specific to registers, be derived from relevance? In fact, all this is part of a very important contemporary debate about the mind; whether it operates at some level in a way which can be made fully explicit as a set of procedures, or whether there is something 'mysterious' about thinking that can't be so represented. This controversy is subtle and ongoing (see Dennett, 1996 for summary; also Boden, 1988, 1990; Dreyfus, 1992).

Relevance theory as a hermeneutic

Another possibility, given that utterance interpretation is perhaps the crucial boundary between scientific psychology and humanistic methodology, would be to deploy relevance theory as a **hermeneutic methodology** (see chapter ten below). Hermeneutics is the theory and practice of textual interpretation. And relevance theory makes very precise, *post facto*, how a text may be read relative to contexts, and possible resulting communicative intentions. Such precision brings into critical consciousness possible strategies of understanding and, in particular, the systems of background beliefs involved. In the remainder of this chapter we shall examine background information in more detail.

Quine's web of belief

Earlier on we said that beliefs form an inferential network. We also drew a clear distinction between meaning and belief. The former were 'coded' and belonged in the mental dictionary. They warranted entailments between sentences and accounted for the necessary truth of analytic sentences – those true by definition. The latter – our beliefs about the world – belonged in the encyclopedia. We can only have empirical beliefs about things which can be true or false. So really belief has to be expressed in sentences which are revisable in the light of experience, have empirical content, namely, synthetic sentences. It is sometimes said that if one denies an analytic sentence, one doesn't understand English. But if one differs from others about the truth of a synthetic sentence, we simply disagree about facts. This distinction is the basis for distinguishing the dictionary, which is part of language, from the encyclopedia, which is not.

The philosopher W. van O. Quine (1953, 1960) draws a picture about belief and language that challenges this clear division between meaning and belief. Quine's overall views about meaning are subtle and complex and go far beyond our scope. I am merely selecting those parts of his views that have consequences for communication and context, especially the notion of 'background knowledge', so crucial above. (In fact, Quine would reject the whole mentalistic framework of our theorizing so far. But that is another ball game.)

For Quine, our beliefs about the world do not stand or fall separately. Rather, everything that we believe is a vast single interwoven web of sentences – to which we assent – which face experience collectively. Many sentences are assigned the values 'true' or 'false' not entirely because of how they relate to observations, but because of this plus their relations to other sentences. It is only sentences at the outer boundary of the inferential network which directly relate to experience. These boundary sentences can be freely assigned the values 'true' or 'false' in the light of observation.

On the other hand, sentences at the centre of what we believe, those most deeply integrated into the network, do not relate to observations, except very indirectly. They appear to us to be necessarily true, analytic sentences. We are not individually free to judge these sentences true or false (nor their negations true) on pain of not appearing to understand them, since they appear to be true by virtue of their meaning alone. We are fairly free in how we assign 'true' or 'false', however, to those sentences neither at the boundary nor at the centre, in order to maintain coherence and simplicity in the overall system.

Pressures ripple through the system from two directions. At the centre are those sentences – the apparently analytic ones – whose truth would be too destabilizing to give up and which *appear* immune from revision in the light of experience. Toward the periphery are sentences expressing those beliefs we are more willing to revise. At the limit are 'observation sentences' whose truth or falsity, we believe, directly depends on a particular occasioned experience. Any observation, or rather belief that the sentence reporting it is true, is thus 'theory laden' in the sense that the effects of assent or dissent ramify in various degrees throughout the system of belief. An observation sentence taken to be true, given one set of background assumptions, could equally be taken to be false, if we were willing to pay the cost in terms of revision of other beliefs. So empirical pressure towards revision ripples inward to meet systematic pressure from the core, which, to varying degrees, resists or is immune to it. Internally, realignments over what we are willing to call 'true' or 'false' take place, but Quine believes that in the interests of coherence the whole system is quite conservative. This kind of **holistic** structure, according to Quine, characterizes the totality of our beliefs – not only our scientific theories, but everyday theories about the world. It also accounts for the relation between steps 1 and 2 in comprehension noted above. The understanding of the utterance of any sentence is always relativized to other sentences in the whole web of belief, as these have been mobilized in this instance.

We can examine this holism by dipping into our beliefs for an example. Let us look at the inferential relations of various types between sentences of the form 'X is pregnant' and other sentences. Our sentence is located somewhere in the middle of the system. Whether it is true or false in any given instance is clearly an empirical matter. But it is not something that can be decided merely by simple observation. If 'X is pregnant' is true, we believe some other sentences whose truth or falsity can serve as a means of verifying it and whose bottom line is observation sentences; for example, when X's last period occurred, whether X has a certain shape of abdomen, whether an expert can feel certain changes in an internal examination, or whether the changes which signify a positive result in a pregnancy test can be seen. Note the complex and indirect inferential links, part of a theory of pregnancy, between our sentence and these observation sentences. We are arguably ambivalent about whether or not knowledge of this kind is part of the 'meaning' of sentences containing 'pregnant'. A person might be said to know English without knowing these things. Presumably only some adults know how a pregnancy test is used, only experts know how it works, and other experts know how to do an internal examination. But if an adult speaker knew too few of these things, they would certainly not just be ill-informed people, they would not be able to speak English in these contexts. Possibly speakers vary about how deeply they understand the 'meaning' of 'X is pregnant'.

Let's agree that our statement 'X is pregnant' is true. Then other sentences are also true in various ways. (The above 'empirical' criteria could be reported by sentences which are true.) We also believe that 'X is a woman' and an 'adult, female human' (if indeed

X is human in this case). We believe that 'X is going to have a baby' and that since a woman who has had a baby is a mother, that 'X is an expectant mother.' These are very tightly linked with 'X is pregnant.' They are so tightly linked that we could argue that they constitute the 'meaning' of the sentence, by virtue of the contribution of the predicate 'pregnant'. Certainly, these are among what we might give, if defining the term for a child or a language learner. 'X is pregnant' might be said to entail 'X is a woman' and 'X is an expectant mother', among other things. And we get the corresponding analytic sentences, e.g. 'All pregnant women are expectant mothers.' These appear to be true by definition.

Other inferentially related sentences are more loosely linked in the network. We might also believe that 'X has a husband Y' and that 'Y is the father of X's baby', depending on what else we knew about X. If we believe that is false, we are almost certain to assent to the alternative claim that 'X had a sexual partner and he was the father'. The choice among this set of beliefs is contingent, their truth or falsity revisable relative to reports and experiences. Myriad other sentences are even more loosely linked to 'X is pregnant'; e.g. whether she will have a long or short labour, welcomes the baby or not for whatever reasons, has an epidural anaesthetic or a Caesarian section. It is easy to see that we are truly dealing with a **web of belief** – each sentence warrants assent to other sentences, tightly by entailment or more loosely, and each of these implies other sentences, and so on, indefinitely. This is sometimes called **infinite semiosis**.

It is the most tightly connected sentences, those which appear analytically entailed by 'X is pregnant', in which we have the most confidence. This type of inference ties our belief to our language in the deepest way, and guarantees sufficient coordination of belief to underwrite communication and get it stated. Because of this we don't think of our assent to analytic statements as a matter of belief, but as 'coded' or 'literal meaning'. But Quine denies that these analytic statements are in principle any less empirical than the more loosely connected sentences. Because the empirical meeting with experience is holistic, these tight inferences are simply the beliefs which are the most deeply integrated into the totality of belief which constitutes our *overall theory of the world.* They are nevertheless beliefs and not meanings. Hence, we get our empirical theory of the world – both everyday and scientific – along with our language.

In saying this, Quine is arguing that there is no analytic-synthetic distinction, that it can't be drawn. This undermines the whole distinction between meaning and background information with which we began this chapter. And it leads to a complex of philosophical and linguistic problems which are beyond the scope of this book.

It is worth exploring these issues in a bit more detail. For one thing, the number of words, such as the classic example 'bachelor', from which one can construct putatively analytic sentences true by definition – 'All bachelors are unmarried men' – is quite small (Putnam, 1962). There are many classes of word and each class behaves somewhat differently. For most classes, constructing putative analytic sentences is problematic.

Consider two candidates for analytic sentences which might be true by virtue of the meaning of 'pregnant'. The phrases to the right of 'if and only if' purport to be synonymous with, and therefore to represent, the 'meaning' of 'X is pregnant':

1. X is pregnant if and only if X is going to have a baby.
2. X is pregnant if and only if X has a foetus inside her body.

Neither of these work as analytic sentences. The trouble with 2 is that it looks to be true as a matter of scientific fact, rather than true as a matter of meaning. As such, it is one, *albeit* widely known, statement from a physical theory. One could imagine a speaker (for example a child) using our sentence quite correctly and not knowing anything about the technicalities of pregnancy, only that mother is going to have a baby. So what about sentence 1? The trouble with 1 is that it does not seem to be necessarily true at all. X may be known to be arranging things so as *not* to have a baby, and, in the case of 'test tube' fertilizations, X may be going to have a baby without being pregnant. If we try to save this definition by introducing the terms 'probably' or 'normally', we make the sentence not necessarily true.

Indeed, we can easily imagine a future world in which we might revise our beliefs about both these statements. At the moment, most of us are probably unwilling to say of a woman whose fertilized ovum resides in the laboratory that she is pregnant. Later, after implantation, we would apply the term. However, imagine a world in which extra-uterine fertilization was the normal way in which conception was engineered (as opposed to intercourse). We would have a uniform state of affairs in which all mothers-to-be found themselves for a time. We have no word for it! In this case, we might be willing to apply the then old-fashioned term 'pregnancy' to this state. Would we have revised our beliefs warranted by sentences of the form, 'X is pregnant', in a way that is extricable from a change of meaning of the term 'pregnant'?

Because it is finally impossible to clearly distinguish between linguistic and factual considerations in assessing the truth of a statement, it is also impossible clearly to distinguish our beliefs about a statement due to its linguistic form, and what Quine calls 'generally shared collateral information' (what we have been calling encyclopedic background information). This is called the **inextricability thesis**. There is no actual distinction between what is coded and what is background.

Some consequences of holism

If the distinction between meanings and background beliefs is changed, so is the distinction between dictionary and encyclopedia. A Quinean view does not compel us to abandon some sort of distinction between beliefs so central to our whole **conceptual scheme** that they appear to be true by definition and beliefs held on more obviously empirical grounds. They are all beliefs, but beliefs with different roles in the overall scheme, and held for different reasons.

How does this change our picture? Instead of the traditional distinction between lexicon and encyclopedia, three sorts of information are linked to a given word or concept. We can illustrate how this information might be organized and contrast Sperber and Wilson's (1995: 87ff. and note 13) view with the more Quinean proposal we have been discussing:

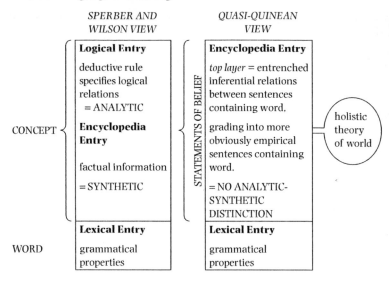

	SPERBER AND WILSON VIEW	QUASI-QUINEAN VIEW	
CONCEPT	**Logical Entry** deductive rule specifies logical relations = ANALYTIC **Encyclopedia Entry** factual information = SYNTHETIC	**Encyclopedia Entry** *top layer* = entrenched inferential relations between sentences containing word, grading into more obviously empirical sentences containing word. = NO ANALYTIC-SYNTHETIC DISTINCTION	holistic theory of world
WORD	**Lexical Entry** grammatical properties	**Lexical Entry** grammatical properties	

(STATEMENTS OF BELIEF)

Both of these views differ from the traditional picture in which the lexicon contains both a semantic representation and grammatical information. Here the lexicon deals only with the latter. In the quasi-Quinean picture, the boundary between knowledge of the world and knowledge of language simply isn't drawn. We escape from the picture in which a pre-given system of representation, the English language, is a fixed instrument to depict the world, something out there, that has little influence on linguistic 'meanings' or what we believe and therefore do. Knowing a language doesn't involve analytic definitions in isolation from their overall pattern of deployment in context. It seems highly implausible, perhaps a reflex of the norms of a standard language (see chapter two above), that knowledge of English simply involves knowing an insulated list of analytic definitions. This is an example of how the ideology of standardization might affect our intuitions/judgements about how language is organized.

The top layer of inferential connectivity is not insulated from other beliefs when examined out of context. Searle (1980) has pointed out that within isolated sentences the contribution of a word to truth conditions is relative to background information. Consider the radically differing states of affairs which any speaker of English believes, if they were to assent to the following sentences:

1. She *cut* him short when he complained.
2. She *cut* his hair short.
3. We can *cut* our staff.
4. You must *cut* the controversial sentences.
5. The criticisms *cut* him deeply.
6. He *cut* classes yesterday.
7. The midwife *cut* the umbilicus.
8. He *cut* the lawn.
9. We must *cut* your salary again.
10. I'm going to *cut* them off with the scissors.
11. I'm going to *cut* them off at the pass.
12. We got *cut* off, I'm afraid.
13. *Cut* that out, it's irritating.

This suggests that we draw inferences – the connections of various kinds between our encyclopedic beliefs – *of varying depths within and between entries* in order to comprehend even what is being 'literally said'; whatever state of affairs would cause us to assent to 1–13. Every English speaker knows that 'cutting staff' involves reducing the number of employees or 'downsizing' by lay-offs or wastage etc. and that this won't be done with scissors or a lawnmower. As noted in stage 2 above, the sentence is merely a set of instructions to employ certain addresses in the encyclopedia to draw inferences, just those the speaker intended to be drawn. It is uniformity of use that stabilizes the patterning.

What we think of as 'meanings' in this picture just *are* the set of relationships between sentences stably held to be true at the most accessible top layer of the encyclopedia entry for a given word or concept. We could represent this top layer, for words, in terms of entailment relations between sentences specified by meaning postulates or some kind of deductive rule. These are the most deeply entrenched beliefs in the system and therefore appear deductive. They most resist disconfirming evidence. In fact, in the case of an obvious linguistic disconfirmation, someone asserting a sentence in a way that appears to contradict these core beliefs, instead of revising our own beliefs we treat the sentence as being used figuratively, thus implicating some other assumption to which we *can* assent.

Besides this top layer, the encyclopedia entry contains all our other assumptions in this domain. The entry is *quasi-holistic* in that the total 'web of belief' has structure and involves inferential relations of different kinds. Each word or concept employed from other domains automatically cross-references a given entry to a multiplicity of other entries, and each of these is likewise connected to other entries, and so on. This network exists at the top-most 'deductive' layer, but also throughout. At most levels the connections are probabilistic. A cut in staff is only *probably* accomplished through lay-offs and to this degree the concept is vague. The exact probability assignment is an inductive matter and reflects degree of confirming experience.

This structure has the effect of potentially reorganizing the system of beliefs within an entry, and with spreading effects across many entries, every time a word is used. In principle even the top layer could be affected, as it would be in the future use of 'pregnant' discussed above. Alternatively, if experience kept disconfirming evidence at the empirical end of the entry, the top level would remain relatively undisturbed. This is the preferred situation since a stable top layer is a *sine qua non* for the inter-subjective reliability of a language. Indeed, it is what makes it 'a language', that is, utterances which are reliable guides to what others believe, at least sufficient to interpret behaviour without too many anomalies.

A consequence of this picture is that all the beliefs in an entry are dynamically related to the actual situations in which they are used. Sense is not separated from patterns of use. This opens the door to a sociology of belief systems in which meaning, the inferential connectivity of beliefs, can be accountably linked to social practice. What we believe accounts for the intelligibility of what we intentionally do. More on this below.

Changes in belief and meaning

This picture presents interesting possibilities for language change since there would be no clear distinction between revisions in belief and changes in language. Changes which we felt were linguistic would occur when systematic changes in beliefs about an area of experience have affected the overall network of encyclopedic information sufficiently, that the most deeply integrated beliefs become dispensable and are revised. This suggests that patterns of revision would affect the broader associations of a word – the background beliefs commonly required for its 'literal' determination – very rapidly as experience changes, although the top layer might remain stable. Indeed, the picture gives us a way of thinking about such associations.

In earlier chapters, we studied the mechanism of linguistic change paying particular attention to the role of social factors. Similar mechanisms might be at work in the way in which we distribute truth values within our inferential network. For example we could propose that redistribution of true and false over sentences will be arranged implicationally in waves. Waves of revision, perhaps ultimately originating in breakdowns in the overall workability of assignments of truth to sentences due to social change or changes in experience, would lead to successive reassignments of truth in inferentially related sentences. Since our approach views the overall 'holistic' relationships of beliefs as both having an internal encyclopedic structure of some kind, and involving different *kinds* of inferential connections, changes might not move evenly through the web of belief, but remain local, spreading through cross-referenced entries later as they are utilized. Since entries relate to domains of social practice, e.g. medicine, obstetrics, childbirth, a change in 'pregnant' would take time to cause revisions in more remote domains, e.g. politics or morality, if and when lack of revision had untoward consequences for practices in those areas. We arrive at a kind of structured 'quasi-holism', reflecting social structures.

In any area, revisions in belief would proceed initially over propositions freer to change truth value because expressed by observation sentences and only finally make their way to the layer of indispensable beliefs. Waves of revision are also embedded in social life. Not only do beliefs constitute and rationalize social practices, but the practices are often distributed unevenly over social groups, with differing network structures. And, depending on such structures, groups exert normative pressure towards conformity of belief. Convergence of beliefs within a social group both originates in and facilitates discourse within that group. Indeed, communality of belief is a part of solidarity and reflects common interests and 'way of life'. But power or differential status is also involved. People find propositions more credible, perhaps, when they are asserted or assumed by individuals of high status; for example, parents, priests, pundits, teachers, journalists and so on. So we can envisage the two dimensions of social structure – superordinate hierarchy (power) and social networks (solidarity) – exerting normative pressure on the structure of belief in a society, just as they do on more properly 'linguistic' structures. It follows that to assign a truth-value can be a symbol of overt or covert prestige and thus serve as part of social identity. If the analogy holds one would expect to find 'belief lames', whose eccentric assumptions make their utterances hard to understand. One would also expect to find waves of revision of belief moving through communities in patterns similar to those for linguistic changes. These would have the same sort of discontinuities, reflecting the differences between groups. One interesting question would be whether revision and its spread are usually gradual or catastrophic, in groups and within larger societies. Illustrations of such patterns of revision are beliefs concerning the economy and the role of government and how they altered during the 1940s–80s, or the catastrophic revision of beliefs about 'heroism', 'duty', 'glory', 'sacrifice' faced with 1914–18.

But, given the inextricability thesis, these processes are not clearly separable from linguistic change. The waves of revision affect the 'tight' inferences warranted by the linguistic form at the top layer. In fact, it is hard to see how these seemingly indispensable beliefs could be maintained or be workable, if large parts of the scaffolding of background encyclopedic beliefs have been revised.

Stereotypes

Thus far we have assumed that the top layer sentences we treat as analytic, those that capture intuitions of literal meaning, are true by definition. This is where we would find uniformity of assent by those who know a language just by virtue of that knowledge, irrespective of experience. Now, in some few cases, like the famous 'All bachelors are unmarried men' – 'If X is a bachelor, then X is unmarried', such analyticity seems discoverable. But for sentences containing 'pregnant' we found it exceedingly difficult to construct sentences which were necessarily true solely because of the meanings of the words they contain. This suggests that the top layer definitions, and the inferential net they establish, might be of different kinds for different kinds of words.

An approach which challenges the orthodoxy has been suggested by Hilary Putnam (1970, 1975). Putnam has argued that at least in the case of words that refer to **natural kinds** (e.g. tigers, lemons or water) what speakers need to know to be competent members of the speech community is a **stereotype** of the kind in question. Consider 'tiger'. To teach a child how to use this English word correctly, we would tell them that the word means a big, orange and black, striped cat etc. or, in another example, that 'water' is a clear, drinkable, odourless liquid. But these statements are not necessarily true, nor are they necessary and sufficient to fix the reference of the terms – to specify the conditions that must hold in the world for something to be a tiger. An albino tiger or undrinkable water are still members of the kind referred to by the term, although they don't satisfy the stereotype.

This is because what makes something a member of a natural kind is its inner structure, its genetic or molecular make-up. Obviously this information is not given to us when we learn a language and the stereotype that guides our use of the natural kind term. There is a **division of linguistic labour**. Most of the time the stereotype will be adequate for our purposes. But in problematic cases we would go to an expert and ask if the sample was *really* water or a tiger. The expertise is available in scientific theory which characterizes the inner structure that makes something a member of the kind, for example, the DNA of a tiger or the atomic structure of water.

Putnam argues that the reference of a natural kind term is first fixed by the original paradigmatic instance of the kind, e.g. the moment that someone 'baptized' the entity with that particular inner structure, 'a tiger'. Afterwards the best scientific account will establish the class of tigers for us. But the statements of a scientific theory are no more analytically or necessarily true than are stereotypes. So 'truth by definition' enters into meaning neither in terms of the speaker's knowledge of the stereotype, nor the expert's scientific knowledge. Analyticity does not seem to figure in the meaning of natural kind terms. Rather the stereotype is a perception based common-sense theory which works for most day to day cases. Putnam quite explicitly refers to it as a *sociolinguistic* phenomenon.

If such stereotypes are what people have to know to be competent speakers of a language with respect to natural kind terms, then the inferential relations at the top layer of the encyclopedia will consist of the stereotypes for these terms. Entailment won't be appropriate. The inferencing performed by the informal reasoning would only transmit a probability that, for example, water is drinkable, not that water is drinkable by definition. And the conclusion will therefore also only be probabilistic. This seems to conform with how people behave with respect to information conveyed by such terms. Coming upon a water hole in the desert, one doesn't just assume that the water is drinkable (by definition) because it is water.

'Pregnant' can be viewed as a natural kind term. Using our example, 'X is pregnant', we can see how Putnam's analysis provides a different kind of structure to the top layer of the encyclopedia entry. This provides a solution to the difficulty we had in finding an analytic definition for 'pregnant'. The notion of 'normally' or 'probably' lets us off the analytic hook in this case. Rather we have at least two kinds of empirical information involved; the common-sense stereotype uniformly employed by any speaker and the specialized scientific theory of the kind available only in the encyclopedias of specialists. The stereotype is a kind of folk or primitive science based on what is perceivable and hence available to anyone. By contrast, the scientific theory is only available through the specialist institutions of science, for example, reference books, experts etc. This differentiation is what one would expect concerning how people's encyclopedias would vary according to their social roles. One might expect the same kind of differentiation to also occur for many different kinds of terms defined for all speakers and for specialists in such domains as technology, law, economics or religion.

Returning now to our two candidate analytic sentences containing 'pregnant', we can say that

1. If X is pregnant, X is going to have a baby

is the central stereotype associated with 'pregnant' and applies in normal cases. It is how one might explain the terms to a child. However, the same child might be able to use the term properly and not know:

2. If X is pregnant, X has a foetus in her body.

This is the first step towards a scientific theory of pregnancy. For specialists in medicine or biology, of course, there are elaborate encyclopedic theories based on science and clinical practices. Lay persons have access to this information when they require it by consulting the specialists.

It is worth drawing our attention here to a distinction between Putnam's notion of stereotype and the notion of a **prototype** as employed by psychologists (for example, Rosch, 1973, 1978). The two notions are not identical. A stereotype can be wrong, while a prototype is both conceptually and empirically the most typical instance of some category. It is possible that the highest level of encyclopedia entries – those equivalent to analytic definitions – could take the form of prototypes.

This points to the diverse kinds of structure in the encyclopedia. It also suggests that for many if not most concepts, an entry contains a warning that the top layer assumptions may be unreliable in problem cases and an instruction to consult an expert. A language then, even at its heart, will only be partially known by any arbitrary speaker.

Representation of belief systems: frames

Almost all scholars who have worked on cognition or discourse comprehension have tried to find some system for representing background information and how it is employed in perception and inference. In our terms, they have tried to describe the structure of the encyclopedia and its role in information processing. The main studies in this area have been within cognitive science, especially cognitive psychology discussed above, and in **artificial intelligence** research (Haugeland, 1985). This has also been an area of concern to linguists and discourse analysts (see, for example, de Beaugrande and Dressler, 1981). There is a huge literature in these areas and it is only possibly to gesture towards it here.

Artificial intelligence, as the name suggests, is the attempt to replicate in computer programs the processes and information required to perform tasks requiring intelligence, those things characteristically done by intelligent creatures such as animals and humans. Such tasks include meaningful interaction with the world in terms of the perception, recognition and manipulation of objects, reasoning, learning and, of course, the use of language. There have been some striking successes in this enterprise, for example, Terry Winograd's (1972) computer system for understanding English. This program can engage in dialogue. It exchanges utterances with the operator about a small and determinate micro-world consisting of blocks of various shapes and colours. The problem of representing systems of knowledge and belief is a central one in artificial intelligence research. Without some solution, a computer system for discourse production and comprehension would prove impossible.

I have been assuming that such a representational system takes the form of some equivalent of sentences or propositions. Data are commonly represented this way by the programming languages used in such research, for example in PROLOG. But within the framework of cognitive science any system using symbols and operations could model the way the mind comprehends and processes information. Indeed, Johnson-Laird (1983, 1993) argues that sentence comprehension and subsequent thinking do not use propositions at all, but rather the construction and manipulation of **mental models**.

One of the most influential proposals has been Marvin Minsky's notion of frames, which was originally advanced in connection with the computer analysis of vision. Minsky writes (1975: 211):

> the ingredients of most theories . . . have been on the whole too minute, local, and unstructured to account – either practically or phenomenologically – for the effectiveness of common sense thought. The 'chunks' of reasoning, language, memory and perception ought to be larger and more structured . . . in order to explain the apparent power and speed of mental activities . . . Here is the essence of the theory:

When one encounters a new situation (or makes a substantial change in one's view of the present problem) one selects from memory a substantial structure called a frame. This is a remembered framework to be adapted to fit reality by changing details as necessary. A frame is a data structure for representing a stereotyped situation, like being in a certain kind of living room, or going to a child's birthday party.

It is most striking that a frame represents not actual situations, but a stereotype of the situation in question. In this respect it is analogous to Putnam's account of a speaker's knowledge of natural kind terms. The obvious move is to suggest that frame-like 'chunks' are the way in which the assumptions of encyclopedia entries are structured and accessed (Sperber and Wilson, 1995: 88).

Minsky suggests that a frame can be thought of as a network made up of nodes or points and the relationships between them. The frame is organized in levels. The top level is fixed and represents things which are purportedly always true of the situation we are processing. This fixed level parallels the top-most layer of the encyclopedia entry we proposed above and would include analytic definitions where those are available.

At the bottom level of the frame are a multiplicity of slots or terminals. These terminals have conditions attached to them which must be matched by the external stimuli being processed. Terminals also include **default assignments**. This is a key property since it allows the actively perceiving mind to supply information that goes beyond that in the stimulus on an 'everything else being equal' basis. Default assignments supply extra information about typical cases which are assumed to hold in the absence of disconfirming evidence. Terminals can also direct us to **subframes** or include instructions on what to do next.

A given situation can also be viewed from different points of view – literally so in the case of visual perception. Minsky allows for this with the notion of a **frame system**. This is a set of formally related frames which share the same terminals. In the case of scene analysis, each of the related frames represents the same scene, systematically transformed, from a different viewpoint. Move a little to the right, for example, and the room will look quite different. The differing viewpoints will be represented by different but related frames in the system.

Minsky (1975: 364ff.) explicitly suggests that the basic principle of frame-system theory can be applied to discourse comprehension, kinds of narrative, word meaning, and **scenarios**, that is, events consisting of a sequence of actions. One can imagine in the event of X *buying* and Y *selling* some *good* for some *value*. Such a representation could simultaneously serve for the comprehension of the event when witnessed, a guide or plan for the performance of such an event, the representation of the meanings of the terms in the lexical field, and the production and comprehension of discourse. Directions to alternative methods of buying and selling and detailed instructions for kinds of purchase would direct the mind to sub-frames and other related frame systems.

There has been a wealth of theories and descriptions along the same line as Minsky's proposals and covering a diversity of domains. Systems for representing common-sense knowledge have been variously termed **frames**, **schemas**, **scripts** and **plans**, and differ somewhat in emphasis. Some, for example scripts, have emphasized the temporal and sequential nature of events and some the way that actions rest on a hierarchy of planned goals (Schank and Abelson, 1975, 1977). Some deal with how narrative is comprehended. It is clear that such systems could also be used to describe the structure of speech events which we discussed in chapter eight.

Ultimately, these proposals don't solve 'the frame problem' as we outlined it above, unless we deal with restricted micro-worlds. They still don't tell us how we are constrained in ordinary conversation to access *just the correct* encyclopedic assumptions, nor how hypotheses might be formed on the basis of past experience.

Nevertheless, there are continuous developments in cognitive science (Johnson-Laird, 1993). One new approach which has become influential and which might have the potential for modelling how the mind-brain learns, remembers and accesses information, is called **connectionism** or **parallel distributed processing** (see Bechtel and Abrahamsen, 1991; Pinker and Mehler, 1988). One striking thing about this model of mental architecture is that it doesn't involve explicit rules. Therefore our seeming inability to write rules that explicitly instruct us how to construct the correct context might be by-passed. We can say that this process is on a lower level, one not involving rule-governed operations on symbols.

In a connectionist network, active units, in our case representations of words/concepts like 'pregnant', 'give birth', 'have a baby', 'in hospital', 'is ill', 'have a husband' etc., would be separate processing units. These would be all actively linked together in such a way that activation of one activates others according to the strength of their connections. Units can be excited when a certain threshold is reached and this excitement can cascade through the system. Certain activations can alternatively inhibit other units. Each unit can be multiply connected to many others and the overall effect is that its role is distributed throughout the system, not localized in one entry. And one can imagine joint input units 'pregnant' and 'hospital' exciting 'give birth' until it reaches a threshold and pops into mind, while simultaneously inhibiting other units such as 'is ill' and 'has a husband'.

However, we need to add a note of caution on connectionism, since there are problems. It works very well at a low, input driven level for forming associations, but seems to require some supplement to account for higher level organization. Some connectionists are looking at **hybrid systems** which combine operations of different types.

A connectionist picture of the mind does represent meaning as distributed holistically throughout a network of active signs in a generally Quinean way. It also suggests a way of making precise the relevance theory problems of accessible contexts and processing effort at a 'lower level'.

Whatever the outcome of further research, both the inferential approach to communication and the notion of frames are crucial for interpretative approaches to text. We shall look at this in chapter ten.

10 Action and critique

> The consideration of linguistic uses associated with any practical pursuit, leads us to the conclusion that language . . . ought to be regarded and studied against the background of human activities and *as a mode of human behaviour in practical matters . . .* language functions as a link in concerted human activity, as a piece of human behaviour. *It is a mode of action and not an instrument of reflection.*
>
> Malinowski (1923)

Action and intention

One theme of the last several chapters has been that to utter, or produce any linguistic token, is to *do* something. In Malinowski's words, it is 'a mode of action'. In considering the prayer in chapter eight we claimed that the text was an activity. We argued that the words 'we pray thee' performed the act of entreating or performing a humble request. It has been a fundamental assumption of pragmatics that utterances are a form of human action (Levinson, 1983: 226). To say something is similar to performing many other types of actions; for example, opening a window, mailing a letter, hitting a ball with a cricket bat, beckoning to someone, and so on. **Speech acts** have their own particular characteristics but also share certain important properties with other types of non-verbal action.

Let us examine two such properties. The first property was described by the philosopher G. E. M. Anscombe in her book *Intention* (1957). Imagine that we are observing a person, X, standing in front of a window doing something. We ask, 'What is she doing?' How can we describe X's action? We could say, 'She's moving her arms' or 'She's moving her arms in that particular manner we describe as "lifting"', or 'She's opening the window' or 'She's airing the room' or 'She's causing the papers to blow all over the place' or 'Because of that, she's annoying me', and so on. The point is that we can describe her action in many different ways. In fact, there are as many ways as there are true statements which describe what X is doing. The point is that the *same* physical behaviour can be subsumed 'under a variety of different descriptions' as long as each statement characterizing it is true.

The second property involves one such type of description. These are **intentional** descriptions. Some human actions are intended by their agents and some are not. Thus, most people would agree that the peristaltic movement of the gut, or the spasm that one's body sometimes gives while falling asleep, is not intentional. By contrast, actions which are intentional are fundamental to understanding human behaviour, including speech acts.

To say a behaviour is intentional in this sense is to describe it in terms of some purpose of an agent to achieve a goal. Notice that this sort of explanation presupposes that the entity to which intention is attributed has inner goings on which are the source of behaviour, in other words has 'a mind'. They believe, desire and intend. Such attributions are called 'intentional descriptions' and entities with such minds – human, some animals, maybe computers – are called 'intentional entities'. An act can be truly described and explained; the entity did X (applying a lifting motion to the window) in order to achieve Y (opening the window). That is *why* the act was performed. It is intelligible in those terms. Social life is important to intentionality because in most cases the intentional explanation of an act demands inferences that draw on encyclopedic social information, as in the reasoning illustrated in chapter nine. We shall return to these issues in chapter eleven.

The point here is that speech acts have this property of intentionality. This is another way of saying that utterances are acts. Also recall that the analysis of communication we gave in chapter nine essentially involved intention as well. That means that Sperber and Wilson's communicative and informative intents are logically also the performances of specialized kinds of acts, **communicative**

acts. The aim of pragmatics as outlined in chapter nine, was to provide a theory of intentionally communicative acts.

The three notions of intending, acting and communicating are involved in *both* verbal *and* non-verbal behaviour. Actions can be intentional or non-intentional whether they are verbal or not. And one kind of intentional act is to intend to communicate. So we can have verbal or non-verbal intentionally communicative acts. (That is why our theory of intentional communication in chapter nine had to cover both verbal and non-verbal stimuli.) The new insight here is that these communicative utterances are actions and can be integrated with our thinking about action in general. (There is also another use of the word 'communicate' in which information is unintentionally 'exuded'; for example, when clouds convey that it might rain, or – to cite a human example – when a shaky voice conveys that one is nervous. For clarity's sake, I will use the term only in the intentional sense here but the other sense will be discussed in chapter eleven.)

A few examples will illustrate the above distinctions. An act may be non-verbal and unintentional; for example, slipping on a banana peel. An act may be non-verbal and intentional but not intentionally communicative; for example, walking to the station with no intention of using the act of walking to communicate the fact that one is going to the station to anyone. Alternatively, the non-verbal act may be intentionally communicative. I may make a gesture to a friend across the street to intentionally convey that I am going to the station (and hence can't stop to talk). The same friend may further truly interpret my activity in ways I never intended. My friend may calculate that I am going to Cambridge to do research. Or my act may be further interpreted in ways that haven't ever *occurred* to me. Perhaps, my travel is taken as evidence of ambition.

These last points allow us to distinguish intentional communication from broader levels of interpretation. For example, the interpretation proposed for the prayer in chapter eight, that it was a social solidarity mechanism, would hardly be intended by those who are praying. If the prayer is sincerely performed as a communicative act surely the addressee must be God. Broader interpretation also shows that although language is used to communicate messages, it is *not* simply a system of communication. A verbal act may have a communicative intention and this class was analysed in chapter nine (Grice, 1957; Sperber and Wilson, 1995). But a verbal act can also be non-communicative although still intentional. Just consider note-taking or talking to oneself aloud to guide one's movement or thinking in words. Alternatively, acts using the vocal apparatus need be neither linguistic nor intentional – a sigh, a moan – or may be intentional but not communicative – whistling in the dark. We tend to think of intentional communication as the prototype linguistic act. This can be misleading as we shall see.

For a moment, however, let us backtrack into the origins of the insight that utterances are a form of human action. Although this insight might appear to be mere common sense, in fact its first appearance in modern literature was in the later philosophical work of Ludwig Wittgenstein and, independently, and somewhat earlier, in the anthropological studies of Bronislaw Malinowski. Both these thinkers emphasized that utterances were activities within the context of social life.

Malinowski spent much of his professional life studying the culture of the Trobriand Islanders of the South Pacific. His view that utterance was an activity embedded in practical social life and culture arose partly because of the difficulty he found in the translation of texts from their exotic language and cultural setting into ours. Utterances, he argued, could only be comprehended (or translated) relative to the culture and situation in which they were inextricably embedded. Likewise, the 'meanings' of linguistic forms should be thought of not as a relationship between a word or sentence and that to which it refers, but rather as a complex of functional relationships between words, sentences and the contexts in which they are used (Malinowski, 1923; Robins, 1971). It was this impetus that influenced J. R. Firth to develop the notion of **contextual meaning**. This is the view that *meaning is function in context*, including the **context of situation** and **context of culture**. From this point of view the description of a register, for example our analysis of the prayer, is just a broad interpretation of the situational and cultural meaning of the text as part of the social process. Linguistic analysis becomes a method of cultural analysis. This socio-functional approach lies behind Halliday's model described in chapter eight (see Figure 8.9).

The philosophy of Wittgenstein, however, is the place where the insight that language is an activity occurs most vividly. As we saw in chapter eight, Wittgenstein (1953) uses the term 'language game' to refer to 'language and the activities into which it is woven', and participant knowledge of 'the technique of using the language'. The term 'language game' is used by Wittgenstein to describe a very wide diversity of kinds of language use. In *Philosophical Investigations* (1. 23), he writes:

> But how many kinds of sentences are there? Say assertion, question, and command? – There are *countless* kinds: countless different kinds of use of what we call 'symbols', 'words', 'sentences'. And this multiplicity is not something fixed, given one for all; but new types of language, new language games, as we may say, come into existence, and others become obsolete and get forgotten.

He lists examples. These include such diverse activities as: 'Giving orders, and obeying them', 'Reporting an event', 'Speculating about an event', 'Guessing riddles', 'Solving a problem in practical arithmetic' and 'Asking, thanking, cursing, greeting, praying'. Wittgenstein stresses that this multiplicity of language games is embedded in forms of life. A language game is only possible within a form of life, the basic communal practices which make up social life. A form of life is 'a way of living in society' (Kenny, 1973: 163). For example, the utterance of a prayer is integrated into the total background of religious practices in a society.

Hubert Dreyfus (1985) points out that the philosopher Heidegger invokes a similar **primordial pre-understanding** involved in interpretation. We saw in chapter nine that comprehension involves encyclopedic background information which is enormously fine-grained. And we saw that there were problems in representing that information. Dreyfus' interpretation of 'primordial pre-understanding' and Wittgenstein's 'forms of life' suggest that such background information may not consist of beliefs at all as that word is normally understood. We do enormously complicated things like dancing, swimming, playing the violin without learning a theory or having a set of beliefs about them. The background knowledge to such practices isn't a system of belief. Such information *can* be represented in propositional terms but it isn't present in that abstract way to the conscious mind. Rather, it is directly encoded in neurology and not accessible to consciousness. These ideas converge with that part of relevance theory in which calculations of relevance only occur at the neurological level (see page 344). We will return to 'unconscious' information again in chapter eleven.

Wittgenstein's later philosophy has been the basis of one approach to the philosophy of language called 'ordinary language philosophy'. We now turn to the work of two philosophers in this tradition, J. L. Austin and John Searle.

Speech acts

J. L. Austin was the originator of the term 'speech act', and in his William James Lectures at Harvard University in 1955, subsequently published as *How to Do Things with Words*, he developed the first systematic theory of utterances as human action. We shall be concerned with only three of Austin's terms. The most useful way of thinking about these is to view them as three different descriptions of the same speech act. To illustrate this, consider the text we examined at the beginning of the last chapter. Here it is again in its full form. Arthur is walking with Brenda, who is married and with whom Arthur has been having a surreptitious affair. We will just concentrate on that part of Brenda's utterance which is in the box.

1. Arthur: What's the matter with you tonight?
2. Brenda: I'll tell you what's the matter with me, Arthur.
3. I'm pregnant. Good and proper this time and it's your fault.
4. Arthur: Oh ay, it's bound to be my fault, ain't it?

Brenda has performed at least one speech act. But this act can be described in three different ways. These are illustrated in Figure 10.1.

To begin with the **locutionary act**: this term deals with the act *of* uttering these words. That is, Brenda made noises which

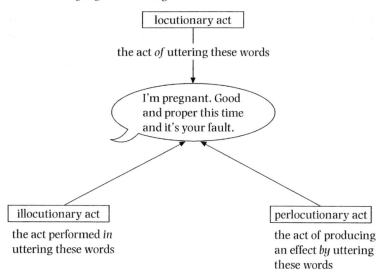

Figure 10.1 Three descriptions of a speech act

happen to have a conventional meaning in English and which realize certain English grammatical forms. We need not discuss this in any more detail now because the more important (for our purposes) descriptions of the speech act are the remaining two.

We'll deal next with the **illocutionary act**. Clearly, Brenda believes she is pregnant. The reason she utters, 'I'm pregnant', is presumably because she intends this utterance to represent an actual situation which she believes is the case. A sentence uttered with this intention is known as a **statement**, when someone states that such and such a state of affairs obtains. Consider the next part of what she utters, 'it's your fault'. Given that she has conveyed that she believes she is pregnant, it is further arguable that she also intends to convey that this outcome is because of some bad or reprehensible thing that Arthur has done. An utterance in which the speaker intends to convey that some act or omission of the hearer is reprehensible is an **accusation**. Both stating and accusing are illocutionary acts. In other words, the illocutionary description of a speech act characterizes the speaker's intention, what sort of thing he or she intended to do *in* making the utterance.

(For example, that he or she intended it to convey the belief that the sentence was true, or intended it to convey that the hearer had done something reprehensible.) Austin (1962: 98–100) defines the illocutionary act in the following words:

> To perform a locutionary act is in general . . . also . . . to perform an *illocutionary act* . . . Thus in performing a locutionary act we shall also be performing such an act as:
>   asking or answering a question,
>   giving some information or an assurance or a warning,
>   announcing a verdict or an intention,
>   pronouncing sentence . . .
> the performance of an 'illocutionary' act, i.e. performance of an act *in* saying something as opposed to performance of an act *of* saying something.

But such actions also have effects on the hearer. It is this that the term **perlocutionary act** describes. One effect of Brenda's utterance is to make Arthur evasive. The perlocutionary force of an utterance covers a multitude of sins, some intended and some not. One example of an intended effect are those acts which require a **perlocutionary uptake** in order to be performed at all. An example of such an act is a bet. I can intend my utterance to count as a proposal that, if there is a certain outcome in the future, I will pay a certain sum to the person with whom I am making the bet or, if the opposite happens, they will pay me the equivalent. Now this can only be happily 'brought off' if the hearer accepts the wager, if there is appropriate uptake. In other cases, the intention to perform the act is sufficient by itself to bring the act off, without the cooperation of the hearer. If we take a question to necessarily involve an intention to elicit information, and that success or not doesn't affect the act of asking a question, then one can happily pose a question even if there is no answer. It is even moot whether the hearer has to recognize that the speaker has asked a question for a question to be posed. Perhaps, hearer recognition that the speaker intends to elicit information is a required 'uptake' in this case. Other perlocutionary effects are purely unintended. For example, if a question throws the interlocutor into a panic. Austin's concepts of illocutionary and perlocutionary acts jointly characterize two features of the overall intentionality of speech acts as a species of intentional action.

Felicity conditions on successful performance

The task of interpreting speech acts is complicated by the fact that the naming of illocutions is unsystematic. All illocutionary acts are mini institutions; some more overtly institutional than others. Some acts such as *making a bid, putting in a tender, voting in an election, making an application, asking or answering an exam question, taking a poll, placing a bet* or *marrying someone* etc. are overtly institutional acts. We have illocutionary force verbs for many acts of this type, for example, *christen, resign, nominate, tender, marry,* etc. – see Searle (1979); Searle and Vanderveken (1985: 205). Other illocutions are more general and cut across many contexts of situation – they are not tied to specific institutions. Examples are, *promise, warn, complain, remind, argue* and so on. Finally, some actions are very general and basic, are **grammaticalized** and not just **lexicalized** (the latter is the term used when we have a specific word for an act). Sperber and Wilson (1995) argue that *say, tell* and *ask* have such a special status (see below). Note also that the range of illocutionary verbs which we have is historically evolved and is fairly arbitrary. There are many 'acts done with words' for which we have no clear single names. If every act performed with words in institutional contexts were distinguished and characterized we would be developing a complex descriptive sociology of the verbal actions of the everyday life world. The traditional vocabulary would need to be put into order and tested for descriptive adequacy.

The systematic study of illocutionary acts has been a major contribution of the philosopher John Searle (1969, 1979; Searle and Vanderveken, 1985). Beginning with his 1969 study *Speech Acts,* Searle has attempted to work out the conditions for the successful, non-defective performance of illocutionary acts, both in general and in particular; the so-called **felicity conditions**.

Searle has schematized the nature of these conditions. The conditions are of various general types; for example, **sincerity conditions** which require speakers to be in certain psychological states, having certain beliefs, intentions, etc. If I am to successfully promise to do A, I must sincerely intend to do A. There are **propositional content conditions**, in which the illocution constrains the content expressed, and other **preparatory conditions** in the context which must be met. The condition mentioned above that Brenda predicate responsibility for her pregnancy to Arthur is a content condition for accusation and the presupposition of its badness is a preparatory condition. Another most important condition is that the illocution has a particular **illocutionary point** which is essential to that type of act. Searle and Vanderveken (1985: 13) define the illocutionary point thus:

> Each type of illocution has a point or purpose which is internal to its being an act of that type. The point of statements and descriptions is to tell people how things are, the point of promises and vows is to commit the speaker to doing something . . . Each of these points or purposes we will call the *illocutionary point* of the corresponding act . . . We mean simply that a successful performance of an act of that type necessarily achieves that purpose.

Searle employs the notion of point to bring classificatory order to sets of illocutionary acts. He argues that there are at base only five broad classes of illocutionary points. All illocutionary forces and verbs can be grouped under just these five categories (Searle and Vanderveken, 1985: 37–62, 179–216). In fact, this is the remarkable claim that humans only perform five basic types of actions using words.

The five fundamental kinds of illocutionary forces and their essential unifying 'points' are:

1. **Assertives** in which the speaker believes that the proposition expressed represents an actual state of affairs and has grounds for so doing. This class includes *accuse, criticize, complain, assert, state, deny, predict,* etc. The basic assertive verb is *to assert.*

2. **Commissives** in which the speaker becomes committed to doing something at some point in the future. The class includes *promise, vow, pledge, guarantee,* etc. The basic commissive verb is *to commit.*

3. **Directives** in which the speaker attempts to get the hearer to carry out a future course of action. The class

includes *request, question, order, command, beg, suggest, urge,* etc. The primitive or basic direct- ive verb is *to direct.*

4.   **Expressives**   in which the speaker expresses some psycho- logical state, feelings or attitudes, about a given state of affairs. The class includes *apologize, com- pliment, deplore, praise, complain,* etc. No one expressive verb is more basic than the others.

5.   **Declaratives**   in which the speaker brings about some state of affairs (usually of an institutional sort) by virtue of the utterance itself. The performance of the act brings about a change in the world. The class includes *endorse, resign, nominate, name, appoint, apply* etc. The primitive or basic verb is *to declare.*

As can be seen, the five fundamental illocutionary points place the verbs into classes. Acts are more finely distinguished within each class according to felicity conditions. Let's look at some assert- ive and directive forces (Searle and Vanderveken, 1985: 182–92, 198–201).

Assertives are central to language use because they are the means by which 'speakers say how things are'. Speakers represent their beliefs. The basic member of this class is *assert. Claim, affirm* and *state* share the same point. *Accuse, criticize, blame* and *complain* can also be seen as variants. As we saw earlier, to accuse X of P is to predicate responsibility for some propositional content to X while also having the preparatory condition that P is bad. These con- ditions are satisfied in Brenda's utterance in 3, 'I'm pregnant and it's your fault.' It is interesting to distinguish this force from closely related ones. According to Searle and Vanderveken, *blame* is like *accuse* with the difference that accusations are public acts as in our example while blaming can be private, an inner act. To *criti- cize* X for P is akin to *accuse* but without the centrality of respons- ibility. The P is asserted to be bad and the hearer or some third party's connection with it is presupposed, e.g. 'It's terrible you getting me pregnant like this.' On the other hand, *complain* has both an assertive and expressive use. For example, in a *complaint* P is asserted. A preparatory condition is that P is bad and the sincerity condition is that the speaker disapproves of P, e.g. 'You never take proper care in doing anything.' To express dissatisfaction for a state of affairs commits the speaker to presupposing both the existence of that state of affairs and that it is bad.

Directives share the point of trying to get the hearer to do something at some future time. The core directive verb is *direct*. Among other directives there are a number of regular contrasting dimensions. One of the most important is between *asking a question* and *telling someone to do something*. These sorts of directives vary in terms of the degree of presupposed coercion they enact; from the very strong directives *command, order, require* or *demand* to the much weaker *request* and *urge*.

The grammar of force: a first approach

Searle's rules for illocutionary acts can be considered as rules for very general language games in Wittgenstein's sense. If we want to abstractly characterize conversational interaction we need to represent what acts are being performed in the utterances. When I say 'abstractly characterize', I mean that we aren't making psychological claims about what necessarily goes on in people's minds or brains as they communicate.

How can we recognize what illocutionary act is being performed when someone says something? Are there overt markers of each illocutionary force attached to the linguistic form itself? This is a difficult question much debated by philosophers and linguists (for a survey of the issues, see Levinson, 1983). The claim that linguistic forms do conventionally convey illocutionary forces is called the **literal force hypothesis**.

The most transparent way to signal an illocutionary force is to use a **performative verb**. These are verbs like *order, promise, accuse, pledge, urge, baptise* and so on. Austin (1962) noticed that when such verbs occur in present tense sentences with 'I' as subject and 'you' as object, for example, 'I (hereby) accuse you of getting me pregnant', then the utterance counts as an actual performance of the act – in this case an accusation – if the felicity conditions are also satisfied. However, such **overt performative formulae** are of little use to the analyst since speakers are only rarely that transparent. At one time, an attempt was made to account for 'literal force' by saying that every sentence contained such a 'covert' performative formula which was subsequently deleted. The semantics of such performative verbs would thus account for the literal force of sentences. However, linguists today believe that such an analysis is untenable (Levinson, 1983: 246–63).

Illocutionary forces are superficially indicated by a number of devices. For example, it is claimed that **grammatical sentence types** (or **moods**) literally indicate illocutionary forces. English has four main sentence types, the **declarative**, the **interrogative**, the **imperative** and the **exclamative**. Traditionally the meaning of each type has been associated with a particular illocutionary force. This is the orthodox version of the literal force hypothesis. For example, it is claimed that the literal meaning conveyed by uttering a sentence in the declarative is that the speaker is performing a statement. The encodings are:

1.	**declarative**	=	**assertive force**	e.g. You are pregnant.
2.	**interrogative**	=	**question force** (information seeking directive)	e.g. Are you pregnant? Who is pregnant?
3.	**imperative**	=	**directive force** (action seeking directive)	e.g. Get yourself pregnant.
4.	**exclamative**	=	**exclamative force** (surprise at truth of p)	e.g. What a pregnancy that was!

This illustrates that the propositional content expressed by a sentence can remain constant – this is called the **sentence radical** – while the force systematically varies by sentence type according to the **mood or force indicator**. The force indicator represents the literal illocutionary force of the sentence.

There are a number of problems with this approach. One problem is that sentence types do not unambiguously signal illocutionary forces. Any of the illocutionary forces can be conveyed by any of the sentence types. Conversely, any one of the sentence types can convey many and various illocutionary forces. To demonstrate this, consider the 'directive' class, the case of getting someone to do something. The imperative is only one rather specialized way of performing this act. Six distinct ways of requesting are illustrated in Figure 10.2. It is clear that all the sentence types are used; declaratives in 1, 3, 5 and 6, imperatives in 2 and interrogatives in 4, 5 and 6. The examples in 6 even show that the act which is requested can be different from the act mentioned in the sentence. As we shall see below, the connection is inferred.

There are further problems with the declarative. It appears to be used in the normal expression of most illocutionary forces. If a declarative sentence incorrigibly and literally means *I am perform-ing an assertive* by virtue of its force indicator, then in performing any non-assertive act I am also asserting something. Thus, Brenda would be asserting that 'It's your fault' as well as simultaneously accusing Arthur. Furthermore, in many cases when speakers utter declarative sentences, they aren't asserting at all. As we have seen, the assertive point involves the speaker believing the proposition expressed, being committed to its truth. But in occasions of irony, hyperbole, metaphor, joking, fictionality and so on, the speaker doesn't believe the proposition literally expressed but is purportedly committed to its truth by virtue of the grammatical form he or she has uttered.

One solution to these problems has been proposed by Searle himself (Searle, 1975). This is the theory of **indirect speech acts**. Because of its form a sentence literally conveys the illocutionary force conventionally associated with its sentence type. So, if I utter a grammatical interrogative, whatever else I may be doing, I am in the first instance asking a question. The theory of indirect speech acts claims that, besides the question, I might also be intending the utterance to primarily count as something else. The speaker is performing a further *non-literal* speech act as well as the one liter-ally signalled by the interrogative grammar. We will call the latter act the **direct illocutionary act** and the former act the **indirect illocutionary act**.

This section was headed 'The Grammar of Force: a First Ap-proach'. This signals that it is possible to relate sentence type and speech act in other ways, which have been termed **the pragmatic**

1 **Performatives**
I order you to eat.
I request that you eat.

2 **Imperatives**
Eat your lunch.
You eat your lunch now.
Let's have lunch.

3 **Peremptory declaratives**
You will eat your lunch this instant. (eat your lunch)
This bar will close at 11.00 sharp tonight. (close the bar at
11.00 sharp)

4 **Requests**

Can
Could   } you come now? (come now)
Will
Would

5 **Interrogatives and declaratives which explicitly contain
the act which is requested**
When are you coming home? (come home)
Are the letters typed yet? (type the letters)
You're the person who can fix my radio. (fix my radio)
This bar needs cleaning. (clean the bar)

6 **Sentences in which the act requested is not explicitly
mentioned**
This house is a mess. (clean the house)
You'll die of lung cancer. (don't light that cigarette)

I'm cold.   (close the windows, door
You look cold.   }   etc. or turn on the heater
How did it get so cold in here?   etc.)

Your water is lovely and hot now. (get into the bath)
She got married yesterday.
She looked ever so nice.   (consider getting married to me)

Figure 10.2 Ways of requesting

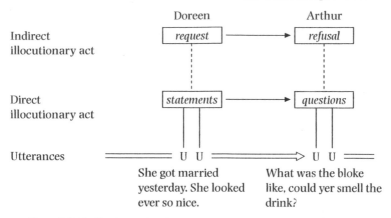

Figure 10.3 Indirect speech acts

analysis. We will look at this later. For simplicity's sake, we will accept Searle's theory of indirect speech acts for now.

Now let us consider an example of an indirect speech act as defined by Searle. Look at Arthur's reply to Doreen's request that they consider getting married, repeated here for convenience.

DOREEN: She got married yesterday. She looked ever so nice.
ARTHUR: What was the bloke like, could yer smell the drink?

Let us assume that Doreen, in fact, intends to perform one of a small number of illocutionary acts such as 'requesting they consider getting married', or 'broaching the topic of marriage', or 'suggesting they consider, or talk about, getting married'.

Arthur's reply in this case could arguably be the following indirect speech act. He has uttered two grammatical interrogatives. These signal that he is performing the act of questioning. But, furthermore, it is arguable that Arthur also intends by his latter question to convey that he *refuses* her request. He does not want to talk about getting married. Thus, his utterance is also a refusal. In our terminology, Arthur's direct speech act is questioning, his indirect speech is refusing. Figure 10.3 illustrates this analysis of the exchange.

The next task is to explain the connection between the direct and indirect illocutionary forces in each case. What is the mechanism

connecting Arthur's question and his refusal, or Doreen's statement and her request? How are we to interpret the dotted lines in
Figure 10.3?

The clue to this is that my interpretation in Figure 10.3 could
be wrong. For example, the reader may have been rebelling at
my interpretation of this exchange all along. One could argue that
it is equally plausible that Doreen merely intended to convey that
she believed the sentences she uttered were true. In other words,
she merely stated them. Arthur, the argument could continue, is
simply replying to her statement in terms which could be para-
phrased: 'She may have looked nice, but he must have been drunk
to get married.' In other words, he is stating, 'Marriage isn't a
state a rational man will enter into', and that's all. I agree that
this is a possible interpretation. I would, however, *argue* that my
analysis in Figure 10.3 is very plausible indeed, and to do so I
would display the chain of inferences which I have constructed
in this context to connect Doreen's statements with her indirect
request, and Arthur's questions with his indirect refusal of the
request.

The crucial point is that the connection between direct and
indirect acts is in terms of inferencing. And the inferencing itself is
dependent on the conversational context of the utterance.

The cooperative principle and its maxims

So we must first *infer* the indirect act. According to Searle (1975),
our starting point in this task is the sentence type of the utterance.
The type chosen conveys the speaker's direct illocutionary act.
This interacts with context and background information so that
the hearer can infer that the speaker intended to convey a further
indirect act. In other words, reasoning out the indirectly conveyed
force of the utterance is another example of the kind of inferences
we draw in context, with which we are already familiar from chapter nine. There we studied Sperber and Wilson's (1995) relevance
theory. Now we will backtrack historically and look at an earlier
theory of contextual implication, one which paved the way for
Sperber and Wilson's work.

The foundational theory of reasoning in conversational contexts has been that of H. P. Grice. In his William James Lectures at Harvard in 1968, Grice provided a first framework for a theory of utterances in context. Such a theory is called a **pragmatic theory**, to distinguish it from a semantic theory or theory of 'literal' meaning. Part of Grice's lectures was subsequently published under the title 'Logic and Conversation' (1975). Sperber and Wilson's (1986) relevance theory is both a critique of and a building upon Grice's pragmatics. His theory also figures crucially in Searle's (1975) view of indirect speech acts. So I will sketch out some of Grice's main ideas and relate them to both these topics in turn.

Grice's pragmatic thought can be divided into two interrelated parts. First, there is a theory of **speaker meaning** discussed in chapter nine (page 325). Grice calls speaker meaning, non-natural meaning or **meaning$_{nn}$** and it is the basis of intentional communication (Grice, 1957). Linguistic meaning and this speaker meaning need not be the same. Indeed, they customarily diverge. This is another way of saying that I can *mean* a great deal more than I actually *say*. We examined this in detail when we saw that the utterance 'Yes, she'll be going to hospital soon' could be used to convey more than its literal meaning. But can we define speaker meaning precisely? We saw above that in speaker meaning or intentional communication the speaker intends the hearer to recognize a message because the speaker also recognizes that there is an intention that this message be recognized. This definition is important because, as we saw above, what people say and do 'exudes' a great deal of information only a small part of which is intentionally communicative in Grice's sense.

How is it possible to convey more than what is literally said? Grice examines this in 'Logic and Conversation' (1975). The theory assumes that intentional communication is a cooperative mutual activity. We assume that each participant is trying to achieve certain goals and interpret their behaviour on that assumption. This is captured by the **cooperative principle**: 'Make your conversational contribution such as is required, at the stage at which it occurs, by the accepted purpose or direction of the talk exchange in which you are engaged' (Grice, 1975: 45). It is claimed that in order to achieve the conversational goals participants must assume of each other that they are obeying the following maxims (Grice, 1975: 45–6):

QUANTITY:		*Don't provide **more or less** information than is required for the current purposes of the exchange*
QUALITY:		*Try to make your contribution one that is **true***
	1.	*Do not say what you believe to be false*
	2.	*Do not say that for which you lack adequate evidence*
RELATION:		*Be **relevant***
MANNER:		*Be **clear***
	1.	*Avoid obscurity of expression*
	2.	*Avoid ambiguity*
	3.	*Avoid unnecessary prolixity*
	4.	*Be orderly*

So when we engage in a conversation with someone, we can assume that they are cooperating to sustain our joint activity; more specifically, that they are trying to follow these maxims.

Now let us see what happens to the maxims in the course of an exchange. Consider this example (Grice, 1975: 51):

A:　Smith doesn't seem to have a girlfriend these days.
B:　He has been paying a lot of visits to New York lately.

Participants work under the assumption that each is observing the maxims. If this is the case, then we have to assume that B's remark is somehow relevant to what A uttered. In order to preserve this assumption we infer the proposition, 'Smith has, or may have, a girlfriend in New York.'

Grice calls this kind of inference a **conversational implicature**, and we can say that B **implicates** the proposition just mentioned. An implicature, therefore, is an inference generated in the course of a conversation in order to preserve the assumption that participants are obeying the maxims. We produce and interpret implicatures over and against the overriding assumption that we are both trying to speak the truth, be relevant, avoid obscurity and so on.

What happens when a maxim is violated or flouted? We do a rescue operation by way of an implicature. We rescue the maxim by reasoning out the 'point' of the violation. Ah, we say, they were being relevant after all. We just have to work somewhat harder to discover what they intended to convey in flouting or violating the maxim. Consider this example (Grice, 1975: 53):

A: X is a fine friend.

Imagine a context in which both A and his or her interlocutor know that X has done something terrible to A – for example, betrayed one of A's secrets. In such a situation A has 'flouted' the maxim of quality. He or she has not spoken the truth. In this case, A will be implicating something by virtue of having flouted the maxim. The hearer's job is to work out the implicature. As Grice points out, the most obvious candidate in this case is that A is implicating the contradictory of what is said. That is, he or she is ironically conveying something that he or she *does* believe is true, that 'X is a rotten friend.'

In summary, then, participants assume that the cooperative principle and its maxims are being obeyed. A conversational implicature is a proposition which makes it possible to preserve this assumption, even when it is apparently violated or flouted. It was violated or flouted for a reason, to convey a 'point'.

It is quite obvious that 'conversational implicatures' are close relatives of Sperber and Wilson's 'contextual implications' discussed in chapter nine. (From now on, I will use Grice's term.) Relevance theory drew attention to many problems with Grice's view. I have assembled some of these together with other criticisms of Grice and display them (for brevity's sake) in Figure 10.4. Relevance theory has in part grown out of Gricean Pragmatics and it is interesting to relate the two theories. To do this involves trying to analyse just what Grice's theory is doing in more detail. I will attempt to point the way to how this might be done.

At bottom, Grice's system is an analysis of the *normatively ideal intentional communicative situation*, a context in which what we mean – *meaning$_{nn}$* – is identical with *literal* meaning. We can group the maxims into two sets. The first is about beliefs and contexts. The second is about the means of communication, how belief is expressed in contexts.

IDEAL INTENTIONAL COMMUNICATIVE EVENT		
1.	**TRUTH** }	*beliefs*
	}	+
	RELEVANCE }	*context*
		+
2.	**BREVITY** }	
	}	*directness*
	CLARITY }	
Apparent deviation. Why? Yields intention as explanation.		

Grice is specifying a norm for communicative events which says that what is meant should be that which is most linguistically direct and transparent, which of course must be relative to the expectations of the context. We should say exactly what we literally mean in the most transparent way possible. The phrase 'literally mean' is important. The Gricean norm is precisely what is required to establish literal meanings. We saw in chapter nine that such meanings are the stabilized core relations represented in the web of beliefs – the network of truth-relations between propositions. Grice requires that we assume that people intend to express themselves as transparently as possible whenever they converse. This would involve expressing themselves literally, as well as relevantly, clearly, compactly, etc.

It is *apparent deviation* from this norm that generates implicatures. Given my beliefs, my interlocutor says something that isn't as transparent as possible, i.e. isn't literal, isn't relevant etc. Since we are cooperating, I assume that there must be *a reason* for this! Therefore, I pose a 'why' question. Why is my interlocutor being (purposely) untruthful or obscure or irrelevant or circumlocutious? I construct a 'passing theory' to explain this anomaly. The implicature is a part of that theory. The theory also includes that the speaker intended that the implicature be drawn (they assumed I would construct just that 'passing theory'). But the way is open to infer *weak or unintended* implicatures as well (see below).

But why does the Gricean norm involve *both* truth and relevance? My hunch is that these are closely intertwined concepts and that relevance serves truth. In their second edition Sperber and Wilson (1995: 264–5) redefine relevance in terms of, not just con-

1. What is the status of the cooperative principle (CP) and its maxims? Is it a social convention, or instead a rational means of teleologically achieving meaning$_{nn}$ and establishing 'literal' meaning?
2. How do the maxims follow from the CP?
3. Why just this disparate set of maxims? Is there anything that might unify them, or are they unrelated?
4. The maxims are not explicit. They take for granted our knowledge of what is 'relevant', 'obscure', etc.
5. In any instance, it is unclear which maxims or combination of maxims produce the conversational implicature. In most cases more than one maxim seems to apply. Why?
6. The distinction between what a speaker 'says', by virtue of sentence meaning, and what a speaker 'implicates' is inaccurate. The semantics of the items uttered under-determines what is 'said' and needs to be pragmatically enriched before even literal meaning is determinable.
7. Which implicatures are intended? Out of the indefinite number of inferences that can be derived from a sentence's literal meaning, context and background information, how can a hearer determine which were meant by the speaker?
8. How are just the right beliefs accessed? How is this process controlled so that an infinite regress of irrelevant information is avoided? (The frame problem referred to in chapter nine.)
9. Many 'standard bridging inferences' are required to make a text cohere. Are these part of meaning$_{nn}$?
10. Since the theory is inexplicit, it cannot be formalized. Therefore, can it be viewed as a scientific theory (it can't be refuted) or be useful for computational models in psychology?

Figure 10.4 Some criticisms of Grice

textual effects, but **positive cognitive effects**. These are effects which satisfy **cognitive goals** among which is the truth of the assumptions in the encyclopedia. We could say that human beings are cognitively designed to **inquire**, to seek the highest quality representation of the world practically possible (the 'cost' dimension) which they also use to construct their intentional behaviour, including utterances. An assumption is relevant to an individual to the degree it produces such positive effects. Relevance is a measure of the empirical impact a stimulus has on assumptions already held and mobilized, a sort of constant testing for truth, but simultaneously constrained by processing cost. Given a willingness to pay, processing 'ought' to constantly improve representations. It automates inquiry (see Downes, 1997; and Dennett, 1996: ch. 13, who gives an evolutionary account of inquiry). This honouring of truth can be assumed of participants in conversational contexts, as Grice claims. (And this is important to underpin literal meanings.) But we don't have to specify it as a separate maxim, it happens automatically.

The above suggests that the thrust of our cognitive activity is utopian; it *ought* to lead to better representations. But you might well ask: 'Why does it seem that both individuals and societies *don't* improve their representations?' Well, in some domains they do! But another possibility is that social factors and their speech acts might **block inquiry**. If someone powerful treats an assumption as true, I may consciouly or unconsciously have to treat it likewise in my practical thoughts and actions, *even* if it contradicts what I believe or the evidence. The assumption is part of an **ideology**. I *am* anyway getting important new information about what authority believes and how I must act appropriately. Society can impose many extra costs on inquiry. This motivates **critique**, the attempt to 'analytically reveal' these blocks. We shall return to this at the end of the chapter.

Inferring an indirect speech act

After this lengthy aside on Grice, let's return to Searle and ask how implicatures figure in the interpretation of indirect speech acts, our current topic. *The answer is that if a speaker implicates that the felicity conditions for some illocutionary act are satisfied, then these can figure as premisses in an argument that the speaker intends to perform that particular speech act.* That is, the most relevant interpretation of the utterance to the hearer is that the speaker intended to perform such and such an illocutionary act or acts. It is through doing '*Gricean' inferencing* that the hearer achieves perlocutionary 'uptake' of the speaker's intentions in those cases where the speech act is indirectly conveyed.

This needs to be illustrated with a concrete example. Let us look again at the exchange between Arthur and Doreen in Figure 10.3. We will concentrate on Arthur's utterance. Consider what happens when a remark appears to be irrelevant to what went before in a conversation. Remember we are always constrained to make our remarks relevant. And Arthur says, 'What was the bloke like, could yer smell the drink?'

The direct act. Arthur has uttered two grammatical interrogatives. We suggested that the literal force of this form conveys that the speaker is asking a question. He is seeking information of Doreen. Now is this a felicitous question or not? Are the felicity conditions on questions satisfied?

To answer this, we look to the context and the background knowledge. But we look at these in relation to the detailed form of the language which Arthur uses. There is nothing problematic in the first clause. But look at the second interrogative! The form of this clause is such that in this context Arthur quietly implicates that he believes that 'the bloke is or had been drinking', and merely asks Doreen if she could smell the results of this on him or not. It is a 'loaded' question. Arthur has no way of knowing whether or not the bloke had been drinking. And, in the context of the bloke's wedding, where the bride looked 'ever so nice', it *seems* an *irrelevant* aspect of the groom about which to ask Doreen.

We have to conclude, I think, that in all likelihood Arthur is neither sincere nor intending his utterance to count as a question. He is, we conclude, intending to convey something else. (Note that he could still be doing this even if the question were felicitous. Defectiveness of the direct act is not a necessary condition for the utterance to convey an indirect act, although direct acts often are infelicitous.)

The indirect act. Our immediate reaction is to look for the connection between what he says and what Doreen has just said. Thus, the deviation between the requirement to be relevant and the seeming irrelevance of the remark forces us to make inferences. These serve to connect the remark to the context and decide what Arthur intended to convey. We perform the same kind of inferencing which we examined in the last chapter under the control of the principle of relevance. I will just sketch out the reasoning informally.

Arthur implicates, given what Doreen has just said, that the bloke must have been drunk or he would not have got married. Given the meaning of the word 'drunk', which includes the inference that its subject is intoxicated or overcome with liquor and therefore not capable of acting in a fully rational way, Arthur further implicates that he believes that you would have to be impaired in this way to get married. It would be a very foolish and irrational man who would get married. Background knowledge tells us that, in general, people don't want to behave in foolish and irrational ways. Now, if we grant, as I argued above, that Doreen has just requested of Arthur that they consider, or at least talk about, getting married, it is easy to see how Arthur intends his utterance indirectly to refuse those requests. He implicates the felicity conditions of a refusal. Nobody in full possession of their faculties would consider getting married. Therefore, he intends his utterance to count as an unwillingness to entertain that proposition.

We have shown that implicatures are crucial in constructing the arguments that connect direct and indirect illocutionary forces. It is inferences of this sort that fill in the dotted lines connecting the directly and indirectly conveyed acts in Figure 10.3. Inferences of the same kind also account for the fact, displayed in Figure 10.2, that a single class of act – for example, directives – can be conveyed by any sentence type. In the more indirect or seemingly opaque ways of requesting (3–6 in Figure 10.2), the illocutionary act is inferred in context, following Gricean principles. (There have been attempts to account for these relations without using Grice explicitly; see, for example, Labov and Fanshel, 1977.)

Discourse analysis: a speech act based model

Now that we have described the machinery, let us try to apply it to the analysis of texts. A methodology developed primarily for textual study we can call **discourse analysis**. But this term is also used to describe various empirically based approaches (especially of spoken mode) developed within linguistics (e.g. Labov and Fanshel, 1977; Sinclair and Coulthard, 1975). Some of the theories described in chapter eight, such as social semiotics or ethnography of communication, might be taken as discourse analytic methodologies (for overviews of the huge range of discourse analytic approaches, see Schiffrin, 1994; Brown and Yule, 1983; Stubbs, 1983). Discourse analysis is ultimately a practically oriented domain, but has to be based on pragmatic theory. Conversely, analysis of texts helps to develop empirically responsive pragmatic theories.

Corresponding to different ways of describing conversation, there are different possible analytic methods for discourse analysis. We shall look at two of these based on pragmatic theory; a method based on intentional communication and one based on speech acts. In chapter nine, we developed a theory of conversation based on beliefs and intentions. In one sense, discourse is the process by which we impact on each other's beliefs in order to assign informative intentions to one another. Each participant can be thought of as having a 'commitment slate' (or 'discourse representation') as that term was defined above. One method for discourse analysis could be based on making explicit the communicative and informative intentions, the beliefs mobilized in context creation and the arguments constructed. We utilized this method in an informal way in chapter nine, but one could imagine a descriptive methodology which was more formal. In another sense, however, the conveying of these beliefs, and the construal of communicative intent, can be conceived of as the performance of communicative acts. And in its illocutionary dimension, speech act theory claims that it has a means of characterizing utterances as actions. We can insist that the belief and intention theory is logically prior, since we need to evaluate participants' beliefs and intentions in order to see if the conditions for a particular illocutionary act from the inventory of institutional social acts have been satisfied. That granted, speech act theory gives us an action based method for discourse analysis. So we have two interdependent methods for the analysis of texts. In the following I will illustrate a **speech act based model of discourse analysis**.

The text is given in Figure 10.5. This also gives us the context and participants. I want to analyse this text in terms of illocutionary

Arthur and Brenda are afraid that Brenda's husband, Jack, may have seen them together in one of their surreptitious meetings. Jack is, at present, drinking in a working man's club, so Arthur decides to make an appearance in order that there should be no suspicion that Brenda and he have been together.

He goes into the club, where men are drinking or playing darts. He greets two of them, Albert and Tom, a union organizer.

1	ARTHUR:	*Hey, Albert!*
2	ALBERT:	*Good evening, Arthur.*
3	ARTHUR:	*Hello, Tom.*
4	TOM:	*How do, Arthur.* (voice from off screen)

Arthur moves on to the bar to buy a beer from the barman, Charlie.

| 5 | ARTHUR: | *Come on, Charlie, give us a pint.* |

Jack is sitting in the club room, alone at a table.

6	ARTHUR:	*Hello, Jack.*
7	JACK:	*Hello, Arthur.*
8	ARTHUR:	*What are you drinking?*
9	JACK:	*Oh ta, I'll have a mild.*
10	ARTHUR:	*Mild and a mild, please, Charlie.*

| 11 | ARTHUR: | *When's the next strike then, Tom?* |

Charlie pulls two beers for Arthur.

12	TOM:	*There's nothing to strike about yet, lad.*
13		*I expect you're too busy with young women for that, anyway.*
14	ARTHUR:	*No, not me, I spend my time with the bookies.*

He picks up the beers and goes over to Jack's table.

| 15 | TOM: | *I believe yer!* |

Figure 10.5 The 'strike' text

acts by focusing on one utterance and teasing out what illocutionary acts it is being used to perform. This is when Arthur says to Tom, 'When's the next strike then, Tom?' There are two theoretical points illustrated by this analysis. The first is to show that the utterance can be revealingly described in speech act terms. The second is to show that an utterance characteristically realizes more than one illocutionary act. This is another way of saying that there is a *complex of intentionality* in the performance of a single utterance.

Our initial problem with utterance 11 is similar to the problem we faced with Arthur's reply to Brenda earlier on. The grammatical form is interrogative. But is this utterance simply a question, or is it an indirect speech act of some kind? Simply in terms of its linguistic form, the utterance presupposes that there is going to be a strike at some future time, and requests that Tom supply the information as to when that strike will be. The form also presupposes, by virtue of 'next', that there have been strikes in the past.

There are very good reasons for supposing that this utterance is not a sincere question. In terms of Searle's felicity conditions on questioning it neither 'counts as an attempt by the speaker to get this information', nor does 'the speaker (sincerely) want this information'. Some of the reasons are overtly available from the context of the utterance. Thus Arthur is physically rather distant from Tom, and he makes no move to enter Tom's personal space. He glances at Tom only very briefly while uttering, and immediately lowers his eyes and engages himself in the purchase of his drinks. In fact, he walks away from the encounter during utterance 14, to join Jack as pre-arranged in utterances 8 and 9. Furthermore, his interrogative has an intonation which often signals that this form is not being used to ask a question (see Sag and Liberman, 1975). In other words, there are ample 'cues' that the question is defective.

But there are other reasons to think this utterance is not intended as a question. One is my judgement as to Arthur's personality and interests, given my previous experience of his talk. Another is the specific linguistic form he chooses to use. Contrast 11 and 11a:

11   When's the next strike then, Tom?
11a When's the strike then, Tom?

'Next' clearly makes an important contribution to the meaning of Arthur's utterance, perhaps in something like the following way. When I ask the time of a strike, I implicate that I believe that this is a relevant question; that there are reasons for us both to assume that a strike is likely soon, and I want to know when. In this case, I would use the form '*the* strike' which, by virtue of 'the', presupposes the existence, in the universe of discourse, of the strike. By contrast, when Arthur uses the form 'next', we can ask what the relevance is of him doing so. In the absence of any information from context that a strike is likely, it could implicate that Arthur's only reason for assuming a question about the time of strikes is relevant at all, is that there has been a strike, or strikes, in the past. This changes the question, because Arthur is indicating that he has no serious assumptions about the immediate relevance of his question regarding time. He does not believe a strike is imminent. Therefore his specific question about its timing is not relevant as a question, and is not a serious request for information.

Be that as it may, we are faced with the question: if Arthur's utterance is not a sincere question, then what illocutionary act might he be performing?

Figure 10.6 displays the illocutionary acts in the exchange. I conclude that 11 is simultaneously *a defective question, a recognition, a compliment* (perhaps defective), *a challenge* and what is termed an act of **phatic communion** (see below). In this case, in contrast with the previous examples, I have concluded that it is plausible that *a single utterance was intended to convey more than one illocutionary force*. In this I follow Labov and Fanshel (1977). I will explain the reasoning involved in deriving each of these indirect illocutionary forces in turn.

Social recognition? If 11 is not a felicitous question, what might it be? What did Arthur intend Tom to conclude he was doing?

We might say that Arthur is simply greeting Tom in a roundabout way. Searle has pointed out that a greeting need not have any specific kind of content, but must essentially count as a 'courteous recognition' of the hearer. It would be quite plausible to greet someone who was, say, characteristically interested in strikes by asking about his or her interest as an act of courtesy. The problem

Arthur's utterance	**Tom's utterance**	
When's the next strike then, Tom?	There's nothing to strike about yet, lad, I expect you're too busy with young women for that, anyway.	
Question as to time of strike	*Answer* no reason for strike	**Direct** (inferences not dependent on context)
Recognition that Tom is active in the union	*Recognition* that Arthur is successful with women	
Compliment that Tom is active in the union	*Compliment* that Arthur is successful with women	**Indirect** (inferences dependent on context)
Challenge (a) that Tom is 'past it' (b) is wasting his time	*Challenge* that Arthur is 'young' and 'silly' and not serious about important issues	
Phatic social relationship established	*Phatic* social relationship established	

Figure 10.6 Illocutionary forces in an exchange

here is that once participants have exchanged greetings, then the act is not repeatable. Try greeting again someone with whom you have just exchanged greetings and you will see what I mean. Tom and Arthur have successfully greeted each other in 3 and 4.

The solution to the problem that this is like a greeting but cannot be a greeting is that very often there are sets of closely related illocutionary acts which have certain features in common, but differ in other respects. Thus, Searle has termed all those acts in which speakers try to get hearers to do something, 'directives' which might include, say, requests and orders. Similarly, we often attempt in our utterances (whatever else we may be trying to do) to include some recognition of the social identity of the hearer. We intend to convey only that we *recognize* some important social attribute which he or she has, or the social relationship we assume we have with them. For example, in the course of a talk with our friendly local bank manager, or our boss, we often intend to include recognitions that they have those roles, whatever else we intend to convey.

The boxes below show explicitly how two distinct recognitions can be inferred from Arthur's utterance. The inferences depend on the interaction of the meaning of 11, the context, and Grice's principles. These show explicitly the relation between the meaning of the actual sentence and an indirectly conveyed act which it is used to perform.

There are a range of other possible interpretations of Arthur's intention above and beyond that of being an act of recognition. I would argue that these are plausible. But I would not argue that a hearer, even in this specific context, would have to take Arthur's remark in the following ways.

Compliment? Arthur implicates that Tom has some privileged access to, or special interest in, the time of the next strike; for example, Tom is a shop steward or is otherwise active in the union. If Arthur also believes, and assumes Tom also believes, that having this information or social attributes is an admirable property of Tom, then Arthur may intend to convey to Tom that he admires this property. But this is the essential condition for complimenting Tom.

That the mirror image of this act is also possible demonstrates the importance of background knowledge in construing an utterance. Thus, if Arthur believed that being active in the union was not admirable, and if Tom believed that Arthur might believe this, then it could just as easily be construed as a criticism of Tom's union activity, or even an accusation that Tom habitually fomented strikes. This is highly implausible in this case. But that is not because of the linguistic form and what it means, but because of what we assume, based on our background knowledge, about Arthur and Tom.

Recognition that Tom is active in the union	Recognition that Arthur and Tom are equal and solidary
1. Arthur has questioned Tom as to when the next strike will occur.	1. Arthur has addressed Tom by his first name only.
2. Tom assumes, because of the relevance maxim, that Arthur's utterance has some relevant point.	2. Since Arthur could not have used Tom's name at all, or chosen some other form of address, Tom can assume that this choice has some relevant point.
3. The conversational setting is not such as to indicate an interest in whether there is to be a strike.	3. The use of first name conveys that the speaker and the one so addressed are equal and solidary.
4. Therefore, Arthur's utterance is probably not just a question. What is it?	4. *Therefore, Arthur intends, probably, to convey to Tom that he recognises himself and Tom as equal and solidary.*
5. In asking the question, Arthur presupposes that Tom has the information necessary to answer the question, information that Arthur doesn't have. Therefore, Arthur is implicating that Tom has privileged access to, or special interest in, such information (e.g. Tom is a shop steward or is active in union affairs).	
6. *Therefore, Arthur intends, probably, to convey to Tom that he recognises that Tom is a shop steward or is active or interested in union affairs.*	

Challenge? There is a sense, however, in which Arthur might be intending to do something other than criticize Tom. There is possibly a kind of good-humoured aggressiveness in Arthur's remark. Such aggressiveness would be consistent with his personality. In this case. Arthur might be seen as possibly conveying a **challenge** such as: 'Tom, you are wasting your time on union affairs when it could be spent in such admirable pursuits as wine, women and song, possibly because you're "past it" or because you are insufficiently cynical.' I leave it to the reader to work out the reasoning involved in these interpretations.

A phatic act? Malinowski first noted that a good deal of human talk seems to exist merely for its own sake, and not to serve any further communicative function. In these cases the intention of the speaker is only to *create* a social relationship by virtue of speaking. 'Talking about the weather' is the classical example of this sort of talk, which Malinowski labelled 'phatic communion'. Notice that this labels an illocutionary act, a phatic act, for which we have no common name as we do for requesting, promising or accusing.

Could Arthur's utterance be a phatic act? The reasoning would go like this:

---

1. Arthur has asked Tom when the next strike will occur.

2. Tom can derive a number of indirectly conveyed acts from this utterance.

3. However, the only act required in this conversational setting is a courteous recognition of Tom's presence and this has already been achieved by the exchange of greetings in 3 and 4.

4. The conversational setting is such that Arthur is under *no* obligation to convey anything further to Tom, yet he has done so. What is the relevance of extra information?

5. *Arthur intended to constitute a social relationship between himself and Tom by virtue of the utterance itself.*

It is worth noting that many of these actions are about the negotiation of social relationships, both on the dimensions of power and solidarity and with respect to strategies of politeness discussed earlier (Brown and Levinson, 1987). Just as we saw in chapter eight that 'complimenting' is a problematic act, so the recognition of the older man, Tom, by the younger man, Arthur, and the sheer 'face management' of the potential encounter could motivate the complex of indirect acts in this situation. Tom and Arthur have *exchanged greetings* (3 and 4) and are co-present, but Arthur has signalled that Jack will be his main involvement, by *offering* him a drink and receiving back the 'preferred' *acceptance* (8 and 9). This is potentially 'face-threatening' to Tom. The richness of implicated solidarity (even down to the solidarity connotations of the word 'strike') can be interpreted in these terms. And the indirect bantering of the *challenge* exercises Arthur's own power and lightens and controls the situation, while at the same time granting the power of knowledge and status to the older man. The point is that some conversational acts implicate information to do with solidarity, power and politeness. As a general point we can say that, whatever else is happening, most conversations possess a *phatic layer* which manages relationships through claims of relative degrees of solidarity. (This ties up with our treatment of accent in chapter seven above and chapter eleven below.)

A schema

Figure 10.7 gives us a way of informally representing Arthur's utterance and the illocutionary forces it conveys. It is adapted from the format used by Labov and Fanshel (1977). The range of illocutionary acts is represented by A on the speaker's side of the utterance, and by α on the hearer's side. The dotted arrows represent the inferencing that connects the utterance with the actions it is being used to perform. Defective acts are starred, and dubious assignments are marked by a question mark. The propositions in the commitment slates contain the beliefs from which the action descriptions are inferred. The interpretation of action depends on belief. It is important to note that all the background information, including the rules for speech events and registers, only figures in

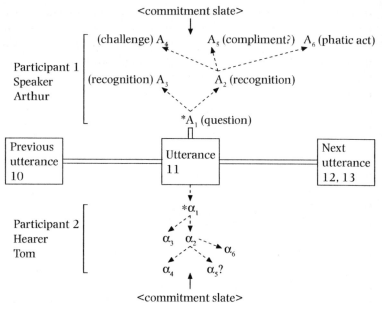

Figure 10.7

discourse as part of the inferential processes by which utterances are produced and construed.

Criticisms of the speech act model

There are persuasive criticisms of the use of illocutionary forces as the basis for a discourse model like the one just presented.

(a) Levinson's critique of speech acts

In his 1981 article, 'The Essential Inadequacies of Speech Act Models of Dialogue', Steve Levinson launches a comprehensive attack on the usefulness of the concept in developing an explicit theory of conversation. He makes three main interrelated points.

The first point is that a model based on speech acts requires the independent identification of two sorts of units: a finite and well defined set of illocutionary acts and a set of utterances, in which there would be a *systematic pairing* between each unit utterance and one or more acts. The 'one or more' possibility is to allow for the fact, illustrated above, that a given utterance can realize more than one layer of acts (e.g. Figure 10.7). Levinson shows that there is simply no well defined set of illocutionary acts available to the theory. Rather there seems to be a network of intentions, based on conversation goals and strategies 'behind' the utterance. One can intend all sorts of perlocutionary effects which are not recognized as illocutionary categories, for example 'pre-closings'. On the other hand *any stretch of speech including silence* can be assigned a perlocutionary intention in a particular context. So neither category of the theory is independently identifiable or well defined. It is better to think of networks of perlocutionary intentions than of illocutionary acts.

Related to this is the fact that there is no *explicit procedure* (or formal rule) which can map utterances and acts on to one another. This is tantamount to saying that there are no formal rules for indirect speech acts; rules which would take as input, for example, a grammatical declarative and yield as output that it must be assigned to the category 'compliment', in some unique set of contexts. Authors like Labov and Fanshel (1977) and Sinclair and Coulthard (1975) who employ speech acts in their theories had attempted to formulate such rules. Instead, Levinson recommends that the interpretation of such phenomena 'is not based on some huge set of *ad hoc* conventional rules for constructing and interpreting indirect speech acts, but some small but powerful set of general principles of inference to interlocutor's communicative intentions in specific contexts' (Levinson, 1981: 482). These would clearly be the principles of an inferential pragmatic theory of a Gricean or Sperber and Wilson type.

Levinson also attacks the notion that the 'sequencing rules' of conversation are determined by the relations between acts – the notion that the ethnomethodological concept of the 'adjacency pair' captures in local dyadic exchanges (see chapter eight above). He shows that in clear cases the sequence of utterances is sensitive to higher level conversational goals and the strategies designed to achieve them, not to immediately preceding acts. Levinson's critique is pessimistic about constructing an explicit theory of conversation, if the theory is to be speech act based. Indeed, there is no 'grammar of discourse' in the sense of 'explicit rule systems' of the kind familiar in linguistics.

(b) Sperber and Wilson's critique of speech acts

Relevance theory also rejects the illocutionary act as understood by Searle as a fundamental category of a theory of communication.

Sperber and Wilson (1995: 244ff.) criticize the notion 'that the assignment of every utterance to a particular speech act type is part of what is communicated and plays a necessary role in comprehension'. Remember that Sperber and Wilson consider the goal of pragmatics to be the development of a cognitive model of intentional communication. Upon reflection, it is obvious that illocutionary acts can be divided into two types. *There is a class of acts in which it must also be explicitly communicated that the act in question has been performed in order for the act in question to be happily performed.* This is a class of institutional speech acts such as *bidding* (in bridge, for example), *promising, thanking* and so on. I just *can't* 'thank' someone without also communicating to them that they are being thanked. Also consider the case of *betting*. This is a very good example of a social institution. And participants who wish 'to bet' have to convey to their interlocutor that they are proposing a bet, quite literally. Then the second party can provide the requisite 'uptake', can agree (or not) to the bet and its conditions. One can imagine that not all cultures might possess this institution. Such acts are part of the sociolinguistic description of a society.

The second type of act is quite different. *The act can be happily performed without also explicitly communicating that the act is being performed.* All that is required for the act to be performed is that its essential condition be satisfied. The hearer need not also explicitly comprehend that the given act has been performed, although he or she can do so. Sperber and Wilson (1995: 245) cite *asserting, hypothesizing, suggesting, entreating, warning* and *threatening* as examples of this type. Consider *accusing* as outlined above. For Brenda to happily 'accuse' Arthur of getting her pregnant, all that Arthur is required to comprehend is that she is telling him that she holds him responsible for something she thinks is bad. Arthur doesn't *also* have to understand, 'Ah hah! She is accusing me.' Although he could understand this, the accusation doesn't require it.

Since an act of this second type isn't communicated, it shouldn't be represented in a model of communication. It would be claiming that something was conveyed when it wasn't. Now consider the Arthur-Tom exchange in Figures 10.5–7. Acts such as 'the compliment', 'the challenge', 'the phatic act' could be acts of this second type. People can establish a social relationship by virtue of the very act of speaking and that also can be the illocutionary point of their utterances without it being explicitly communicated that this is happening between them; ditto with being polite. If this is the case, speech act based representations of conversational communication like Figure 10.7 are wrong as analyses of 'communication'. However, it is also important to note that *studying utterances as social actions* is an important role for discourse analysis in social science and this is true *even if* the acts don't figure in intentional communication. It is just a *different* sort of study. More on this sort of 'non-intentional' interpretation later on.

The grammar of force: new approaches

Sperber and Wilson (1995: 246ff.) also argue that three speech acts are of special interest to pragmatics because they have a special relation to the sentence types. These are the acts of *saying*, *asking* and *telling*. They argue that rather special interpretations of these illocutions expressing the speaker's attitudes to the propositional form are grammaticalized into the sentence types. This is another possible approach to the issue of 'literal force' discussed above. These three special acts will be included in a model of communication as input to the process of pragmatic inferencing warranted by the meaning of the grammar.

In Figure 10.8, I contrast Searle's version of the literal force hypothesis – which entails a theory of indirect speech acts – with Sperber and Wilson's relevance theory account of coded propositional attitudes. To complete the picture I have also schematized two other accounts of the relationship between form and force. These are Hudson's (1975) **sincerity conditions** analysis and a

	DECLARATIVE	INTERROGATIVE	IMPERATIVE
Searle (1975) LITERAL FORCE HYPOTHESIS. THE SENTENCE TYPES CONVENTIONALLY ENCODE CLASSES OF ILLOCUTIONARY FORCE.	CONVENTIONALLY ASSOCIATED with *Assertive Force*	CONVENTIONALLY ASSOCIATED with *Question Force*	CONVENTIONALLY ASSOCIATED with *Directive Force*
Sperber and Wilson (1995) THE LINGUISTIC FORM OF AN UTTERANCE CONSTRAINS THE ATTITUDE IT MAY BE USED TO EXPRESS. SYSTEMATIC CORRELATION BETWEEN SENTENCE TYPE AND THREE SPEECH ACT TYPES, SAY, TELL AND ASK, WHICH ARE UNIVERSAL AND GENUINELY COMMUNICATIVE.	*saying that P* the thought that P represents (which need not be the same as P and isn't in non-literal cases) is entertained as a true description of a state of affairs.	*asking wh-P* the thought that P represents would be desirable if true, that is, a true answer to the question would be relevant.	*telling to P* the thought that P represents is entertained as describing a desirable hypothetical state of affairs
Hudson (1975) SINCERITY CONDITIONS. THESE ARE LITERAL PROPERTIES OF THE SENTENCE TYPE ENCODING SPEAKER'S RELATION TO THE PROPOSITION, WHICH ARE NOT ILLOCUTIONARY FORCES, BUT WHICH CONTRIBUTE TO THE DETERMINATION OF VARIOUS FORCES IN CONTEXT.	In normal utterance of a declarative it is necessary for the speaker to believe the proposition to be true.	In normal utterance of an interrogative it is necessary that the speaker believes that the hearer knows, at least as reliably as the speaker does, whether the proposition is true or false.	—
Radical Pragmatic Analysis THERE IS NO CONVENTIONAL OR LITERAL FORCE CONNECTED WITH THE SENTENCE TYPES. THE COMMUNICATED FORCE OF AN UTTERANCE IS ALWAYS DERIVED FROM CONTEXT AND SPEAKER ATTITUDE IS ONLY ENCODED 'CONTRASTIVELY'.	Speaker issues a sign that can be interpreted as a proposition and this act invites interpretation relative to the Gricean norm. Why has the sign been issued?	Speaker issues a sign that can be interpreted as a proposition but which is marked (or incomplete) with respect to truth relative to the Gricean norm. Why can't truth be unproblematically assigned, or a complete proposition issued?	Speaker issues a sign that must be interpreted as a proposition which specifies a hypothetical action of the hearer. Why, relative to the Gricean norm?

Figure 10.8 The grammar of force

purely **pragmatic analysis** (for an overview of the issues in this area see Levinson, 1983: 274ff.).

Let's contrast these approaches. Searle's theory is straightforward. Each sentence type conventionally encodes and therefore must convey a single literal force. Other indirect forces are the non-literal 'indirect speech acts' and must be inferred. Now compare this to Sperber and Wilson's (1995) approach. Three propositional attitudes are encoded, *saying, asking* and *telling*. These three acts are given a precise definition by relevance theory. *Saying* P communicates that the thought conveyed by uttering P is true – 'is entertained as a description of an actual state of affairs' (Sperber and Wilson, 1995: 247). The propositional content of the thought being expressed is determined by calculating the optimal relevance of the utterance and it may differ from that of the proposition literally expressed. *Asking* conveys that the true answer to the question will be relevant – whether the hearer ought to answer it is worked out in context. Finally, *telling* indicates that the thought expressed is desirable – whether the hearer ought to do it is worked out in context. Hudson (1975) develops a similar approach in which literal meanings are encoded but these fall short of full illocutionary forces. The last alternative, at the bottom of Figure 10.8, is the most thoroughgoing pragmatic analysis. It claims that the meanings of the sentence types are very minimal and all of the work is done automatically through inferences generated by general pragmatic principles. The utterance of a declarative simply demands interpretation like *any* intentional behaviour. Why has the sign been issued? The 'unmarked' possibility, if there is no good reason to the contrary, is that the speaker believes it and is following the maxims. An assumption of truthfulness is automatic but not *necessary*, if there are contextual reasons for doubt. The interrogative is 'marked' with respect to the declarative and this mark simply conveys that there is 'a problem' with respect to the truth of the proposition or its true completion. As John Lyons (1977: 754) puts it, 'the difference between declarative sentences and interrogative sentences . . . results from a grammaticalization of the feature of doubt'. Everything but these minimum assumptions is inferred. A speaker uttering a declarative may only be performing an assertive, but equally might be speaking ironically, figuratively or loosely, or accusing, complaining or performing virtually *any* illocutionary act. With respect to the interrogative, one reason for conveying doubt may be to see if the addressee can provide the information, but there are many other possible motivations for not conveying a high degree of belief – putting the truth value of the proposition into play. Likewise, the imperative simply defines a hypothetical proposition with the addressee as subject and leaves the intended consequences to be inferred – perhaps to make the proposition true (see Downes, 1977).

Strong versus weak implicatures

For any utterance, we can derive many more implications than those that the speaker intended. It isn't always clear which were intended, which were not.

It is always possible to enlarge context and so obtain further implicatures. Consider this fairly ordinary exchange from the Channel 4 TV programme *Faces of the Family*, broadcast on 4 March 1994:

> INTERVIEWER: *Did you ever, ever think . . . that you might have an abortion . . . was that one of your alternatives?*
> INTERVIEWEE: *I think I would have considered it but . . . uh . . . I found out I was pregnant too late for it to be an option.*

It is clear that the interviewee implicates that having an abortion was not one of her alternatives. This is the obvious intended answer to the question. But does she also want to implicate that she has no objection to abortions? Or that she has no *moral* problems about termination? Or that she is not susceptible to social pressures in favour of abortion so as 'not to be a single parent', a topic broached earlier by the interviewer? Or that she is not a 'pro-lifer'? Or, that being the case, that she is not influenced by religious doctrine in this area? And so on. What is communicatively intended and what unintentional, yet derivable?

Sperber and Wilson (1995) recognize degrees of strength of implicatures with respect to speaker's intentions. Those implicatures which are clearly intended by speakers are called **strong**

implicatures. These fade off into those implicatures for which hearers take responsibility and which are termed **weak implicatures**. Strong implicatures are those that the hearer is strongly encouraged to draw if the interpretation is to be optimally relevant. Gradually the encouragement to draw an inference gets weaker and weaker until the hearer takes all the responsibility. Both the form of the language chosen and the type of social context can encourage or discourage weak implicature.

This distinction between implicatures is extremely important because it recognizes that there are *valid interpretations which do not involve intentional communication*. There can be non-communicative texts, or textual situations which encourage readings which *can transcend meaning$_{nn}$, the intentions of its source*. This is a crucial property of language.

If we think of how we handle texts in terms of contexts of situation, this occurs whenever we separate the act of interpretation from the speaker's or writer's communicative intent. For example, I can interrogate a text in a context which consists of my own interests and it will achieve a high degree of relevance to me. The premises and conclusions thus weakly implicated are relevant but have nothing to do with the speaker's or writer's communicative or informative intent. Thus, if I am interested in abortion as a result of pressure not to be a single parent, the interviewee may weakly implicate to me that she is not susceptible to that pressure without intending to do so.

The social sciences and humanities deal with texts and in general they create interpretative situations which depend on weak implicature. Such interpretative methods **recontextualize** a text or behaviour as an object of inquiry, making it relevant in a new way. For example, a historian may truly interpret the divorces of Henry VIII in a way that Henry could not have imagined. Or a Marxist or Freudian literary critic may interpret a play by Shakespeare in a manner impossible in Shakespeare's time. Yet in the context constructed by psychoanalytic or Marxist thought, the text weakly implicates that conclusion. In fact, in conversational contexts, I think we perform parallel interpretations, simultaneously drawing *both* strong and a penumbra of weak implicatures. We employ such material in formulating responses as the conversation unfolds.

Weak implicature is relative to background information mobilized by interpreters and/or by interpretative contexts of situation. For example, a psychoanalytic interpretation might be proposed such that such an utterance is a symptom of a repressed wish. In terms of the analyst's context such a reading is highly relevant. If denied by the speaker – 'I didn't *mean* that' – it might be attributed to an 'unconscious' intent. But one reading of the 'unconscious' is that it is simply another term for the collective encyclopedic material which is not presently accessible. And if it is made accessible, a participant may retrospectively accept the intent – 'Oh! I *must have meant* that'. It is the phenomenon of weak implicature that accounts for the 'openness' of texts so often noted in literary studies.

Hermeneutic and critical understanding

We have established two contrasting kinds of interpretation. The first reconstructs the speaker's communicative and informative intentions in the Grice or Sperber and Wilson sense. Let us call this **hermeneutic interpretation**. It is tied to the context of production and explicates strong implicature or meaning$_{nn}$.

This can be distinguished from interpretations which uncover those weak implicatures which are relevant to some interpreters' interests. The text or action becomes data for some hypothesis which is independent of the source's communicative intent. Let us call this second kind **critical interpretation**. In fact it covers any kind of non-intentional explanation of text or action. The context of critical interpretation employed by an interpreter may be 'folk' theories drawn from the encyclopedia, or sophisticated theories of the human sciences.

In chapter nine, I pointed out some problems with relevance theory as cognitive psychology. Most pragmatics suffers from similar problems. One possible strategy faced with this is to consider pragmatic theories, not only as psychology, but as hermeneutic and critical methodologies in the human sciences. They offer unparalleled rigour and insight when used as metalanguages for interpretation. For example, background information can be made fully explicit.

Linguistic turns

New theories which are critically interpretative in the sense just defined have become influential in social theory, literary and cultural studies, history and human sciences. There is a tangled web of influences drawn from linguistics, semiotic and structuralism, Marxism and psychoanalysis which is sometimes called the **linguistic turn in social science** (for an overview, see Skinner, 1985).

It is appropriate to indicate some aspects of this thought in the broad context of language and society. Perhaps the most important single influence is that of the French social theorist, Michel Foucault (for surveys of his thought, see Skinner, 1985; Gutting, 1994). Foucault's project was to understand the profoundly socio-historical way in which 'knowledge' is produced. Such conditions of knowledge production are called a **discursive formation** or **discourse**. These are rules constituting what is true or false in some domain. They form a mode of thinking, for example, the Enlightenment concept of 'Man' involved in the origins of the human sciences: sociology, medicine, criminology, psychiatry etc. This broader concept of discourse is included in our synoptic diagram Figure 8.9, at the top right, as a higher level semiotic, a 'context of culture', which motivates how texts operate in many registers. For example, all 'bureaucratic/administrative' registers realize a discourse that constitutes social control within the institutions of modern societies. They are a socio-historical language game.

Such discourses create **subjects**, persons made by the representations, and in so doing create, legitimate and reproduce the **power relations** by which a modern society controls its population. Kinds of knowledge create kinds of people. And battles about knowledge in this sense are also sites where power can be contested. Foucault's project provides perspective about the world creating and power laden nature of representations. The influence of Foucault can be seen in the many studies which examine the way discourses constitute social reality in diverse domains, from his own studies of madness, incarceration and sexuality to Edward Said's (1978) **orientalism**, the creation of 'the East' as part of the mentality of the modern West, Benedict Anderson's (1983) notion of **imagined communities** and its role in the discourse of nationalism and J. Fabian's (1983) concept of **othering** or how anthropology constructs the object of its study.

Critical linguistics and critical theory

There has been considerable interdisciplinary work employing discourse analysis or pragmatics as a critical methodology in various domains, for example in political theory (Thompson, 1984, 1990), in studies of the press (Fowler, 1991; Van Dijk, 1988; Fairclough, 1995), in particular socio-political domains (Chilton, 1985; Sarangi and Slembrouck, 1996), in literature and history (Fowler, 1996; Downes, 1991) and as general studies of power and control (Fowler, 1981; Fowler *et al.*, 1979; Fairclough, 1989, 1995, 1995a).

These employ linguistics in the development of a critique of linguistic practices which conceal how they are socially manipulative. That is, texts function socially in covert ideological ways, ways that serve the interests of power in the social system. The core notion is that the sociolinguistic phenomena we have studied enact the interests and conflicts of power in society by means of mechanisms of which participants are generally unconscious or deny. This is particularly marked in terms of various public discourses and registers, for example the media, bureaucratic, legal, academic, technical-scientific, advertising etc., but is also inescapably pervasive since all texts are part of the social process.

Critical linguistics or critical discourse analysis systematically displays any divergence between (1) a text viewed as intentional communication (what participants overtly would say is going on) and (2) social processes covertly constituted by the text of which at least the 'subjected' participant, and probably both participants, are unaware and which serve to produce and reproduce the social system and its encyclopedic beliefs. It is 'systematically distorted communication' because of the repressions and evasions motivated by power relations. In Richardson's (1987) terms, there is a disjunction between 'official meaning' and 'diagnostic reading', that which reveals the ideological level of texts. Such critical interpretations 'see through' the official meaning and thus serve an **emancipatory function** (Habermas, 1971).

We can't develop a new example here. But reconsider the 'prayer' in chapter eight. This can serve as an example of critical linguistics using social semiotics as a method. In our examination of the social activity of 'praying', we saw that whatever else is 'officially' going on, the participants are acting out their own solidarity in a hierarchical social and metaphysical order. The text is a model of such an order, and a device for creating it. Similarly, in Downes (1991), I analysed Paul Robeson's testimony before the House Committee on UnAmerican Activities and tried to show that the committee's famous question, 'Are you now a member of the Communist Party?' is *not* a genuine question. Instead, it is a form of public accusation and serves as a device of stigma attachment, which invalidates its object as a credible political or civil subject. This is the social activity or field of discourse of the hearings.

Such an analysis is a critique in the sense that perhaps Robeson and certainly the public at large were unaware of the social process that was happening. Indeed the committee itself was probably unconscious of what it was doing and might deny any such intent. Yet I would argue that my critique is true and any disinterested critic would draw similar weak implicatures. It is a way of 'seeing through' participant transcendent socio-historical worldmaking processes of belief and practice.

To conclude, we shall glance at the German philosopher and social theorist, Jurgen Habermas. Habermas is the inheritor of one strand of western Marxist thought, the **critical theory** of the Frankfurt School (Giddens, 1985; Held, 1980). One of the most serious problems with critique is how it can be justified. This applies to critical linguistics as much as it does to critical theory. (The move of critical linguistics is the recognition of the role of language in belief and action, ideology and practice.) On what basis is the critic's diagnostic reading to have the authority to see through the official meaning of the participants, or to suggest that they might 'slenderly know themselves'? (Richardson, 1987). Habermas attempts to provide this justification. Communication is said to presuppose a Grice type norm which demands intelligibility, truth, warrant and sincerity. This norm defines an 'ideal pragmatic situation' in which communication is undistorted by social factors like tradition or power. In this ideal situation a warranted 'rational consensus' can be arrived at by free and disinterested argument and such consensus is the best concept of truth available to us. A critical analysis, a step towards such truth, can thus be rationally justified by the 'force of the better argument' between rational participants. Pragmatics can be the basis for a critical linguistics which is even more effective since it rigorously lays bare the reasoning processes and encyclopedic background involved in interpretation.

11 Language and social explanation

> Where, finally, does linguistics stand as a science? Does it belong to the natural sciences, with biology, or to the social sciences? . . . Behind the apparent lawlessness of social phenomena there is a regularity of configuration and tendency which is just as real as the regularity of physical processes . . . though it is a regularity of infinitely less apparent rigidity and of another mode of apprehension on our part. Language is primarily a cultural or social product and must be understood as such. Its regularity and formal development rest on considerations of a biological and psychological nature to be sure. But this regularity and our underlying unconsciousness of its typical forms do not make linguistics a mere adjunct of either biology or psychology.
>
> Sapir (1929)

When we do an analysis as we did in Figure 10.6 of 'When's the next strike then, Tom?', in what sense can we be said to have explained the utterance? In chapter ten we looked at a discourse theory based on the idea that utterances are actions. That theory yields an account of Arthur's utterance as an array of illocutionary acts and demonstrates how the acts were inferentially derived. Alternatively, chapter nine showed how we could have interpreted Arthur's utterance as a communicative act, having an informative intent. Relevance theory would allow us to identify that intent by calculating the optimal relevance of the utterance. It is likely that the phatic dimension of the behaviour is not part of any *conscious* intent. Instead it is revealed by a 'critical' or 'functional' explanation offered as a form of social analysis. There are many different

415

ways that language can be socially explained. What kinds of explanation are available?

Kinds of social explanation

The topic of this chapter is the social explanation of language. We will look at some of the types of explanation that have been used or mentioned in this book, their relationship with one another and their role in linguistics. Many of the theories have originated not in linguistics but other disciplines; for example, speech act theory and implicature from philosophy, accommodation theory from social psychology. In fact, the advances made in the study of language and society have been through the adoption of research methods from other disciplines. Labov's use of quantitative social science, social network theory employed by Milroy and Milroy, the adoption of the cognitive science model and Grice's philosophical inquiry by Sperber and Wilson spring to mind. In this area, it is perhaps more useful to think of patterns of influence or research programmes often associated with particular names like Labov, Chomsky, Sperber and Wilson, Halliday, etc. rather than a homogenous discipline. Furthermore, there have been other major developments in social thought in the last decades which mainstream linguists have been slow to take on board, for example 'hermeneutics' or 'critical theory' (see Giddens and Turner, 1987; Skinner, 1985).

Four major kinds of explanation used in this book are presented in Figure 11.1. We will concentrate on and develop the relationship between two of these in this chapter, types 1 and 3 in the figure. The first, type 1, develops *empirical theories which predict and explain large-scale patterns in social behaviour*. The other, type 3, involves *the interpretation of the intentional actions of individuals*. Although we will concentrate on these two explanatory types, cognitive and functional accounts will also be discussed later on.

In earlier chapters, we examined many studies which used Labov's methodology. These offered explanations of the first type. Such explanations are modelled on the methods of the natural sciences. Correlational sociolinguistics obtains statistical relationships between social constructs, mainly class, style, sex, age, social

1. EMPIRICAL SOCIAL SCIENCE THEORY of large-scale patterns of social behaviour

    (i) Correlational statistical study

    (ii) Interpretation by explanatory model
    (invoking underlying 'causal' mechanism/analogy, etc.)

2. COGNITIVE SCIENCE

    (i) Chomskyan mentalist linguistics
    (studies 'knowledge of language')

      (a) universal and innate
      (b) instantiated in brain as biological system
      (c) differentiated from performance

    (ii) Relevance theory as cognitive theory

    Mind performs computations on mental representations, which process information.

3. INTENTIONAL INTERPRETATION OF ACTION
    (belief/desire explanations)

    (i) Hermeneutic of communicative and speech acts

      (a) communicative + informative intents
      (b) illocutionary + perlocutionary intents

    (ii) Critical/Explanatory interpretation

    Interpret acts in ways that transcend the conscious intentions of the actor.

      (a) ethnomethodology
      (b) social semiotics
      (c) critical linguistics/discourse analysis

4. FUNCTIONAL EXPLANATIONS

      (a) functional interpretation of behaviour in terms of containing social system or context
      (b) functional etiology or origin of behaviour
      (c) evolution

Figure 11.1 Explanation of linguistic behaviour

network and linguistic variation. The social factors are the independent variables and the index scores reveal the dependency between them and the linguistic variants. This allows the investigator to make general statements which can be displayed in sociolinguistic structure diagrams or represented by variable rules. We discover empirical regularities in our statistical statements. For example, social class, if style is held constant, predicts average linguistic scores for a population. Of course, the facts can get a great deal more subtle and complex than this.

Issues about the status of this sort of explanation arose in chapter four. We argued there that such generalizations represent 'social facts'. Because of the social nature of these facts, grammars which globally represented them couldn't be directly internalized by individual speakers although speakers clearly knew with what frequency to perform the variables. A purely individual interpretation of the results in terms of any individual's 'mind' would be unrevealing to the degree that the language pattern being studied is an autonomous social fact which only emerges in the behaviour of groups.

Another issue is to what degree a correlation by itself explains anything. We shall return to this later on. Here it is sufficient to note that a scientific theory is expected to involve more than just the discovery of mathematical regularities. It is expected to *account* for the regularities in causal terms. The descriptive part, the 'lawlike' and 'predictive' formal theory, needs to be interpreted with a causal model that suggests why the relationships obtain. In 'hard' as opposed to social science, we have the mathematical structure which *is* the theory and which makes empirical predictions (e.g. *quantum mechanics* where the predictions are said to be very successful). On top of that is the interpretation which offers, in more or less everyday English, an *explanation* of what the mathematics describes. But as the century long debate about how to model quantum mechanics shows, this is very difficult.

Likewise, as noted in chapter four, Labov's variationist method is also incomplete until an interpretation is provided which explains why the variables are related as they are in terms of some underlying mechanism. We can't say that social class directly 'causes' the statistical result. We need to show what underlying mechanism might explain how the social variables and individual scores come to be related, also taking language internal factors into account. As we left the story earlier, this has to do with 'acts of identity'.

Now contrast correlational sociolinguistics with the way we explained Arthur's utterance. It is a radically different sort of explanation. For one thing, there is no attempt to account for linguistic facts by correlating them with social facts. The utterance is not a dependent variable. We do not correlate Arthur's utterance with features of the situation. So, our explanation was not predictive. In fact, I believe it would be impossible to propose a theory which would predict that Arthur would say, 'When's the next strike then, Tom?', even statistically. Our explanation makes no generalizations in this sense. This is because we were trying to explain Arthur's utterance in terms of the illocutionary acts he intended to perform. We have no way of theoretically predicting people's intentions; whether, for example, they intend their utterances to count as questions, recognitions, accusations or compliments, and so on. We also said that alternative interpretations were possible, that there was some 'risk' in our explanation.

It follows from this indeterminacy and this lack of predictive power that our explanation is not refutable by observation in the normal way. Indeed, the sort of fact involved is not even observable. Arthur's utterance can be observed, but the sort of act he intended it to be taken as cannot be observed. If I said, 'He accused Tom of being an agitator', mere observation of his utterance could not refute my claim. If you rightly wanted to dispute my interpretation, you would have to refer to Arthur's beliefs, and these are equally unobservable. So what kind of explanation are we offering, when we describe utterances in intentional terms?

Teleological explanation

In order to discuss this, we need to delve into issues which are typically of concern to philosophers. However, they are also very important in linguistics. The mere fact that studies in variation and discourse analysis use such different methods shows this. The first area we must look at is the philosophy of action and its explanation.

Later on, I will try to relate this to other kinds of explanation in both science and social science. The issues involved are very complex, and in a book like this we can only deal with things in the barest outline.

Let us see what we are doing when we give an account of a speaker's action in terms of his or her intention. What I am going to say here is based on the views of the philosopher G. H. von Wright whose book, *Explanation and Understanding* (1971), is a major treatment of the problem of explaining action within the social sciences. (For a series of articles which relate to von Wright's work in this area, see Manninen and Tuomela, 1976.)

Von Wright distinguishes two main traditions in the history of scientific method, that of **causal** and that of **teleological explanation**. Such traditions provide differing conditions on what we are to expect from a scientific explanation. Most of us are familiar, at least in a rough way, with causal explanations in the natural sciences. Indeed, causal explanation has such prestige, due to its success in explaining the physical world, that it is popularly viewed as the only valid sort of scientific explanation. (However, there are many different kinds of explanation which we offer and accept in everyday life – reflect for a moment on the many different ways you commonly use the words 'why' and 'because' in ordinary talk.) The kind of empirical theory we discussed above and illustrated from Labov's paradigm shows how models of explanation based on the methods of the physical sciences are commonly used to explain social phenomena. Later, we will look at some differences between natural and social science, when empirical theories and methods are used in the two different domains.

It can be argued, as von Wright does, that teleological explanation provides a more adequate account of human action. In a teleological explanation, an action is explained by saying it was performed in order that a specific object or goal be achieved. In a causal explanation we say, 'This happened, *because* that had occurred.' In a teleological explanation we say, 'This happened, *in order that* that should occur' (von Wright, 1971: 83).

So we can give a causal account in answer to the question, 'Why did the window open?' – someone applied physical pressure to it. But this is very different from the appropriate answer to the question, 'Why did that person open the window?' A teleological explanation is that he or she opened it in order to cool the room.

Now to the crucial part of the argument. If the connection between the inner aspect of action, various mental states and events, and the basic act is not causal, what is it? According to von Wright, the connection is inferential.

Practical inference and teleological explanation

Intention and action are connected by the **practical inference**. Behind the inference will be a motive: that A wants or desires p. The simplest version of the practical inference is:

Inference	Premisses	A *intends* to bring about p
		A *believes* that they cannot bring about p unless they bring about q
	Conclusion	Therefore, A sets themself to bring about q

Inferences of this form provide a connection between the volitional-cognitive complex 'behind' a basic act and the act itself. The connection is logical. In von Wright's analysis, the relation of intention and action is not causal in the usual sense in which 'causality' deals with a physical connectedness between events which can be stated as a law. But the role of causation in action explanations is one of the thorniest in this area of philosophy. We cannot explore the issues more fully here, but for both sides of the argument see Davidson (1980), Manninen and Tuomela (1976), Macdonald and Pettit (1981: esp. 80ff.), Romaine (1984: 31–2) and von Wright (1971: 96ff.).

Let's go through the practical inferences involved in the action of cooling the room. Say I intend to cool the room. I believe I cannot bring this about unless I open the window. This produces a second intention and so I now further intend to open the window. I further believe I cannot bring this about unless I apply upward muscular pressure to the window. Therefore, I set about doing this. The action involves reasoning. It is a rational act. The practical inference is the form which this reasoning takes. Now imagine that someone else in watching me. How would they go about explaining my action? The description of my basic act – applying the upward muscular pressure – though true, is certainly not a satisfactory explanation of what I did, although the only evidence for any explanation is the observation of the basic act and its context. To say 'why' I performed the act, in the intentional sense of 'why', the observer has to work backwards from the action to the intention, *via* my beliefs. They must construct an argument which starts from the observation of the basic act and concludes with the understanding of my intention. They have constructed a teleological explanation of my action. So the observer who wishes to explain an action constructs a teleological explanation which is the agent's (the performer of the act) practical inference '*turned upside down*' (von Wright, 1971: 96). The observer *re*constructs the agent's reasoning and thus comprehends it. It provides an answer to the 'why' question in teleological terms; that is, in terms of the agent's intention to bring about the object of that intention, their goal in acting.

Our elementary example has been cooling the room. But reflection on the verbal acts examined in the last few chapters shows that this pairing of *practical inference* and *teleological explanation*, illustrated in Figure 11.2, also applies to utterances. Recall Brenda's 'I'm pregnant. Good and proper this time and it's your fault.' Brenda *intends* to convey to Arthur that he is culpably responsible for something reprehensible, namely, her pregnancy. Perhaps she also intends that he act on this responsibility and help her. Her practical inference is that she must utter this sentence to produce these effects in this context.

This figure illustrates the pairing of *practical inference* and *teleological explanation* in the interpretation of actions and utterances. *Communication* is the special case whereby the actor/speaker has the intention that a specific message be understood 'as intended' by virtue of the mere recognition of that intention. Or in Sperber

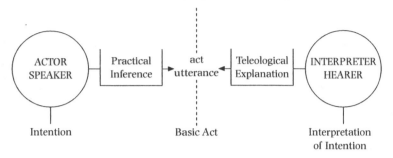

Figure 11.2

and Wilson's theory that the ostensive stimuli achieve relevance by being treated as having communicative and informative intents. Arthur's response is to construct a teleological explanation which concludes with an understanding of Brenda's intentions.

In Figure 11.1 section 3(i), I labelled this sort of intentional interpretation of action a *hermeneutic of communicative and speech acts*. I further distinguished *communicative acts* and *illocutionary acts* within this category. Grice's speaker meaning or meaning$_{nn}$ and Sperber and Wilson's communicative and informative intents were analyses of communicative acts while illocutions were examined under the heading of speech acts. As illustrated in Figure 11.2, a communicative act is a special case of the practical reasoning pattern, since it involves the extra layer of intention to communicate. As we saw above, non-verbal acts are also commonly communicative in this sense. As for illocutionary acts, Sperber and Wilson (1995) point out that which act is being performed does not also have to be communicated as a piece of information. Brenda's accusation, just discussed, is a case in point. Her practical inference and Arthur's teleological explanation do *not* have to also literally communicate the fact that he is being accused for her to successfully accuse him. She must simply convey that Arthur is *responsible for the bad act*; that is what is essential to an accusation. Illocutionary acts like this are 'little institutions'; a repertoire of recognized things people can do with words in a culture, for example to accuse, or pray, or perform phatic communion as prepackaged intentional acts. Felicity conditions are rules for these acts, language games in Wittgenstein's sense. When someone reports that someone warned them, or accused them, we immediately know what the speaker's intention was. We can paraphrase it by stating the essential conditions of the act. *The names we have for illocutionary acts are 'packaged up' teleological explanations of action made available by our lexicon. They are conventional ways of assigning intentional descriptions to utterances, a repertoire of language games.*

But the set of teleological explanations of utterances is larger than the set of illocutionary acts for which we have names, or clear conventional rules. This means that a method of discourse analysis which simply assigned speech act labels to utterances (accuse, warn, state, compliment etc.) would be very misleading. A more revealing methodology is to construct teleological explanations for utterances. Each explanation will conclude, 'Therefore, the speaker intends, probably, to convey' etc. It will be obvious if this is the essential condition for a familiar act, one for which we have a name.

But very often it will not be. Contrast an 'accusation' with 'phatic communion', which is an act for which, before Malinowski, we had no name. Probably most illocutionary acts have no common names; especially so, since we are not required to explicitly communicate what act we are currently performing. A teleological analysis of utterances allows the social scientist explicitly to work out the intentionality and the encyclopedic background information on which the hermeneutic understanding depends, even in the absence of a common name for the speaker's action. In this way, access is gained to the social activities ('fields of discourse' in register theory) that constitute a culture. So we have a linguistic methodology, based on speech acts, for the deep understanding of social life and the interweaving of verbal and non-verbal action. (For the application of this hermeneutic method to 'King Lear's question to his daughters', see Downes, 1988.)

How does von Wright's pairing of practical inference and teleological explanation illustrated by Figure 11.2 relate to Sperber and Wilson's pragmatics in chapter nine and Grice's in chapter ten? I would suggest that both conform to its general logic. Both reconstruct the actor/speaker's non-demonstrative practical reasoning and how the perceiver/hearer comes to comprehend intentionality, but give the process contrasting accounts in terms of relevance on the one hand and the CP and maxims on the other. There is not space here to compare these three analyses. It is clear, however, that each theory could be used as a revealing hermeneutic, an interpretative methodology.

Issues of intentionality

There are complex issues involved with intention in the explanation of actions. We shall just look at two such issues here. First, intentions multiply rapidly when an action is analysed. How many intentions should lie behind any one action? Related to this is a second issue; how do intentions relate to the consciousness of an actor or speaker?

Complexes of intentions. We noted in chapter ten that when he said, 'When's the next strike then, Tom?', Arthur was performing more than one action at the same time and therefore had a complex intention or multiple intentions. The single behaviour was doing a number of jobs simultaneously.

It turns out that this is a characteristic of the intentions behind any sort of action. And complexes of intentionality can have structure of various kinds. A second intention may follow from a first intention. Think again about the window-opening activity. Let us assume that the agent intends, first, to cool the room. Practical reasoning leads him or her to the conclusion that, in order to do this, the window must be opened. This generates a second intention. The agent now intends to open the window. Practical reasoning leads from this to the muscular activity involved, and so he or she sets to do it. The point here is that the **primary intention**, to cool the room, generates a **secondary intention**, to open the window. Thus, we characteristically get intentions arranged in chains, the one following from the other (Kim, 1976).

Multiplicity of intentions of this sort was pointed out by Anscombe (1957: 37ff.). We can get as many answers to the 'why' question as there are separate intentional descriptions of the action. We saw how a primary intention can generate another secondary intention to do what is sufficient to bring about the first intention. There are also intentions which are *conditional* on the action required to bring about another prior intention. For example, say I intend to go to a conference in London on 12 June. In order to do this, I need to travel from Norwich to London by that date. This generates a chain of secondary intentions. I must go to the station, buy a ticket, etc. Now, say my mother lives near London. My first intention can generate another intention to visit my parent before going on to the conference. This is a **conditional intention** (Kim, 1976). The intention to visit my mother is conditional on my other, prior intention to attend the conference.

So, on 11 June, I perform the action of purchasing a train ticket in Norwich. This has behind it a complex of intentionality which might be described by a scheme such as,

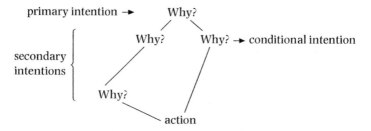

This is precisely the kind of complex of intentions we need to describe the intentionality of an utterance. Normally, if we ask 'why' a speaker performed an utterance, we get a complex of teleological answers each of which concludes, 'The speaker intends, probably, to convey that . . .'

Multiplicity of intentions has been implicit in much of what we have said about utterances in previous chapters. Thus, we saw in chapter eight how initial exchanges perform greetings while they at the same time serve to identify participants. This was typical of many metaconversational acts. Questions, for example, could be used not only to elicit information but to select the next speaker. In chapter seven, we saw how any utterance could also be viewed as an act of identity. In chapter ten, we teased out a complex of intentions from Arthur's utterance to Tom. In this last example, the various illocutionary acts form a complex of primary, secondary and conditional intentions. Say we assume that the phatic act is primary, perhaps motivated by the requirements of politeness. Arthur's practical inference would be that one way sufficient to bring this about is to produce a sentence which shows that he recognizes Tom's social identity and conveys that they are equal and solidary. However, conditional on this, he can also, in passing, challenge Tom's values in an aggressive but playful way. He reasons that asking a question, insincerely, about the next strike, using Tom's first name, etc. ought to be able to achieve these aims, given the context and the rule of relevance. In analysis, we construct teleological explanations to try to get at these intentions. We ask 'why' questions about each detail of the form the utterance takes, see what implicatures are generated, and deduce from them the acts Arthur probably intended to perform.

How does this multiplicity of intents relate to communication? We have already seen that some speech acts, although intended and performed, aren't also explicitly communicated to the hearer. For example, although Arthur communicates his solidarity to Tom, he *doesn't also communicate* that he is performing a phatic act. Nevertheless, it is clear that a communicative act can involve a multiplicity of intended messages.

Conscious and unconscious intentions. This leads to another problematic issue. In action explanations, we explain outward behaviour by attributing inward mental states to the actor, namely intentions and beliefs. To say that an actor has an intention is simply to say that the actor behaves as if he or she has a goal and the act is best understood as a means of achieving that goal. There seems to be no logical requirement that the actor be conscious of this for it to be a good explanation. But we need to make some further distinctions.

First, some of the intentions behind an act need not be explicitly part of the communication. We have already seen this with respect to Arthur's phatic act. Also, it is arguable that some of the complex of conditional and secondary intents attributed to any utterance may also not be communicated. This is very nicely illustrated by an example used by Grice (1975: 51):

> A is standing by an obviously immobilized car and is approached by B; the following exchange takes place:

A: *I am out of petrol.*
B: *There is a garage around the corner.*

(Gloss: B would be infringing the maxim 'Be relevant' unless he thinks, or thinks it possible, that the garage is open, and has petrol to sell; so he implicates that the garage is, or at least may be, open, etc.).

But isn't the meaning$_{nn}$ or informative intent only 'I think you can obtain petrol at place X'? To convey that primary intent, is there also a conditional intent to *communicate* that the garage is open? But is it possible to have a non-communicative implicature? This leads to the question of consciousness. Would 'that the garage is open' be *consciously* entertained as a communicated message for one moment by either participant?

This leads to the second point. Does a communicated message have to be consciously produced by the speaker and consciously understood by the hearer? We remarked above that there was no logical requirement that a true intentional description of an action be conscious. But some philosophers might disagree. Should an actor's 'knowledge without observation' – the ability to truly report that the act was intended to achieve a goal and that was *why* it was done – be a requirement of its intentional status (Anscombe, 1963)? In that case, it would seem that a requirement of intentional communication is that the actor either be conscious of this knowledge or able to retrieve it. One could not have an intention and it be irretrievably unconscious. Much of the mentalistic language used to describe action connotes that the mental processes attributed are conscious or at least in principle available to introspection; terms like 'meant', 'formulate an intent', 'have a purpose', 'to aim at a goal', to 'entertain a belief', 'communicate a message' etc. These terms have a bias towards consciousness. The stereotype is of conscious deliberations, giving *pros* and *cons* and working out the best means to the end.

The alternative claim is that we can and do perform intentional actions without having *access* to the mental states involved, even in principle. A true account of our behaviour in terms of intended goals can be given which does not and perhaps could not enter into conscious awareness. (That's not to say that many communications aren't conscious and deliberative.) But let us consider sources of 'unconscious intents'.

This phrase is not as bizarre as it sounds. The claim that there are complex cognitive activities which are not accessible to consciousness is a commonplace of cognitive science. Chomsky's tacitly known grammars involve unconscious knowledge of this type. On reflection, it is obvious that if consciousness was aware of all the details of the operations of the mind-brain in, for example, visual perception, it would be swamped by information. There has been research on what is variously termed **the cognitive unconscious** or **implicit cognition** (see Reber, 1993; Underwood, 1996). Knowledge can affect behaviour but still be below the level of a subjectively experienced cognitive representation.

Recently, the theory of consciousness has become a highly visible part of cognitive science. Whether consciousness, for example, a conscious intent, can causally affect brain mechanisms is a matter of controversy; this is part of the debate, mentioned above, concerning causality and the mental. Compare the views in Johnson-Laird (1993: 353f.) and Jackendoff (1987). Johnson-Laird argues that consciousness is a 'high level monitor from the web of parallel processes' which 'sets goals for lower level processes and monitors their performance' (Johnson-Laird, 1993: 356). The idea is that the mind consists of a hierarchy of parallel levels of cognitive processing most of which is normally inaccessible to consciousness. This is 'unconscious cognition'. There is a highest level, however, which has an 'executive function'. This comes into play if there are conflicts at the lower levels. Using an ability to construct successively higher models of its own operation, the cognitive system becomes 'self aware and reflective' in consciousness where it can both formulate and monitor intentions and actions. This higher conscious level informationally interacts with unconscious lower levels. It is also suggested that it is the conscious level that manipulates symbols, conceptual representations. The lower levels operate with something more like the connectionist networks described in chapter nine. (This parallels the difference in relevance theory between the conscious awareness of what is perceived as relevant and the calculation of relevance at the lower level neurophysiological substrate.)

Such a picture accounts for some differences between conscious and unconscious intentions. Some goal-directed behaviour may originate at the lower levels of mental architecture as part of a chain of intents, only the highest level of which was conscious. This could account for the fact that Grice's implicature 'the garage is open' was both intended and communicated but didn't enter consciousness. Exploring this notion further, perhaps the intentionality of some goal-directed behaviours is usually or always tacit; we would then have unconscious intents. This would especially arise if the goals were not personal, but socially given and unconsciously picked up through socialization; behaviour that although intentional does not seem usually to require deliberation or conscious thinking. The use of accent variation to signal solidarity and power, politeness phenomenon, phatic acts may all be intentional acts of this type – for example, the phatic goal of Arthur's utterance to Tom in Figure 10.7. The utterance act is unconsciously intentional; its goal is a *social function*. Only if something 'went wrong' in the act's functional efficacy would it enter consciousness. It would be a 'violation' in the language of ethnomethodology.

This suggests that there is a scale between conscious and unconscious behaviour. In Figure 11.3, I have arranged accessibility to consciousness and various intentional phenomena on a scale from the typically conscious to the typically unconscious. In the former case, there is conscious control and intention and agentivity is unproblematic. This is deliberative behaviour. In the latter case, intentionality is tacit and agentivity is impersonal. Such unconscious roots of behaviour have their origins either in biology, automatic cognitive processes or social function. (We shall consider the implications of this for accent variation later on.) Conflicts or problems at the bottom of Figure 11.3 can sometimes manifest themselves at the top of the scale in order to be consciously resolved.

Critical interpretation is included in Figure 11.1 as an explanation of linguistic behaviour. We can now add to the definition given there that this form of explanation 'interprets acts in ways that transcend the conscious intentions of the actor'. Critique addresses itself to the unconscious teleology of our language behaviour; the functioning of language caused by factors to which we don't have access (see chapter ten above). *To offer a critical interpretation is to explicate that functioning, when it is social, and make it conscious.* But the origins of such unconscious teleology may be:

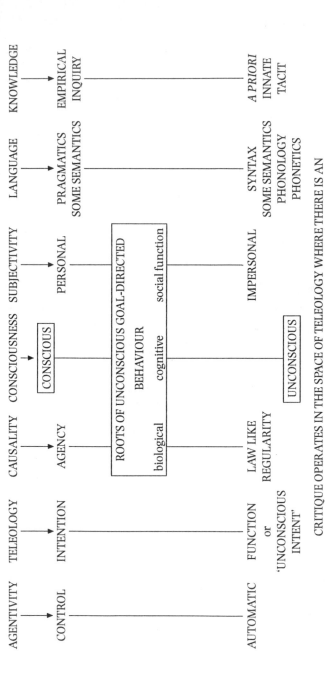

Figure 11.3 Scale of conscious and unconscious processes (*see Agentivity Continuum in Romaine, 1984: 34*)

1.   **biological** – *evolutionary*
2.   **cognitive** – *psychological*
3.   **social** – *norms/regularities*

These three origins can overlap. The latter two may have a historical dimension while the first is evolved. For example, it might be that primate evolution sees to it that humans are biologically compelled to tactical deception (see LaFrenière, and Savage-Rumbaugh and McDonald, in Byrne and Whiten, 1988). Likewise, such cognitive properties as perception of accents in terms of stereotypes – for example, the perception noted above that RP speakers are more intelligent that speakers of other accents – would unconsciously militate against truth and lead to 'systematically distorted communication' (for example, in schools). Similarly, social functions of power and solidarity – phatic communion, politeness, gossip etc. – are intentional, but automatic and unconscious. Biological and social functioning may also be related. Dunbar (1996) has placed the evolutionary origins of language in its phatic function; gossip as verbal grooming. Explanation of language in terms of critical interpretation serves to bring into awareness unconscious or repressed biological, cognitive and social functionings which produce distortions or internal conflicts to the detriment of the organism or society. It is a form of applied pragmatics or sociolinguistics which aims to make transparent the compulsive and unconscious aspects of discourse.

Summary so far

Let us now summarize where we have got to in looking at social explanations of language. Broadly speaking, following the mainstream of correlational sociolinguistics and pragmatics, we have distinguished two main types:

(1)   Empirical theories modelled on the methods of the natural sciences (1 in Figure 11.1)
(2)   Teleological explanations of action (3(i) in Figure 11.1).

The first type explains language as aggregate behaviour in terms of social structures and categories. The second type explains language in an intentional idiom. The two types might be contrasted as 'institutional' and 'interpersonal', respectively. Note that hermeneutic explications of social norms and contexts, social meanings, tacit beliefs etc. are prerequisites for explanations in terms of a speaker's intentions. They are bridges between the two explanatory types.

I have presented the teleological or intentional approach in terms of von Wright's (1971) work in the philosophy of action as it developed after Wittgenstein. However, intentionally oriented, hermeneutic approaches to the understanding of society have also arisen in other traditions and have a long intellectual history both in philosophy and the social sciences. For a discussion of the intellectual background, see Giddens (1976), Hollis (1994: esp. ch. 7).

As a matter of daily talk, in order to live, everybody assigns intentional descriptions to actions, including speaker meanings to communicative acts. Every normal child learns how to use the language of intention and action, to understand the minds of others. This makes intelligible both the actions of others and the child's own actions. It constructs the social semiotic. The child becomes a social agent and interpreter. **Autism** is the failure of this ability, which appears to be a distinct mental function of the mind-brain (Baron-Cohen, 1995). Interpretative methods in the social sciences, such as teleological explanations of action, merely make this fundamental analysis of action explicit. Science often proceeds by making common-sense folk theories rigorous. Ethnomethodology is also a method of this type. The analyst's interpretation hermeneutically reconstructs everyday understanding. However, the explicitness itself leads to insights about what people are doing and why they are doing it at a level of self-consciousness beyond that we normally have in social life. For example, Schegloff's analysis of how people identify themselves in telephone conversations, or our own analysis of the complex of intentions behind Arthur's utterance, go beyond our consciousness of practical reasoning in everyday life. So intentional analysis tends towards critique. It draws the unconscious into consciousness and demonstrates how the utterance functions in interactive context – its unconscious goal-directedness or teleology. These features make it a valid form of social explanation.

Scientific and social explanation

This method is very different from the form of inquiry we saw in Labov's paradigm of sociolinguistic research. There the aim was to develop an empirical 'scientific' theory which could give an account of linguistic variability and change. The Labov 'variationist' research paradigm is an example of empirical theory building in social science (type 1 in Figure 11.1). It constrasts not only with the intentional hermeneutic and critical types just discussed (type 3 in Figure 11.1) but the psychological cognitivist methods of the Chomsky research programme, which we will examine later (type 2 in Figure 11.1).

One central question which has preoccupied the philosophy of social explanation is whether or not social behaviour can be adequately explained using methods like Labov's. That is, does normal scientific explanation work for aggregate human behaviour; for example, economic phenomena or linguistic variation. In chapters four to seven, we just assumed that it did. There are those such as von Wright (1971) or Winch (1958) who argue that it cannot, or that hermeneutic methods provide more revealing accounts in history and social science. In fact, it is an odd idea that we could get an explanatory, predictive theory of social change, i.e. history, in any social domain including language, since we wouldn't expect it in history itself. By contrast, Popper (1957) maintains that social explanations can be, with certain reservations, both theoretical and empirical. Empirical theories in social science, such as Labov's, are based on the model of explanation believed employed in natural science. What is at stake here is the 'logical empiricist' doctrine of **unified science**; that all scientific inquiry is methodologically guided by the same set of principles. When Popper wrote in 1957, this was the orthodoxy among social scientists. Empirical theories modelled on natural science yielded 'objective' theories of social facts. Theories based on the interpretation of action were 'subjective' and not explanatory. Here, we will try to integrate the two kinds of theorizing. For a discussion of these issues, see Ryan (1970), Hollis (1994) and Giddens and Turner (1987).

This is perhaps the most complex issue that has arisen in this book. Before relating the two types of social explanation of language, it should be pointed out that there has been a series of very influential criticisms of the logical empiricist conception of science, criticisms of which mainstream linguists seem only dimly aware. There has been a crisis of confidence in the culture with respect to the scientific-technical worldview dominant for much of the modern period. This has had an effect on social science; see Giddens and Turner (1987), Hollinger (1994), Skinner (1985) – the title of this last work, *The Return of Grand Theory in the Human Sciences* is revealing in itself. Among the criticisms of the logical empiricist view of science are: (1) an awareness that science itself is a socio-historical phenomenon, that there is a **sociology of science** (Hesse, 1980); (2) that science has ideological 'power' interests which may affect objectivity; and (3) scientific inquiry itself depends on the interpretation of its language. The truth of scientific statements has tended to be relativized to cultural or at least conceptual schemes by some writers. *In other words, scientific practice has itself been subjected to a socio-historical, hermeneutic and critical analysis.* It has been suggested that knowledge itself is a social and linguistic construction.

We can't go into more detail here, but it is worth noting that correlational sociolinguistics is susceptible to aspects of this critique. We have seen such work already in Cameron and Coates' (1988) discussion of gender. The correlational method also depends on 'borrowed' social descriptions for its social variables. And these are taken out of context and their significance in social theory is often not explored. Each 'borrowed' category – social stratification, class, status, role, situation, gender, ethnicity, network, etc. – *seems to generate the observation of systematicity in linguistic variation.* The methodology seems to 'construct' the particular variation that is described. The social and historical context of correlational sociolinguistics, how its results are interpreted, publicized and consumed, is of relevance. With respect to language, the methods of research seem to half-construct and half-discover the facts. But this may be a normal feature of scientific inquiry.

For the present, let us just accept Labov's variationist paradigm as an empirical social science theory, which is scientific in Popper's sense.

At the beginning of this chapter we mentioned some features of a normal scientific theory. It is a set of explicit hypotheses which explain and predict facts. It has deductive rigour – the facts can be deduced from the statements of the theory. It is refutable. The predictions which it makes must not be falsified by observation. If they are, and there is no alternative explanation of why this should be so from common sense or a secondary theory, then the hypothesis must be either revised or abandoned. Agreement of observation with prediction corroborates the theory.

Let us see how the explanation of a particular event works. There are three parts: the event to be explained, a set of initial conditions, and a **covering law**, which is part of the scientific theory. The law explains the event by saying that if the initial conditions obtain, then this is sufficient to bring about the event.

Here is an example of a covering law from Popper (1957: 25). 'For light of any given wavelength, the smaller the aperture through which a light ray passes, the greater is the angle of diffraction.' Now say we want to explain an event – we observe an increase in the angle of diffraction of a light ray. If we take the covering law and combine it with the initial condition that someone has decreased the width of the aperture through which the ray is passing, we can deduce our observation. It follows from the covering law, given the initial conditions.

It is clear that this 'covering law' picture of science really only yields the kind of descriptive and predictive theory discussed earlier on. Its laws make predictions but don't explain why they should occur, other than that they are in conformity with the law. Any given covering law describes a regularity in isolation. In fact, we would prefer to have sets of laws which fitted together into a logically connected whole, as a system of rules (Harré, 1985: 170).

It is the rigorous description, ideally in a mathematical form, and consequent predictive power of such theories that are their justification. They have technical payoffs in the control of nature and can be justified in those terms alone. But as we noted in chapter four and at the beginning of this chapter, there is a *desire for explanation* as well. We want an explanatory as well as a descriptive theory. This demands a causal narrative that also 'explains' the formal results in terms of general hypotheses from which those results may be deduced and which thus tells us why things are the way they are. Because this is couched in ordinary language, albeit in a specialized register, the senses of the words used may be vague or underspecified and make unconscious metaphysical assumptions, for example about materialism or mechanisms of causation, which are embedded in the culture. The explanation itself begs interpretation, as well as simplifying re-writings for popular dissemination, if it is to have an ideological impact or become part of educational curricula. Explanations as interpretations are also 'underdetermined by data', or if Quine is right, are 'indeterminate' in things to do with the mind. Thus, alternative explanations are *always* available. The persuasiveness of an explanation has partly to do with how it fits into the overall web of belief discussed in chapter nine. Both Hesse and Harré point out that scientific explanations also rest on underlying analogies or metaphors and that this is crucial to the creativity of science (Harré, 1985: 168f.; Hesse, 1980: ch. 4; see also Gentner, 1982). For example, the germ theory of disease rests on a warfare metaphor. We saw the computer analogy for the mind-brain. Modern linguistics has usually conceived of language as a calculus. What kind of metaphor underpins correlational sociolinguistics? This is a complicated case because the analogies are 'borrowed' from sociology along with the social variables like class and social network. One basic analogy underlies the categories of **social structure and social function** – the picture of a machine or a biological organism. The structure of linguistic variation is a statistical parallel to social structures (e.g. class stratification) and serves social functions (e.g. the signalling of class identity; reproduction of class norms).

To return to the distinction between description and explanation, we can agree with Lass that correlational sociolinguistics 'explains' nothing as it stands, although it generates suggestive empirical generalizations (Lass, 1980: 166f.). These are social facts which are not visible from or accessible to individual points of view and are in that sense irreducible. However, an explanatory theory of variation and change needs to be developed and this is being done (see above, esp. chapter seven). There is an intuitive urge to say that the social categories 'cause' the variation. Indeed, in the first edition of this book I said they 'weakly caused' it. But that is inappropriate. Class, gender, social networks by themselves don't have causal powers. To develop an explanation of social factors in variation and change we need to explain the mechanisms at the intentional level that functionally motivate individual utterance acts such that the aggregate behaviour described at the correlational level will emerge. This means we have to link our two kinds of explanation, the empirical social scientific and the teleological explanation of action. This is also why this book has covered *both* sociolinguistics and pragmatics. The key issue in social explanation is to bring together the two levels of inquiry. We will now try do this more explicitly.

Expressive and explanatory autonomy

So we have two valid kinds of social explanation. Using methods modelled on natural science, we offer descriptions of sociolinguistic patterns. By contrast, using teleological explanations modelled on the way we understand action in everyday life, we gain insight into the speech acts which constitute discourse. Shall ever the twain meet?

In order to link the two kinds of explanation, we need first to look at a distinction made by MacDonald and Pettit (1981: 115ff.) between the **expressive** and **explanatory autonomy** of institutions. The term 'institutions' here refers to social groups and their practices. Here is a rough and ready account of their ideas.

Say we have a set of terms to refer to some entities in a given area of experience. Examples of such terms might be 'class', 'style' and 'social network'. If this set of terms allows us to give expression to truths which cannot be expressed without those terms, then the entity in question is expressively autonomous. The referring terms make possible the expression of truths which we could not state without referring to those entities. MacDonald and Pettit argue convincingly that institutions are expressively autonomous. It is hard to see, for example, how one could express the truths in a sociolinguistic structure graph without reference to class and style. The pattern of variability is just not visible from the point of view of the individual.

Now let us contrast this with explanatory autonomy. Imagine this time we have two contrasting sets of terms that refer to different things. For example, an institutional and an intentional vocabulary:

institutional: *class, style, social network*, etc.
intentional: *speaker, attitude, intention, action*, etc.

In a sociolinguistic structure diagram we explained events by referring to things like class and style. If we *can* explain the same event in individualist terms, then institutions like class and style do not have explanatory autonomy. That is, these concepts only have explanatory autonomy if we *cannot* also explain the same events by referring to the attitudes and intentions of individual speakers.

In other words, the collective patterns revealed by using terms like class or social network may be expressively autonomous and reveal truths that cannot otherwise be put into words. At the same time, they may not be explanatorily autonomous. We may be able to explain the same events in terms of the attitudes and intentions of individual speakers.

The importance of MacDonald and Pettit's case for social science is the claim (which they argue convincingly) that institutions are expressively, but *not* explanatorily, autonomous. They can always also be accounted for in teleological terms.

If this is true, then the twain shall meet. *We ought to be able to explain the large-scale patterns revealed by Labov's sociolinguistics in terms of the intentional account of discourse developed in the second part of the book.*

Sociolinguistic patterns and individual intentionality

Can aggregate scores for sociolinguistic variables also be explained in terms of the attitudes and intentions of individual speakers? I think they can. In fact, we were on our way to doing this earlier in the book.

We began by studying the social distribution of linguistic variables. Striking correlations emerged from this kind of investigation. Variants were regularly distributed according to various dimensions of social structure.

In chapter seven we moved from the social to the individual. Social distribution could be accounted for in terms of norms of pronunciation within a community. Because of these norms, variants had 'social meanings' – they stood for certain social identities and values. The uniformity of speakers' attitudes to variants revealed their awareness of both norms and meanings. This was more regular than their actual pronunciations. But clearly, to speak one way or another means something in social terms. With LePage's notion of an act of identity (page 273 above) these meanings informed individual speech acts. Each speaker's every utterance 'placed' him or her in terms of degree of affiliation to the identities available in the community, and encoded in its norms. Each utterance claims a social identity. The act of identity, therefore, adds another dimension to the complex of intentionality behind an utterance.

The outcome of uniformity of norm and meaning (reflected in speakers' attitudes to varieties) is that individual speakers' intentions are realized in more or less regular ways throughout the community. We observe regularity in the social distribution of linguistic variables. The structure we observe reflects speakers' differing positions in relation to the norms which come about for social and historical reasons. But we are able to account for the collective patterns in terms of individual attitudes, intentions and actions.

We can conclude that two kinds of social explanation are both necessary for an understanding of variation. The Labov paradigm reveals the pattern. The teleological tells us why individuals should act in such a way as to produce the pattern.

Hypothesis: the pragmatics of social meaning

We can tie sociolinguistic patterns even more closely to pragmatics and our account of intention. In earlier chapters, the notion of social meaning was very important. In the first edition of *Language and Society*, I suggested that we could reinterpret social meaning in terms of Grice's concept of implicature. The claim was made that social meanings were conventional implicatures. This needs to be reconsidered. I will recapitulate my earlier suggestion and then criticize it.

An implicature arises when the use of a particular form of words conveys something which is not part of what has actually been *said*, nor entailed by what has been said. An implicature makes no contribution to whether the sentence is true or false. Now Grice (1975) distinguishes different kinds of implicature (for a discussion see Levinson, 1983: 126ff.; Gazdar, 1979: 37ff.). Only two of these need concern us here. The first type are the conversational implicatures which we studied in chapter ten. They were generated in context by the speaker's apparent violation of the cooperative principle and its maxims. The second kind are **conventional implicatures**. These are also conveyed in spite of not being part of what the speaker actually *said*, and also make no contribution to whether his sentence is true or false. They differ in being attached by convention to particular linguistic forms.

Our claim here is that the use of sociolinguistic variants conventionally implicates a speaker's affiliation with particular groups within the community. For example, think of 'When's the next strike then, Tom?' pronounced in a variety of different accents. In each case, the speaker has said exactly the same thing. Each utterance of the sentence would be true or false under exactly the same conditions. Each utterance has the same entailments. Nevertheless, each utterance conveys something different by virtue of the accent in which it was pronounced. By producing different values of the variable features available, each speaker conventionally implicates, at least, a claim to a different social identity. We also saw that speakers can alter their pronunciation of variable features. A speaker, for example, can increase or decrease the frequency with which he or she produces a constricted *r* variant or can code-switch between separate dialects or languages. In different contexts and between people in different relationships the use of one variant rather than the other would be considered appropriate. For example, between people who were equal and solidary the use of their mutual vernacular would signal this relationship. Such norms of appropriateness depend on the meanings conventionally associated with each form.

But such norms can also be violated. In this case, the hearer looks to the Gricean maxims. He or she can ask, what is the relevance of the speaker producing such an unexpected frequency for this variable feature in this context? We are supposedly equal and solidary – why switch away from our common vernacular? In other words, speakers can use choice of variant or changes in frequency to produce the other kind of implicature. They can *conversationally implicate* propositions by their use of variants. The argument is that changes in variables over and against what is expected within the conversation raise questions of relevance in Grice's sense just as they do on the other levels of language. Therefore, they can produce conversational implicatures.

This might give us a way to look at the origin of sound changes. Labov (1974: 253ff.) has argued that three factors motivate a sound change. These are identity, solidarity and the strengthening of the force of expression. Let us look at this third factor. Say a given vowel height or a given frequency for a variable conventionally implicates a social identity. It can also, therefore, be used to convey solidarity with those of the same identity. Now say for some reason an individual wants to emphasize identity or solidarity. He or she can do this by violating the maxim of quantity, producing a higher frequency or a more open vowel than normal. He or she conversationally implicates that affiliation with the group and its values is very strong in this context. He or she has increased the force of expression for communicative purposes. In a community, such implicatures would keep pushing the norm of pronunciation further along in the direction of change.

Recasting social meaning in terms of Grice's theory further integrates our two ways of investigating language in social terms. It suggests a mechanism through which the intentional use of language in acts of identity systematically employs variability for communicative ends.

However, there are criticisms of this Gricean understanding of social meaning. Seven distinct points can be made.

1. *Is social meaning conventional?* I suggested above that the relation of a sociolinguistic variant and its 'meaning' was conventional. In fact, the meaning has its ultimate origin in the actual speech of the group which the variant comes to signify. In terms of the theory of signs, the signifier – the statistical production of one variant rather than another in some context – is an **index**. An indexical sign isn't arbitrary, rather it is interpreted as a sign because it has a causal relation to its object, that which it represents. In our case, the cause is affiliation with a social group. An

accent is also a **metonymic index**; one attribute of the group, use of a linguistic variant, comes to represent the whole identity of the group, much as 'The White House' represents the US presidency. But the situation is more complex, since to some degree the variant gets detached from actual causal properties of its group of origin and becomes a **symbol** of the group – a bit like a flag! In this respect, the sign comes to have a conventional dimension.

2. *Symbolism and stereotypes.* We saw in chapter seven that attitudes took the form of stereotypes or schematas about the group represented. This seems to be a general feature of cognitive information processing, so the perception of linguistic variation is not unusual in this respect. We saw the role of such stereotypes as regards both encyclopedic information and word meaning in chapter nine. Group stereotypes can be seen as a form of conventionalized information arbitrarily mobilized by an indexical sign. They are a 'folk theory' of its object, the social group, and constitute the symbolic dimension of social meaning. Stereotypes of region and class, ethnicity and gender – which have separate ideological origins – become symbolically melded into the indexical statistical structure of variation as it is communicatively perceived in context. The accent can access a conceptual address, just like a word can. It is in this sense that 'conventional implicature' is an apt label.

3. *Accommodation theory: solidarity and power.* In chapter seven, we saw that participants adjusted their production of variables to addressee and situation. Affiliation and difference were signalled in this way. This relates both to strategies of politeness and the enforcement of norms and resistance to that enforcement. Here let us query what sort of 'communication' is taking place in accommodation. Is accommodation a matter of conversational implicature? In relevance theory terms – 'Is there an incorrigible layer of communicative content where perceived frequency of sociolinguistic variables is input to the calculation of relevance with respect to social affiliation or distance in all spoken interaction?' Deviation or otherwise from contextual expectations, including those of politeness, with respect to social relationships would generate a layer of contextual effects and be a part of the calculation of relevance as a

matter of course. Such social meanings would be implicated, and thus propositional in form.

4. *Are social meanings propositional?* There is no doubt that speakers *can* produce variants on particular 'marked' occasions in order to convey a definite conversational implicature in the full sense of having an informative intent. However, this seems to differ from the subtle adjustments of accommodation theory. It seems bizarre to suggest, for example, that the accommodative use of *r* in everyday conversation would engender a propositional belief in its recipient. It would be more an almost physical 'sense' of being drawn closer or being pushed away. One solution to this lies in the fact that there are types of knowledge and intentional behaviour which are non-propositional in form. Examples are the knowledge of how to walk, ride a bicycle, dance or return a serve in tennis. There is meaningful information 'embodied in our practices' which Dreyfus (1985), following the philosopher Heidegger, calls **practical understanding** or **primordial preunderstanding** (page 372 above). This is a form of background to speech that is so pervasive and involving of motor skills that it can't plausibly be viewed as a 'belief system'. Dreyfus explicitly links such preunderstanding to Wittgenstein's forms of life. We could apply these ideas to social meaning. The social meanings communicated by the motor finetuning described by accommodation theory are *pre-propositional* or primordial in this sense. Therefore, they are not best considered either as implicatures or as a layer of contextual effects; although they could be input to the calculation of relevance when they are used in a 'marked' way to convey specific informative intents. However, they don't normally do this. Rather they are an affective-affiliative background and claim social identity as a subliminal aspect of personal presence.

5. *Subliminal or unconscious intention.* On the other hand, the remarkable adjustment of sociolinguistic variables is best explained as teleological, as behaviour generated by a goal. *This would be a case of unconscious intention as discussed at length above.* A speaker may intentionally yet unconsciously communicate affiliation or difference with a hearer or a group. Respondents make complex

judgements in speech evaluation and self-reporting tests. This form of intentional, yet non-propositional meaning, being systematic and expressive of identity yet not consciously controlled, is *a candidate for the mechanism by which individual intentionality interacts with statistical group and structural factors in linguistic change.* Being non-propositional, it isn't an informative intent as normally understood.

6. *Subjectivity and the impersonal system of identities.* If the intention behind an utterance with respect to social meaning is unconscious, then the conscious will of a personal subject is not an explanatory source for language change. Rather the processes are impersonal. Our explanation is not individualistic in any simple sense in spite of the use of intentional idioms. *An utterance event is a token or instance of the impersonal socio-historical mapping of structural inherent variation on to systems of social identity.* The dialectic of these two systems serves this social and psychological function. Because of this, the global structure of sociolinguistic variation is also **iconic**; it is an analogue of the system of social identities. On the level of the individual the production of a variant is therefore also an **iconic sign** of the social relation being enacted. That is, more of the variant perceived as similar signifies that we are 'the same'; more of the variant perceived as dissimilar signifies our 'difference'. The linguistic variation is a subtly adjustable icon of our relationship because variation is an analogue of the system of social identities.

7. *Critique.* The making of the unconscious conscious is the role of critique. The explication of the unconscious social functioning of variability in individual utterances is the role of critical interpretation as outlined in chapter ten (see also 3(ii) in Figure 11.1 and Figure 11.3). The critical analyst will interpret variability in terms of impersonal psychological and social functions to which the speaker hasn't access and which are expressed through institutions like standardization. There will usually be a difference and therefore conflict between the subject's consciously held encyclopedic beliefs and the results of criticism, for example, as discussed with respect to standardization in chapter two. Critique is 'liberating' in the sense that it allows people and society at

large to 'see through' – see the functional motivation of consciously held aspects of the web of belief; to be relatively freed from 'not knowing what they are doing'. Put this way, all science has a critical role in a culture.

Psychological versus social explanation

We have looked at the social explanation of language. How does it relate to the dominant Chomskyan paradigm in linguistics? What is the appropriate relationship between psychological and social or teleological explanations as far as language is concerned? Do the forms of explanation presuppose incommensurable conceptions of language?

Following the tradition of Saussure, Chomsky defines language as the object of linguistic inquiry very precisely. As pointed out in chapter one, linguistics is a theory of I-language, internalized language, as opposed to E-language or externalized language (Chomsky, 1986). The former is the system of language, equivalent to Saussure's *langue*. The latter includes all the diversity of speech, equivalent to *parole*. The distinctions are displayed in Figure 11.4. All through its history, linguistics has conceived of language in a specialized way that both claims to determine its essence and be explainable by the methodology of linguistics. To some degree, what language 'is' is produced by the theoretical approach adopted. Each approach foregrounds some aspect of the phenomenon. One has to decide upon the plausibility, not only of particular descriptions but of the whole paradigm.

Chomsky's conception of language is psychological, universalistic and biologically based. He specifies that I-language, the object of the theory, is knowledge of language. This is a determinate state of the human mind, ultimately reducible to brain structures and processes. It is the job of linguistics at this time – since the brain cannot be directly investigated – to abstractly characterize that state of knowledge of language in any way possible (by developing arguments about formal grammars, doing psycholinguistic experiments etc.). In language acquisition, knowledge of a specific language spontaneously 'grows' by virtue of the application of these biological principles intrinsic to every normal child's mind-brain to

CONCEPTION OF LANGUAGE	OBJECT OF INQUIRY	COGNITIVE LOCALE MODULARITY	EXPLANATION TYPE
I - language Saussure's *langue*	**knowledge of language** as a property of the mind-brain. *competence*	**language faculty** as a module of mind, localized in the brain.	cognitive, psychological, universal, biological.
E - language Saussure's *parole*	**use of language;** set of utterance acts. *performance*	**non-linguistic cognitive faculties** involved in language use.	social empirical, teleological intentional, cognitive relevance theory of non-linguistic processes, functional, critical.

Figure 11.4 Distinctions underlying Chomsky's mentalistic paradigm in linguistics

early linguistic experience. This system of principles, or I-language, is the essence of language. Since it is a coherent mental system or module of mind, it is natural to claim that it is physically localized in a specific region of the brain. This is Chomsky's explanatory narrative which 'explains' the formal descriptions or grammars which are the result of linguistic investigations. Chomsky notes that only this picture 'grounds' linguistics as having a real object, a state of affairs that makes the theory really true or false. The object is the biological basis of language, a faculty of the mind-brain.

We shall look at some weaknesses of this approach in a moment. First I-language as the object of linguistics must be contrasted with E-language. The difference is summarized in Figure 11.4. E-language is the *conception of language as the set of all possible utterance acts under all true non-I-language descriptions*. These are all the uses to which knowledge of language is or could be put. In psychological terms, it is the output of the interaction of the language faculty with other cognitive faculties or modules of mind; for example, intention, encyclopedic information, memory or reasoning. The consequent diversity of E-language reflects the fact that this is language as it actually functions. But Chomsky's position is that E-language is not the proper object of linguistics. It is a reflex of aspects of the brain which are not part of the language module. And E-language is not even a coherent object. It follows that there can be no correct theory of it (Chomsky, 1986: 19–24). Predictably, with E-languages, we get a conclusion like Quine's that there is no determinate theory of language, no object of explanation that would make a theory true. That is the cost of rejecting mentalism and modularity. For Chomskyans it is not a sensible cost to bear. But this means that they must exclude E-language as the object of linguistics. Of course, I-language casts its net to *whatever* can be plausibly included in the language module or system. That is, whatever would form part of a simple and convincing unitary theory of I-language when all the evidence is in. If one accepted mentalism, but without I-language and therefore a concomitant language module, language could be a **distributed system** scattered all over the mind-brain and **inextricable** from other aspects of mind. Then linguistics would have no unique object of description and no basis as a unique science. Since Saussure linguists have always claimed that, suitably idealized, 'language is a system'; but how much of that systematicity is a result of methodologically excluding all the ways language inextricably pervades other aspects of both mind, social life, culture and historical change?

So, like Saussure, in order to make an autonomous science of linguistics possible, Chomsky makes language autonomous. Methodologically, they draw a sharp boundary (the bold line in Figure 11.4) between *knowledge* and *use*, *langue* and *parole*, *competence* and *performance*, the *language module* and *other faculties of mind*. Language is explained in terms of the first of these dualisms. First, we describe and explain I-language, then how it is put to use, how it functions.

This dualism between I- and E-language defines the relationship between psychological and social explanations of language. It ought to be clear that everything we have discussed in this book are aspects of the theory of E-language or performance in terms of Chomsky's methodology. They are outside the realm of linguistic theory. Variability and language change, the rules of conversation, convention, speech acts, meaning$_{nn}$ and communicative/informative intents, the encyclopedia, the inferencing involved in utterance comprehension, are all features of how language is used, not knowledge of language. The distinctions drawn in Figure 11.4, made by Saussure and Chomsky in different ways, are an empirical hypothesis about language, but of a methodological kind. *They establish the autonomy of linguistics as a theory of language conceived of as an autonomous abstract system or mental module.* This hypothesis is called **arbitrariness**; the hypothesis that language is inexplicable in terms of any of its uses or functions. On this view, whatever we have been describing in this book, it *isn't* language in this sense.

The Chomsky-Saussure paradigm runs into a number of problems at this point. The first is to do with semantic inextricability. In chapter nine, we saw that Quine argued that it was impossible to distinguish between beliefs held because of the meaning properties of sentences and beliefs held because of the way the world was; between the analytic and the synthetic. There was *no distinction* between 'knowledge of language' and 'knowledge of the world', between meaning and background information. If this is true, it is impossible to have a semantic theory which is either 'autonomous' or 'arbitrary' with respect to a theory of knowledge or belief fixation. Far from being arbitrary, the semantics of natural languages is an empirical theory of the world. (A consequence of this is our intuition that the 'meanings of language' pervade all the world representations that constitute thought and culture, so that the study of language underlies all inquiry into the human.) Responses to this dilemma form boundaries between views of language in linguistics, philosophy and cognitive science. The Saussure-Chomsky hypothesis can be preserved by withdrawing from 'real semantics'; the relation of language and the world. Linguistic semantics only deals with formal properties of language itself. Also, it can be claimed that the relation of language and the world is mediated by non-linguistic but language-like cognitive representations (concepts, ideas) which are *not* part of the language module, but map on to language. The first solution is Chomskyan and the second that of cognitive science, including relevance theory.

The second problem involves the inextricability of data. In abandoning real semantics, syntax becomes the main concern of Chomskyan theory. One piece of basic data which is evidence for the linguistic faculty is native speakers' judgements about sentences. But are such judgements really extricable from the pervasive variability within E-language, features due to processes of change, attitudes to variables deriving from standardization, or the pragmatics of utterance comprehension? Can judgements about which strings are part of the syntax of language L, and which are not, judgements of grammaticality, really be extricated from judgements about utterances? In other words – is evidence for the language module extricable from evidence about other aspects of mind? If not, then linguistic theory is unempirical and insulated from falsification.

The answer is that this problem of data is a feature of any theory in the social sciences. A theory itself constructs the relevance of its data; selects what to observe, draws its boundaries, extricates itself. Linguistics accepts any sort of relevant observation from any source. It is the overall descriptive and explanatory success of the theory that is important and decides what factors are relevant and irrelevant, assigned to I-language or to E-language.

We are thus led to consider the overall satisfactoriness of the Saussure-Chomsky conception of language as a description and explanation of language phenomena. This depends on social factors; group affiliation, ideology, accidents of biography and the purposes of linguistics – what Halliday (1968) called 'Syntax and the Consumer'. The bottom line of the theory presented in Figure 11.4 is autonomy and arbitrariness. *Language as defined and thus described is explained because this is the way the mind-brain is arbitrarily constructed. Full stop.* But many linguists have found this circumscription of language and this explanatory destination unsatisfactory with respect to their interests. Arbitrariness cuts linguistics off from all the most important dimensions of language; to represent the world, to communicate, to criticize and interpret, to constitute social life and culture, and so on. More importantly, it makes the functions of language irrelevant to an account of its form. The purposes or socio-historical dynamics of E-language have *no possible effect* on I-language. From this perspective the hypothesis of arbitrariness looks incredible!

Functional explanations

We can ask of any linguistic structure the role it plays in some context, the purpose which it has. That is, we can ask for a **functional explanation** (type 4 in Figure 11.1). A functional explanation is a generalized subtype of teleology, to interpret something in terms of the purpose or goal of its output. For example, a functional interpretation of a heart would describe its purpose in a circulatory system. In a brief survey for *The Encyclopedia of Language and Linguistics* (Downes, 1994), I distinguished two types of this sort of explanation. (These are distinct from the teleological explanation of action described earlier in this chapter.) The two types are a weaker **functional interpretation** and a stronger **functional aetiology**.

In the weaker type of functional analysis, an item is described in terms of the role it plays in the context of some larger system. This is a sort of 'engineering' analysis. For example, chlorophyll functions to enable plants to perform photosynthesis or a carburettor to mix fuel and air and distribute it to the combustion chamber in an internal combustion engine, and so on. Usually, a function can be achieved in alternative ways, has alternative 'engineering solutions'. For example, an engine may have fuel injection. Now any linguistic structure is amenable to this type of analysis. **A functional grammar** will interpret linguistic structures in terms of an analysis of proposed functions of language (see for example Halliday, 1994). When we interpreted sociolinguistic variables, for example the centring diphthongs on Martha's Vineyard, in terms of social meaning, we were describing them as having a social function.

The stronger type of functional explanation is more exciting. In a functional aetiology we claim that the linguistic item *comes into being and takes the form it does because of* the role it plays in the containing system. It is this stronger aetiological claim that some functional linguists like Halliday (1970: 141–2) make when they say that 'the particular form taken by the grammatical system of language is closely related to the social and personal needs that language is required to serve' or 'Language has evolved to serve human needs; and the way it is organized is functional with respect to those needs – it is not arbitrary' (Halliday, 1994: xiii). In artificial systems like an internal combustion engine, the previously mentioned carburettor clearly has a functional aetiology in terms of intentions and actions. These called it into being. As far as language is concerned, there is no doubt that the registers described in chapter eight are the way they are because of the effects they achieve. Only consider the example of the prayer. Note that a functional aetiology which is the result of social processes is not likely to be conscious. On the individual level, it generates the sort of unconscious intent discussed earlier and is 'critical' to the degree it reveals such unconscious origins of action (see Figure 11.3). Consider also sociolinguistic variables like (aw) on Martha's Vineyard or (r) in New York. It is the unconscious significance of tiny variations in pronunciation (statistically produced relative to context) in the complex processes of enacting the 'social meanings' discussed earlier in the chapter that actually 'brings into being' the sociolinguistic marker as an entity. They have a functional aetiology. Variables wouldn't have the structure they have, revealed in sociolinguistic structure diagrams, without the social functions.

Functional aetiology is the precise opposite of Saussurean or Chomskyan arbitrariness. It clearly operates within E-language. Aetiological penetration into I-language, for example, syntactic structures, *pace* Halliday, is usually considered more problematic. (Although there is no problem giving functional *interpretations* of syntactic structures.) There are a number of schools of functional linguistics, a survey of which would go beyond the brief of this book (see Downes, 1994). However, functional aetiologies for I-languages could be of a number of types.

Features could be produced because they are adaptive in evolution. Chomsky's biological approach to I-language does not preclude functional aetiology (for discussions see Dennett, 1996; Pinker, 1994). But for a function to bring into being innate features of the language faculty would likely require them to have an adaptive, Darwinian origin. The only alternative is for the structural properties to be 'preadapted', originating without being directly selected for, as a concomitant of some other features of the mind-brain, and *then* assembled for use as E-languages by human groups. But that leaves another space for functional aetiology. What context and what purposes initially elicited this coordinative exploitation of the pre-adapted mental and physical properties and turned a non-language array of cognitive capacities into 'modern language'? Furthermore, if language was the result of pre-adaption, then wouldn't it reveal this mosaic of origins by being a more 'distributed system', rather than a specific 'module'? In fact, this is exactly what we do observe! The evolution of language is a controversial issue. It partly depends on how you define 'language'. If the whole 'language' complex can be broken down into

(1)   cognitive representations: real semantics, Fodor's 'thought'
(2)   the process of communication: 'Sperber and Wilson's' pragmatics
(3)   grammar: syntax, linguistic meaning, phonology: Chomsky's 'language'
(4)   the physical exponence: speech, signing, writing etc.
(5)   inherent and sociolinguistic variation in time,

then it can be seen as a synergistic assemblage brought together by evolution in social contexts (see Dingwall, 1988). Within grammar itself there are signs of adaptive advantage (see Downes, 1994;

Newmeyer, 1991). Much work in contemporary linguistics will be on the interfaces between these five. It is their interaction that makes locating functional aetiologies difficult.

Obvious candidates for one context which functionally turned the coordination of preadapted elements into 'language' would be pragmatic, or to do with the psychological processing of language, including perception. Cognitive representations and the interpretation of perceptual stimuli, including intentional action, could have already been in place, providing a functional context for the emergence of language from a mosaic of different capacities. By contrast, leaving evolution aside and rejecting linguistic nativism, the same functional needs could reproduce linguistic structures for each generation in turn in an ongoing functional aetiology. This would be the strongest possible functional hypothesis. There have been investigations of these hypotheses (see, for example, Sankoff and Brown's (1976) *The Origin of Syntax in Discourse*). In Downes (1977), I attempted to give such an alternative account of the English imperative construction. There are functional interpretations of sentence topics or themes and of the stylistic variations of word order illustrated in chapter seven as an example of pervasive variability at the syntactic level. The existence of pairs such as

> The vicar killed the *shark*
> The shark was killed by the *vicar*

can be viewed as a resource for communicating meanings motivated in discourse terms – what Halliday has termed the textual function of language (Halliday, 1970, 1994; Firbas, 1964). Both sentence topic and the variations in word order of related sentences are input to pragmatic processing. They direct attention to conceptual addresses in the encyclopedia and give clues for the calculation of relevance. There has long been interest in the interpretation of syntax in functional terms. See for example, as well as Halliday and the school of systemic functional linguistics, Grossman *et al.* (1975), Givon (1979, 1995), Sankoff and Brown (1976), Foley and Van Valin (1984), and Dirven and Fried (1987).

How do functional explanations figure with respect to sociolinguistic variation and change? We argued above that register variation and sociolinguistic markers have functional aetiologies. Each sociolinguistic area should be examined in turn. It appears inescapable that the evolution and maintenance of standard languages and therefore their concomitant vernaculars have a socio-functional aetiology (see Figure 2.6). Does this have a reflex in the characteristics of vernaculars? Chambers (1995: 207f.) reminds us that standard varieties in general are more restricted in variation than vernaculars, since they limit variation. Standardization is functionally designed by a society to carry out the ideological task of creating normative uniformity and social unity. However, Chambers also describes a small set of purely linguistic processes – consonant cluster simplification is an example – that typify vernaculars across many languages. This shows that the function of standardization may be 'marked', in the case that it impedes linguistic processes that would otherwise occur. The ideological function of standardization generates types of varieties in a universal way.

But we must be careful in the use of functionalist thinking. Purely formal properties have a great deal of autonomy and interact with communication in complex ways. *It has been a central argument of this book that the two sorts of social description of language, the empirical descriptions of variation in sociolinguistic surveys and the pragmatic teleological-intentional level can be integrated. Individual unconscious acts of identity enact social and psychological functions realized through normative pressures, taking the form of social meanings, transmitted in social networks which differ in type by class. This is the coordinative mechanism that partially 'explains' the patterns observed at the higher level. However, at each stage, purely structural features of language interact to affect the observed outcome.*

Conclusion

There are as many theories of shape-shifter language as there are paradigms and methods for its investigation. We have surveyed some explanations which account for language in social terms as promised by our broad definition of sociolinguistics in chapter one:

- sociolinguistics proper (Labov, Trudgill, Milroys)
- traditional and urban dialectology
- language change, historical linguistics, creole studies
- the sociology of language, bilingualism, language planning

- ethnography of communication, code-switching
- register theory, social semiotics
- ethnomethodology, conversation analysis, politeness
- pragmatics, speech acts, relevance theory
- background information, knowledge representation
- philosophy of language, Quine, Wittgenstein
- philosophy of social science
- functional linguistics, critical linguistics

Much of the most fruitful work in the understanding of language and society has been through the adaptions of methods and theories from other disciplines by linguists (social network theory, philosophy of language) or within other disciplines (sociology, cognitive psychology). There are also further approaches which investigate contextual interpretations of language which we have not looked at, notably literary theory and discourse analysis. It ought to be clear that there are very diverse methods and influences coming from various research communities all of which provide different means for the analysis of language in social context and different insights. Some approaches not surveyed or only mentioned in passing are:

- structuralism and post-structuralism, literary theory
- postmodernism in contemporary social theory
- Habermas and critical theory
- literary stylistics, linguistics and literature
- literary and philosophical hermeneutics
- Bakhtin's dialogism, literary theory
- anthropological linguistics, language and culture
- discourse analysis in linguistics
- text linguistics
- cognitive psychology, computational linguistics
- cognitive linguistics, G. Lakoff, M. Johnson

The object of inquiry is truly both encyclopedic and web-like because of the pervasiveness of language and the institutional nature of inquiry. The next steps for research and essay writing for the student of language and society, including suggestions on using new technology, are outlined in the Further Reading which follows.

Further reading

Chapter 1. Linguistics and sociolinguistics

This section aims to be a guide to further and private study, as well as essay writing. In this first chapter, an overview of how to get more information on any topic is provided. We also survey the main textbooks in the field.

Reference books

Reference books and surveys are useful sources of information. There are three which are particularly useful. Asher, R. (ed.) (1994), *The Encyclopedia of Language and Linguistics*, 10 volumes (Pergamon) contains up to date entries on virtually any topic in linguistics. Newmeyer, F. J. (ed.) (1988), *Linguistics: The Cambridge Survey*, 4 volumes, esp. volume 4, *Language: The Socio-Cultural Context* (Cambridge) contains survey articles on areas of sociolinguistics, with references. The third is Ammon, U., Dittmar, N. and Mattheier, K. (vol. 1, 1987 and vol. 2, 1988), *Sociolinguistics, An International Handbook of the Science of Language and Society*. Your library reference section may also have specialist linguistics bibliographies on specific topics.

Resources online and journals

It is also useful to search university library catalogues. This is now possible using the COPAC and other similar access systems on the World Wide Web. COPAC is an online public access catalogue which gives the user access to the holdings of major UK university research libraries. There are some sites which now provide abstracts of articles in journals and these services may be available in your library. Also, as noted above, search engines – ALTA VISTA is the most academically oriented of the major ones

– can be used to hunt for sites on linguistic topics. It is also useful to use the major journals in the field such as *Language in Society*, *Journal of Sociolinguistics*, *Journal of Pragmatics*, *Behavioral and Brain Sciences*, etc.

Some selected textbooks in sociolinguistics

There are a number of textbooks in sociolinguistics and all contain references.

1. Chambers, J. (1995), *Sociolinguistic Theory*.
   (Theoretically sophisticated and up to date. Concentrates on variation studies. Cites research from all over the world. Quite advanced but very good.)
2. Fasold, R. (1984), *The Sociolinguistics of Society* and (1990), *The Sociolinguistics of Language*.
   (These two volumes are comprehensive. The second includes coverage of pragmatics/discourse. Intermediate in difficulty.)
3. Graddol, D., Leith, D. and Swan, J. (1996), *English: History, Diversity and Change*.
   (About English. Covers the external history and sociolinguistics of the language and is very well presented and illustrated. Especially good on standardization and globalization. Introductory level.)
4. Holmes, J. (1992), *An Introduction to Sociolinguistics*.
   (Covers multilingualism, variation and language use at a fairly introductory level. Contains exercises and many examples from around the world.)
5. Hudson, R. (1996 2nd edn.), *Sociolinguistics*.
   (Theoretical and wide-ranging. Original in its approach. Contains a chapter on language and culture.)
6. Montgomery, M. (1995 2nd edn.), *An Introduction to Language and Society*.
   (Elementary introduction. Contains sections on language development in social context, register, anti-languages, and critical linguistics. A Halliday oriented textbook.)
7. Romaine, S. (1994), *Language in Society*.
   (An excellent survey of mainstream sociolinguistics. Covers variation, gender, language change, pidgins and creoles. Good value. No treatment of pragmatics or discourse.)
8. Trudgill, P. (1995 3rd edn.), *Sociolinguistics*.
   (The 1974 edition was the first introduction to modern mainstream sociolinguistics and dialectology for the general reader. Largely Labov oriented in its approach, but with chapters on language and nation and language and interaction. Still very good.)

9. Wardhaugh, R. (1992 2nd edn.), *An Introduction to Sociolinguistics* (Comprehensive in its coverage at intermediate level of difficulty Mainstream approach. Thorough with good further reading.)

Sociolinguistics around the world

Much of the early research was in the USA and the UK. More recently, there have been investigations in many other speech communities; see contributions to Ammon *et al.* (1987/1988). A special issue of the *International Journal of the Sociology of Language* 115 (1995), edited by E. H. Jahr, is dedicated to sociolinguistics in Norway. Bolton and Kwok (eds.) (1992), *Sociolinguistics Today* contains articles from a 1988 Hong Kong conference and the introductory article by Bolton surveys sociolinguistic research in Asia and the West, with references. Below are textbooks and readers in English containing research useful for students of the most studied European national languages.

English language books in French, German and Spanish sociolinguistics.

1. Ager, D. (1990), *Sociolinguistics and Contemporary French.*
2. Barbour, S. and Stevenson, P. (1990), *Variation in German.*
3. Battye, A. and Hintze, M. (1992), *The French Language Today.*
    (Contains external history of French, phonology, grammar and varieties.)
4. Dittmar, N. and Schlobinski, P. (1988) (eds.), *The Sociolinguistics of Urban Vernaculars.*
    (Contains studies of the Berlin vernacular.)
5. Mar-Molinero, C. (1997), *The Spanish-Speaking World.*
6. Sanders, C. (1993) (ed.), *French Today: Language in its Social Context.*

Some selected textbooks in pragmatics

1. Blakemore, D. (1992), *Understanding Utterances.*
    (Introduces pragmatics but solely from a relevance theory point of view.)
2. Levinson, S. (1983), *Pragmatics.*
    (The basic textbook, although by now somewhat old. Definitive coverage of much of the subject, including conversation analysis/ ethnomethodology. Nothing on relevance theory.)
3. Mey, J. (1993), *Pragmatics.*
    (A survey covering the main approaches. Continental European in its outlook.)

.   Yule, G. (1996), *Pragmatics.*
    (Brief and basic but up to date survey. Doesn't cover relevance theory.
    Excellent further reading provided.)

Some selected textbooks in discourse analysis

1.   Brown, G. and Yule, G. (1983), *Discourse Analysis.*
     (Develops its own analysis of discourse and texts, drawing on a
     number of approaches, including Halliday and cognitive science.)
2.   Coulthard, M. (1985 2nd edn.), *An Introduction to Discourse Analysis.*
     (A clear and brief introduction with chapters on pragmatics, conver-
     sation analysis/ethnomethodology, ethnography of communication,
     as well as discourse intonation and the Sinclair-Coulthard 'Birming-
     ham' model of discourse analysis.)
3.   Schiffrin, D. (1994), *Approaches to Discourse.*
     (A wide-ranging survey of many approaches to 'language in con-
     text', including pragmatics, each illustrated by an analysis. There is a
     chapter on definitions of discourse.)
4.   Stubbs, M. (1983), *Discourse Analysis.*
     (Comprehensive textbook also generally oriented to the Sinclair-
     Coulthard 'Birmingham' model originally based on the descriptive
     analysis of classroom discourse.)

Practical research methodology

There are discussions of how research on language in use is carried out for **sociolinguistics** in L. Milroy (1987a), *Observing and Analyzing Natural Language*, and for **discourse** in Stubbs (1983), ch. 11 and Schiffrin (1994), Appendix 1. The latter gives extensive references. The important issue of the ideological significance of research both for the researcher and the informants is considered in Cameron *et al.* (1992), *Researching Language: Issues of Power and Method.* Both Levinson (1983: 369–70) and Schiffrin (1994) give systems for transcribing conversation, the latter more extensive. (See also further reading for chapter four below.)

Linguistics: background in Chomsky's theory

1.   Chomsky, N. (1986), *Knowledge of Language.*
     (The clearest account by Chomsky himself of his conception of the
     language faculty and its philosophical implications.)
2.   Cook, V. and Newson, M. (1996 2nd edn.), *Chomsky's Universal
     Grammar.*

(A very clear introduction, aimed at the beginner or someone from another related discipline, of the nuts and bolts of Chomsky's grammar and its theoretical basis. Completely up to date.)
3. Pinker, S. (1994), *The Language Instinct.*
    (An enthusiastic exposition of the compelling evidence for the Chomskyan position that a language module of the mind-brain is part of our biological endowment and all its ramifications. Written for the educated general reader.)

Linguistics as sociolinguistics

For an alternative socio-functionalist account of language in general, see Halliday, M. (1978), *Language as Social Semiotic* and the further reading for chapters eight (for Halliday) and eleven (for functional explanations).

Chapter 2. A tapestry in space and time

An excellent theoretical introduction to dialectology is Chambers and Trudgill's (1980) *Dialectology.* The question 'What is a Language?' is discussed in Hudson (1996: 30f.). Nancy Dorian (1973, 1981) is the key figure in the study of language death. Dorian (1989) is a collection, while Dressler (1988) and Campbell (1994) provide surveys. Pidgins and creoles have been the subject of intensive research since the 1960s. For comprehensive discussions, see Romaine (1988) or Mühlhaüsler (1986). *Linguistics: The Cambridge Survey* (Newmeyer 1988) contains a number of articles from different points of view, including Bickerton's. For standard languages, Haugen's (1966) article still merits study. Milroy and Milroy (1991) is an important treatment. The standardization of English is extensively treated and well illustrated with historical source materials in Graddol *et al.* (1996) and is also treated by Lass (1987). Standard and dialect in some other European national languages are treated in Ammon and Fishman (1979) and for the historical standardization of French, see Lodge (1993). Trudgill (1984) *Language in the British Isles* contains useful articles on both the history and varieties of English in Britain and other British languages. For globalization and English as a world language, see Crystal (1997) and for descriptions of English throughout the world there is Trudgill and Hannah (1994) and Cheshire (1991). Stubbs (1986), *Educational Linguistics* discusses standard English from a teacher's point of view. The concept of 'anti-language' originates in Halliday (1978) and is discussed (with exercises) in ch. 5 of Montgomery (1986). For further reading on language change, see chapter seven below.

Chapter 3. Language varieties: processes and problems

This chapter used Canada as a case study of bilingualism, language maintenance and shift and language planning. General treatments of bilingualism are Romaine (1995 2nd edn.) and Hoffman (1991). Wardhaugh (1987) treats language conflict in *Languages in Competition*. Issues of ethnicity and identity in relation to language are introduced in Edwards (1985). The later work of Fishman (1989, 1991) is a prolonged reflection on ethnic identity and language planning, maintenance and shift. On Canada, detailed references are given in the chapter. A recent description of Canadian English is Chambers (1991, in Cheshire (ed.)) and of Canadian French, Blanc's article in Sanders (1993). The socio-politics of Canadian language conflict is treated in Fishman (1991) and Wardhaugh (1987). With respect to diglossia, Ferguson's (1959) article is a must and is easily available in Giglioli (1972). There are now extensive bibliographies on the topic construed broadly: by Alan Hudson (1992) in *Language and Society* 21 (also his article in Asher, 1994), and in Fernandez (1993). The best place to start a study of code-switching is Blom and Gumperz's article on Hemnesberget in Gumperz and Hymes (eds.) (1972). There has been much development since then. Blom and Gumperz's work has been criticized by Norwegian sociolinguists, see Trudgill (1995a). In particular, look at Heller (ed.) (1988). Eastman (ed.) (1992) has studies of urban code-switching from Africa, and Milroy and Muysken (eds.) (1995) has a section on grammatical constraints. Also see the research of Myers-Scotton (1993, 1993a).

Chapter 4. Discovering the structure in variation

Labov's methods are presented both in Labov's (1966) New York City study and in his *Sociolinguistic Patterns* (1972). His more recent field methods are in Labov (1984). For the methodology of investigating primary groups, see Blom and Gumperz (1972) and Labov *et al.* (1968). Milroy's original use of the social network methodology was published in Milroy (1987 2nd edn.) and she has provided a general, critical account of sociolinguistic method in Milroy (1987a). David Sankoff (1988) is a philosophically oriented contribution on sociolinguistic method in *Linguistics: The Cambridge Survey* (Newmeyer (ed.), 1988). See Romaine (1981) and Sankoff (1988a) on variable rules. For more on explanation in sociolinguistics, see chapter eleven below.

Chapter 5. Rhoticity

A definitive treatment of the accents of English is John Wells' (1982) three volume survey. Rhoticity is treated in volume 1, pages 212–20.

Besides the specific references made in the body of chapter five abc
there is a historically oriented discussion in Lass (1987: 94–5) *The Sha*
of English.

Chapter 6. At the intersection of social factors

Traditional dialectology mapped variation over geographical space. For
discussion and Trudgill's work see Chambers and Trudgill (1980: chs. 2,
7, 8 and 11) and Trudgill (1983) *On Dialect*, chs. 2, 3 and 4. The basic
text on social networks is L. Milroy (1987 2nd edn.). The uncritical use of
the sociological category of class has been criticized. A look at this issue
and the attempt to relate class and social network is found in Milroy and
Milroy (1992); see also the stimulating essays in Dittmar and Schlobinski
(1988). With regards style, social psychological approaches to language
are relevant – see further reading for chapter seven. For language and
gender, Coates' (1993 2nd edn.) textbook *Women, Men and Language* is a
good place to start. The critique of sociolinguistic methodology, including
the use of class, by Cameron and Coates is in Coates and Cameron (eds.)
(1988). Recent readers are Cameron (1990) and Mills (1995). For American Black English, there is Labov's (1972a) *Language in the Inner City*.
Another standard is Dillard (1972) and there is a summary chapter in
Dillard (1992). A fascinating book is Bailey, Maynor and Cukor-Avila
(1991) which includes transcriptions of early recordings of former slaves
with linguists' commentaries, but see Wald (1995). Aspects of Black
British English are described by Sutcliffe (1982), Edwards (1986) and
Sebba (1993).

Chapter 7. Change, meaning and acts of identity

There are some excellent introductions to historical linguistics.
Aitchison (1991 2nd edn.) in this series is reliable and accessible. Bynon
(1977) is more advanced and Lehmann (1992 3rd edn.) more traditional
in its coverage of the comparative method. For social factors, begin with
Aitchison, then Labov (1972) ch. 1 for his study of Martha's Vineyard.
Chapters 7 and 9 are also relevant. Labov (1980) and (1982a) present
later and more general views, the latter being a reassessment of the programmatic article by Weinreich, Labov and Herzog (1968), which began
modern studies of change in progress. Labov (1994 and forthcoming)
advertises a three volume study of *Principles of Linguistic Change* of which
vol. 1 on *Internal Factors* is available. James Milroy (1992) is an excellent
book on variation and change; ch. 6 deals with the actuation problem

.J on this, see also Milroy and Milroy (1985). Social psychological
.ork on attitudes to language and accommodation can be surveyed in
Giles (1994), Giles and Coupland (1991) and more broadly in Giles and
Robinson (1990). Acts of identity are discussed in LePage (1980) and
more fully in the broader context of LePage's work in Lepage and Tabouret-
Keller (1985).

Chapter 8. The discourse of social life

Levinson's *Pragmatics* (1983) contains an excellent overview of conversation analysis in chapter 6. From there, it is useful to look at some of
the original ethnomethodological analyses: Schegloff (1968), Schegloff
and Sacks (1973) and Sacks, Schegloff and Jefferson (1974). Garfinkel
(1967), a founder of ethnomethodology, and the posthumously published
Lectures on Conversation of Harvey Sacks (1994) are interesting background.
A sociological look at ethnomethodology is Sharrock and Anderson
(1986). On conversation, besides the various readers referred to in the
chapter are also Atkinson and Heritage (1984) and Boden and Zimmerman
(1991). For politeness, the original source is Brown and Levinson (1987
is a reissue of 1978, in Goody). Goffman's (1955) notion of 'face' is the
one employed and his sociology is of general interest for conversation
analysis. There is a bibliography on linguistic politeness by Dufon *et al.*
(1994) in the *Journal of Pragmatics* 21. Two recent discussions of the issue
in the same journal are Mao (1994) and O'Driscoll (1996). Saville-Troike
(1989 2nd edn.) is an introduction to the ethnography of communication. But it is useful to start with the essays of Hymes, especially (1972)
and (1977). Schiffrin (1994) has a good chapter on this approach. For
register and social semiotics M. A. K. Halliday is a must; for the latter see
also Hodge and Kress (1988). His conception of register has undergone
development. Halliday, McIntosh and Strevens (1964) and Gregory and
Carroll (1978) use earlier versions. In *Language as a Social Semiotic*, Halliday
(1978) integrates register into a comprehensive socio-functional model
(use his index). See also Ghadessy (ed.) (1993) and, for a non-Halliday
survey of work on register, Biber and Finegan (eds.) (1994). There is a
chapter on register from a literary linguistic point of view in Fowler (1996).

Chapter 9. Communication, words and world

Levinson (1983) is the basic textbook in pragmatics, but doesn't cover
relevance theory for which Sperber and Wilson (1995 2nd edn.) is the
basic source. (Contrast their theory of intentional communication with

that in Grice's 'Meaning', 1957; see also Schiffer, 1972.) Begin with Blakemore (1992) which introduces relevance theory in textbook form. An earlier precis of the theory by Sperber and Wilson followed by a critical discussion is in *Behavioral and Brain Sciences* 10 (1987), 697–754. But the best critique is Levinson's (1989) review. *Lingua* 87 (1992) is a special issue on relevance theory. The footnotes in the 2nd edn. of Sperber and Wilson are an excellent guide. For Quine on the 'analytic–synthetic distinction' see Quine (1953) and for 'holism', Quine (1960), ch. 2. Martin (1987), *The Meaning of Language* is an excellent simple introduction to the analytic philosophy of language. Fodor and LePore (1992) is about holism and its consequences, and for a radically different approach there is Dreyfus (1985). For cognitive science, see Johnson-Laird (1996) and Crane (1995). Haugeland's (1985) *Artifical Intelligence: The Very Idea* is a good introduction to AI and has a section of the 'frame problem'. Dennett (1996) discusses heuristic algorithms and formalization.

Chapter 10. Action and critique

For speech acts, begin with Searle (1969: ch. 3, reprinted in Giglioli, 1972), then Searle's 'Indirect Speech Acts' (1975). There is a good account in Levinson (1983). Speech act based discourse analysis can be seen in Labov and Fanshel (1977) and Sinclair and Coulthard (1975). Critiques are Levinson (1981) and Sperber and Wilson (1995: 243–54). For implicatures begin with Grice (1975) and then Sperber and Wilson (1995, esp. ch. 4). A very useful introduction to developments in social thought is Skinner (ed.) (1985), *The Return of Grand Theory in the Human Sciences*, especially the essays on Foucault, Althusser and Habermas. Held (1980) introduces Frankfurt school critical theory, and for Habermas see Skinner above and White (1995), *The Cambridge Companion to Habermas*. For critical linguistics, begin with Fowler's (1981) essay 'Linguistic Criticism' and then Fairclough (1989, 1995a). From a social theory perspective there is John B. Thompson (1984, 1990). Specific studies of power and control are Fowler *et al.* (1979) and more recently Sarangi and Slembrouck (1996).

Chapter 11. Language and social explanation

General studies in the philosophy of social explanation are Ryan (1970) and Hollis (1994). There are not many philosophical studies of sociolinguistic and pragmatic explanation but important overviews are Pateman (1987), Romaine (1984) and Sankoff (1988). A largely non-social approach to the explanation of change is Lass (1980). Contrast Lass with Labov's methodological stance and Lesley Milroy (1987, 1987a), Milroy and Milroy (1992) and Dittmar and Schlobinski (1988). My main source for teleological explanation is von Wright (1971). The intentional stance is discussed in Dennett (1979) and more broadly in Dennett (1996a), ch. 2. For consciousness, see Johnson-Laird (1993) and Jackendoff (1987). There is an interesting difference regarding consciousness between Dennett (1993) and Chalmers (1996). Dingwall (1988) surveys the evolution of communicative behaviour while Aitchison (1996) introduces the evolution of language; see also Pinker (1994) and Dennett (1996). I surveyed functional explanation in Downes (1994). A generative approach to functional explanation is Newmeyer (1991), while Givon (1995) begins with a general discussion. Chambers (1995) has a chapter on the adaptive significance of linguistic variation.

References

Abelson, R. (1973), 'The Structure of Belief Systems', in *Computer Models of Thought and Language*, R. C. Schank and K. M. Colby (eds.), San Francisco: W. H. Freeman and Company.

Ager, D. (1990), *Sociolinguistics and Contemporary French*, Cambridge: Cambridge University Press.

Aitchison, J. (1991 2nd edn.), *Language Change: Progress or Decay?*, Cambridge: Cambridge University Press.

 (1996), *The Seeds of Speech*, Cambridge: Cambridge University Press.

Althusser, L. (1977 2nd edn.), *Lenin and Philosophy and Other Essays*, trans. by Ben Brewster, London: NLB.

Ammon, U. and Fishman, J. (1979), *Dialect and Standard in Highly Industrialized Societies*, International Journal of the Sociology of Language.

Ammon, U., Dittmar, N. and Mattheier, K. (2 vols. 1987/8), *Socio-linguistics, An International Handbook of the Science of Language and Society*, Berlin: De Grutyer.

Anderson, B. (1991 2nd edn.), *Imagined Communities: Reflections on the Origin and Spread of Nationalism*, London: Verso.

Anscombe, G. E. M. (1957), *Intention*, Oxford: Basil Blackwell.

Anshen, F. (1975), 'Varied Objections to Various Variable Rules', in *Analyzing Variation in Language*, Papers from the Second Colloquium on New Ways of Analyzing Variation, R. W. Fasold and R. W. Shuy (eds.), Washington, DC: Georgetown University Press.

Asher, R. (1994) (ed.), *The Encyclopedia of Language and Linguistics, Volumes 1–12*, Oxford: Pergamon Press.

Atkinson, J. and Heritage, J. (1984) (eds.), *Structures of Social Action: Studies in Conversation Analysis*, Cambridge: Cambridge University Press.

Austin, J. (1962), *How to Do Things with Words*, The William James Lectures, 1955, Oxford: Clarendon Press.

467

ach, K. and Harnish, K. (1979), *Linguistics Communication and Speech Acts*, Cambridge, MA: MIT Press.

Bailey, B. (1965), 'Towards a New Perspective in Negro English Dialectology', in Wolfram and Clarke (1971).

(1966), *Jamaican Creole Syntax: A Transformational Approach*, Cambridge: Cambridge University Press.

Bailey, C.-J. (1973), *Variation and Linguistic Theory*, Arlington, VA: Center for Applied Linguistics.

Bailey, C.-J. and Maroldt, K. (1977), 'The French Lineage of English', in *Langues en Contact-Pidgins-Creoles-Languages in Contact*, J. M. Meisel (ed.), Tübingen: TBL Verlag Gunter Narr.

Bailey, G. and Maynor, N. (1987), 'Decreolization', *Language in Society* 16, 449–73.

(1989), 'The Divergence Controversy', *American Speech* 64, 1 (cited in Butters, 1989).

Bailey, G., Maynor, N. and Cukor-Avila, P. (1991) (eds.), *The Emergence of Black English: Text and Commentary*, Amsterdam: Benjamins.

Bailey, R. (1982), 'The English Language in Canada', in Bailey and Gorlach (1982).

Bailey, R. and Görlach, M. (1982) (eds.), *English as a World Language*, Ann Arbor: University of Michigan Press.

Barbour, S. and Stevenson, P. (1990), *Variation in German*, Cambridge: Cambridge University Press.

Baron-Cohen, S. (1995), *Mindblindness*, London: MIT Press.

Barthes, R. (1967), *Elements of Semiology*, trans. by A. Lavers and C. Smith, London: Jonathan Cape.

Bastarche, M. (1989), *Language Rights in Canada*, Montréal: Les Editions Yvon Blais.

Battye, A. and Hintze, M.-A. (1992), *The French Language Today*, London: Routledge.

Baugh, J. (1980), 'A Reexamination of the Black English Copula', in *Locating Language in Time and Space*, W. Labov (ed.), London: Academic Press.

Bauman, R. and Sherzer, J. (1974) (eds.), *Explorations in the Ethnography of Speaking*, Cambridge: Cambridge University Press.

de Beaugrande, R. and Dressler, W. (1981), *Introduction to Text Linguistics*, London: Longman.

Bechtel, W. and Abrahamson, A. (1991), *Connectionism and the Mind*, Oxford: Basil Blackwell.

Berger, M. (1980), 'New York City and the Antebellum South: The Maritime Connection', in *Perspectives on American English*, J. L. Dillard (ed.), The Hague: Mouton Publishers.

Berger, P. and Luckmann, T. (1971), *The Social Construction of Rea*ʲ Harmondsworth, Middlesex: Penguin Books.

Berk-Seligson, S. (1986), 'Linguistic Constraints on Intrasentential Code Switching: A Study of Spanish/Hebrew Bilingualism', *Language in Society* 15, 313–48.

Biber, D. and Finegan, E. (1994) (eds.), *Sociolinguistic Perspectives on Register*, Oxford: Oxford University Press.

Bickerton, D. (1971), 'Inherent Variability and Variable Rules', *Foundations of Language* 7, 457–92.

(1973), 'The Nature of a Creole Continuum', *Language* 49, 640–69.

Birch, D. and O'Toole, M. (1988) (eds.), *Functions of Style*, London: Pinter.

Blakemore, D. (1992), *Understanding Utterances*, Oxford: Blackwell.

Blanc, M. (1993), 'French in Canada', in Sanders (1993).

Bloch, B. (1939), 'Postvocalic *r* in New England Speech, a Study in American Dialect Geography', in *Readings in American Dialectology*, H. B. Allen and G. N. Underwood (eds.), New York: Appleton-Century-Crofts, 1971.

Blom, J.-P. and Gumperz, J. (1972), 'Social Meaning in Linguistic Structures: Code-Switching in Norway', in Gumperz and Hymes (1972).

Bloomfield, L. (1933), *Language*, London: George Allen and Unwin.

Bobrow, D. and Collins, A. (1975) (eds.), *Representation and Understanding*, London: Academic Press.

Boden, D. and Zimmerman, D. (1991) (eds.), *Talk and Social Structure*, Cambridge: Polity Press.

Boden, M. (1977), *Artificial Intelligence and Natural Man*, Hassocks: Harvester Press.

(1988), *Computer Models of Mind*, Cambridge: Cambridge University Press.

(1990), *The Philosophy of Artificial Intelligence*, Oxford: Oxford University Press.

Boissevain, J. (1974), *Friends of Friends: Networks, Manipulators and Coalitions*, Oxford: Basil Blackwell.

Bolton, K. and Kwok, H. (1992), *Sociolinguistics Today*, London and New York: Routledge.

Bott, E. (1971), *Family and Social Network: Roles, Norms, and External Relationships in Ordinary Urban Families*, London: Tavistock.

Bourhis, R. (1984) (ed.), *Conflict and Language Planning in Quebec*, Clevedon, Avon: Multilingual Matters 5.

(1984a), 'The Charter of the French Language and Cross-Cultural Communication in Montreal', in Bourhis (1984).

...thillier, G. and Meynaud, J. (1972), *Le choc des langues au Québec, 1760–1970*, Montréal: Les Presses de L'Université Du Québec.

Bradley, R. and Swartz, N. (1979), *Possible Worlds*, Oxford: Basil Blackwell.

Bronstein, A. (1960), *The Pronunciation of American English*, New York: Appleton-Century-Crofts.

Brown, G. and Yule, G. (1983), *Discourse Analysis*, Cambridge: Cambridge University Press.

Brown, P. and Levinson, S. (1987 2nd edn.), *Politeness*, Cambridge: Cambridge University Press. Previously published as Brown, P. and Levinson, S. (1978), 'Universals in Language Usage: Politeness Phenomenon', in E. Goody (ed.) *Questions and Politeness*, Cambridge: Cambridge University Press.

Brown, R. and Ford, M. (1961), 'Address in American English', in Laver and Hutcheson (1972).

Brown, R. and Gilman, A. (1960), 'The Pronouns of Power and Solidarity', in Laver and Hutcheson (1972).

Butters, R. (1989), *The Death of Black English*, New York and Frankfurt: Peter Lang.

Bynon, T. (1977), *Historical Linguistics*, Cambridge: Cambridge University Press.

Byrne, R. and Whitten, A. (1988) (eds.), *Machiavellian Intelligence*, Oxford: Clarendon Press.

Cameron, D. (1985), *Feminism and Linguistic Theory*, London: Macmillan. (1990) (ed.), *The Feminist Critique of Language*, London: Routledge.

Cameron, D. and Coates, J. (1988), 'Some Problems in the Sociolinguistic Explanation of Sex Differences', in Coates and Cameron (1988).

Cameron, D., Frazer, E., Harvey, P., Rampton, M. and Richardson, K. (1992), *Researching Language: Issues of Power and Method*, London: Routledge.

Campbell, L. (1994), 'Language Death', in Asher (1994), vol. 4.

Cartwright, D. (1987), 'Accommodation Among the Anglophone Minority in Quebec to Official Language Policy: A Shift in Traditional Patterns of Language Contact', *Journal of Multilingual and Multicultural Development* 8, 187–212.

(1988), 'Language Policy and Internal Geopolitics: the Canadian Situation', in *Language in Geographic Context*, C. Williams (ed.), Clevedon, Avon: Multilingual Matters.

Caudwell, G. (1982), 'Anglo-Quebec on the Verge of its History', *Language and Society* 8, 3–6, Ottawa: Office of the Commissioner of Official Languages.

(1984), 'Anglo-Quebec Demographic Realities and Options for the Future', in Bourhis (1984).

References

Census Canada 1986, R. Bourbeau, 'Canada, a Linguistic Profile', in
    on Canada, Statistics Canada Catalogue 98–131.

Census Canada 1991, 'Mother Tongue', Statistics Canada Catalogue ⁹
    313.

Chalmers, D. (1996), *The Conscious Mind*, New York: Oxford University
    Press.

Chambers, J. (1975) (ed.), *Canadian English, Origins and Structures*, Toronto:
    Methuen.

   (1979) (ed.), *The Languages of Canada*, Montreal: Didier.

   (1979a), 'Canadian English', in Chambers (1979).

   (1991), 'Canada', in Cheshire (1991).

   (1995), *Sociolinguistic Theory*, Oxford: Blackwell.

Chambers, J. and Trudgill, P. (1980), *Dialectology*, Cambridge: Cambridge
    University Press.

Cheshire, J. (1984), 'Indigenous Nonstandard Language Varieties and
    Education', in Trudgill (1984).

   (1991) (ed.), *English Around the World*, Cambridge: Cambridge University
    Press.

Chilton, P. (1985) (ed.), *Language and the Nuclear Arms Debate*, London:
    Pinter.

Chomsky, N. (1957), *Syntactic Structures*, The Hague: Mouton.

   (1965), *Aspects of the Theory of Syntax*, Cambridge, MA: MIT Press.

   (1980), *Rules and Representations*, Oxford: Basil Blackwell.

   (1986), *Knowledge of Language*, New York: Praeger.

Clark, H. (1977), 'Bridging', in Johnson-Laird and Wason (1977).

Clark, H. and Marshall, C. (1981), 'Definite Reference and Mutual
    Knowledge', in *Elements of Discourse Understanding*, A. K. Joshi, B. L.
    Webber and I. Sag (eds.), Cambridge: Cambridge University Press.

Coates, J. (1993 2nd edn.), *Women, Men and Language*, Harlow: Longman.

Coates, J. and Cameron, D. (1988) (eds.), *Women in their Speech
    Communities*, London: Longman.

Coleman, W. (1984), 'Social Class and Language Policies in Quebec', in
    Bourhis (1984).

Cook, V. and Newson, M. (1996 2nd edn.), *Chomsky's Universal Grammar*,
    Oxford: Blackwell.

Coulthard, M. (1985 2nd edn.), *An Introduction to Discourse Analysis*,
    London and New York: Longman.

Cox Report (1989), DES/WO *English for Ages 5–16*. London: HMSO.

Crane, T. (1995), *The Mechanical Mind*, Harmondsworth: Penguin Books.

Crystal, D. (1997), *English as a Global Language*, Cambridge: Cambridge
    University Press.

st, D. (1984), 'Francization and Terminology Change in Quebec Business Firms', in Bourhis (1984).

rnell, R. (1971) (ed.), *Linguistic Diversity in Canadian Society*, Edmonton, Alberta, and Champaign, IL: Linguistic Research Inc.

Davidson, D. (1980), *Essays on Actions and Events*, Oxford: Clarendon Press.

Denis, W. and Li, P. (1988), 'The Politics of Language Loss: A Francophone Case From Western Canada', *Journal of Education Policy* 3, 4, 351–70.

Denison, N. (1972), 'Some Observations on Language Variety and Plurilingualism', in Pride and Holmes (1972).

Dennett, D. (1979), *Brainstorms*, Hassocks, Sussex: Harvester Press.

(1984), 'Cognitive Wheels: The Frame Problem of AI', in *Minds, Machines and Evolution*, C. Hookway (ed.), Cambridge: Cambridge University Press, also in Boden (1990).

(1987), *The Intentional Stance*, Cambridge, MA: MIT Press.

(1993), *Consciousness Explained*. Harmondsworth: Penguin Books.

(1996), *Darwin's Dangerous Idea*, Harmondsworth: Penguin Books.

(1996a), *Kinds of Minds*, London: Weidenfeld and Nicolson.

Deuchar, A. (1988), 'A Pragmatic Account of Women's Use of Standard Speech', in Coates and Cameron (1988).

Dillard, J. (1972), *Black English*, New York: Random House.

(1975) (ed.), *Perspectives on Black English*, The Hague: Mouton.

(1992), *A History of American English*, Harlow, Essex: Longman.

Dingwall, W. (1988), 'The Evolution of Human Communicative Behavior', in Newmeyer (1988), vol. 3.

Dirven, R. and Fried, V. (1987) (eds.), *Functionalism in Linguistics*, Amsterdam: J. Benjamins.

Dittmar, N. and Schlobinski, P. (1988) (eds.), *The Sociolinguistics of Urban Vernaculars*, Berlin and New York: Walter de Gruyter.

Dittmar, N., Schlobinski, P. and Wachs, I. (1988), 'The Social Significance of the Berlin Urban Vernacular', in Dittmar and Schlobinski (1988).

Dorian, N. (1973), 'Grammatical Change in a Dying Dialect', *Language* 49, 413–38.

(1981), *Language Death: The Life Cycle of a Scottish Gaelic Dialect*, Philadelphia: University of Pennsylvania Press.

(1989), *Investigating Obsolescence: Studies in Language Contraction and Death*, Cambridge: Cambridge University Press.

Downes, W. (1977), 'The Imperative and Pragmatics', *Journal of Linguistics* 13, 77–97.

(1988), 'Discourse and Drama', in *The Taming of the Text*, W. van Peer (ed.), London: Routledge.

(1991), 'Language and Interpretation: Paul Robeson Before the Hou⸱ Committee on Un-American Activities', in *Language, Class and History*, P. Corfield (ed.), Oxford: Basil Blackwell.

(1994), 'Functional Explanations', in Asher (1994), vol. 1, 314–17.

Dressler, W. (1988), 'Language Death', in Newmeyer (1988) vol. 4.

Dreyfus, H. (1985), 'Holism and Hermeneutics', in *Hermeneutics and Praxis*, R. Hollinger (ed.), Notre Dame, IN: Notre Dame University Press.

(1992 2nd edn.), *What Computers Still Can't Do*, Cambridge, MA: MIT Press.

Dufon, M., Kasper, G., Takahashi, S. and Yoshinaga, N. (1994), 'Bibliography on Linguistic Politeness', *Journal of Pragmatics* 21, 527–78.

Dunbar, R. (1997), *Grooming, Gossip and the Evolution of Language*, London: Faber.

Durkheim, E. (1938), *The Rules of Sociological Method*, G. E. Catlin (ed.), translated by S. A. Solovay and J. H. Mueller, New York: The Free Press, Macmillan, 1964 (8th edn.).

Eastmam, C. (1992) (ed.), *Codeswitching*, Clevedon, Avon: Multilingual Matters; also in *The Journal of Multilingual and Multicultural Development* 13, 1–2, 1992.

Eco, U. (1976), *A Theory of Semiotics*, Bloomington: Indiana University Press.

Edwards, J. (1985), *Language, Society and Identity*, Oxford: Basil Blackwell.

Edwards, V. (1984), 'British Black English and Education', in Trudgill (1984).

(1986), *Language in a Black Community*, Clevedon, Avon: Multilingual Matters.

Elyan, O., Smith, P., Giles, H. and Bourhis, R. (1978), 'RP-Accented Female Speech: the Voice of Perceived Androgyny?', in Trudgill (1978).

Engel, W. V-R. (1979), 'The Language of Immigrant Children', in Chambers (1979).

Fabian, J. (1983), *Time and the Other: How Anthropology Makes its Object*, New York: Columbia University Press.

Fairclough, N. (1989), *Language and Power*, Harlow, Essex: Longman.

(1992), *Discourse and Social Change*, Cambridge: Polity Press.

(1995), *Media Discourse*, London: Edward Arnold.

(1995a), *Critical Discourse Analysis*, London: Longman.

Fasold, R. (1969), 'Tense and the Form *be* in Black English', *Language* 45, 763–76.

(1970), 'Two Models of Socially Significant Linguistic Variation', *Language* 46, 551–63.

(1972), *Tense Marking in Black English*, Arlington, VA: Center for Applied Linguistics.

(1975), 'The Bailey Wave Model: A Dynamic Quantitative Paradigm', in *Analyzing Variation in Language*, Papers from the Second Colloquium on New Ways of Analyzing Variation, R. W. Fasold and R. W. Shuy (eds.), Washington, DC: Georgetown University Press.

(1984), *The Sociolinguistics of Society*, Oxford: Blackwell.

(1990), *The Sociolinguistics of Language*, Oxford: Blackwell.

Ferguson, C. (1959), 'Diglossia', *Word* 15, 325–40; also in Giglioli (1972).

(1970), 'The Role of Arabic in Ethiopia, a Sociolinguistic Perspective', in Pride and Holmes (1972).

Fernandez, M. (1993), *Diglossia: A Comprehensive Bibliography 1960–1990*, Amsterdam: John Benjamins.

Firbas, J. (1964), 'On Defining the Theme in Functional Sentence Analysis' *Travaux Linguistiques de Prague* 1, 267–80, updated version in Dirven and Fried (1987).

Firth, J. R. (1950), 'Personality and Language in Society', in J. R. Firth, *Papers in Linguistics 1934–1951*, London: Oxford University Press.

(1951), 'Modes of Meaning', in J. R. Firth, *Papers in Linguistics 1934–1951*, London: Oxford University Press.

(1957), 'A Synopsis of Linguistic Theory', in *Selected Papers of J. R. Firth 1952–59*, F. Palmer (ed.), London: Longmans.

Fischer, J. (1958), 'Social Influences in the Choice of a Linguistic Variant', *Word* 14, 47–56.

Fishman, J. (1968) (ed.), *Readings in the Sociology of Language*, The Hague: Mouton.

(1971), 'The Relationship Between Micro- and Macro-Sociolinguistics in the Study of Who Speaks What Language to Whom and When', in Pride and Holmes (1972).

(1972), *The Sociology of Language*, Rowley, MA: Newbury House.

(1989), *Language and Ethnicity in Minority Sociolinguistic Perspective*, Clevedon, Avon: Multilingual Matters 45.

(1991), *Reversing Language Shift*, Clevedon, Avon: Multilingual Matters 76.

Fodor, J. (1983), *The Modularity of Mind*, Cambridge, Massachusetts: MIT Press.

Fodor, J. and LePore, E. (1992), *Holism: A Shopper's Guide*, Oxford: Basil Blackwell.

Foley, W. (1988), 'Language Birth: The Process of Pidginization and Creolization', in Newmeyer (1988), vol. 4.

Foley, W. and Van Valin, R. (1984), *Functional Syntax and Unive Grammar*, Cambridge: Cambridge University Press.

Foster, M. (1982), 'Canada's First Languages', *Language and Society* 7, 7 16, Ottawa: Office of the Commissioner of Official Languages.

Fowler, R. (1981), 'Linguistic Criticism', in *Literature as Social Discourse*, London: Batsford.

  (1991), *Language in the News*, London: Routledge.

  (1996 2nd edn.), *Linguistic Criticism*, Oxford: Oxford University Press.

Fowler, R., Hodge, B., Kress, G. and Trew, T. (1979), *Language and Control*, London: Routledge and Kegan Paul.

Frake, C. (1969), '"Struck by speech": The Yakan Concept of Litigation', in Gumperz and Hymes (1972).

  (1975), 'How to Enter a Yakan House', in Sanches and Blount (1975), also in Frake (1980).

  (1980), *Language and Cultural Description*, essays selected and introduced by A. S. Dil, Stanford: Stanford University Press.

Fraser, C. and Scherer, K. (1982) (eds.), *Advances in the Social Psychology of Language*, Cambridge: Cambridge University Press.

Gagné, R. (1979), 'The Maintenance of the Native Languages', in Chambers (1979).

Garfinkel, H. (1967), *Studies in Ethnomethodology*, Englewood Cliffs, NJ: Prentice-Hall.

Gazdar, G. (1979), *Pragmatics*, London: Academic Press.

  (1981), 'Speech Act Assignment', in *Elements of Discourse Understanding*, A. K. Joshi, B. L. Webber and I. Sag (eds.), Cambridge: Cambridge University Press.

Gazdar, G. and Good, D. (1982), 'On a Notion of Relevance', in Smith (1982).

Geertz, C. (1960), 'Linguistic Etiquette', excerpt from C. Geertz, *The Religion of Java*, Glencoe, IL: The Free Press, in Pride and Holmes (1972).

Gentner, D. (1982), 'Are Scientific Analogies Metaphors?', in *Metaphor: Problems and Perspectives*, D. Miall (ed.), Brighton: Harvester.

Ghadessy, M. (1993) (ed.), *Register Analysis*, London: Pinter.

Giddens, A. (1976), *New Rules of Sociological Method: A Positive Critique of Interpretive Sociologies*, London: Hutchinson.

  (1985), 'Jürgen Habermas', in Skinner (1985).

Giddens, A. and Turner, J. (1987) (eds.), *Social Theory Today*, Cambridge: Polity.

Giglioli, P.-P. (1972) (ed.), *Language and Social Context*, Harmondsworth: Penguin.

Giles, H. (1970), 'Evaluative Reactions to Accents', *Educational Review* 22, 211–27.

971), 'Patterns of Evaluation in Reactions to RP, South Welsh and Somerset Accented Speech', *British Journal of Social and Clinical Psychology* 10, 280–1.

(1977) (ed.), *Language, Ethnicity and Intergroup Relations*, New York: Academic Press.

(1980), 'Accommodation Theory: Some New Directions', in *York Papers in Linguistics, 9, Festschrift R. B. LePage*, M. W. S. de Silva (ed.), York: Department of Language, University of York.

(1994), 'Accommodation in Communication', in Asher (1994).

Giles, H. and Coupland, N. (1991), *Language: Contexts and Consequences*, Milton Keynes: Open University.

Giles, H. and Powesland, P. (1975), *Speech Style and Social Evaluation*, London: Academic Press.

Giles, H. and Robinson, W. (1990) (eds.), *Handbook of Language and Social Psychology*, Chichester and New York: John Wiley.

Giles, H. and Ryan, E. (1982), 'Prologomena For Developing a Social Psychological Theory of Language Attitudes', in Ryan and Giles (1982).

Gimson, A. C. (1962), *An Introduction to the Pronunciation of English*, London: Edward Arnold.

Givon, T. (1979) (ed.), *Syntax and Semantics*, volume 12, *Discourse and Syntax*, London: Edward Arnold.

(1995), *Functionalism and Grammar*, Amsterdam: J. Benjamins.

Goffman, E. (1955), 'On Face-Work: An Analysis of Ritual Elements in Social Interaction', in Laver and Hutcheson (1972).

(1967), *Interaction Ritual*, New York: Doubleday.

Graddol, D., Leith, D. and Swan, J. (1996), *English: History, Diversity and Change*, London and New York: Routledge in association with The Open University.

Gregory, M. (1967), 'Aspects of Varieties Differentiation', *Journal of Linguistics*, 3, 177–98.

Gregory, M. and Carroll, S. (1978), *Language and Situation*, London: Routledge and Kegan Paul.

Grice, H. P. (1957), 'Meaning', *Philosophical Review*, LXVI, 3, 377–88, reprinted in *Readings in the Philosophy of Language*, J. Rosenberg and C. Travis (eds.), Englewood Cliffs, NJ: Prentice-Hall, 1971.

(1975), 'Logic and Conversation', in *Syntax and Semantics*, volume 3, *Speech Acts*, P. Cole and J. Morgan (eds.), London: Academic Press.

Grice, H. P. and Strawson, P. (1956), 'In Defense of a Dogma', in *Readings in the Philosophy of Language*, J. Rosenberg and C. Travis (eds.), Englewood Cliffs, NJ: Prentice-Hall, 1971.

Grossman, R., San, L. and Vance, T. (1975) (eds.), *Papers from the Para* sion on Functionalism, Chicago: Chicago Linguistic Society.

Gumperz, J. (1975), 'Foreword' to Sanches and Blount (1975).

(1982), *Discourse Strategies*, Cambridge: Cambridge University Press.

Gumperz, J. and Hymes, D. (1972), *Directions in Sociolinguistics*, New York: Holt, Rinehart and Winston.

Gutting, G. (1994) (ed.), *The Cambridge Companion to Foucault*, Cambridge: Cambridge University Press.

Guy, G. (1980), 'Variation in the Group and the Individual: The Case of Final Stop Deletion', in *Locating Language in Time and Space*, W. Labov (ed.), New York: Academic Press.

Habermas, J. (1971), *Knowledge and Human Interests*, trans. J. Shapiro, London: Heinemann.

Halliday, M. (1967/1968), 'Notes on Transitivity and Theme in English', *Journal of Linguistics* 3, 37–81, 199–244, and *Journal of Linguistics* 4, 179–215.

(1968), 'Syntax and the Consumer', in *Georgetown University Round Table Selected Papers on Linguistics 1961–1965*, Washington, DC: Georgetown University Press.

(1970), 'Language Structure and Language Function', in *New Horizons in Linguistics*, J. Lyons (ed.), Harmondsworth: Penguin Books.

(1973), 'Linguistic Function and Literary Style: An Inquiry into the Language of William Golding's *The Inheritors*' in *Explorations in the Functions of Language*, M. Halliday, London: Edward Arnold, reprinted in *The Stylistics Reader* (1996) J-J. Weber, (ed.), London: Edward Arnold.

(1978), *Language and Social Semiotic*, London: Edward Arnold.

(1994 2nd edn.), *An Introduction to Functional Grammar*, London: Edward Arnold.

Halliday, M., McIntosh, A. and Strevens, P. (1964), *The Linguistic Sciences and Language Teaching*, London: Longmans; 'The Users and Uses of Language', reprinted in Fishman (1968).

Hamblin, C. (1971), 'Mathematical Models of Dialogue', *Theoria* 37, 130–55.

Hancock, I. (1977), 'Appendix: Repertory of Pidgin and Creole Languages', in *Pidgin and Creole Linguistics*, A. Valdman (ed.), Bloomington: Indiana University Press.

(1984), 'Romani and Angloromani', in Trudgill (1984).

Harré, R. (1985), *The Philosophies of Science*, Oxford: Oxford University Press.

Haugeland, J. (1985), *Artificial Intelligence: The Very Idea*, Cambridge, MA: MIT Press.

~agen, E. (1966), 'Dialect, Language, Nation', in Pride and Holmes (1972).

(1967), 'Semicommunication: The Language Gap in Scandinavia', in *Explorations in Sociolinguistics*, S. Lieberson (ed.), The Hague: Mouton.

(1968), 'Schizoglossia and the Linguistic Norm', in *Georgetown University Round Table Selected Papers on Linguistics*, R. O'Brien (ed.), Washington, DC: Georgetown University Press.

Hawkes, T. (1977), *Structuralism and Semiotics*, London: Methuen.

Held, D. (1980), *Introduction to Critical Theory*, Cambridge: Polity Press.

Heller, M. (1988) (ed.), *Code-Switching: Anthropological and Sociological Perspectives*, Berlin: Mouton de Gruyter.

(1988a), 'Strategic Ambiguity: Code-Switching in the Management of Conflict', in Heller (1988).

Hesse, M. (1980), *Revolutions and Reconstructions in the Philosphy of Science*, Brighton: Harvester Press.

Hill, A. (1940), 'Early Loss of [r] Before Dentals', *Publications of the Modern Language Association* 55, 308–21, reprinted in Williamson and Burke (1971).

Hintikka, J. (1962), *Knowledge and Belief*, Ithaca, NY: Cornell University Press.

Hodge, R. and Kress, G. (1988), *Social Semiotics*, Cambridge: Polity Press.

Hoffman, C. (1991), *An Introduction to Bilingualism*, Harlow, Essex: Longman.

Hollinger, R. (1994), *Postmodernism and the Social Sciences*, London: Sage Publications.

Hollis, M. (1994), *The Philosophy of Social Science*, Cambridge: Cambridge University Press.

Holmes, J. (1992), *An Introduction to Sociolinguistics*, London: Longman.

Hudson, A. (1992), 'Diglossia: A Bibliographic Review', *Language in Society* 21, 611–74.

Hudson, R. (1975), 'The Meaning of Questions', *Language* 51, 1–31.

(1996 2nd edn.), *Sociolinguistics*, Cambridge: Cambridge University Press.

Hughes, A. and Trudgill, P. (1979), *English Accents and Dialects*, London: Edward Arnold.

Hung, H., Davison, J. and Chambers, J. (1993), 'Comparative Sociolinguistics of (aw)-Fronting', in *Focus on Canada*, S. Clarke (ed.), Amsterdam and Philadelphia: John Benjamins.

Hymes, D. (1962), 'The Ethnography of Speaking', in *Readings in the Sociology of Language*, J. Fishman (ed.), The Hague: Mouton, 1968.

(1964), 'Introduction: Toward Ethnographies of Communication', in *The Ethnography of Communication*, J. Gumperz and D. Hymes (eds.), *American Anthropologist* 66, 6, part II, 1–34.

(1972), 'Models of the Interaction of Language and Social Life
Gumperz and Hymes (1972).

(1977), *Foundations in Sociolinguistics*, London: Tavistock Publication

Ignatieff, M. (1994), *Blood and Belonging: Journeys into the New Nationalism*,
London: BBC Books/Chatto and Windus.

Jackendoff, R. (1987), *Consciousness and the Computational Mind*, London:
MIT Press.

Jesperson, O. (1954), *A Modern English Grammar on Historical Principles*,
Part I, *Sounds and Spellings*, London: George Allen and Unwin.

Johnson-Laird, P. (1983), *Mental Models*, Cambridge: Cambridge University
Press.

(1993 2nd edn.), *The Computer and the Mind*, London: Fontana.

Johnson-Laird, P. and Wason, P. (1977) (eds.), *Thinking: Readings in
Cognitive Science*, Cambridge: Cambridge University Press.

Judge, A. (1993), 'French: A Planned Language?', in Sanders (1993).

Karttunen, L. and Peters, S. (1979), 'Conventional Implicature', in *Syntax
and Semantics*, volume 2, *Presupposition*, C.-K. Oh and D. Dineen (eds.),
London: Academic Press.

Kaye, J. (1979), 'The Indian Languages of Canada', in Chambers (1979).

Kenny, A. (1973), *Wittgenstein*, Harmondsworth: Penguin Books.

Kim, J. (1976), 'Intention and Practical Inference', in Manninen and
Tuomela (1976).

Klein, A. M. (1948), 'Montreal', stanza IV, in *The Rocking Chair and Other
Poems*, Toronto: The Ryerson Press.

Kress, G. (1988), 'Textual Matters: The Social Effectiveness of Style', in
Birch and O'Toole (1988).

Kurath, H. (1965), 'Some Aspects of Atlantic Seaboard English Considered
in Their Connection with British English', in Williamson and Burke
(1971).

Labov, W. (1963), 'The Social Motivation of a Sound Change', *Word* 19,
273–309, reprinted in Labov (1972).

(1966), *The Social Stratification of English in New York City*, Washington,
DC: Center for Applied Linguistics.

(1967), 'The Effect of Social Mobility on Linguistic Behaviour', in
Explorations in Sociolinguistics, S. Lieberson (ed.), The Hague: Mouton;
also in Williamson and Burke (1971).

(1971), 'Methodology', in *A Survey of Linguistic Science*, W. O. Dingwall
(ed.), Linguistics Program, University of Maryland.

(1972), *Sociolinguistic Patterns*, Philadelphia: University of Pennsylvania
Press.

(1972a), *Language in the Inner City*, Philadelphia: University of Philadelphia Press.

References

974), 'Linguistic Change as a Form of Communication', in *Human Communication: Theoretical Explorations*, A. Silverstein (ed.), Hillsdale, NJ: Lawrence Erlbaum Associates.

(1975), 'Empirical Foundations of Linguistic Theory', in *The Scope of American Linguistics*, R. Austerlitz (ed.), Lisse: The Peter de Ridder Press.

(1980), 'The Social Origins of Sound Change', in *Locating Language in Time and Space*, W. Labov (ed.), London: Academic Press.

(1982), 'Objectivity and Commitment in Linguistic Science: The Case of the Black English Trial in Ann Arbor', *Language and Society* 11, 165–201.

(1982a), 'Building on Empirical Foundations', in *Perspectives in Historical Linguistics*, W. Lehmann and Y. Malkiel (eds.), Amsterdam: Benjamins.

(1984), 'Field Methods of the Project on Linguistic Change and Variation', in *Language in Use: Readings in Sociolinguistics*, J. Baugh and J. Sherzer (eds.), Englewood Cliffs, NJ: Prentice-Hall.

(1994), *Principles of Linguistic Change, Vol. 1: Internal Factors*, Oxford: Basil Blackwell.

Labov, W., Cohen, P., Robins, C. and Lewis, J. (1968), *A Study of the Non-Standard English of Negro and Puerto Rican Speakers in New York City*, Report on Co-operative Research Project 3288, New York: Columbia University Press.

Labov, W. and Fanshel, D. (1977), *Therapeutic Discourse*, London: Academic Press.

Laferriere, M. (1979), 'Ethnicity in Phonological Variation and Change', *Language* 55, 603–17.

LaFrenière, P. (1988), 'The Ontogeny of Tactical Deception in Humans', in Byrne and Whiten (1988).

Lambert, W. (1967), 'A Social Psychology of Bilingualism', in Pride and Holmes (1972).

Laporte, P. (1984), 'Status Language Planning in Quebec: An Evaluation', in Bourhis (1984).

Lass, R. (1980), *On Explaining Language Change*, Cambridge: Cambridge University Press.

(1987), *The Shape of English*, London: Dent.

Laver, J. and Hutcheson, S. (1972) (eds.), *Communication in Face to Face Interaction*, Harmondsworth: Penguin Books.

Lehmann, W. (1992 3rd edn.), *Historical Linguistics: An Introduction*, London: Routledge.

LePage, R. (1980), 'Projection, Focussing, Diffusion', in *York Papers in Linguistics 9, Festschrift R. B. LePage*, M. W. S. DeSilva (ed.), York: Department of Language, University of York

LePage, R. and Tabouret-Keller, A. (1985), *Acts of Identity*, Cambric. Cambridge University Press.

Levine, L. and Crockett, H. (1966), 'Speech Variations in a Piedmon. Community', in *Explorations in Sociolinguistics*, S. Lieberson (ed.), Bloomington: Indiana University, and the Hague: Mouton; also in Williamson and Burke (1971).

Levinson, S. (1981), 'The Essential Inadequacies of Speech Act Models of Dialogue', in *Possibilities and Limitations of Pragmatics*, H. Parret, M. Sbisa and J. Verschueren (eds.), Amsterdam: Benjamins.

(1983), *Pragmatics*, Cambridge: Cambridge University Press.

(1989), 'A Review of Relevance', *Journal of Linguistics* 25, 455–72.

Lewis, D. (1969), *Convention*, Cambridge, MA: Harvard University Press.

Lieberson, S. (1965), 'Bilingualism in Montreal: A Demographic Analysis', *American Journal of Sociology* 71, 10–25; also in Lieberson (1981).

(1970), *Language and Ethnic Relations in Canada*, New York: Wiley.

(1970a), 'Linguistic and Ethnic Segregation in Montreal', in *International Days of Sociolinguistics*, Second International Congress of Social Sciences of the Luigi Sturzo Institute, Rome: Luigi Sturzo Institute; also in Lieberson (1981).

(1981), *Language Diversity and Language Contact*, selected by A. S. Dil, Stanford: Stanford University Press.

Lightfoot, D. (1979), *Principles of Diachronic Syntax*, Cambridge: Cambridge University Press.

Lodge, R. (1993), *French: From Dialect to Standard*, London: Routledge.

Lyons, J. (1977), *Semantics, Vol. 2*, Cambridge: Cambridge University Press.

MacDonald, G. and Pettit, P. (1981), *Semantics and Social Science*, London: Routledge and Kegan Paul.

Malinowski, B. (1923), 'The Problem of Meaning in Primitive Languages', Supplement I to C. K. Ogden and I. A. Richards, *The Meaning of Meaning*, London: Kegan Paul, Trench, Trubner and Co., 1945 (7th edn.).

Mallea, J. (1984), 'Minority Language Education in Quebec and Anglophone Canada', in Bourhis (1984).

Manninen, J. and Tuomela, R. (1976) (eds.), *Essays on Explanation and Understanding*, Synthese Library 72, Dordrecht, Holland: D. Reidel.

Mao, L. (1994), 'Beyond Politeness Theory: "Face" Revised and Renewed', *Journal of Pragmatics* 21, 451–86.

Mar-Molinero, C. (1997), *The Spanish-Speaking World*, London: Routledge.

Martin, R. (1987), *The Meaning of Language*, Cambridge, MA: MIT Press.

McDavid, R. (1947), 'Postvocalic -r in South Carolina: A Social Analysis', in *Language in Culture and Society*, D. Hymes (ed.), New York: Harper and Row, 1966.

1975), 'The Urbanization of American English', in R. McDavid, *Varieties of American English*, Stanford: Stanford University Press, 1980.

McDavid, R. and O'Cain, R. (1977), 'Southern Standards Revisited', in Shores and Hines (1977).

McDermott, D. (1987), 'A Critique of Pure Reason', *Computational Intelligence* 3, 151–60, also in Boden (1990).

Mencken, H. L. (1919), *The American Language*, New York: Alfred A. Knopf, 1980, 4th edition.

Metzing, D. (1980) (ed.), *Frame Conceptions and Text Understanding*, Berlin: de Gruyter.

Mey, J. (1993), *Pragmatics*, Oxford: Blackwell.

Mills, S. (1995), *Language and Gender: Interdisciplinary Perspectives*, London: Longmans.

Milroy, J. (1984), 'The History of English in the British Isles', in Trudgill (1984).

(1992), *Linguistic Variation and Change*, Oxford: Basil Blackwell.

Milroy, J. and Milroy, L. (1978), 'Belfast: Change and Variation in an Urban Vernacular', in Trudgill (1978).

(1985) 'Linguistic Change, Social Network and Speaker Innovation', *Journal of Linguistics* 21, 339–84.

(1991 2nd edn.), *Authority in Language*, London: Routledge.

(1993), 'Mechanisms of Change in Urban Dialects: The Role of Class, Social Network and Gender', *International Journal of Applied Linguistics* 3, 57–78.

Milroy, L. (1987 2nd edn.), *Language and Social Networks*, Oxford: Basil Blackwell.

(1987a), *Observing and Analyzing Natural Language*, Oxford: Basil Blackwell.

Milroy, L. and Margrain, S. (1980), 'Vernacular Language Loyalty and Social Network', *Language and Society* 9, 43–70.

Milroy, L. and Milroy, J. (1992), 'Social Network and Social Class: Toward an Integrated Sociolinguisitic Model', *Language in Society* 21, 1–26.

Milroy, L. and Muysken, P. (1995) (eds.), *One Speaker, Two Languages*, Cambridge: Cambridge University Press.

Minsky, M. (1975), 'A Framework for Representing Knowledge', in *The Psychology of Computer Vision*, P. H. Winston (ed.), New York: McGraw-Hill, see also Johnson-Laird and Wason (1977) for shortened version under different title.

Mitchell, R. (1994), 'Diversity or Uniformity? Language "Standards" and the English Teacher in the 1990s', *Modern English Teacher, MET*, 3, 7–13.

Mitchell-Kernan, C. (1972), 'Signifying and Marking: Two Afro-American Speech Acts', in Gumperz and Hymes (1972).

Montgomery, M. (1995 2nd edn.), *An Introduction to Language and Soci* London and New York: Routledge.

Mougeon, R. and Beniak, E. (1989), 'Language Contraction and Linguistic Change: The Case of Welland French', in Dorian (1989).

  (1991), *Linguistic Consequences of Language Contact and Restriction*, Oxford: Clarendon Press.

Mühlhaüsler, P. (1986), *Pidgin and Creole Linguistics*, Oxford: Basil Blackwell.

Muysken, P. (1988), 'Are Creoles a Special Type of Language?', in Newmeyer (1988), vol. 2.

Myers-Scotton, C. (1988), 'Code-Switching as Indexical of Social Negotiations', in Heller (1988).

  (1993), *Social Motivations for Codeswitching*, Oxford: Clarendon Press.

  (1993a), *Duelling Languages: Grammatical Structure in Codeswitching*, Oxford: Clarendon Press.

Myhill, J. (1988), 'Postvocalic /r/ as an Index of Integration into the BEV Speech Community', *American Speech* 63, 203–13.

Newmeyer, F. (1988) (ed.), *Linguistics: The Cambridge Survey, Volumes 1–4*, Cambridge: Cambridge University Press.

  (1991), 'Functional Explanation in Linguistics and the Origins of Language', *Language and Communication* 11, 1/2, 3–28.

O'Driscoll, J. (1996), 'About Face: A Defence and Elaboration of Universal Dualism', *Journal of Pragmatics* 25, 1–32.

Parslow, R. (1971), 'The Pronunciation of English in Boston, Massachusetts: Vowels and Consonants', in Williamson and Burke (1971).

Parsons, T. (1951), *The Social System*, Glencoe, IL: The Free Press.

Pateman, T. (1987), *Language in Mind and Language in Society*, Oxford: Clarendon.

Pellowe, J. and Jones, V. (1978), 'On Intonational Variability in Tyneside Speech', in Trudgill (1978).

Pfaff, C. (1976), 'Functional and Structural Constraints on Syntactic Variation in Code-Switching', in *Papers from the Parasession on Diachronic Syntax*, B. Steever *et al.* (eds.), Chicago: Chicago Linguistic Society, 248–59.

  (1979), 'Constraints on Language Mixing: Intrasentential Code-Switching and Borrowing in Spanish/English', *Language* 55, 2, 291–318.

Pinker, S. (1994), *The Language Instinct*, Harmondsworth: Penguin.

Pinker, S. and Mehler, J. (1988) (eds.), *Connections and Symbols*, Special Issue of *Cognition*, Cambridge, MA and London: MIT Press.

Pomerantz, A. (1978), 'Compliment Responses: Notes on the Co-operation of Multiple Constraints', in *Studies in the Organization of Conversational Interaction*, J. Schenkein (ed.), London: Academic Press.

Poplack, S. (1980), 'Sometimes I'll Start a Sentence in English Y Termino En Espagñol: Towards a Typology of Code-Switching', *Linguistics* 18, 581–618.

—— (1981), 'Syntactic Structure and Social Function of Code-Switching', in *Latino Language and Communicative Behavior*, R. Duran (ed.), Norwood, NJ: Ablex.

—— (1988), 'Contrasting Patterns of Code-Switching in Two Communities', in Heller (1988).

Popper, K. (1957), *The Poverty of Historicism*, London: Routledge and Kegan Paul.

Pride, J. and Holmes, J. (1972) (eds.), *Sociolinguistics*, Harmondsworth: Penguin Books.

Putnam, H. (1962), 'The Analytic and the Synthetic', in *Readings in the Philosophy of Language*, J. Rosenberg and C. Travis (eds.), Englewood Cliffs, NJ: Prentice-Hall.

—— (1970), 'Is Semantics Possible?', *Metaphilosophy* 1, 187–201.

—— (1975), 'The Meaning of "Meaning"', in *Minnesota Studies in the Philosophy of Science*, Volume 7, K. Gunderson (ed.), Minneapolis: University of Minnesota Press.

Quine, W. (1953), *From a Logical Point of View*, New York: Harper Torchbooks.

—— (1953a), 'Two Dogmas of Empiricism', in Quine (1953).

—— (1960), *Word and Object*, Cambridge, MA: MIT Press.

Quirk, R. (1968 2nd edn.), *The Use of English*, London: Longman.

Reber, A. (1993), *Implicit Learning and Tacit Knowledge*, Oxford: Oxford University Press.

Richardson, K. (1987), 'Critical Linguistics and Textual Diagnosis', *Text* 7, 145–63.

Richler, M. (1992), *Oh Canada! Oh Quebec!*, London: Chatto.

Rickford, J. (1977), 'The Question of Prior Creolization in Black English', in *Pidgin and Creole Linguistics*, A. Valdman (ed.), Bloomington: Indiana University Press.

—— (1986), 'The Need for New Approaches to Social Class Analysis in Linguistics', *Language and Communication* 6, 3: 215–21.

Robins, R. (1971), 'Malinowski, Firth, and the Context of Situation', in *Social Anthropology and Language*, E. Ardener (ed.), London: Tavistock Publications.

Romaine, S. (1981), 'The Status of Variable Rules in Sociolinguistic Theory', *Journal of Linguistics* 17, 93–119.

—— (1982), *Socio-Historical Linguistics*, Cambridge: Cambridge University Press.

References

(1984), 'The Status of Sociological Models and Categories in Expla
Language Variation', *Linguistische Berichte* 90, 25–37.

(1988), *Pidgin and Creole Languages*, London: Longman.

(1994), *Language in Society*, Oxford: Oxford University Press.

(1995 2nd edn.), *Bilingualism*, Oxford: Blackwell.

Rosch, E. (1973), 'Natural Categories', *Cognitive Psychology* 4, 328–50.

(1978) 'Principles of Categorization', in *Categorization and Cognition*,
E. Rosch and B. Lloyd (eds.), Hillsdale, NJ: Lawrence Erlbaum.

Ryan, A. (1970), *The Philosophy of the Social Sciences*, London: The
Macmillan Press.

Ryan, E. and Giles, H. (1982), *Attitudes Towards Language Variation*,
London: Edward Arnold.

Sacks, H. (1994), *Lectures on Conversation*, G. Jefferson (ed.), Oxford: Blackwell.

Sacks, H., Schegloff, E. and Jefferson, G. (1974), 'A Simplest Systematics
for the Organization of Turn-Taking for Conversation', *Language* 50,
696–735.

Sag, I. and Liberman, M. (1975), 'The Intonational Disambiguation of
Indirect Speech Acts', *Papers from the 11th Regional Meeting Chicago
Linguistic Society*, R. Grossman, L. San and T. Vance (eds.), 487–97.

Said, E. (1978), *Orientalism*, New York: Pantheon, London: Penguin edition
(1991).

Saint-Jacques, B. (1979), 'The Language of Immigrants: Sociolinguistic
Aspects of Immigration in Canada', in Chambers (1979).

Sanches, M. and Blount, B. (1975) (eds.), *Sociocultural Dimensions of
Language Use*, New York: Academic Press.

Sanders, A. (1993), *French Today: Language in its Social Context*, Cambridge:
Cambridge University Press.

Sankoff, D. (1978) (ed.), *Linguistic Variation: Models and Methods*, New
York: Academic Press.

(1988), 'Sociolinguistics and Syntactic Variation', in Newmeyer (1988),
vol. 4.

(1988a), 'Variable Rules', in Ammon *et al.* (1987/8).

Sankoff, D. and Laberge, S. (1978), 'The Linguistic Market and the
Statistical Explanation of Variability', in Sankoff (1978).

Sankoff, D. and Rousseau, P. (1979), 'Categorical Contexts and Variable
Rules', in *Papers from the Scandinavian Symposium on Syntactic
Variation*, S. Jacobson (ed.), Stockholm: Almqvist and Wiksell.

Sankoff, D., Cedergren, H., Kemp, W., Thibault, P. and Vincent, D. (1989),
'Montreal French: Language, Class and Ideology', in *Language Change
and Variation*, R. W. Fasold and D. Schiffren (eds.), Amsterdam: John
Benjamins.

References

.off, G. (1971), 'Language Use in Multilingual Societies: Some Alternative Approaches', in Pride and Holmes (1972).

(1975), *The Form of Language*, London: Weidenfeld and Nicolson.

Sankoff, G. and Brown, P. (1976), 'The Origins of Syntax in Discourse', *Language* 52, 631–66.

Sapir, E. (1929), 'The Status of Linguistics as a Science', *Language* 5, 207–14.

(1933), 'Language', in *Encyclopedia of the Social Sciences*, New York: Macmillan.

Sarangi, S. and Slembrouck, S. (1996), *Language, Bureaucracy and Social Control*, London: Longman.

Saussure, F. de (1915/1959), *Cours de Linguistique Générale*, Paris: Payot 1915. English translation by W. Baskin, *Course in General Linguistics*, New York: The Philosophical Library, 1959; London: Fontana, 1974.

Savage-Rumbaugh, S. (1988), 'Deception and Social Manipulation in Symbol Using Apes', in Byrne and Whiten (1988).

Saville-Troike, M. (1989 2nd edn.), *The Ethnography of Communication*, Oxford: Blackwell.

Sawyer, J. (1959), 'The Speech of San Antonio, Texas', in Williamson and Burke (1971).

Schank, R. and Abelson, R. (1975), 'Scripts, Plans and Knowledge', in Johnson-Laird and Wason (1977).

(1977), *Scripts, Plans, Goals and Understanding*, Hillsdale, NJ: Lawrence Erlbaum Associates.

Schegloff, E. (1968), 'Sequencing in Conversational Openings', *American Anthropologist* 70–6, reprinted in Gumperz and Hymes (1972).

(1979), 'Identification and Recognition in Telephone Conversation Openings', in *Everyday Language: Studies in Ethnomethodology*, G. Psathas (ed.), New York: Irvington Publishers.

Schegloff, E., Jefferson, G. and Sacks, H. (1977), 'The Preference for Self-Correction in the Organization of Repair in Conversation', *Language* 53, 361–82.

Schegloff, E. and Sacks, H. (1973), 'Opening Up Closings', in Turner (1974).

Schiffer, S. (1972), *Meaning*, Oxford: Clarendon Press.

Schiffrin, D. (1994), *Approaches to Discourse*, Oxford: Blackwell.

Scotton, C. (1983), 'The Negotiation of Identities in Conversation: A Theory of Markedness and Code-Choice', *International Journal of the Sociology of Language* 44, 115–36.

Searle, J. (1969), *Speech Acts*, Cambridge: Cambridge University Press.

(1975), 'Indirect Speech Acts', in *Syntax and Semantics*, volume 3, *Speech Acts*, P. Cole and J. Morgan (eds.), New York: Academic Press.

(1979), *Expression and Meaning*, Cambridge: Cambridge University Pres.

(1980), 'The Background of Meaning', in *Speech Act Theory an Pragmatics*, J. Searle, F. Kiefer and M. Bierwisch (eds.), Dordrecht, Holland: D. Reidel.

Searle, J. and Vanderveken, D. (1985), *Foundations of Illocutionary Logic*, Cambridge: Cambridge University Press.

Sebba, M. (1993), *London Jamaican*, London: Longman.

Sharrock, W. and Anderson, B. (1986), *The Ethnomethodologists*, Chichester: Ellis Horwood.

Shores, D. and Hines, C. (1977), *Papers in Language Variation*, Alabama: University of Alabama Press.

Sillitoe, A. (1961), *Saturday Night and Sunday Morning*, screenplay adapted from his novel by Alan Sillitoe, film directed by Karel Reisz, in *Masterworks of the British Cinema*, introduction by J. R. Taylor, London: Lorrimer Publishing.

Sinclair, J. and Coulthard, M. (1975), *Towards an Analysis of Discourse*, London: Oxford University Press.

Skinner, Q. (1985) (ed.), *The Return of Grand Theory in the Human Sciences*, Cambridge: Cambridge University Press.

Smith, N. (1982), *Mutual Knowledge*, London: Academic Press.

Smith, N. and Wilson, D. (1979), *Modern Linguistics*, Harmondsworth: Penguin Books.

Spears, A. (1992), 'Reassessing the Status of Black English', *Language in Society* 21, 675–82.

Spender, D. (1985 2nd edn.), *Man Made Language*, London: Routledge and Kegan Paul.

Sperber, D. and Wilson, D. (1982), 'Mutual Knowledge and Relevance in Theories of Comprehension', in Smith (1982).

(1995, 2nd edn.), *Relevance*, Oxford: Blackwell.

Stalnaker, R. (1978), 'Assertion', in *Syntax and Semantics*, volume 9, *Pragmatics*, P. Cole (ed.), London: Academic Press.

Steele, R. and Threadgold, T. (1987) (eds.), *Language Topics, Vols. 1–2*. Amsterdam: Benjamins.

Stephenson, E. (1977), 'The Beginnings of the Loss of Postvocalic /r/ in North Carolina', in Shores and Hines (1977).

Stewart, W. A. (1967), 'Sociolinguistic Factors in the History of American Negro Dialects', in Wolfram and Clarke (1971).

(1968), 'The Functional Distribution of Creole and French in Haiti', in *Georgetown University Round Table Selected Papers on Linguistics 1961–65*, R. O'Brien (ed.), Washington, DC: Georgetown University Press.

(1968a), 'A Sociolinguistic Typology for Describing National Multilingualism', in Fishman (1968).

Strevens, P. (1984), 'The State of the English Language in 1982: An Essay in Geo-Linguistics', in *Language Standards and their Codification*, J. Woods (ed.), Exeter: University of Exeter Linguistic Studies.

Stubbs, M. (1983), *Discourse Analysis*, Oxford: Basil Blackwell.

(1986), *Educational Linguistics*, Oxford: Blackwell.

Sutcliffe, D. (1982), *British Black English*, Oxford: Basil Blackwell.

Thakerar, J., Giles, H. and Cheshire, J. (1982), 'Psychological and Linguistic Parameters of Speech Accommodation Theory', in Fraser and Scherer (1982).

Thompson, J. (1984), *Studies in the Theory of Ideology*, Cambridge: Polity.

(1990), *Ideology and Modern Culture*, Cambridge: Polity.

Threadgold, T. (1987), 'Changing the Subject', in Steele and Threadgold, vol. 2 (1987).

Trudgill, P. (1972), 'Sex, Covert Prestige and Linguistic Change in the Urban British English of Norwich', *Language in Society* 1, 215–46.

(1974), *The Social Differentiation of English in Norwich*, Cambridge: Cambridge University Press.

(1974a), 'Linguistic Change and Diffusion: Description and Explanation in Sociolinguistic Dialect Geography', *Language in Society* 2, 215–46.

(1978) (ed.), *Sociolinguistic Patterns in British English*, London: Edward Arnold.

(1979), 'Standard and Non-Standard Dialects of English in the United Kingdom: Problems and Policies', in Ammon and Fishman (1979).

(1983), *On Dialect*, Oxford: Basil Blackwell.

(1984), (ed.), *Language in the British Isles*, Cambridge: Cambridge University Press.

(1984a), 'Standard English in England', in Trudgill (1984).

(1995 3rd edn.), *Sociolinguistics*, Harmondsworth: Penguin.

(1995a), 'Sociolinguistic Studies in Norway 1970–1991: A Critical Overview', *International Journal of the Sociology of Language* 115, (*Sociolinguistics in Norway*), 7–23.

Trudgill, P. and Hannah, J. (1994 3rd edn.) (eds.), *International English*, London: Edward Arnold.

Turner, R. (1974) (ed.), *Ethnomethodology*, Harmondsworth: Penguin Books.

Underwood, G. (1996) (ed.), *Implicit Cognition*, Oxford: Oxford University Press.

Urion, C. (1971), 'Canadian English and Canadian French', in Darnell (1971).

Van Dijk, T. (1977), *Text and Context. Explorations in the Semantics ⸤ Pragmatics of Discourse*, London: Longman.

(1988), *News as Discourse*, Hillsdale, NJ: Lawrence Erlbaum.

Vanek, A. and Darnell, R. (1971), 'Canadian Doukhobor Russian in Grand Forks, B.C.: Some Social Aspects', in Darnell (1971).

Voloshinov, V. (1973), *Marxism and the Philosophy of Language*, translated by L. Matejka and I. Titunik, New York: Seminar Press.

Von Wright, G. (1971), *Explanation and Understanding*, Ithaca, NY: Cornell University Press.

Wald, B. (1995), 'The Problem of Scholarly Disposition' (Review of Bailey *et al.* 1991), *Language in Society* 24, 245–57.

Walker, D. (1979), 'Canadian French', in Chambers (1979).

Wardhaugh, R. (1987), *Languages in Competition*, Oxford: Blackwell.

(1992 2nd edn.), *An Introduction to Sociolinguistics*, Oxford: Blackwell.

Weinreich, U. (1964), *Languages in Contact*, The Hague: Mouton.

Weinreich, U., Labov, W. and Herzog, M. (1968), 'Empirical Foundations for a Theory of Language Change', in *Directions for Historical Linguistics*, W. P. Lehmann and Y. Malkiel (eds.), Austin: University of Texas Press.

Wells, J. (1982), *Accents of English*, volume 1, *An Introduction*: volume 2, *The British Isles*: volume 3, *Beyond the British Isles*, Cambridge: Cambridge University Press.

White, B. (1995) (ed.), *The Cambridge Companion to Habermas*, Cambridge: Cambridge University Press.

Whitney, W. (1875), *The Life and Growth of Language* (Documenta Semiotica, Serie 1. Linguistik), Hildesheim: Olms, 1970, facsimile, originally published London: King, 1875.

Williams, R. M. (1968), 'The Concept of Norms', in *International Encyclopedia of the Social Sciences*, volume 11, D. L. Sills (ed.), London: Crowell, Collier and Macmillan.

Williamson, J. and Burke, V. (1971) (eds.), *A Various Language: Perspectives on American Dialects*, New York: Holt, Rinehart and Winston.

Wilson, B. (1970) (ed.), *Rationality*, Oxford: Basil Blackwell.

Wilson, D. and Sperber, D. (1981), 'On Grice's Theory of Conversation', in *Conversation and Discourse*, P. Werth (ed.), London: Croom Helm.

Winch, P. (1958), *The Idea of a Social Science and its Relation to Philosophy*, London: Routledge and Kegan Paul.

Winograd, T. (1972), *Understanding Natural Language*, Edinburgh: Edinburgh University Press.

Wittgenstein, L. (1953), *Philosophical Investigations*, translated by G. E. M. Anscombe, Oxford: Basil Blackwell.

olfram, W. (1969), *A Sociolinguistic Description of Detroit Negro Speech*, Washington, DC: Center for Applied Linguistics.

   (1971), 'Black-White Speech Differences Revisited', in Wolfram and Clarke (1971).

   (1974), 'The Relationship of White Southern Speech to Vernacular Black English', *Language* 50, 498–527.

Wolfram, W. and Christian, D. (1976), *Appalachian Speech*, Washington, DC: Center for Applied Linguistics.

Wolfram, W. and Clarke, N. (1971) (eds.), *Black-White Speech Relationships*, Washington, DC: Center for Applied Linguistics.

Woodward, F. L. (1973), *Some Sayings of the Buddha, According to the Pali Canon*, translated by F. L. Woodward, London: Oxford University Press.

Wyld, H. (1920), *A History of Modern Colloquial English*, Oxford: Basil Blackwell.

Yule, G. (1996), *Pragmatics*, Oxford: Oxford University Press.

Index

accent, 17, 40, 133f., 138f., 225;
  acquisition of, 225f.; attitudes to,
  261f.; distinguished from dialect,
  17, 40; loyalty, 263; in
  pronunciation of 'butter', 7f.
accommodation theory, 225, 271,
  272, 443
action: act sequences in Hymes
  SPEAKING, 302; assessment acts,
  285; communicative, 291, 369,
  415, 417, 422f.; complex of, 287,
  296, 415, 425f.; constituted by
  rules, 276f., 291, 300–1, 308,
  423–4; conventions and, 257f.;
  coordination of, 282; explanation
  of, 419f.; illocutionary, 371f.;
  intelligibility of, 258, 277;
  intention and, 368f., 396, 440;
  in language games, 308, 372;
  language-like nature of,
  277; locutionary, 373;
  metaconversational, 300–1;
  norms and, 257f., 271, 273–4,
  291, 440; perlocutionary, 375;
  prayer as, 318; rationality and,
  291; register, field as, 315;
  regulated by rules, 291;
  situations/speech events and,
  304; social action, 276, 405;
  supportive acts, 285; utterances
  and, 368–9, 371, 419; verbal
  v.s. nonverbal, 368f., 370;
  see also speech acts and
  intention
acts of identity, 272f., 440; and
  system of identities, 445

adjacency pairs, 279–85;
  compliment/responses, 285–90;
  definition of, 282; examples of,
  281; in identification, 296; in
  speech events, 302; in turn-
  taking, 297; preferences, 284,
  287, 291; summons/answer, 279f.
age differentiation, 167f., 173, 181f.,
  189, 197, 211, 215–16, 223–7;
  acquisition of accent, 225; age
  grading, 223f., 238f.; language
  change and, 167f., 180f.,
  189–90, 235, 238f.; networks
  and, 211f.
analytic *v.s.* synthetic, 4, 226–7,
  331, 350f.; holism and, 350f.,
  354–60, inextricability thesis
  and, 355, 449
Anscombe, G., 368, 425, 428
analogy: between variation and
  systems of identity, 445; in
  science 437
antilanguage, 44, 461
arbitrariness, 6, 449f., 450–1;
  convention, coding and, 6; non-
  arbitrariness in functional
  explanation, 6, 452f.
artificial intelligence (AI), 363f., 465
attitudes to language, 62, 64, 84, 134,
  161, 223, 244–5, 261–70; covert
  and overt, 265; regularity of, 262,
  264; semicommunication and,
  26; social meaning and, 65, 245;
  standardization and, 36; *see also*
  social meaning, prestige, stigma
Austin, J., 373

Printed in the United States
54099LVS00001B/1-30